1997

The Content of America's Character

THE CONTENT OF AMERICA'S CHARACTER

Recovering Civic Virtue

Edited by
Don E. Eberly

Foreword by
George Gallup, Jr.

MADISON BOOKS
Lanham • New York • London

Published by Madison Books
4720 Boston Way
Lanham, Maryland 20706

3 Henrietta Street
London WC2E 8LU, England

Distributed by National Book Network

⊖™ *The paper used in this publication meets the minimum requirements of*
American National Standard for Information Sciences—Permanence of
Paper for Printed Library Materials, ANSI Z39.48–1964.
Manufactured in the United States of America.

Library of Congress Cataloging-in-Publication Data

The content of America's character : recovering civic virtue / edited by Don E. Eberly
p. cm.
1. Character. 2. Values—Political aspects—United States. 3. United States—Politics
and government—1993– I. Eberly, Don E.
BJ1531.C66 1995 170'.973—dc20 95-8944 CIP

ISBN 1–56833–055–3 (cloth : alk. paper)

Contents

Foreword

With its careful and comprehensive examination of character development in the United States, this book makes a timely appearance. Americans today are more concerned about the state of morality and ethics in their nation than at any other time in the six decades of scientific polling.

Described as major problems by heavy majorities of citizens interviewed in a Gallup Institute survey for William Moss are "lawlessness among young people" and the "weakening of family values." Those surveyed also describe the level of ethics and honesty of individual citizens as only average or low. The law, business, and politics as well as other major professions all test poorly on the ethics scale.

The picture does not improve when the focus shifts from professions to institutions. The church leads the list of nine institutions tested in the survey for doing a good job of raising moral and ethical standards, although only 36 percent hold this view. Far behind, and next in order, are recent U.S. presidents, newspapers, advertising, individual role models in the news, big business, movies, television, and Congress.

The spotlight in many chapters in this book falls appropriately on young people who will set the moral tone for society in the future. At the root of many problems afflicting teens today are uncertain values. A reassuring fact does come from the Gallup Youth Survey—teenagers, like their parents, overwhelmingly support values instruction.

We live in a time of moral relativism and a "do your own thing" or "anything goes" mentality. Yet, remarkably, a solid majority of Americans think it is possible to secure community agreement on the basic values that should be taught in schools. And the public has an answer to the question often asked by critics of character education: "whose values?" A Gallup Institute survey conducted for Phi Delta Kappa shows that 97 percent of citizens believe honesty should be taught; 93 percent belief in democracy; 93 percent acceptance of people of different races and ethnic backgrounds; 91 percent caring for family and friends; 91 percent moral courage; 90 percent the golden rule; and 87 percent acceptance of unpopular political and society views.

Vital to a discussion of character formation is the faith dimension. For many Americans who believe in a personal god who rewards and judges peoples and answers prayers, values are rooted in a living faith and in absolutes.

Americans are discouraged and even alarmed over the state of morals in our society. But they are also hopeful and they believe that the institutions of society have great potential for raising the moral and ethical standards of this country. For example, only five percent say the movies are currently doing a good job in raising the moral and ethical standards of the nation. However, 60 percent say they *could* have such an effect.

Further encouragement is gained from the fact that despite the bewildering array of societal problems afflicting our nation, a majority of Americans believe our democracy remains in a healthy state. Still another hopeful sign: most Americans adhere to a belief that humankind is basically good.

In *The Content of America's Character: Recovering Civic Virtue,* experts from many disciplines explore this topic in the unique context of American society. This is a much needed book, and an important resource for educators, social workers, clergy, parents and many others. Each of the book's contributors writes out of the conviction that democracy is not viable without a solid moral foundation

The good news is that there are programs described in this book, either being tested or already in place, that promise solid results. This book offers a fascinating historical perspective on the content of character, but is it also a call to action—one that the public appears increasingly ready to answer.

George Gallup, Jr., Chairman
The Gallup International Institute

Preface

The Greek philosopher Heraclitus said that character is destiny. This is especially true in a democratic society that wishes to function with minimal and nonintrusive government. Character was regarded by many of the nation's founders as central to citizenship and indispensable to the maintenance of a healthy, free, and civil society. It was clearly understood that the less individuals practiced self-regulation the more they could expect external controls to expand in the form of costly and meddlesome government.

For most of America's history, it was simply taken for granted that character was central to a well-ordered society and that citizens and leaders everywhere would continue to embrace their responsibility to help maintain it. For reasons detailed in this book, the work of fostering character can no longer be taken for granted as a society-wide priority. Powerful philosophical currents and cultural influences have steadily undermined this consensus and weakened society's character-shaping institutions.

The replacement of time-honored universal values with a relativized system of morality in which values are individually designed and self-authenticated is a very recent phenomenon, but one which has become deeply embedded in the public mind. When values become completely contingent upon individual choice, moral life is soon regarded as strictly a matter of private, not public concern. In other words, my values are no one else's business. Not surprisingly, in this environment, the discussion of moral responsibility frequently produces defensiveness and skepticism. "Whose values?" someone is bound to quickly ask when the subject comes up.

The basic ethos of American society has shifted in recent decades away from a desire to preserve character to an ever widening search for liberation from moral requirements.   Little is offered in either American culture or politics to keep alive a broad search for values that society has long held in common.   The shapers of culture often seem more preoccupied with expanding the horizons of expressive freedom and escaping conventional morality than in fostering an approach to life that celebrates sturdy and sound character.

Similarly, the political debate for several decades has focused almost exclusively on impersonal systems, either the state or the marketplace, with little room made available for discussing the more important matters of culture and individual character.   Few debates provide a place for discussing foundational questions such as the duties and rights of citizenship, or the strengthening of character and the mediating institutions that make its preservation possible.   A public philosophy centering on the pursuit of what is best for all has long been replaced by an ideology of self-expression, self-interest, and individual entitlement.

The public debate until recently has placed all hope for human advancement in economic growth, public program improvements, breakthroughs in science, or faith in the transforming power of new technology.   But these concrete structures and instruments make too little contribution by themselves to the development of citizens who desire to know the good and to live out a commitment to civic virtue and responsibility.

Signs that this shrunken view of society is finally running its course are now multiplying. The chief ingredients of America's social regression are increasingly understood to involve factors that are less susceptible to fiscal and programmatic adjustments.   Public opinion polls reveal deep and broad consternation over the collapse of elementary civic values and personal restraints. The concept of character, if not always understood in the affirmative, is increasingly noted by its absence in a culture that drifts steadily toward the vulgar and violent.

America's new frontiers lie in the realm of social change and girding up the institutions that impart character.   Public conversation is filled with lament over the loss of self-restraint, respect, and basic ethics reflected in the rise of pervasive lying, cheating, and stealing.   Fortunately, the movement to restore character is finding a vast field of common ground, even in a society riddled with deep disagreement over politics and public policy.

Transmitting values has always been the work of civilization.   This means that an entire society must take the enterprise seriously. Aristotle held that virtue did not naturally or spontaneously arise. Moral self-regulation had to be cultivated by moral exemplars, starting with parents and including other authority figures and cultural role models. What is seldom understood is that character is rarely the achievement of solitary individuals. Turning conditions that corrode character into conditions that foster it will require the involvement of leaders from all value-shaping institutions—from our churches, schools, and a host of other private and public institutions.

Restoring character as a preeminent concern will not be easy. It will likely require a moderation of the expressive individualism that has arisen in America. Widespread character may not flower amidst a libertine culture that often refuses to acknowledge the public consequences of private morality. Nor will the restoration of character be likely as long as strategies focus strictly on individuals, not institutions. Knowing what we now know, for example, about the vital role of parent-child relations in the formation of character and conscience, it is difficult to imagine a return to character without a widespread reembracing of the family as the central character forming institution of society.

Then there is the role of the voluntary associations of civil society. If it is not the business of the state to inculcate morality, and if families are too weak to carry the burden entirely themselves, the voluntary institutions of society—neighborhood associations, charities, civic groups, and churches and temples—must assist.

The Content of America's Character: Recovering Civic Virtue is an attempt to build a framework for understanding the importance of character, the roots of character, and the shaping of character through the many sectors of life that affect it, for good or bad. The book makes no attempt to steer clear of asserting normative values. It would be impossible for an entire volume on the subject of character to be completed without assuming that character is a good thing; that a free society requires it in abundance to prosper; and that it should thus be expected of all, not just a few. If character is destiny, it affects us all and must be applied to all. This volume is an attempt to inform and mobilize citizens, leaders, and scholars, in the work of strengthening character.

Acknowledgments

I am very grateful for the generous staff support that was offered in producing this volume by Clifford Frick, Communications Director for the Commonwealth Foundation who guided the project from beginning to end and by Research Assistant Scott Bishop who edited the volume with relentless scrutiny. My thanks also go to Research Associate Keith Bashore, Administrative Assistant Wendy Lentvorsky, and Senior Policy Associate Charles Greenawalt, each of whom provided valuable administrative and editing assistance. I also thank Deb Strubel for her technical editing contributions. I am indebted to the pioneering work of so many authors and programmatic leaders who are attempting to reconstruct the architecture of character in America. They are far too numerous to mention here, and many are included in this volume. They include scholars who are laboring in academia to rebuild the philosophical foundations of virtue and morality, business leaders who are working to restore a code of professional ethics in the marketplace, social theorists who are calling for the renewal of character-shaping community institutions, and countless policy advocates who are attempting to renew society's appreciation for the family as the primary seedbed for the cultivation of character.

I. Character in America

Chapter 1

The Quest for America's Character

Don E. Eberly

This century has seen a progressive relaxation of many of our standards of behavior and the souring of many commonly held beliefs. Taken one by one, most are of little importance. Taken together, I believe they show that we have lost our way.

Dr. Benjamin Spock[1]

People feel like there is nothing they can depend on, there is nothing certain.

Stanley B. Greenberg, President Clinton's Pollster[2]

There is a great yearning in the country to provide our national life and institutions with a larger moral dimension.

Mortimer B. Zuckerman, Editor-in-Chief, *U.S. News and World Report*[3]

To have people who are well informed but not constrained by conscience is, conceivably, the most dangerous outcome of education possible. Indeed, it could be argued that ignorance is better than unguided intelligence, for the most dangerous people are those who have knowledge without a moral framework. It is not the lack of technological information that threatens our society; it is the lack of wisdom, and we run the risk today of having our discoveries outdistance our moral compass.

Ernest Boyer, President of the Carnegie Foundation for the Advancement of Teaching[4]

Standards of morality matter no less than standards of excellence. We are not automatons. To understand all may indeed be to forgive all, but no civilization can survive when the capacity for understanding is allowed to supersede the capacity for judgment.

Stephen Carter, Author, *The Culture of Disbelief*[5]

The real answer to the perils of our time is that we simply must become more civilized. We must pay attention to something that every civilized society has given preeminent importance: instilling in our children certain fundamental traits of character—traits like honesty, compassion, courage, perseverance, altruism, and fidelity to one's commitments.

Former U.S. Secretary of Education William J. Bennett[6]

INTRODUCTION

The growing interest in character may be one of the most socially significant developments in the latter part of the twentieth century and one of the most telling in what it signifies about America's moral and social condition. If it is true, as is often said, that interest in the study and application of values is inversely tied to the perceived morality of society, the current level of interest suggests the depth of modern morality's descent. Opinion polls have never indicated so deep a state of anxiety about the condition of society, and rarely, in a country with a long history of apocalyptic forebodings, have so many diverse leaders gathered together around the basic proposition that America suffers from a deficit in character. From the fields of academia, business, education, journalism, and politics comes the sound of alarm: our children, our society, and our heritage face a deepening peril.

Joseph Josephson, founder of the Character Counts Coalition, states bluntly, "There is a hole in the moral ozone." William Kirkpatrick, author of *Why Johnny Can't Tell Right From Wrong,* charges that our schools have produced a generation of "moral illiterates." Norman Lear, long a critic of religious influence in public life, is now concerned mostly about the impact of secularization. He laments the public banishment of values, blaming it in part on "the sophisticates of our politics, our culture and the media" who are embarrassed to "talk seriously about the life of the spirit."[7]

None of this is unique to the American continent. The moral disintegration now widespread in America is rooted in cultural and philosophical forces that are producing the same corrosive effects throughout the entire Western world. English historian Paul Johnson sees a common collapse of ethical finalities throughout Western culture as the root cause of the rise of such primitive and irrational behaviors as racism, ethnic triumphalism, xenophobia, and hatred of refugees. Today's students, says Johnson, have become "fitter candidates for a mob than for a citizenry."[8]

Marian Wright Edelman of the Children's Defense Fund describes our nation as courting serious risk because of a weakening conscience. She sees a society witnessing the collapse of "nurturing families and communities," where people are turning to guns and gangs. It is a society that delivers relentless cultural messages "glamorizing violence, sex, possessions, alcohol and tobacco" and comprises "too few adult role models." It is time, says Edelman, "for all parents and adults to stop our hypocrisy and break the code of silence about the breakdown of spiritual values and parental and community responsibility to nurture and protect children."[9]

The conditions which concern these leaders were once confined to the back alleys of society. Now, they seem so close and are creating a palpable fear and visible nervousness in large cities and small towns alike, on the streets, in the schools, and at work. The portrait of American society presented in the images and language of today's popular culture is of a country in retreat from the notion of society. It is a portrait, not of self-governing citizens, but of autonomous, isolated, and self-absorbed individuals governed by an ideology of "me-ism."

America is a society in which both the individual and the state are in constant advance, while the intermediary institutions which preserve a civil and humane society are in retreat.

Political discourse rings, not with the unifying sound of moral vision but with the impoverishing and polarizing demands for either individual entitlement or government dismantlement. The good life is explained almost entirely as the pursuit of pleasure, not purpose. The highest end of life advertised by the economic marketplace is, simply, making a purchase, by credit card if necessary. In schools, children without childhoods pass through metal detectors on their way to instruction in personal safety, conflict resolution, and the avoidance of deadly transmittable diseases. In higher education, learning to think with moral clarity has been traded in for learning to sympathize with new claims of victim status. The field of law beckons the aggrieved to sue for damages, drowning the courts in the most trivial of litigation.

This is a vision not of society, but its negation. The rise of antisocial behavior in recent decades must be explained, not just by the collapse of private conscience, but by the disintegration of the social institutions that cultivate character. Morality is not simply an abstract set of principles—it is cultivated in a society's seedbeds of virtue: the family and community institutions. Thus, the work of rebuilding character must be fused with the work of rebuilding moral community and reasserting social norms.

The recovery of individual character must be rooted in an understanding not just of the individual but of society. Most of society's most pressing social problems—from teen pregnancy, crime, and violence to the abuse and neglect of children, to our vulgar and violent culture—are just that, they are social. They will not be solved predominantly through public policy reforms—by simply applying better rewards or penalties through our tax, criminal, and welfare codes. Nor will they be solved through great and polarizing campaigns of moral rearmament. They will be solved through society-wide efforts to revitalize the institutions of civil society, to strengthen individual capacity for self-government and to renew a lost ethical order. The extent of society's crisis of character is too universal to think that change will be produced from one sector alone.

FACTS OF A CHARACTER-STARVED CULTURE

Pollster George Gallup, Jr., who has long tracked societal attitudes about values, describes having "a sinking feeling" when he looks over current computer printouts. A recent Gallup poll showed that large majorities of the American people perceive a world of despair and division. Large majorities believe it is unsafe to visit the nation's largest cities, much less live there. Significantly, more blacks than a generation ago are convinced that America is moving toward two societies, separate and unequal, and that racial problems cannot be solved. According to Gallup, "There is a harsh and mean edge to society, a society in which the very notion of a good person is often ridiculed, a society increasingly litigious, in which retribution is the operative word."[10]

The greatest signs of erosion can be found among the young. Author and character education expert Tom Lickona has surveyed the ethical conditions of youth and has identified ten troubling trends: rising youth violence; increasing dishonesty (lying, cheating, and stealing); growing disrespect for authority; peer cruelty; a resurgence of bigotry on school campuses, from preschool through higher education; a decline in the work ethic; sexual precocity; a growing self-centeredness and declining civic responsibility; an increase in self-destructive behavior; and ethical illiteracy.[11]

Lickona's ten troubling trends are more than his own personal observations. They are substantiated through extensive social data and scientific surveys.

1. Since 1965, the juvenile arrest rate for violent crimes tripled, making children the fastest-growing segment of the criminal population.

2. The U.S. homicide rate for 15- to 24-year-old males is seven times higher than Canada's and 50 times higher than Japan's.

3. The United States has one of the highest teen pregnancy rates, the highest teen abortion rate, and the highest level of drug use among young people in the developed world.[12]

4. The rate of unmarried teenagers becoming pregnant has nearly doubled since 1972, to nearly one out of ten high school girls.

5. Youth suicide has tripled over the past 25 years.

6. A survey of more than 2,000 Rhode Island students, grades six through nine, found that two out of three boys and one out of two girls thought it "acceptable for a man to force sex on a woman" if they had been dating for six months or more.

7. Scholastic Aptitude Test scores dropped 73 points from 1960 to 1993.

8. A survey of 7,000 students conducted in 1993 revealed that 61 percent had cheated on an exam in the past year; 33 percent had stolen something from a store; and 33 percent said they would lie on a resume.[13]

9. Ten percent of all teachers and 25 percent of all students had been the victim of an assault in their schools during the past year. Some type of weapon is regularly taken to school by 20 percent of all high school students.[14]

Then there are the press reports of increasingly commonplace tales of horrific crimes:

1. A teenager in Lonoke, Arkansas was shot dead by a friend just because she spoke. Six teenagers were hanging out on the porch of Nina Scott's grandmother's house, when Kevin Barnes told the group that "I'm going to shoot whoever says the next word." When Nina opened her mouth, Kevin

shot her through the forehead. Nina was fourteen, and Kevin was eighteen.[15]

2. Twelve-year-old Polly Klas was kidnapped from her own bedroom during a slumber party while her parents were in the adjoining room. She was raped and murdered.

3. In Brooklyn, three teenage boys doused sleeping homeless persons with gasoline and set them on fire. At the police station, one of the boys stated that they "just like to harass the bums."[16]

4. In 1990, a group of teens beat, raped, and stabbed a woman 132 times and left her for dead in a Boston park. Some of the youths said they were simply bored.

5. A *New York Times* headline story "Where Boys Will Be Boys" tells of teenage boys in Lakewood, California who have been accused of molesting and raping girls as young as ten, all the while keeping score as if the challenge compared to a slam dunk or quarterback sack. "We didn't do nothing wrong, cause it's not illegal to hook up," declares Billy Shehan, who boasts of leading the competition with 66 such "hookups."[17]

Finally, there is the corrosive influence of pervasive and seemingly mundane acts of dishonesty, as documented in repeated studies. Here are some of the findings of recent surveys on honesty:

1. The Josephson Institute, a California foundation devoted to the study of personal ethics, has discovered an alarmingly high number of students who steal, lie, and cheat at school, at work, and in their personal relationships. The institute found that honesty has simply ceased to be a goal for many students. Honesty ranked sixth among high schoolers' list of priorities, behind getting into college, getting a well-paying job, and paradoxically, "having trusting relationships" and "being respected for your integrity."[18]

2. One-third of all high school students said they were willing to lie on a resume, job application, or during a job interview to get a desired job; one out of eight college students admitted to have engaged in each of the following forms of theft or fraud: lying to an insurance company, inflating expense claims, falsifying financial aid forms, and borrowing money with no intention of paying it back; three out of five high schoolers and one in three college students admitted to cheating on an exam.[19]

3. In a different study, 67 percent of American high school seniors said they would happily inflate an expense account, 50 percent would pad an insurance

claim, and 66 percent would willingly lie to achieve a business objective.[20]

Like crime and other more serious offenses, basic dishonesty can be found through all ranks of society. The expectation that dishonesty may be more prevalent among the "down and outers" is contradicted by research indicating that the highest achievers in society frequently set the lowest standards. In a survey of 6,000 graduate students nationwide by Rutgers University Graduate School of Management, 57 percent admitted to cheating to get into graduate school. A 1992 survey by Shearson Lehman Brothers, Inc., a Wall Street stock brokerage firm, found that about 80 percent of people between the ages of 18 to 29 agreed that "corruption was an important factor in getting ahead."[21] In a survey of high-achieving students taken by Who's Who Among American High School Students, 80 percent of the students admitted to dishonesty such as copying someone else's homework or cheating on an exam.[22]

CHARACTER: A CONCEPT IN RETREAT

Interest in character is anything but new. The pages of history reveal a pattern of character's emergence, its retreat, and then its reemergence out of concern for ethical standards. Character has been a central concern in societies dating back to antiquity, across all civilizations. It was a preeminent interest of America's Founders, and it was part of the defining purpose for public education throughout most of that institution's history; indeed, it was the reason public schools were created.

Throughout most of recorded history, education concerned itself with the ends, not just the means, of human existence. This was especially true during classical antiquity, but also for most of the history of America's education system. Public education had been committed to two equally important goals: helping kids to become smart and helping them to become good. The learning of facts was thought inseparable from the cultivation of habits such as trustworthiness, respect, responsibility, justice and fairness, civic virtue and citizenship, and caring.

It is not surprising, then, when education professionals rush to point out that the educational enterprise has always been committed to values. This is partly true of course, but it fails to take into account the nature and scale of the retreat that has occurred over the past three decades. Any serious investigation would reveal that, with regard to the ebb and flow of concern for character, American education has clearly been operating in the down cycle.

Why has character been in such retreat? It is tempting to offer simplistic theories for why morality in the latter part of the twentieth century is at such a low ebb. There are the more obvious and plausible explanations, such as the weakening of the family and the arrival of relativism, as we will see. But there are many more, less obvious, but equally consequential factors, including the rise of individualism and consumerism, and their fragmenting impact on community.

One reason values change is because the structure of societies and the patterns of work, family, and social life change. The transitions from agriculture to industrialization to the information age each produced radical differences in social life and values. Many of the sterner virtues of early America endured because they were linked to a way of life filled with unrelenting demands and risk. Most folks were well acquainted with their neighbors and lived in small villages or on the land where self-reliance and restraint toward others was valued and where individual failure or nonconformity imposed a far greater price on the community.

Whereas these older character traits were considered imperative for preparing the individual for an environment that was often harsh and demanding, these character-producing conditions have largely been eliminated by the managed economy and social welfare functions of modern society. Many question whether character can be fully restored without a return to this older way of life. Says David Frum, "If the old American culture and the old American character were rational responses to the riskiness of life, you cannot alleviate that riskiness and expect the old culture to persist."[23]

Another variation of this theory is the idea that prosperity itself is destructive to the underlying virtues which brought wealth about in the first place. There appears to be support for this in sociological theory and in surveys of public attitudes over time. Sociologist Daniel Bell speaks of the cultural "contradictions of capitalism," a phenomenon describing the collapse of virtues such as industry and thrift under the softening effects of the prosperity they create. Pollster Daniel Yankelovich has surveyed shifting public attitudes on values and finds an "affluence effect" that exerts a powerful influence on cultural values.

As a basic rule, Yankelovich's "affluence effect" theory holds that people permit their commitment to values to soften when they perceive their economic futures to be relatively secure. The perception of prosperity's durability encourages "new forms of self-expression and individuality" that were thought unthinkable during earlier, less economically stable periods. By contrast, periods of economic contraction generally produce a return to the sterner values of sacrifice, work and saving, and a repudiation of the ethos of unlimited personal expression and choice. The "affluence effect" cycle completes itself in the return of prosperity and a renewed desire for self-fulfillment, spending, living for the moment, and less conformity and self-sacrifice.[24]

A final explanation for the collapse of character is the loss of influence by those institutions in society which have traditionally been responsible for inculcating character—parents, churches, and schools—to other cultural influences, particularly the entertainment industry, whose purpose is more tied to commercial success than public purpose. Deep and broad change has come to society, and it would be wrong to single out schools for blame. Even as the world has changed around them, schools have continued to prepare students for participation in a democratic society.

Nevertheless, the commitment to this work, as well as the content of it, was dramatically altered over the past three decades. The values education program conceived by early architects of public education focusing unreservedly on desired moral outcomes lost out to other dominant cultural and intellectual influences in the latter half of the twentieth century. Thomas Lickona identifies several powerful philosophical and cultural forces to which public schools became vulnerable: philosophical Positivism, "personalism," and "pluralism."

The Fact-Value Dichotomy

One powerful intellectual influence was the arrival from Europe of the philosophy of Logical Positivism which sought to establish a radical distinction, in the name of scientific inquiry, between facts and values. While facts existed in the objective world of research and observation, values were relegated to the subjective realm of preferences, feelings, and tastes. Facts were objective; values and notions of truth were entirely relative. As a result, says Lickona, "morality was relativized and privatized—made to seem a matter of personal 'value judgment,' not a subject for public debate and transmission through the schools."[25]

Schools, like the society they served, steadily turned away from enforcing any common understanding of values, even of the most elementary kind. Relativism produced a paralysis over the fear that moral education involved indoctrination. The result was that schools sought to substitute "situational" ethics for transcendent and universal moral principles. The older form of moral learning involving the telling of stories with tales of courage, discipline, sacrifice, and honor was out; the presentation of ethical ambiguities in which there were no obvious heroes or villains, vice or virtue, was in.

Situational ethics eased the pressures posed by relativism by offering a vague, uncertain, and self-directed approach to morality. With situational ethics, there were endless moral dilemmas, usually involving highly remote circumstances and always weighted down with abstraction and uncertainty; for example, the lifeboat with seven passengers and provisions for only four, or the case of the doctor who considered stealing a drug to save his dying wife, and so on. The right answer was always located somewhere inside the "situation" and the person's own self-understanding. Unlike real-life experience in which common standards of right conduct could be asserted in the great majority of cases, most of the situations in situational ethics could be argued either way, and as the determined relativism of the day would have it, never really settled.

The directive approach to moral education that was steadily cast away was hard to sustain because it involved judging right from wrong, good from bad. The practice of judging conduct and the content of character has become, according to ethics professor Jean Bethke Elshtain, "in bad odor. It is equated," she says, "with being punitive, or with insensitivity," or with various "phobias" or "isms," and thus has been replaced with "sensationalistic tales of victimization and equally sensationalistic proclamations of immunity from responsibility."[26]

The abandonment of rendering judgment in the name of being open-minded and tolerant produces a paradoxical result: a loss of respect for individuals. Elshtain maintains that "judging is a sign, a mark, of our respect for the dignity of others and ourselves. The elimination of the possibility of judgment, the evacuation of the very capacity of judging, would spell the end of the human subject as a self-respecting, accountable being."[27]

This subjectivism and its privatized concept of social values leads to another costly consequence: it produces a society in which any concept of a common moral vision is nearly impossible to come by. As columnist George Will describes it, "The idea is abroad that there is no moral heritage worth 'imposing' on children, respect for whom requires that their selection of 'values' be regarded as a mere matter of taste."[28]

Sociologists dating back to Emile Durkheim have warned about societal disintegration resulting from the erosion of shared beliefs and common purpose. Alexis de Tocqueville worried about excessive individualism and materialism producing an atomistic society. What Tocqueville was describing was not a society at all, but a collection of individuals living in resistance to the notion of enduring common interests, pursuits, traditions, or beliefs that make up a society.

The myth of value neutrality left the public in a baffled sense of drift over what, if anything, could be asserted without making someone uncomfortable. *Newsweek* captured this reflexive nonjudgmentalism with its cover story in 1992 entitled "Whose Values?"[29]

Could the schools not even teach honesty as superior to dishonesty, responsibility as more important than self-indulgence? Apparently not. According to educator William Moloney, the implied message became "Hitler and Gandhi both qualify as philosopher-kings."[30]

The consequence of relativism is that institutions of learning themselves are now paralyzed under the weight of their own unworkable relativist philosophy. Educators became incapacitated in setting the standards of conduct that make a learning environment even possible. Former Secretary of Education William Bennett reports that in the 1940s teachers identified talking out of turn, chewing gum, making noise, running in the halls, cutting in line, dress code violations, and littering as the primary sources of disruption in school. By the 1990s, teachers identified drug abuse, alcohol abuse, pregnancy, suicide, rape, robbery, and assault as top concerns.[31]

Values as Subjective Self-Expression

A second cultural development eroding character, according to Lickona, and somewhat an extension of the first, was the emergence in the 1960s of "personalism." Whereas relativism simply argued against asserting objective truth out of a desire to be nonjudgmental, personalism celebrated the subjective self. Personalism exalted not just the individual over against society, but a concept of the autonomous self that distinguished itself radically from the American tradition of tempered individualism. In personalism, individualism represented a revolution in self-realization that was antagonistic toward the very notion of moral norms. Older substantive notions of character lost out to more superficial categories such as "personality," which concerned itself more with image and style than content.

Modernity has placed the sovereign, autonomous self at the center of all things, and has made moral decision-making strictly contingent upon human choice. If there is no objective basis for truth, perhaps one should simply search for meaning in human will, passion, and imagination. Self-sublimation for the sake of purposes larger than the self are, with the full blessing of this philosophical system, traded in for self-preoccupation.

According to social historian Fred Siegel, America has "conducted a 30-year experiment with desublimation," and the results, he says, have been "a disaster."[32]

Another term for personalism is what philosopher Alasdair MacIntyre calls "emotivism," which is a mindset that links morality to feelings, emotions, and therapeutic notions. This morality, according to MacIntyre, holds that "all moral judgments are nothing but expressions of preference, expressions of attitude or feeling."[33]   In other words, morality not only lacks objective grounding, the search for moral meaning within is pursued with self-reverential fascination. The result was the search for values that were "authentically mine," but not necessarily anyone else's.

Personalism was aided by various educational movements that sought to assure the student in his or her self-directed search for moral meaning. One of the primary objectives of the "values clarification" movement, for example, was to show teachers how, when it came to values, to avoid teaching all together. How one "felt" about shoplifting, for example, was frequently presented as though there was no objective standard, moral or legal, against which to judge whether one drew the right conclusion.

Personalism was also fueled by a self-esteem movement which frequently drifted toward narcissistic self-love divorced from any expectation of effort or achievement.   The self-esteem movement, according to Boston University professor Steven Tigner, encouraged a willful blindness to people's shortcomings in inducing them to feel good about themselves." The problem with this, says Tigner, is that a failure to discriminate between a person's excellent work or shoddy performance "is to deprive them of one of the chief incentives to grow, improve, and mature. If I don't distinguish their finer efforts from their failures," says Tigner, "I am not serious about that person."[34]

Unlike previous concepts of self-respect which entailed respect for others, this is self separated from others, "narcissistic and solipsistic," according to Gertrude Himmelfarb.   "The current notions of self-fulfillment, self-expression and self-realization derive from a self that does not have to prove itself by reference to any values, purposes, or persons outside of itself."   Esteem is presumed, she says, "to adhere to the individual regardless of how he behaves or what he accomplishes."[35]

It was inevitable that an ethos of self-fulfillment, advanced often in the name of rejecting social arrangements thought to be oppressive and notions of truth deemed antiquated, had to produce unexpected consequences: a weakening of social commitments, a decline in institutions such as marriage, and a weakening regard for manners and elementary mores.

In a world in which facts and values were assigned to wholly segregated compartments, and in which personality triumphed over performance, the very notion of objective moral norms had to be forcefully cast off. The unsurprising result of this liberationist ethos was that traditional sources of moral authority were delegitimized. A Louis Harris survey of 5,000 young people asked the question: "What do you take to be the most believable authority in matters of truth?" One to two percent said science or the media. Three to four percent said religion or their parents. Most of the kids said simply "me."[36]

In a separate poll of adults by the Gallup organization, 63 percent rejected the notion of "moral absolutes." So strong has been the commitment to relativism that even religion, still one of the most powerful forces in society, has become an appendage to subjective self, losing most of its authoritative dimensions. In the Gallup poll, 91 percent identified religion as very important in their lives, but 43 percent said "their own experience" was the most reliable guide to truth.[37]

Secular Pluralism

The final factor in the erosion of character, according to Lickona, was the combined role of a "rapidly intensifying pluralism" and "the increasing secularization of the public arena." As America became more culturally diverse, public leaders became less, not more, inclined toward asserting a common culture consisting of core values. For schools, this represented a dramatic departure from the original vision and central mission of the public school enterprise: assimilation.

As secularism took on the form of pseudo-religion, public schools, being public and secular, simply assumed that they were forbidden from asserting any values that might be linked to religion, even though the values in question were common to virtually all cultures and religions. The result was a concept of society based on a discordant embrace of our differences, the pursuit of divergence not convergence, and the prizing of nonconformity over conformity.

The problem with this is that nations live by their myths and traditions, and in America's case, the story of America and its ideals may be the only unifying idea. Societies pay dearly when unifying ideas and myths are cast aside. Historian Arthur Schlesinger, Jr., worries that "the historic idea of a unifying American identity is now in peril." He believes the end result will be "the fragmentation, resegregation, and tribalization of American life."[38]

Learning respect for the accomplishments of a nation's past is necessary to preserve a society's identity and heritage, and this job falls largely to educators. In an ethnically diverse nation like America, that means honoring the contributions of all, but the contributions of all to America, a land and a nation in which the many somehow become assimilated into the one. Schlesinger maintains that "the militants of ethnicity" now view the main objective of public education, not as assimilation, but "the protection, strengthening, celebration and perpetuation of ethnic origins and identities." But this separatism, he says, "nourishes prejudices, magnifies differences, and stirs antagonisms."[39]

The rich heritage and contributions of all immigrant groups must be honored, and no group has a monopoly on heroes, a corner on human virtues, or a special exemption from human vices. Human heroism and individual accomplishments in science, arts, and enterprise come in all colors and creeds. But in the struggle to build student self-esteem and achievement around ethnic identity, the search for shared values and common democratic interests can be quickly subordinated to more narrow objectives. Ethnic pride is a good thing, but it should not come at the expense of "ethical pride."

CHARACTER RECONSIDERED: BEYOND NEUTRALITY

Debates over values tend to raise deeper questions about social and political agendas that are frequently attached to those debates. Laments over the loss of values in society frequently produce a simple search for a guilty party or an easy theory on how the erosion came about, followed by a comforting call for a return to a lost golden age. An honest approach to restoring character will move beyond these impulses.

The sixties counterculture movement certainly produced excesses, but in many respects it merely supplied fresh impetus to a trend toward relaxing standards of conduct and expression that had been gaining strength since the beginning of the century. Moreover, the cultural revolt, in spite of its obvious excesses, was fueled by an aversion to a strict and stifling regiment of social conformity that had as much to do with power and status as with elevating traditional moral ideals.

Some of the change that came about during and after the cultural convulsions of the 1960s nearly all Americans support and few would reverse. Most acknowledge that the change opened up new horizons of opportunity and individual choice in society, especially for those who had long been denied it. The key to making new advances in individual character may be in accepting that, while the worst excesses of cultural change must be moderated, the best results are here to stay.

Reconsidering Relativism

If it is true that schools are losing their way on values due to cultural and philosophical forces, the public debate has done little to help. A major detriment has been the tendency of the political debate to repeatedly present the public with false choices. On values, the false choice was either secularism or sectarianism, relativism or absolutism, implying there was no common ground to be found across cultural and religious heritages.

As is frequently the case, however, fragmented debates only open up opportunities for others to enter the process in search of synthesis. The Character Counts movement represents a rare attempt to transcend political and ideological boundaries. Character, as a concept, is neither liberal nor conservative because it is not primarily about political ideology or competing policy programs. It is pre-political. The character movement includes diverse figures ranging from liberal Barbara Jordan to conservative William Bennett. According to Jordan, "there is no ideological tension here." The movement's literature announces a desire simply to replace situation ethics and moral relativism with the advancement of character in "a common language."[40] This is done by promoting the six pillars of character: trustworthiness, respect, responsibility, fairness, caring, and citizenship.

The coalition reflects what majorities believe. According to polls, substantial majorities believe it is possible to find common agreement on the core principles and values that should be imparted to youth. According to pollster George Gallup, "surprisingly high" agreement can be found on such key tenets as the golden rule and religious tolerance. Two adults in three (69 percent) think it is possible to secure community agreement on the basic values that should be taught. Ninety-seven percent believe honesty should be taught; 93 percent, belief in democracy; 91 percent, caring for family and friends; 91 percent, moral courage; 90 percent, the golden rule; 93 percent, acceptance of people of different races and ethnic backgrounds; 87 percent, acceptance of unpopular political and social views; and 73 percent, teaching sexual abstinence outside of marriage.[41]

The project of restoring sound character can be undertaken independent of political debate over issues that divide; indeed, a broad embrace of character throughout society might make those debates more fruitful.

Moral and ethical questions need not produce partisan or ideological responses. As William Bennett said in the introduction to his *Book of Virtues:*

> Good people—people of character and moral literacy—can be conservative and good people can be liberal. We must not permit our disputes over thorny political questions to obscure the obligation we have to offer instruction to all our young people in the area in which we have, as a society, reached a consensus: namely, on the importance of good character, and on some of its pervasive particulars.[42]

Both the Left and Right frequently confuse the quest for ethics with social policy debates: the Left with poverty, injustice, and racism; the Right with abortion, alternative lifestyles, and destruction of the family. These are important public issues which cannot be separated entirely from private moral convictions, but they are public issues, and are no substitute for the pursuit of virtuous individual behavior.

The shortsightedness of this approach is displayed in an experience related by ethics professor Christina Hoff Sommers. A colleague of hers insisted that discussions of ethics focus on such issues as corporate corruption, capital punishment, or Third World transgressions. The concern of ethics, according to this professor, was whether private institutions, the government, or society itself is moral. Discussion of private morals such as honesty, decency, responsibility, or honor were automatically assumed to be of secondary importance, if not avoided altogether. The professor in question was stunned when she discovered that many of her students had cheated on their social justice take-home exams. She conceded that ethics had to include matters of private morality.

The quest for character is not primarily about resolving issues of public or institutional ethics, although it should certainly contribute to improved thinking about these things, as well as more reasonable public debate about them. There is far less disagreement over the core principles of character than there is over divisive social issues. Before aspiring to transform a society along ethical lines, the person of character is encouraged to seek the development of his own integrity and moral wisdom. Professor Andrew Oldenquist says, "Principled behavior is simply more important than reasoning about controversies, though both are important." The inculcation of civilized moral habits, he says, logically precedes the study of social dilemmas if the society in which those controversies are argued is "to be minimally safe and satisfying."[43]

This confusion of character with either vexing situational ethics or divisive public policy debates has contributed to the continuing doubt over the nature of moral education; whether it is little more than the imposition of one particular view on others. The question of what is morality, and whether it can be taught, as opposed to caught, is essential. Is the knowledge and practice of morality a function of hearing morality or of habituation into it? Is it mostly about making and enforcing external rules, or is it about making self-regulating people? Is it a result of self-discovery, inculcation, indoctrination, habituation, or a combination thereof?

Efforts to impart morality in youth have followed dramatically different approaches in recent decades. As discussed earlier, there were the movements of situation ethics and values clarification in the 1960s and 1970s. There were new approaches in the 1970s promoted principally by Lawrence Kohlberg involving "rational decision" making, which were less relativistic and more oriented toward the development of moral reasoning skills. Character education, an even more recent development, differs from both the values clarification approach and the Kohlbergian moral development approach. Character programs typically endorse specific content, such as the moral virtues of honesty, courage, and kindness, and they attempt to guide the student toward behaviors consistent with those relevant values. It assumes that certain moral claims are, in fact, legitimate; that not all values are equal.

In effect, character education represents a return to a more classical notion of moral education that bases itself on expected behaviors rooted in values that are universally found in successful societies.

Character's Universality

Because of the confusion over what exactly the enterprise of moral education entails, its advancement is usually impeded by doubts relating to "whose values?" should be taught. The concern is that a system of values cannot be constructed or taught without favoring one religion or culture over another. Yet as C. S. Lewis, himself a devout Christian, pointed out in *The Abolition of Man*, there are certain universal ideas of right and wrong that recur in the writings of ancient Egyptians, Babylonians, Hebrews, Chinese, Norse, Indians, and Greeks, along with Anglo-Saxon and American writings.

Lewis calls these transcendent principles the *Tao*, a term borrowed from the Chinese which means simply "the way." Rooted in the laws of nature, the *Tao* is a road that leads to the good life, and to harmony with nature and its maker. This concept bases such moral imperatives as the care for the young and veneration of the old, not on subjective human psychology, but in universal principles of justice that transcend individuals and cultures.

That these core principles emerged around the globe throughout the millennia, independent of one another, on vastly different soil, producing the same successful civilizations, regardless of race or religion, confirms Lewis's suggestion that they are rooted in the natural laws of the universe, not just Christian doctrines of revelation, for example.

The common core virtues that C. S. Lewis identifies are not ethnocentric; they span time, cultures, and religions. To abandon them, says Lewis, is to sap a civilization of its dynamism, creativity, and coherence. When societies abandon the *Tao*, according to Lewis, they produce "men without chests," of whom society then vainly expects "virtue and enterprise." To step outside the *Tao*, according to Lewis, is to have "stepped into the void"—it is socially suicidal.[44]

What was this *Tao* that could not be abandoned?

1. THE LAW OF BENEFICENCE. This rule recognizes the importance of kindness, shared generously for the sake of society. For example, do not murder, oppress, bear false witness, hate; be kind and good; give alms. The Egyptians: "I have not brought misery upon my fellows." The Hindu: "He who is cruel and calumnious has the character of a cat." Chinese: "He whose heart is in the smallest degree set upon goodness will dislike no one."

2. DUTY TO FAMILY. Family is recognized everywhere as deserving of special love and the highest form of loyalty. Children are owed unique care and responsibility by their parents. Marriage involves specific rights as well as responsibilities. According to the ancient Hindu and Jewish traditions, honoring your father and mother is one of life's first duties. Respecting and caring for our aging kin is an unavoidable obligation, according to Jewish and Egyptian traditions. According to the ancient Greek, Epictetus, marrying and begetting children is a great honor and sacred duty because it is upon this foundation that the commonwealth rests.

3. THE LAW OF JUSTICE. This principle establishes standards of right and wrong in the area of human conduct, such as respecting private and common property, treating one another with basic honesty, not offering or taking bribes, and not avenging wrongdoing in violation of the law. The Egyptians encouraged fairmindedness and impartiality before the law: "Regard him whom thou knowest like him whom thou knowest not."

Ancient Jewish standards guarded against partiality on the basis of means or social status: "Do not consider the fact that one party is poor nor the fact that the other is a great man."

4. THE LAW OF GOOD FAITH AND VERACITY. This ancient law issued the sternest warnings against general falsehood: lying, cheating, defrauding. The ancient Chinese admonished: "Be of unwavering good faith." An Anglo-Saxon writer boasted: "I sought no trickery, nor swore false oaths." "The foundation of justice is good faith," said Cicero of ancient Rome. "Anything is better than treachery," said the ancient Norse.

5. THE LAW OF MERCY. This law summons the strong to care for the weak, infirmed, and dying. For example, "give bread to the hungry" (Egyptian); "never strike a woman" (Hindu); "make intercession for the weak" (Babylonian); "take care of widows, orphans and old men" (American Indian).

6. THE LAW OF MAGNANIMITY. This principle encourages the citizen to seek to live a good life of courage and honor. Some things, for many ancients, were worse than death, like treachery, murder, betrayal, and torturing another person. "Death is better for every man than life with shame," said the Anglo-Saxons. "Praise and imitate that man to whom, while life is pleasing, death is not grievous," said Seneca the Stoic. "Love learning and if attacked be ready to die for the Good Way," wrote the ancient Chinese.

These universal principles embodied what C. S. Lewis called "a common human law of action which can overarch rulers and ruled alike." Belief in the *Tao* is necessary to "the very idea of a rule which is not tyranny."[45]

Many of the purveyors of these human values on the American continent were originally "white European males," as today's multiculturalists would describe them, owing to the homogeneous makeup of America at the time of the country's founding. Yet, the framers were drawing from a deeper and more diverse well of antiquity than simply European culture. The virtues not only transcend cultures, they predate the Victorian Age and terms like "bourgeois" values by thousands of years.

Ben Franklin's comprehensive list of virtues—temperance, silence, order, resolution, industry, sincerity, justice, moderation, cleanliness, tranquillity, chastity, and humility—are virtues that humane societies everywhere have sought to keep in wide practice. These were thought to be virtues that nourished human civilization. Only the modern mind would view them skeptically and consider itself wise enough to invent moral principles that are newer and better.   The ancient Greeks had a word for this: *hubris.*

CONCLUSION

If there is a basis for optimism in America it is that the nation harbors a unique capacity for self-renewal. Periodically, major social reform movements have come along seeking to address society's basic deficiencies—community standards gone lax, behavioral norms gone soft, public ideals in retreat.

This volume is offered by its editor and contributing authors as a critical analysis and hopeful guide of the job that now lies ahead for refurbishing the nation's slumping regard for individual character and social values. It examines the theory and origins of character as well as the many practical strategies for renewing character.

It is offered in the hope that many Americans from diverse walks of life will discover a new vision for citizenship based on character and will apply it in their neighborhoods and professional fields of endeavor.

NOTES

1.   Benjamin M. Spock, *A Better World for Our Children: Rebuilding American Family Values* (Bethesda, MD: National Press Books, 1984), 93.

2.   From Ronald Brownstein, "America's Anxiety Attack," *Los Angeles Times Magazine*, 8 May 1994, 14.

3.   Mortimer B. Zuckerman, "Where Have Our Values Gone?" *U.S. News and World Report*, 8 August 1994, 88.

4.   Kristen J. Amundson, "Teaching Values and Ethics: Problems and Solutions," *AASA Critical Issues Report* (1991): 13.

5.   Jean Bethke Elshtain, "Judge Not," *First Things*, October 1994, 39.

6.   William J. Bennett, "How to Teach Values," *Ladies Home Journal*, September 1994, 142.

7.   Norman Lear, "A Call For Spiritual Renewal," *Washington Post*, 30 May 1993.

8.   William J. Moloney, "Are Students 'Moral Illiterates'?" *Philadelphia Inquirer*, 2 February 1993, A7.

9.   Marian Wright Edelman, "The Character Crisis: A Nation, and Its Children, At Risk," *The Josephson Institute* (May/June 1994), 2.

10.   Princeton Religion Research Center, *Emerging Trends* 5 (1994), 5.

11.   Thomas Lickona, "The Return of Character Education," *Educational Leadership*, November 1993, 9.

12.   Lickona, "Return of Character Education," 9.

13. Carol Innerst, "Bennett Sees Ruin in U.S. Behavior," *Washington Times*, 9 February 1994.

14. Mary Jordan, "Summit Searches for Cease-fire in Violence Enveloping Children," *Washington Post*, 22 July 1993.

15. "What's With These Kids?" *Washington Times*, 22 October 1994, D2.

16. Thomas Lickona, *Educating For Character: How Our Schools Can Teach Respect and Responsibility* (New York: Bantam Books, 1991), 4.

17. Suzanne Fields, "Rape as Sport: The Culture is at the Root," *Insight*, 3 May 1993, 19.

18. Richard Morin, "Honesty May No Longer Be The Best Policy," *Washington Post*, 7-13 December 1993, national weekly edition.

19. Morin, "Honesty May No Longer."

20. Lawrence Reed, "As Values Collapse, Government Grows," *The Mackinac Center*, 24 February 1992.

21. Dan Guido, "Speaker: Ethical Slide Could Spell Disaster in 21st Century," *Lancaster Sunday News*, 17 January 1993.

22. Carole Feldman, "A Survey of Students Finds Lots of Cheating," *Philadelphia Inquirer*, 20 October 1993.

23. George Will, "Up From Geniality," *Newsweek*, 5 September 1994, 76.

24. Daniel Yankelovich, "How Changes in the Economy Are Reshaping American Values," in *Values and Public Policy* (Washington, DC: Brookings Institution, 1994), 18-19.

25. Lickona, "Return of Character Education," 6.

26. Elshtain, "Judge Not," 37.

27. Elshtain, "Judge Not," 39.

28. George Will, "A Trickle Down Culture," *Newsweek*, 13 December 1993, 84.

29. Joe Klein, "Whose Values?" *Newsweek*, 8 June 1992, 19-27.

30. Moloney, "'Moral Illiterates'?" A7.

31. Noel R. Card, "The Condition of America," *FYI, The American Legislative Exchange*, 26 March 1993, 7.

32. Klein, "Whose Values?"

33. John Leo, "Who Gets Invited to the Table?" *U.S. News and World Report*, 18 July 1994, 18.

34. Steven S. Tigner, "Character Education: Outline of Seven Point Program," *Network News & Views* (Hudson Institute), August 1994, 5.

35. Gertrude Himmelfarb, "A Demoralized Society: The British/American Experience," *The Public Interest*, Fall 1994, 80.

36. Reed, "As Values Collapse."

37. Associated Press, "For Many, 'Situation Ethics' Are Replacing Moral Absolutes," *Washington Times*, 4 April 1992.

38. Arthur M. Schlesinger, Jr., *The Disuniting of America: Reflections on a Multicultural Society* (New York: Norton, 1992), 17.

39. Schlesinger, *Disuniting of America,* 17.

40. Josephson Institute of Ethics, press announcement, 8 October 1993.

41. Princeton Religion Research Center, newsletter 15 (1994), 1.

42. William J. Bennett, *The Book of Virtues* (New York: Simon and Schuster, 1993).

43. Andrew Oldenquist, "Directive Moral Education," *Letters From Santa Fe,* (St. John's College Newsletter), Fall 1992, 2.

44. C. S. Lewis, *The Abolition of Man* (New York: Macmillan, 1947), 77.

45. Lewis, *Abolition of Man,* 84.

Chapter 2

Building the Habitat of Character

Don E. Eberly

THE ACQUISITION OF CHARACTER

Being convinced of what character is, and of its need, is not enough. The restoration of character must be guided by sound theories of how it is imparted. Good character, according to Tom Lickona, consists of "knowing the good, desiring the good, and doing the good."[1]

In other words, character has cognitive, affective, and behavioral dimensions. It requires use of the head, the heart, and the hands. The cognitive side supplies the knowledge of right and wrong. The emotional side provides the bridge between personal judgment and responsible action. It includes conscience as well as empathy, which supplies the sense of obligation to do something with what you know. To possess and live out good character, the individual must desire the good, must be aware of specific moral qualities that are expected in a character-centered society, and must be able to apply these qualities to concrete cases through rational, moral decision-making.

THE HABITS OF CHARACTER

Aristotle differentiated between mere learning of facts, which was the function of pedagogy or of intellectual search, and acquiring wisdom. The

/5 8, 4 0 6

Aristotelian view suggests that individuals do not come by good character simply through moral instruction, but rather through the repetitious doing of good and heroic deeds. Character is not compartmentalized in a class: it is caught in the daily routines of ordinary life.

Moral virtues, such as courage or honor, come about as a result of "habit," says Aristotle. We become "just by doing just acts, temperate by doing temperate acts, brave by doing brave acts."[2]

Sound character, according to this school, is acquired through the development of sound habit, or through "habituation," to use James Q. Wilson's familiar term. Family habituation in particular, according to Wilson, is "the chief method by which every society induces its members to exercise a modicum of self-control and to assign a reasonable value to the preferences of others."[3]

Wilson defines the term habituation to mean "the process whereby people acquire a constant, often unconscious, way of doing something, a regular inclination to behave in ways that are either impulsive or reflective, self-indulgent or other-regarding, decent or indecent."[4]

> When right actions are regularly, promptly, and consistently followed by approval and rewards and when wrong actions are regularly, promptly, and consistently followed by disapproval and punishments, good behavior becomes more common and bad behavior less so.[5]

At the core of character are the notions of respect and responsibility. To act with responsibility for one's actions, one must be willing to take into account the consequences of one's behavior on others. To act consistently with respect toward others, one must have high regard for their inherent worth, which is acquired predominantly through a complex developmental process in early childhood in which impulsiveness is controlled out of sympathy for others.

Strategies for renewing character must be consistent and comprehensive, which means that certain primary sources such as family and kin are vital. Countless studies confirm the basic conclusion that human bonds—primarily those of the family—are indispensable to achieving emotional and cognitive well-being. In the family individuals develop the capacity for self-control and respect for the worth of others. Many ordinary problems of youth are rooted in the weakness or complete absence of the restraints that are acquired through parental nurturing. The most extreme forms of antisocial behavior, such as ruthless crime, are often explained by the lack of parental competence.

When this direct ordering of moral life is attempted in the schools, some may mistake it as a form of indoctrination. To be introduced to the habits of character, the student must indeed be predisposed toward a certain conception of the good, and reinforced for pursuing it. It is difficult to imagine how such a process could be avoided in any moral training program. Schools have always operated in accordance with some elementary notion of the good, if for no other reason than preparing citizens for democracy, and this requires imparting the virtues of self-government and respect for the rights of others. Moreover, this aspect of character education is consistent with the responsibility that has fallen to adults for the care and training of children throughout all of history.

While character education seeks to impart a clear moral understanding, it does so by virtue of an approach that develops the student's capacity for moral decisionmaking. The student is taught to think critically and to present justification for his actions. Aristotle himself affirmed the importance of both acquiring moral wisdom as well as granting the individual a choice in his actions.

THE HABITAT OF CHARACTER

Character development is not just an individual process, nor is it simply a function of pedagogy. Man does not stand alone in a universe of moral abstractions; he is a social being who comes by his moral development through a process that is social. In a free and democratic society, the individual and the society influence one another. Because free and just societies depend upon virtuous people for their success, they normally take the work of preserving virtue in the people seriously. The root meaning of the Greek word for ethics (*ethikos*) signifies an ethos that is rooted in community and transmitted through customs.

Restoring character, therefore, also requires a sociology of character. The problem with many efforts to guide moral reform, according to communitarian Amitai Etzioni, is that they are "asociological," which is to say that they address moral life as though it is simply a matter of developing individual conscience. In the process, says Etzioni, "many Americans disregard the crucial role of the community in reinforcing the individual's moral commitments."[6] Individuals are powerfully affected by "the approbation and censure" of others, especially those with whom we have close relations, such as family and neighbors. A society that wishes to preserve character, then, will encourage these voices in the community to speak in "unison and with clarity" in a way that strengthens individual judgments about right and wrong.[7]

Similar to Etzioni is Robert Nisbet's notion of a sociology of virtue, focusing on the protection and nurturing of "the varied groups and associations which form the building blocks of the social order."[8] These are the voluntary associations through whom a society nourishes the habits of citizenship, strengthens the ideals of self-improvement, and fortifies the foundations of character. Alexis de Tocqueville marveled at the force of "voluntary associations" and what he called the "spirit of township" through which the habits of citizenship and generous regard for the public interest flourished. Building character in and through these structures requires building what Harvard professor Robert Putman calls "civic community,"[9] or what David Green, author of *Reinventing Civil Society*, calls "communal liberalism."[10]

This sector is civil society, the realm between the individual and the state in which citizens conduct much of their lives and join together to mediate decisions and conflicts. A well-functioning society depends upon what Edmund Burke called "little platoons,"[11] Emile Durkheim called "the little aggregations,"[12] and Christopher Dawson called the "interpenetrating orders—political, economic, cultural, and religious."[13]

BUILDING A CULTURE OF CHARACTER

Children learn values from life—from family, from teachers and peers, church, athletics, the media and movies, the library, travel, and a host of other social activities. In decrying the corruption of character in individuals, it is easy to single out for blame the primary shapers of an individual's character, namely parents and teachers, while ignoring the tide of influence coming from sources well beyond their control.

Culture exerts a powerful force over the entire enterprise of character formation. Culture functions as society's thermometer and thermostat: it shapes and reflects society's deeper values and meaning. Thus, the content of culture can easily overwhelm other functions in society, such as politics and economics, by its force. In fact, a nation's political and economic systems are vessels into which the culture's preeminent values are constantly poured.

A healthy culture is not indifferent to its effect on individual character. Culture either elevates or debases, summons the noble or ignoble, generates public spiritedness or self-absorption. In other words, culture either cultivates or corrupts character. If a society wishes to see character flourish, it must create a culture of character operating throughout all spheres of society—the home, neighborhood, schools and workplace, and the powerful character-shaping institutions of media and entertainment.

Individual resistance to negative cultural influences is a fine and heroic pursuit, but as any parent knows, solitary efforts rarely succeed. Gertrude Himmelfarb says, "Individuals, families, churches, and communities cannot operate in isolation, cannot long maintain values at odds with those legitimated by the state and popularized by culture. It takes a great effort of will and intellect for the individual to decide for himself that something is immoral and to act on that belief when the law declares it legal and the culture deems it acceptable."[14] Values, she says, require legitimization.

Parents, teachers, and community leaders operating at the bottom of society need a lot of help from the intellectual, journalistic, and entertainment elites operating at the top of culture. George Will suggests that much of the moral corruption of society "comes from the top down." We live, he says, in "a trickle-down culture that begins with the idea that the good life consists of satisfying every impulse." Many cultural leaders, he says, have helped supplant those moral categories essential to civilized living, replacing them with a thin-gruel vocabulary of 'lifestyles' and 'values' and 'self-esteem.'[15]

C. S. Lewis maintained that moral principles were learned indirectly from others around us—moral exemplars—and that it was difficult to preserve virtuous individuals apart from a virtuous society. Unfortunately, the tendency of culture shapers is often to offend and disturb, as Lionel Trilling said in his famous essays entitled *Beyond Culture*. It is to generate, Trilling says, a "disenchantment of our culture with culture itself."

Michael Josephson particularly blames the "incredibly bad parade of examples" of public figures from sports, business, and politics. He says that, based upon cultural programming, kids "grow up believing that successful people lie and cheat and steal. That's the environment in which they're learning values today."[16]

Media/Entertainment

Until very recently, society made a concerted effort to protect childhood as a period of relative innocence from premature negative influences. Children were to be nurtured in an unhurried environment, protected by all adults from the coarse and cruel influences that would come.

That was before the rise of an entertainment and media culture in which the marketplace is king and increasingly exasperated parents struggle to remain moral guardians of their children. No strategy to restore character to American life will be successful unless it includes a plan to raise the level of responsibility within the national media and entertainment for the sake of children.

So dominant is the media in American culture that we are becoming "a society created by the media," according to Henry Johnson.[17]   The direction of society is more and more determined by massive media enterprises employing the techniques of mass media and determined, by whatever means necessary, to reach and hold mass audiences. In a society in which the medium is the message, the medium itself dominates, if not completely determines, the conversation over who we are and ought to be. The omnipresence of the media has fundamentally affected all aspects of American life, private and public.   It has even radically altered our understanding of the public sphere, and how we view and talk about our public problems.   By any measurement, our discourse has become superficial and debased.

From the revolutionary period, through the Civil War and until the recent rise of electronic media, the heart of the American democratic experience was the rhetorical tradition. Through the printed word, colonial Americans read Thomas Paine's *Common Sense* and nineteenth-century Americans read George Whitefield's sermons and *McGuffey's Readers*, by the tens of millions.   Society celebrated the printed word. According to Neil Postman, when Charles Dickens visited America in 1842, he received the adulation that is reserved today for TV celebrities and football quarterbacks.[18]

The records of history suggest that just about everybody read. Under the governance of the printing press, says Postman, discourse in America was "generally coherent, serious, and rational."   Under television, he says, it has become "dangerous nonsense...shriveled and absurd." With television, the viewer is ushered into a world of images and emotions in which fact and fiction are blurred.   The viewer becomes passive, his mind largely disengaged, his moral sensibilities neutralized. Rational forms of discourse and human exchange are traded in for entertaining fantasy.   Even otherwise serious matters—like religion, children's programming, and the evening news—is transformed through television into the same entertaining format. Compared to debates over slavery in which each antagonist was given up to three hours to make his case, complex reality is conveyed via television in 15-second snippets of sights and sounds.

Mortimer Zuckerman, editor in chief of *U.S. News and World Report*, has said that the nation's moral "redemption" must begin in two areas: education and television. It is hard to imagine moral reform coming to a nation without the help of television executives. Society, says Zuckerman, must find some way for television to have a higher purpose than merely making money.[19]

For many kids, television may exert more influence than parents and teachers combined. Children spend more waking hours at school than with their parents, but even more hours annually in front of television than in the classroom. The average teenager spends 1.8 hours a week reading, 5.6 hours a week on homework, and 21 hours a week watching television. Quality time with parents, according to numerous studies, is facing near extinction in many households.

The content that comes from the television tutor is not encouraging. Children are being raised in a social environment drenched in violence. A 1990 study by the American Psychological Association concluded that by his or her tenth birthday, an American child typically witnesses 8,000 simulated murders and more than 100,000 other acts of simulated violence.[20] In many distressed neighborhoods, television fiction increasingly blends with reality as poorly socialized kids are raised on a daily desensitizing diet of TV violence which portrays real-life crimes previously unthinkable.

Then there is the permeating presence of sexual themes and innuendo. *Time* describes "the saturation of American culture with sexual messages, themes, images, and exhortations." According to the Center for Population Options, teens typically watch five hours of television a day—which in a year means they have seen nearly 14,000 sexual encounters. Whether TV, MTV, Calvin Klein ads, or the heavy-breathing movies of mainstream theater, everywhere kids turn adults seem to be undressing. The results? More than a third of 15-year-old boys and 27 percent of 15-year-old girls have had sex. By the end of teen years, it is 75 percent. One-fourth of teens contract some venereal disease each year. Teens are the fastest-growing segment of the population infected with the AIDS (HIV) virus.[21]

This is the media environment in which all countervailing movements, such as teen abstinence, parental responsibility, and the character movement, must operate. Not surprisingly, polls reveal a deep discouragement among parents over the loss of parental control and the demise of childhood. Writing for *Newsweek*, author and playwright Joy Overbeck describes the experience of raising her eight-year-old daughter in a culture in which she is "bathed in the fantasy of bodies and beauty that marinates our entire culture. The result is an insidious form of premature sexual awakening that is stealing our kids' youth." The message of our popular culture for any observant eight-year-old, says

Overbeck, is "sex rules."[22]

Character and the Marketplace

America is the world's most successful market economy. Billions of daily marketplace transactions exert a powerful, often unseen, influence over the individuals who participate as producers, workers, and consumers of goods, services, and values. Most adults spend the greater part of their waking hours pursuing some remunerative activity in the marketplace. Business professionals and managers carry a heavy responsibility in determining whether the corporate culture is one that values or devalues character.

For decades, the pursuit of ethics in business received little encouragement from the nation's top business schools. In 1979 the retiring chairman of the Securities and Exchange Commission, John Shad, endowed the Harvard Business School with a grant of $20 million for the purpose of teaching "business ethics." The receipt of this generous contribution was appreciated, but the purpose to which the money had been targeted generated immediate confusion.[23]

The money arrived long after the consensus in academia over whether there was such a "discipline" as ethics had collapsed. The suggestion that a classroom enterprise such as this could possibly make men and women moral in the marketplace seemed anachronistic. This work, if it was to be conducted at all, belonged to parents and religious institutions, not scholars engaged in rational pursuits. How can matters of conscience be cultivated in a learning environment, much less applied in any systematic way?

Harvard was not unique. Many universities have long abandoned an interest in morality as inconsistent with the higher calling of scientific inquiry, preferring instead the radically rationalist and oxymoronic term "value free." There are the rigorous scientific fields of biology, geometry, and economics; then there are the unscientific and highly normative fields of moral ethics that were always seen as located adjacent to the religion department. One represents the objective world of fact and rationality, the other allegedly occupies the subjective realm of private opinion and theological speculation.

A decline in business ethics, documented extensively elsewhere, produces, in hundreds of measurable ways, declining economic opportunity for those entering the marketplace. An erosion in business ethics supplies government with the rationale to resort to regulation, and forces the private sector on the defensive in countless ways from litigation to regulatory compliance. The general pattern of decline in personal moral responsibility contributes to lower worker well-being as drug and alcohol use and family stress turns businesses into social agencies.

Business schools have recently shown signs of renewed interest in the pursuit of economic wealth by ethical means. Popular literature emphasizing quality, ethics, and character is proliferating. Stephen Covey, for example, promotes the "character ethic," which he says is based upon the basic idea that "there are principles that govern human effectiveness—natural laws in the human dimension that are just as real, just as unchanging and unarguably 'there' as laws such as gravity are in the physical dimension."[24] In reviewing 150 years of "success" literature, Covey found the character ethic as the consistent foundation of success—principles such as courage, integrity, justice, industry, and temperance.[25]

Stories abound about how renewed commitment to ethics translates into quality, more satisfied customers, and improved profits. Visionary leaders who enjoy influence at the top of American business and industry can play a powerful role in guiding the commercial sector back to an embrace of ethics as the key to an economy more self-regulated and less fettered by external control.

Character and Public Discourse

Civil society involves the exchange of ideas—even vigorous arguments over competing ideas and values. In no area of public life are society's extremes of individualism more evident than in its public debate. Rarely is there the faintest reference to any concept of the common good. The ancients viewed politics as a means of improving man's capacity to better himself and to practice self-government. Politics was rarely separated from the deeper normative questions regarding the purposes for which citizens lived, individually and corporately. Statecraft meant more than simply advancing individual interests within the realm of government; in large measure it was soulcraft.

Politics, practiced as soulcraft, concerned itself with the condition of a person's mind and soul, his or her habits of industry, moderation, courage, public spiritedness, and capacity for sound democratic judgment—characteristics which republican forms of government were thought to depend upon for survival.

The classical philosophers were concerned about rhetoric and the public discourse. The story of the Roman Empire is the record of one monumental success heaped upon another, only to be followed by the internal collapse of civilization into disorder. Disorder was fueled in part by the endless polemics that broke out between warring factions during the latter stages of the republic, producing bitter and eventually violent recriminations. Historian Lewis Mumford described "a leaching away of meaning and a loss of faith" in the Roman Republic, and a "barbarization from within."[26]

In other words, public discourse can contribute to, even compound, the erosion of mutual trust and respect. Without acknowledging the other's humanity, debates generate into shrill mutterings, plunging into the "objectivization"[27] of human beings. Whoever wins, society loses, and "the barbarian is at the gates of the city."[28]

Anyone concerned about character in public life will be concerned about character in public discourse. To Thomas Hobbes, author of *Leviathan*, the one irreducible requirement for civil debate was possessing a genuine respect for the rights and dignity of one's fellows. He suggested the establishment of a "golden rule" for public life which held high a basic moral principle: "do not that to another which thou wouldst not have done to thyself."[29] He said no practitioner of democracy should "by deed, word, countenance, or gesture declare hatred or contempt for others." The reemergence of the golden rule as a unifying moral principle for children in schools might be preceded by a return to use by adults in public debate.

Policy

The work of moral habituation was once entirely the work of private institutions. But there is no denying that today's government touches nearly every aspect of life with its countless programs, messages, rewards and penalties, and by so doing either reinforces or undermines individual responsibility.

Public law and policy, like culture, play a critical role in the legitimization of values. The refusal of politicians to reform tort law only encourages litigation. The increasing support of rights to the exclusion of responsibilities in government policy sends a powerful message that society exclusively values the individual, and devalues the community. Unrestrained growth in public debt undoubtedly signals approval for equal levels of private borrowing.

Few would recommend turning the U.S. government into a national nanny. It was not designed for moral reformation and should not be entrusted with it. Still, government is too pervasive for policy-makers to be indifferent to its influence over character and culture. Former

Department of Education Undersecretary Chester Finn maintains that the vitality of culture "is a key factor in the success and durability of nations and peoples," and thus the maintenance of core cultural values is essential for the preservation of a free society and in a nation's long-term interest. That society, "including the government," he says, must play an active role in the maintenance of values. All that Finn is recommending is that government policy "send the right messages and teach proper lessons to the whole society, and especially the young, about good behavior, sound habits, and acceptable practices."[30]

Private institutions are superior by far and will meet less resistance than government in undertaking this function. Where policy-makers could help is in consciously strengthening the role of private value-shaping organizations which frequently suffer from government encroachment. James Q. Wilson urges policy-makers to encourage "local, private efforts that seem to do the best job at reducing drug abuse, inducing young people to marry, persuading parents, especially fathers, to take responsibility for their children, and exercising informal social control over neighborhood streets."[31]

Character and Parenting

No institution is as central to character formation as the home. Even if all other societal institutions were somehow functioning well, and the home was dysfunctional, individuals would be poorly prepared for life and social decline would soon follow. Chicago sociologist James Coleman has long argued that the strength of families is *the* variable that shapes all others. He said, "I believe the causes of the downward trends in youth character lie primarily outside the school—in the changes that have taken place in the American family."[32]

Parents are under enormous stress. Not only must the family compete with powerful influences from outside the home, as discussed above, but the families have less time to pursue quality family life inside the home. The combined rise of single-parent households and the growing employment of each parent where both exist, has resulted in a precipitous drop in available time for parenting. Once the primary source of care and instruction at home, upwards of two-thirds of women have some employment outside of the home, leaving far less time for face-to-face communication with children. More instruction is delegated to television, teachers, and other caregivers.

According to Harvard professor Robert Cole, who has studied and observed children for decades, parental busyness is the primary culprit for why "children are no longer being cared for by their parents in the way they once were." Cole blames the rise of materialism for much of the phenomenon. He says "parents are too busy spending their most precious capital—their time and energy—struggling to keep up with the MasterCard payments. They're depleted." The trade-off is that parents work longer hours so that the kids are left with "Nintendo or a pair of Nikes...big deal."[33]

Every effort, including government policy reforms, must be directed at strengthening parental time, financial capacity, and competence in the care of children.

CHARACTER AND THE COMMONWEALTH—THE JOURNEY TOWARD A NEW PUBLIC PHILOSOPHY

As pointed out in the beginning of this section, Americans are in a somber mood about the state of society. Cynicism and fear are combining to erode their confidence in prevailing policies and values as well as their respect for the democratic and cultural institutions responsible for them. As polls confirm, large majorities now feel the consequences of society's decades-long process of weakening regard for character and responsibility.

The preservation of virtue was thought by many of America's Founders to be the central concern of statecraft. Madison thought it chimerical to believe a republican form of government could last without the preservation of republican virtue. As originally designed by America's Framers and as observed over the years by visitors such as G. K. Chesterton and Alexis de Tocqueville, citizenship and character were the very centerpiece of what has been called the American creed. The Founders fully expected that self-interest in the pursuit of commercial advantage was a good and natural impulse but that it would be equally matched by concerted efforts to instill civic virtue. Combined, commerce and character would build a civilization rich in opportunity and civil in its manners and mores.

The existence of self-interest as a motivating force was a given; as the Founders saw it, rooted in nature. Neither was there any doubt, given man's natural tendency toward vice and faction, that the nation's leaders would take necessary steps to preserve virtue. The thought that the pursuit of virtue could be abandoned entirely for the pursuit of interests and wealth alone would have been considered inconceivable during the nation's early years.

Yet, with very few exceptions, politics in recent decades has given scant recognition to the republican virtue thought so central to American success. Current ideologies appear either unwilling or incapable of commanding unselfish devotion to anything that might be defined as the common good; they do not even try. The language of common good or of commonwealth—a term implying shared ideals—has fallen completely out of use.

The vision of progress that has dominated Western imagination ever since the Enlightenment, according to David Walsh, has been one of "unending technological, industrial, social, and political progress."[34] But with the persistence of deep and seemingly intractable social problems and the arrival of a postmodernism, a weariness and wariness has set in. According to Walsh, "The age that began with the glory of the Renaissance, the bright expectations of the enlightenment, and the energies of the scientific, industrial, and political revolutions has devolved in the horror, vacuity, and mediocrity of the twentieth century." The search for human progress in the form of technical and material advances has created a society wedded to the pursuit of happiness through power, interest group privilege, litigation, and crass consumerism. The result has been the triumph of the private over the public, the individual over the community, the secular over the sacred, and commerce over character.

This is a vision for progress that assumes that continued improvement can be engineered for society from outside of man through endless economic growth (the political Right) or endless bureaucratic interventions (the political Left). The result of this vision of progress in the twentieth century has been what Peter Drucker calls "salvation by state," an almost messianic zeal for power. The striving for social progress through power was matched in fervor by a self-aggrandizing abandonment of self-governance.

Contrary to expectation, the restless search for human progress through power has done nothing to transfigure human nature. A society that was prepared to place an almost religious faith in reason, technology, and administrative expertise to deliver progress was also one that was prepared to abandon virtue. This is a republic in which the forms of thought are ideological and the mode of public action is self-interest; where the only community is faction, where public discourse consists of "rights talk," and where justice becomes a zero-sum game of gains and losses for groups.

This is a republic not of ideals or of virtue, but of commerce, legal procedure, and bureaucratic fiat. And it is not the nation that Tocqueville observed in the 1830s, which sought to "elevate the mind and teach it to regard the things of this world with generous feelings, to form and nourish strong convictions and keep alive the spirit of honorable devotedness." This is a republic that, as the late Russell Kirk put it, has "committed taxidermy on moral categories, draining them of their richness and stuffing them full of sawdust talk of 'rights' and 'interests' and 'interstate commerce.'"[35]

This is a politicized society in which every public problem is seen as partisan property, where every public dispute is cast in the language of the tribe: "us versus them." Harvard professor Mary Ann Glendon has compared the recent tendency of our politicized society to assert political hegemony over other spheres of authority to the tendency during the French Revolution to destroy all intermediary institutions in society under the slogan "there are no rights except those of individuals and the state."

There is little wonder so many Americans now fear that their public life resembles war. Societies differ in thousands of ways, but cross-cultural studies indicate that the decisive characteristic is whether the culture favors and privileges its groups—family, community, corporation, or state—or whether it strictly rewards the individual.

America has always been regarded as a highly individualistic society, and a well-moderated individualism is good. It supplies society with enormous energy or achievement resulting in expanding goods and opportunities for the betterment of all. But the individualism of today, coming from both the Left and the Right, celebrates untrammeled freedom from restraint or obligation. The mere mention of favoring the community over the individual, or responsibilities over rights, even if by voluntary means, provokes a fear of statism on the libertarian Right and of reaction on the Left. Efforts to build shared values are dismissed as majoritarianism, collectivism, or worse, fascism, even though the more likely path to any of those destinations is the kind of moral relativism and cultural nihilism that is currently afflicting the entire West.

There is nothing either exalted or noble, says David Walsh, about "a humanity composed of a mass of atomistic individuals, each claiming prerogative of unfettered self-expression and the limitless gratification of desire." The loss he says is respect for man as a moral and spiritual being who possesses freedom and dignity.[36] The autonomous person, subscribing to relativized morality, basing all ethical decisions entirely on human choice, is a person in descent.

Reversing the decline of human respect and dignity presents a new challenge for those seeking progress: viewing the challenge as mostly spiritual, psychological, and social. The chief frontiers of the future are not those of science, technology, or administrative improvements, but finding the capacity, as Robert Bellah put it, of uniting the tremendous possibilities opened up by modern technologies with "a coherent pattern of living together."

The Paradigm of Civil Society

The American debate must move beyond the two competing paradigms of either laissez-faire or the welfare state, into the paradigm of a civil and humane society. Born of a growing dissatisfaction with prevailing approaches, a growing number of historians and social critics are turning to a tradition which the late Christopher Lasch described as "republicanism" or "civic humanism," which has historically been a strong competitor of liberal individualism.

The new vision of civic republicanism responds to the refusal of current ideologies to inspire constructive action beyond political organizing. It is a vision for reordering society, not just reforming government. It is a vision for achieving social change, not just ballot box victories aimed at control of Congress. It is a vision for the empowerment, not only of individuals, but of the communities that prepare individuals for citizenship.

Character and the New Localism

As pointed out previously, leaders operating at the top of society bear a heavy responsibility. Still, because of the nature of the work, renewing character will be done, as it must, at the lowest levels of society, and particularly in the noncoercive sector of civil society. This is a decentralized world conceptualized by Robert Bellah, author of *The Good Society*, as a "new localism," what Josiah Royce long ago called "provincialism," or what Lewis Mumford called "settlement."

These are visions for community, not separated from the notion of nation, but joined in local commitment to the nourishment of habits and customs which are the seedbeds of character. They offer a bold call to social reformation; they seek to mobilize citizens and leaders from all sectors of society, and unashamedly call for a return to the American creed of character, self-government, and community.

Civic republicanism affirms spiritual dimensions of America's longing for renewal and seeks to confront the power of secular ideologies and intellectual paradigms that crowd out the sacred from community life. It replaces a humanism which is secular with a humanitarianism which embraces the whole man, including his spiritual and social nature.

The relationship between the health of the soul and the well-being of the commonwealth has long been recognized in Western thought. Society is a spiritual community, said Edmund Burke. It is not an artificial construction; it is a spiritual partnership, not just between those who are living, but "between those who are living, those who are dead and those who are yet born."[37]

The search for a transcendent foundation for law, politics, economics, and society need not be a sectarian undertaking. Civic republicanism offers a framework for transcending religious and ideological factionalism by reviving a language that is neither secular nor sectarian. It is a language of social fraternity, strengthened neighborhoods, and shared values. It is a public philosophy committed to advancing claims on society through moral means—rooted in Martin Luther King Jr.'s call to avoid the politics of resentment and bitterness. Above all, it places the focus of concern on the strengthening of those institutions which mediate between the individual and the state—family, religious, civic, and voluntary associations.

THE JOURNEY OUTWARD: CHARACTER-CENTERED SOCIAL CHANGE

Margaret Mead is said to have warned on her deathbed that if civilization is to survive, it will be saved, not by a reformed government, but by citizen volunteer associations "going out and taking social action." Mead was describing the restoration of civil society premised upon the strengthening of character and citizenship.

If Mead is correct, Americans have been led to expect too much change through the ballot box. Public cynicism is rooted both in a government that underperforms while overextending and in a politics that dramatically oversells itself as a source of national renewal. The result: politics asserts greater hegemony over spheres of human life and society which were never before thought to be its proper domain.

As stated by the late Russell Kirk, "A society in which men and women are morally adrift, ignorant of norms, and intent chiefly upon gratification of appetites, will be a bad society—no matter how many people vote and no matter how liberal its formal constitution may be."[38]

When public life is dominated by the impulse to politicize, the state becomes society's master, not its servant. Greater by far than the cost of government to the taxpayer may be its harm to character-building institutions of civil society, such as the family, church, neighborhood, and other mediating structures that provide individuals meaning and social solidarity.

As polls indicate, the public is most worried about social regression. As currently defined, politics is presented as the only instrument to change America even though many of America's weaknesses lie in the civic, cultural, and moral realms where government solutions are often deficient and unworkable. It is difficult to imagine significant breakthroughs coming from city hall or state or federal lawmakers to reduce crime, teen pregnancy, family fragmentation, dependence on drugs and alcohol, or the decline in manners and morals.

The restoration of character throughout society will require new social movements which are committed to transcending an exhausted ideological politics that defines all social and cultural problems as the appropriate target for policy agendas, not a renewed civil society, to solve.

There are signs that as the twentieth century draws to a close the century's most destructive scourge, political salvationism, may be in retreat. On the pro-government Left, growing numbers of government officials privately voice exasperation over the limited capacity of even fully funded programs or fully staffed policy departments, social agencies, and prisons to cope with spiraling social problems.

On the laissez-faire Right, the idea that government is always the problem and thus the answer is simply getting rid of it appears increasingly naive. There is scant evidence to support the assumption that this action alone, in a time of deepening social disorder, will cause civil society, individual virtue, and strong communities to magically reappear.

What is needed to save families, make neighborhoods friendly and safe, and restore lost virtues are dynamic new social movements centered on the restoration of character such as have come along periodically in American history. What made the difference during earlier periods of American history was the development of voluntary societies and social reform movements which sought to socialize males, curb adolescent crime, and take sterner measures to protect vulnerable children.

There is little evidence from the record of either American history or other cultures to suggest that a rise in crime, for example, correlates with either weak economies or defective public policies. It is rather the case that the rise of general criminality tends to accompany a softening of social sanctions against radical individualism and its celebration of the release rather than restraint of impulse.

The pattern of the past suggests that change begins when growing numbers of people are appalled enough at disorder to reassert older notions of informal social control against a too dominant libertine subculture. Values of permissiveness are forced to yield to values emphasizing the mastery of passion out of respect for the good of society.

Until recent decades, the work of moral uplift for the sake of society was thought by cultural elites to be progressive, not reactionary work. A good, progressive, and tolerant society was one that bothered to solicit good character in its citizens. Because preserving morality was not assumed to be coercive or the business of government, it was reinforced predominantly through voluntary means throughout all sectors of society.

During the nineteenth century, for example, Americans created hundreds of voluntary associations and societies aimed at social reform and moral uplift. There were spiritual awakenings, temperance movements, private charity campaigns, and children's aid societies. For the churched, there was the Sunday School movement; for the unchurched, there were YMCAs and rigorous character education programs in the public schools.

Works of charity treated the whole man. Temperance cadets took aim at morally reckless youth. Poorly socialized young males were mentored by adult men. Churches did not wait for a change in Congress to rescue neglected and abandoned children. The unemployed were drawn into church-sponsored training programs that developed the habits of self-motivation as well as the skills of industry.

The results of these nineteenth-century voluntary social movements to inculcate internal controls were large declines in alcohol consumption, criminality, sexual license, and a host of other social problems.

The true citizen does more than participate in elections. He or she organizes his or her community against crime, develops strategies against teen pregnancy, volunteers at the local soup kitchen, and joins the PTA. The true politician does more than simply attend to the affairs of government; he or she leads movements to strengthen the character-shaping institutions of civil society—family, neighborhood, church and synagogue, and voluntary associations.

Generating social change will require resuscitating an older and richer concept of both citizenship and politics—a tradition rooted in character.

NOTES

1. Thomas Lickona, "The Return of Character Education," *Educational Leadership,* November 1993, 9.

2.   Aristotle, *Nichomachean Ethics*, bk. 1, chap. 1 in *The Basic Works of Aristotle*, ed. Richard McKeon (New York: Random House, 1941).

3.   James Q. Wilson, "Culture, Incentives, and the Underclass," *Values and Public Policy* (Washington, DC: Brookings Institution, 1994), 62.

4.   Wilson, "Culture, Incentives, and the Underclass," 55.

5.   James Q. Wilson, "Public Policy and Personal Character," in A. Anderson and D. L. Bark, eds., *Thinking About America: The United States in the 1990s*, (Palo Alto, CA: Hoover Institution, 1988), 493.

6.   Amitai Etzioni, "Restoring Our Moral Voice," *The Public Interest,* Summer 1994, 109.

7.   Etzioni, "Restoring," 110.

8.   William Kristol, "The Future of Conservatism," *The American Enterprise*, July-August 1994, 32.

9.   David Boldt, "The Anatomy of Democracy," *Philadelphia Inquirer*, 30 August 1994.

10.   David G. Green, *Reinventing Civil Society: The Rediscovery of Welfare Without Politics* (London: Institute of Economic Affairs, 1993), 3.

11.   Peter L. Berger and Richard John Neuhaus, *To Empower People: The Role of Mediating Structures in Public Policy* (Washington, DC: AEI Press, 1977), 4.

12.   Berger and Neuhaus, *To Empower People.*

13.   Christopher Dawson, *Beyond Politics* (Freeport, NY: Books For Libraries, 1971), 21.

14.   Gertrude Himmelfarb, "A Demoralized Society: The British/American Experience," *The Public Interest*, Fall 1994, 74.

15.   George Will, "A Trickle Down Culture," *Newsweek,* 13 December 1993, 84.

16.   David O'Reilly, "Ethics of Adolescents: A Plan to Clear Up Moral Confusion," *Philadelphia Inquirer*, 20 October 1993.

17.   Henry C. Johnson, "Society, Culture and Character Development," in K. Ryan and G. F. McLean, eds., *Character Development in Schools and Beyond* (New York: Praeger, 1987), 59.

18.   Neil Postman, *Amusing Ourselves to Death* (New York: Penguin Books, 1985), 30-40.

19.   Mortimer B. Zuckerman, "Where Have Our Values Gone?" *U.S. News and World Report,* 8 August 1994, 88.

20.   Thomas F. Curran, "Our Children Live in a Violent World," *Philadelphia Inquirer*, 14 July 1994.

21.   Karen R. Effrem, "Where Do Children Fit Our Priority List?" *Center For The American Experiment*, August 1993, 3.

22.   Joy Overbeck, "Sex, Kids, and the Slut Look," *Newsweek*, 26 July 1993, 8.

23.   Irving Kristol, "Ethics Anyone," *Wall Street Journal*, 15 September 1987.

24.   Stephen R. Covey, *The Seven Habits of Highly Effective People* (New

York: Simon and Schuster, 1989), 32.

25. Covey, *Seven Habits*, 18.

26. Norman Lear, "A Call For Spiritual Renewal," *Washington Post*, 30 May 1993.

27. Dietrich Bonhoeffer, *The Cost of Discipleship* (New York: Macmillan, 1955), 23.

28. John Courtney Murray, *We Hold These Truths: Catholic Reflections on the American Proposition* (New York: Sheed and Ward, 1960), 11-12.

29. Thomas Hobbes, *Leviathan* (1651), chaps. 14-15.

30. Chester E. Finn, Jr., "Giving Shape to Cultural Conservatism," *The American Spectator*, November 1986.

31. Wilson, "Culture, Incentives, and the Underclass," 74.

32. Kevin Ryan and Thomas Lickona, "Character Development: The Challenge and the Model," in K. Ryan and G. F. McLean, eds., *Character Development in Schools and Beyond* (New York: Praeger, 1982), 6.

33. Kristen J. Amundson, "Teaching Values and Ethics:　Problems and Solutions," *AASA Critical Issues Report* (1991): 13.

34. David Walsh, *After Ideology* (San Francisco: Harper, 1990), 3.

35. Russell Kirk, *The Politics of Prudence* (Bryn Mawr, PA: Intercollegiate Studies Institute, 1993), 30.

36. Walsh, *After Ideology*, 257.

37. Russell Kirk, *The Conservative Mind* (Washington, DC: Regency Books, 1986), 17.

38. Kirk, *The Politics of Prudence*, 18.

II. The Theory and Origins of Character

Chapter 3

The Cultural Roots of Virtue and Character

Michael Novak

INTRODUCTION

The word "virtue" today is commonly associated with sexual behavior, as when in saying that a woman has lost her "virtue," we mean her chastity. In this weak meaning, the term has become only a faint shadow of its former self. For free societies today, we need a more robust meaning of the term, of at least the depth that the ancient Greeks and Romans gave it—and, to account for the responsibilities imposed by modern freedoms, considerably more ample range.

The ancient city states of Greece were typically quite small; Athens at the height of its power consisted of 30,000 inhabitants, most of them slaves. To defend their city against their enemies, therefore, and to attain the sort of civilization to which they aspired, the relatively few free Greek males of Athens had to develop a broad repertoire of military and civil skills. In their own lives, they needed a certain degree of discipline, self-control, and concentration of attention. With regard to their common life, they needed to learn arts of expression and persuasion, civic duty and public honor, reliability, and wisdom. They needed to learn how to use arms—dagger, sword, and spear—and they needed skill with horses and chariots. A young lad of 10 or 12 had quite a lot to learn by the time he reached 18. The city needed him to learn these things. His fellows expected him to learn them. In this context, the word "virtue" corresponded to an obvious necessity of Greek education.

A Greek male needed to be able to act in many different capacities because the demands of civilization were so many while the citizens were few. At one moment, he would need to employ the arts of peace; at another, the arts of war. It was useful, therefore, to have a term like "virtue" to designate these settled dispositions, these learned skills, these tendencies or capacities (and to act quickly, with some degree of excellence and pleasure—in one field of activity and then in another), of which Greek city states had such manifest need. The most general term for such settled dispositions or capacities is "habit."[1] From the point of view either of the individual or of the community, one can, however, speak of *good habits* and *bad habits*. The good habits were called "virtues"; the bad habits, "vices."[2]

The habits were thought of as tendencies or dispositions; in this respect, they were regarded as properties of the human *mind* and *will*. The word "mind" came into play when human actions needed to be informed by acts of insight and judgment. Typical evidences of the human mind in action are getting the point of a joke or a story, sizing up a situation, grasping what needs to be done, or forming a judgment that one should proceed in this way rather than that. All these are acts of insight and judgment—and all these are also acts in which experience and preparation, nourishing native wit, matter a lot.

CLARIFICATION OF TERMS

Getting the point about the habits of the mind was, for the Greeks, as natural as opening their eyes; becoming conscious of the meaning of the word "will" was a little more difficult. Permit me to use a modern example. Suppose that in going to bed at night you remember that you need to get up the instant the alarm rings because of an early commitment. However, when the alarm rings, it penetrates your grogginess only gradually. Your sense of hearing and your remote memory awaken first. Eventually, you become sufficiently aware of the cause of the jangling to recognize that it comes from the alarm. Slowly, the association is made with the need to arise immediately. Instinctively, your arm begins to move toward the clock to shut it off. But neither your mind nor your will is sufficiently focused to direct the arm efficiently toward its target. Your mind awakens slowly as you become dimly conscious of where you are, what is happening, what that sound means, and what you are supposed to do. But your body is still wed to sleep, and the desire for continued union with sleep is strong. The imperative concerning what you *ought* to do is at war with what your body *wants* to do. Two parts of yourself are at war —the part attuned to "want" and the part attuned to "ought." As your mind gets clearer, this inner conflict comes into sharper focus. You experience within yourself, in fact, the slow awakening of *will*, over against the inclination of the rest of you. Your will is, in a sense, the last and deepest of your inner capacities to come awake. It is the hardest to bring into exercise. You can feel the struggle to summon it up, in order to force yourself to get out of bed.

From this example, it is fairly easy to see why moral education needs to focus on the training of the will. Will is the capacity that makes us choose to do something; it makes us want to follow the dictates of what we know we should do, and to want to do so badly enough to overcome the most intense resistance of the rest of us. (My father used to joke that he had no problems with will power; what caused him trouble, he said, was *won't* power. What he wanted, he wanted; saying "no" was the harder exercise.) The will is the power to carry the judgment of the mind—"yes" or "no"—into action. It is the power of self-government, self-mastery, and self-discipline.

GREEK PHILOSOPHY OF VIRTUE

In relation to the history of philosophy, the modern example of heeding the alarm clock achieves another purpose. In Greek thought, particularly in Aristotle, there was considerable clarity about the nature of a voluntary act. But of what St. Paul was later to call "the inner war in our members," there was considerably less awareness. The Greeks tended to be fascinated by the power of mind and reason, on the one hand, and the power of the passions of sensuality and pride, on the other hand. They did not give as much scope to will as, later, Roman and especially Christian thought did.

The Greeks had an acute sense of the war between reason and the passions. This war reflects in part the famous mind/body problem which still plagues those parts of modern philosophy which owe most to the retrieval of Greek thought by the Enlightenment. (One can see this war between reason and the passions still vividly at work in the novels of Nikos Kazantzakis, for example, in *The Last Temptation of Christ*.) But this war reflects, as well, and in some ways more profoundly, the hidden work of the passions in subverting, overpowering, or co-opting the mind, of which the Greeks with their love for mind were painfully aware.

One should not, as moderns often do, think of passion solely in terms of sensuality or erotic desire. The passions of the spirit are far deeper and more potent than the passions of the flesh—perhaps especially so such passions as the desire for power, the pride of life, and the desire for self-sufficiency (the desire to be like God). This fact is reflected in our instinctive association of the passions of the spirit with the strong, and the passions of the flesh with the weak. The first are certainly more lasting and more deeply driven. The latter, while for a time fully and sweetly absorbing, are more quickly sated and in their swift passing leave a disquieting emptiness.

The Greeks, indeed, had a great respect for the passions of the mind, to which they were deeply committed. So much power did they ascribe to the mind, indeed, that they sometimes seemed to say that if you *knew* what you should do, *really knew*, you would necessarily do it. They thought of the Good, fully seen, as overpowering the mind. They did not allow—or did not allow much—for weakness of the will. The action of the will hardly figured in Greek thought. Thus was left to Christian thinkers, especially to St. Paul, St. Augustine, and St. Thomas Aquinas, the task of explaining how it could happen that what we know we should not do, we do, and what we know we should do, we do not. Regarding both the concept of conscience and the concept of will, Christian philosophy was to add a great deal of light to the unfinished psychology of the Greeks.[3]

This brief digression into the psychology of the passions might seem to have taken us far from the point; but it has not. One can only understand the theory of the virtues in the context of the theory of the passions and emotions.[4] In Greek thought, one of the roles of the chief virtues, on which sound human action most often hinges (thus the term "cardinal" virtues, from the Latin *cardo*, hinge), is to order the passions in such a way that mind and will can do their best work. Mind and will need the equanimity afforded by tempered passions; the courage to still fears of various kinds; and learned instincts of practical wisdom and the right touch in giving to each person and each matter its due: thus, as we shall see, "the four cardinal virtues": temperance, fortitude, practical wisdom, and justice. The inner life of the human being, experience had taught the Greeks, is complex. One part of ourselves, then another part, seems to take the lead in our consciousness and to display itself in our actions. We act from reason; we act from passion; we act from whim. Thus, the imperative "Know Thyself," a fundamental imperative of human life, gives scope to a wide-ranging inquiry into everything our consciousness touches.

In applying the imperative of self-knowledge to understanding their own human actions, the Greeks laid special stress on those dispositions or capacities from which actions are elicited as situations demand. A man of well-developed habits in a broad range of fields of activity, a well-rounded man, will at one time be called upon to think clearly, on another occasion to speak persuasively, on yet another to lead a group of fellow citizens decisively and wisely, and on a fourth occasion to meet the enemy in deadly and fateful combat. To perform well in all these fields of activity—and to perform well on demand, with excellence, and with pleasure—is to draw on the considerable human capital of inherited and acquired habit. So, up until the modern era, the ancient Greeks and Romans, and later the medieval Jews and Christians, imagined the arena of human action.

ATTRIBUTES OF HUMAN VIRTUES

I mentioned earlier that the human virtues were thought to reside chiefly in the mind and will. The two sets of abilities—the mind to gain insight and to make judgments, and the will to lock onto goals and commitments—were, together, recognized as distinctively human. To become adequately human is to seek to understand and to summon up the will to act accordingly. Each of us does these two exercises with a distinctive signature. These give us our individuality or, at least, the individuality for which we are responsible.

Each cat, for example, may be an individual unlike every other cat. Within limits, cats have a kind of insight, but at certain points cats simply refuse to understand a great many things one would wish them to understand. As lovable as cats might be, and as highly individual as each is, only a human being has the capacity to reflect upon his or her own actions, to repent *or* to approve of some of them, and to choose from among an array of possible futures. These capacities to reflect and to choose give rise to a distinctive language about humans; we are not only "individuals" (as cats are) but "persons" (as cats are not). Our dignity as persons derives from our capacities to reflect and to choose, that is, our capacity to be self-determining. We are (each of us) responsible for our own destiny. Our dignity lies in this responsibility. Our dignity lies— above all else—in the quality of our reflecting and our choosing.

In this light, to take possession of one's own capacity for personhood is to train oneself in the full range of habits that allow one to make in everyday life as many free acts of reflection and choice as possible. In a sense, a human being at birth is not yet a realized person, but does have (even before birth) the potential to become one. To become a fully developed person is to learn the many habits that allow one to increase the frequency of one's acts of reflection and choice. Note the paradox here. One must learn many habits in order to be able to bring reflection and choice into play frequently; that is, to act from *more* than mere habit: to act from choice.

It is not as easy to act from reflection and choice as one might at first think. If you are capable of self-criticism, you will discern soon enough that a great many of the actions you have already taken today were performed mostly by routine, "out of habit," without much reflection and choice. And even where "choice" may have been thought to enter, as when one chose orange juice rather than apple juice at breakfast, an outsider may doubt whether this was more than a learned preference, a matter of taste and inclination. Such "choices," a skeptical observer might say, are not matters much thought about and consciously chosen, not at least with that degree of determination and commitment we intend by the word "will." Indeed, it is rather surprising to become aware of how seldom throughout each long day we exercise our capacities for fresh reflection and conscious choice of the will. Perhaps it is just as well. Perhaps that would be far too tiring. Whatever the reasons, we do not often act at the top of our spiritual nature, in the realm of insight and will. We typically live in their derived light, in the moonlight, so to speak, cast from a distance. A lot of our living is spent in a kind of sleepwalking.

OTHER APPROACHES TO VIRTUES

We should by now have developed some fairly clear notions of "habit," "virtue," "mind," "will," and "person"—and the reader here is urged on reading these words to pause and give a clear definition to each. After that it may then be useful to name and to describe some of the virtues that the Greeks, Romans, and medieval Christians thought to be most important to leading a good human life.

Chief among these was the virtue of "wisdom," that is, "practical wisdom" (*phronesis*), the capacity to order all the parts of the self and all the components of action in a realistic, appropriate, and effective way.[5] The person of practical wisdom is like an archer, Aristotle said. In action, there are an infinite number of ways to get things wrong; but to act in the right way, at the right time, with the right emphasis, with regard to the right persons, and with exact appreciation for all the relevant circumstances, is to "hit the mark exactly," like an arrow thudding into a bull's-eye.[6] A good archer has to account not only for the wind but for the weight of his own arrowhead, the defects of his own shaft, the perfection of the feathering, the tensile strength of his bow, the quality of his string, the tightness in his arm, the habits of his own eye, and a whole host of other factors grasped better by instinct and habit than by conscious articulation.

Furthermore, practical wisdom must suffuse all the other virtues, if they are to be on target. Given the Greek love for form, for the shaping loveliness of things, it was natural for them to speak of practical wisdom as the form of all the other virtues.[7] Practical wisdom directs and gives shape to each of them, while organizing them together in as beautiful a way as possible.

Indeed, the Greeks spoke of goodness under a word, *Kalos*, that works as well for beauty as for loveliness. *Kalos* signifies a kind of grace in action. Goodness is to get everything right, to pay the proper reverence to every aspect of things. A good action hits the mark in all respects. When an action is in some way deficient, from one point of view or another, its goodness is marred.

It may be worth noting how distant this approach to the moral life is from approaching it through the lens of duty. The modern tradition after Immanuel Kant speaks of morals largely in terms of "duty," "ought," "thou shalt," and "thou shalt not." Whether or not there is some ancient and classical warrant for this, it is worth noting that throughout the *Nicomachean Ethics*, when Aristotle needs a metaphor for goodness in action, he turns to athletics rather than to law or command or duty, as in his example of the archer "hitting the mark." For the Greeks, ethics was, in a sense, closer to the aesthetic than to the deontological. A good action represents not so much a law obeyed as an instance of beauty. The Greeks sought the Good as an elusive ideal, a goal up ahead to aspire to, a power of attraction and beauty drawing one onward by its radiance. The Greeks felt drawn by something, attracted by something, pulled toward it as by some law of the spirit parallel to the physical law of gravity. They called this force that attracted them from the future, up ahead, the Final End. They thought of ethics, in this sense, as teleology, the pursuit of this attractive and compelling end.

This conception is quite different from modern utilitarianism. The latter, a modern philosophy developed most extensively by Englishmen Jeremy Bentham (1748-1832) and John Stuart Mill (1806-1873), is an adulterated version of the former. In teleology, the end is a vision of the highest possible development of the human person or, perhaps, at the highest flights of Greek thought, the unity of this highly developed human person with God. Utilitarianism is much more prosaic, as its name itself suggests. It is a theory for choosing the most useful means toward whatever ends it is that one happens to seek. Utilitarianism's strongest suit lies in its application to worldly fields such as politics, law, and economics, more or less flatly considered, in terms rather of worldly objectives met than of the full development and fulfillment of the person meeting them.

Let us linger on this contrast for a moment. Where teleology has in view the human person, utilitarianism has in view the efficiency of means and ends. From the one to the other there is a visible and quite long step, described by the ancients and medievals as the step down from nobility to utility. In the eighteenth century (although perhaps not so in America), this step was quite consciously taken.[8]

In the ancient and medieval view, to reflect on ethics is to try to imagine what sort of person one wishes by the end of one's life to have become. The idea is that one must, in one sense, discover oneself—learn who one is, who one was made to be—and, in another sense, one must make oneself, shape oneself according to the model of the ideal man or woman, as best one can discern that ideal. The best path here is to make choices as a living model, like Pericles, would make them; it was to Pericles, in any case, that Aristotle is said to have turned when he needed an exemplar. This, Aristotle says, is the path of practical wisdom—to make choices as an exemplar of practical wisdom does.[9] To become such a man, one must single out this exemplar in advance and then begin working to develop the habits required to live like that exemplar.

Among these habits, the Greeks thought (as we have seen), one would need not only practical wisdom but also justice (to give each person his or her due),[10] temperance (the disciplining of one's appetites so that one's capacities for reflection and choice are as unimpeded as possible by the "noise" and gyroscopic disturbances the appetites bring in their train),[11] and courage (the steady capacity to pursue the good unswervingly and to allow one's spirit to see truly).[12]

To these four cardinal virtues (practical wisdom, justice, temperance, and courage) must be added a host of others: magnanimity,[13] liberality,[14] patience, perseverance, sympathy, fellow-feeling, benevolence, and the like, not to mention such distinctly Judeo-Christian virtues as faith, hope, charity, humility, kindness, and (in this context only one among many, but a jewel) chastity.

The list of virtues beloved by the premoderns eventually became quite long. For one had only to observe or to feel the need for new human excellences to name them and to add them to the list.

Some of these virtues are obviously in conflict with one another; when is patience cowardice, or temperance pettiness? Besides, few persons, probably none, are endowed by nature with all of the virtues, or have time to master all of them equally. In practice, different persons choose different favorites. Every person develops a fairly unique blend of habits. We call this unique blend of habits, good and bad, "character." To have character is to have a fairly defined profile of habits that can be relied upon, that have, as it were, a kind of personal signature. "That sounds just like him." "That is completely out of character for her; I never saw her do anything like that." From virtue, therefore, we arrive at character. Character is a personal quiverful of virtues (and vices), a distinctive repertoire of more or less predictable dispositions.

There we have it. A rather rough and ready definition of terms. Henceforth, at least, when we speak of habit and virtue, character and act, reflection and choice, mind and will, and passions of the spirit and passions of the flesh, we should have a fairly clear idea of what we mean.

TOWARD A CULTURE OF MORAL DEVELOPMENT

Ethics, Aristotle wrote, is a branch of politics.[15] From a very early age, we learn both by instruction and by observing what goes on around us whatever range of habits the city we live in chooses, more or less consciously, to instruct us in. Long before we are able to choose for ourselves, throughout our childhood and even adolescence, our city shapes us more than we shape ourselves. But this is not the whole story. We dare not discount those acts of rebellion and self-appropriation, dissent and enthusiastic approbation, that each person makes as he or she goes along, nodding or frowning at, imitating or rejecting the panoramic scene and passing parade. However strong their conditioning, persons do define themselves. That is why persons are so endlessly fascinating in their inexhaustible variety.

Nonetheless, as Aristotle also noted, city differs from city, and constitution from constitution. The shape of the institutions we live under goes a long way toward determining the kinds of character its citizens are likely to develop. Thus, many persons today do not like the modern city they are living in. Still, in reacting against modern utilitarianism and the modern preoccupation with social engineering, when such persons demand a return to the ancient moral virtues, they sometimes falsify the past. In reaction against the too easy politicalization of modern life, they seek refuge in the more quiet gardens in which the practice of the personal virtues is assiduously cultivated, as if in a cloister. They forget that Aristotle was not writing about life in the cloister, but life in the city. They forget the public nature and the public role of the virtues he was describing. Such public virtues were absolutely necessary to the survival and the flourishing of Athens. Insofar as Athens was one high point of civilization, its resources lay in the human spirit and depended on the development of specific capacities of that spirit, the Athenian virtues. One must not imagine that these virtues were merely private; their role was public and visible. Perish those virtues, perish Athens.

So it is with the United States or any other nation today. To be sure, societies constructed around sets of institutions different from the institutions of Athens no doubt call forth a different panoply of human virtues. But human virtues they do require. As James Madison once said, it is chimerical to think that a republic (such as he wished the United States to be) can thrive without the practice of republican virtues.[16]

Above all, then, virtue is learned in social contexts. We learn how to improve our moral skills from others. We are encouraged—or ridiculed—by others. If in society as a whole we wish again to make every criminal "an enemy of the human race,"[17] we need also again to praise every man and woman of virtue as our friend.

Several obstacles stand in the way. First, our high culture—composed of intellectuals, professors, and artists—is quite ambivalent about praise for virtue and for character, as it is also ambivalent about strengthening the family. For many, such realities smack of "traditional values," i.e., those residues of the dark past that "enlightenment" is supposed to "enlighten" us *from*.

Second, our academic tradition in the study of ethics has largely ignored the concepts of virtue and character. Neither the utilitarian tradition derived from Bentham nor the deontological tradition derived from Kant, neither the "pessimistic" image of human nature sketched in Thomas Hobbes nor the "romantic" image sketched in Jean-Jacques Rousseau, offers illumination about virtue and character. While the Aristotelian tradition is kept alive in Great Britain, and (outside the Catholic intellectual tradition) rather less so in the United States, it seldom counts for a great deal in contemporary ethical discussion and its concepts are almost never clearly grasped or accurately presented. If one were to ask contemporary intellectuals to define virtue and character, there is reason to doubt, first, whether discussions of significant clarity would be forthcoming, and second, whether the powerful arguments of the past would be known well enough to be embodied within them. Instead, amid allusions to the Victorian Age and to bourgeois morality, it is often suggested that virtue and character connote a straightlaced, stiff, hypocritical, and conservative moral posture, from which liberalism or progressivism intends to liberate us.

These are serious intellectual errors of distortion and omission. Their consequences are also serious, because if clear concepts of virtue and character are not available at the highest intellectual level, it is not likely that they will be taken seriously in textbooks, curricula, and informed public discussion, even if they were there to be found, as typically they now are not.

Third, the needs of the entertainment media to some extent fly in the face of virtue and character and to some extent totally depend upon them. The essential dependence of the media upon virtue and character follows from the inherent demands of the art of storytelling. Without character, "characters" would lack intelligibility; without virtue, they could not be attractive. Courage, kindness, tenderness, persistence, integrity, loyalty, and other virtues are indispensable to the storyteller's art. On the other hand, knowing well the burdens imposed upon them by virtue, audiences necessarily love plots in which heroes and heroines are tempted, fall, flout conventions, "kick against the goad," and in other ways rebel—at least against excessively conventional ways of understanding virtue and —character. In a profound sense, such real-life battles deepen our understanding of true virtue, true character, andone almost wishes to add —"true grit."

In a superficial sense, however, popular entertainment often depends on "shock value" and titillation. Its producers are always tempted to violate ethical norms just enough to offer a taste of "forbidden fruit," yet without creating too high a sense of alarm. When this is done cheaply and in tawdry fashion—through unnecessary nudity, sexual suggestion, violent behavior, and impulse gratification—critics properly attack such products both on aesthetic and on moral grounds. Their work sometimes described as a moral "wasteland," producers of television shows and popular films at times seem to want it both ways: both to pay conventional respect to traditional values and to pander. It is plausible that ratings systems reward such compromises. Hungers for greater depth in programming usually go unfulfilled.

In particular, there is in the mass media a striking balance of significant drama about the specific struggles for virtue and character characteristic of the Jewish and Christian religious traditions. Ordinarily, persons do not learn "virtue in general," rather, through their families and religious traditions they learn *particular* paths to virtue, taught somewhat distinctively within each religious body. Some religious bodies are quite impulsive, for example, placing great stress on vivid emotional experiences in moments of conversion ("I accepted Jesus on May 27, 1972," one such communicant may recall). Others have more sober, restrained traditions that appeal much less to subjective experience and far more to objective disciplines and rites. Virtue, in the concrete, is typically communicated through particular communities of understanding, of method, and of style.

About many such matters, our intellectual and academic elites are remarkably incurious, and our national communications media have been (at least until recent years) remarkably reticent. By contrast, most seem eager to explore new moralities, fresh liberations, new imperatives of consciousness-raising, and the ongoing saga of progressive attitudes. The bias is pronounced. It exacts several social costs.

One such cost appears to be a gap between the cultures of academic and intellectual elites and those of the ordinary public. Another seems to be the vacuum created by the separation of the three major subsystems (political, economic, and moral-cultural) of our political economy.[18] This point needs some explication.

While explicit about the republic's dependence upon the virtue and religiousness of its citizens, the American Founders did not assign to government the task of "soulcraft." This is left to the leaders of the nation's moral and cultural institutions: principally to families, of course, and local communities but also to the churches, the press (today, the "media"), and the universities and schools. For generations, the primary task explicitly assigned to the public schools of the nation was character formation.[19] *McGuffey's Readers* exemplify the methods employed in teaching reading, writing, and arithmetic; one learned from them, not only techniques, but classic statements of American purpose and American (northern Protestant) virtue.[20]

In recent decades, by contrast, the teaching of virtue and character has explicitly *not* been the primary function of the American state-run public schools. Further, the American mainline churches seem nowadays less to emphasize their long traditions of instruction in virtue and character and more to emphasize counseling, therapeutic methods, and social causes. In the university world, emphasis upon virtue and character would now seem to many not only quaint but perhaps threatening and even impermissible.

Thus, at present, no major institution appears to concern itself with the standing of virtue and character in modern culture; virtue and character have been orphaned.

Understandably, then, families concerned to instruct their children in virtue and character feel isolated and alone, even when not under assault from the glowing screen in their own living rooms, and not infrequently even in church.

CONCLUSION

All this is not to say that the future is bleak. On the contrary, the family and local communities have shown themselves to be amazingly resilient and persistent in continuing to instruct their youngsters in the classic paths of virtue and of character. In some ways, such institutions of immediate culture may prove to be far more powerful than the more remote cultures represented through larger institutions. There are significant indications, indeed, that a quiet moral revolution is under way, affecting not only communications elites but, in particular, some of the more influential intellectual and academic elites. In America, even "progressive" elites are thinking and writing more these days about the family, local communities, civil society, and traditional values. William Bennett's skillful anthology *The Book of Virtues* has wrung warm praise from left and right alike— even from the often-sour Martha Nussbaum in *The New Republic*.[21] For even "progressives" in the end depend upon appeals to commitment, integrity, sacrifice for a cause, comradely bonds, honesty, and individual initiative. Like Moliere's bourgeois surprised (and pleased) that he had been speaking prose for many years, many former socialists are expressing newfound pleasure in having practiced the old, prosaic virtues for decades now, even though they had forgotten to speak of them.

In free societies, the language of virtue and character is indispensable— so indispensable as to be prosaic, indeed. For how can a people profess to be capable of self-government—of government of, by, and for the people —if they cannot govern their own passions? How can a people govern a whole society that cannot, each of them, govern themselves? In the free society, virtue is a sine qua non. Where there is no virtue, the free society perishes and the very idea of liberty becomes chimerical.

NOTES

1. Aristotle first proposes a threefold division: "A state of the soul is either 1) an emotion, 2) a capacity, or 3) a disposition; virtue therefore must be one of these three things...The capacities are the faculties in virtue of which we can be said to be liable to the emotions, for example, capable of feeling anger or pain or pity. The dispositions are the formed states of character in virtue of which we are well or ill disposed in respect of the emotions; for instance, we have a bad disposition in regard to anger if we are disposed to get angry too violently or not violently enough, a good disposition if we habitually feel a moderate amount of anger; and similarly in respect of the other emotions" (*Nicomachean Ethics*, 1105b19-29). After considering each in turn, Aristotle concludes, "If then the virtues are neither emotions nor capacities, it remains that they are dispositions" (*Nicomachean Ethics*, 1106a12-13).

2. Aristotle builds up our concept of virtue dialectically, by causing us to reflect on our own experience quite carefully. His first, tentative definition of any man's virtue is "the disposition that renders him a goodman and also will cause him to perform his function [as a man] well" (*Nicomachean Ethics*, 2. 6. 1106a23-24). Later, he sharpens this to a fuller definition, each term of which he has taken care to build up slowly: "Virtue is 1) a habit of mind, 2) determining the choice of actions and emotions, 3) consisting essentially in the observance of the mean 4) relative to us, this being determined 5) by the principle *as the man of practical wisdom* [a man like Pericles]*would determine it*" (*Nicomachean Ethics*, 2. 6. 1106b36-1107a2). Note the flexibility added by characteristic 5. The translation is my own free rendering of the Greek translation by H. Rackham in the Loeb Classical Library.

3. See Eric D'Arcy, *Conscience and Its Right to Freedom* (New York: Sheed and Ward, 1961); Albrecht Dihle, *The Theory of the Will in Classical Antiquity* (Berkeley: University of California Press, 1982); A. J. Kenny, *Aristotle's Theory of the Will* (New Haven: Yale University Press, 1979); Brian O'Shaughnessy, *The Will*, 2 vols. (Cambridge: Cambridge University Press, 1980).

4. "Habits are the formed states of character in virtue of which we are well or ill disposed in respect of the emotions" (*Nicomachean Ethics*, 2. 5. 1105b26).

5. "...moral virtue...is concerned with emotions and actions, in which one can have excess or deficiency or a due mean. For example, one can be frightened or bold, feel desire or anger or pity, and experience pleasure and pain in general, either too much or too little, and in both cases wrongly; whereas to feel these feelings at the right time, on the right occasion, towards the right people, for the right purpose and in the right manner, is to feel the best amount of them, which is the mean amount—and the best amount is of course the mark of virtue. And similarly there can be excess, deficiency, and the due mean in actions. Now feelings and actions are the objects with which virtue is concerned" (*Nicomachean Ethics*, 2. 6. 1105b16-25). Aristotle does not speak of "the mean" as a

mathematical notion. He speaks of it, rather, as athletes or artists do, "hence the common remark about a perfect work of art, that you could not take from it nor add to it—meaning that excess and deficiency destroy perfection, while adherence to the mean preserves it" (11065.b10-13). He gives as examples the wrestler, the runner, the expert in any art, and most vividly the archer. "If virtue, like nature, is more accurate and better than any form of art, it will follow that virtue has the quality of hitting the mean" (1106b14-16). And he adds, "it is easy to miss the target, and difficult to hit it" (1106b32-34). That is why, for him, "in point of excellence and rightness [virtue] is an extreme" (1107a7-8). *Phronesis* is defined at *Nicomachean Ethics*, 6. 5. 1140b20-22.

6. *Nicomachean Ethics*, 2. 6. 1106b29-35.

7. *Nicomachean Ethics*, 6. 13. 1144b18-33.

8. "Reason ought to be viewed, the modern theory proposes, not as somehow constituting the end or purpose of human existence; instead it is the marvelously effective servant of the passions. More precisely, reason is best understood as the servant of those strongest self-regarding passions that, when enlightened by their servant, point toward forms of competition and cooperation that bring about 'the common benefit of each' (a striking phrase coined by Machiavelli and then imitated by Locke)." Thomas L. Pangle, "Republicanism and Rights," in Robert A. Licht, ed., *The Framers and Fundamental Rights* (Washington, DC: AEI, 1991), 112. Cf. also Ralph Lerner, *The Thinking Revolutionary: Principle and Practice in the New Republic* (Ithaca: Cornell University Press, 1987), 202-3: "Everything had more or less utility and hence could be hefted and judged with a trader's savvy. Because knowledge was seen to be a source of power, because knowledge paid, people sought it. The market mentality shrugged off that 'inconsiderate contempt for practice' typical of aristocratic ages; the *use* to which the discoveries of the mind could be put became the leading question...Among commercial republicans, even religion was brought down to earth: 'in the very midst of their zeal one generally sees something so quiet, so methodical, so calculated that it would seem that the head rather than the heart leads them to the foot of the alter.' Where the central concern was with utility, there could be little room for the play of the imagination, for poetry; people not only spoke prose but thought prose, all the days of their lives."

9. "Virtue is a habit of the mind determining the choice of actions and emotions, consisting essentially in the observance of the mean relative to us, this being determined by principle, that is, *as the prudent man would determine it*" (*Nicomachean Ethics*, 2. 6. 1106b36-1107a2). And note 6. 5. 1140b8-11: "Hence men like Pericles are deemed prudent, because they possess a faculty of discerning when things are good for themselves and for mankind; and that is our conception of an expert in domestic economy or political science."

10. *Nicomachean Ethics*, 5. 1129a1-1133b15.

11. *Nicomachean Ethics*, 3. 10-12. 1117b23-1119b19.

12. *Nicomachean Ethics*, 3. 6-9. 1115a6-1117b22.

13. *Nicomachean Ethics*, 4. 3. 1123a34-1125a35.

14. *Nicomachean Ethics*, 4. 1. 1119b20-1122a118.

15. "...the most authoritative of the sciences...is manifestly the science of politics; for it is this that ordains which of the sciences are to exist in states, and what branches of knowledge the different classes of the citizens are to learn, and up to what point; and we observe that even the most highly esteemed of the faculties, such as strategy, domestic economy, oratory, are subordinate to the political science. Inasmuch then as the rest of the sciences are employed by this one, and as it moreover lays down laws as to what people shall do and what things they shall refrain from doing, the end of this science must include the ends of all the others. Therefore, the good of man must be the end of the science of politics. For even though it be the case that the good is the same for the individual and for the state, nevertheless, the good of the state is manifestly a greater and more perfect good, both to attain and to preserve. To secure the good of one person only is better than nothing; but to secure the good of a nation or a state is a nobler and more divine achievement" *(Nicomachean Ethics*, 1. 2. 1094a27-1094b12).

16. Jonathan Elliott, ed., *Debates in the Several State Conventions on the Adoption of the Federal Constitution* (Philadelphia: Lippincott, 1907), Virginia, June 20, 1788.

17. See Alexis de Tocqueville, *Democracy in America*, trans. George Lawrence, and ed. J. P. Mayer (New York: Doubleday, 1966), 96: "In Europe the criminal is a luckless man fighting to save his head from the authorities; in a sense the population are mere spectators of the struggle. In America he is an enemy of the human race and every human being is against him."

18. Michael Novak, *Spirit of Democratic Capitalism* (Lanham, MD: Madison Books, 1991), 171-186.

19. "The origins and aspirations of the public school movement were thoroughly entwined with...moralistic reform movements. From the beginning, the purpose of the tax-supported public school was character formation subordinate to the 'goals of character building,' even in programs that emphasized manual arts." Wilson and Hernnstein, *Crime and Human Nature* (New York: Simon and Schuster, 1985), 433.

20. See John Silber, Commencement Address to Boston University (Boston: Boston University, 1981).

21. William J. Bennett, *The Book of Virtues* (New York: Simon and Schuster, 1993).

Chapter 4

Incivility and Crime: The Role of Moral Habituation

James Q. Wilson

INTRODUCTION

Of late, modernization has been accompanied by criminality. Although there are some noteworthy exceptions (Japan being the most prominent), the economic advancement of a nation has been purchased at the price, among other things, of higher levels of property crime and to a lesser extent of violent crime. Yet the evidence is also quite clear that those individuals who are most likely to commit crimes are not the most obvious beneficiaries of modernization; the criminals today, like the criminals of yesteryear, tend to be the poor and the unschooled. How can we explain the failure of economic progress to produce higher levels of law-abidingness, especially since that progress has reduced the relative size of the population most likely to break the law?

The question is all the more puzzling when we realize that only economic progress in its *contemporary* form seems to be associated with increased criminality. In the early nineteenth century crime and disorder were quite common in the large cities of Europe and the United States but then became less so during the second half of that century, though the size and density of these cities were increasing dramatically. Ted Robert Gurr found that in London, Stockholm, and Sydney the number of murders, assaults, and thefts that came to the attention of the police declined irregularly, but consistently, for half a century or more. Public safety continued to improve in these cities well into the twentieth century. In Boston, Philadelphia, Rochester, Muncie, and New York City, crime rates rose in the early nineteenth century and then began to decline beginning around the middle of that century. Philadelphia is the best-studied city in this regard. There Roger Lane counted 3.3 murder indictments per hundred thousand persons in the middle of the nineteenth century but only 2.1 by century's end, a decline of 36 percent.

The nineteenth century's second half was a period of industrialization and urbanization and, in the United States, one in which millions of immigrants entered the nation. Despite rapid economic growth and convulsive social changes, crime rates appear to have declined or at worst to have traced an irregular pattern around a relatively stable trend line.

The contemporary period has also been one of economic growth and urbanization, but unlike a century ago these changes have been accompanied by higher rates of crime. In the United States between 1960 and 1978, the robbery rate more than tripled, the auto theft rate more than doubled, and the burglary rate nearly tripled. Beginning around 1955, the rate of serious ("indictable") offenses in England began increasing at about 10 percent per year. Murder rates during the 1960s rose in, among other cities, Amsterdam, Belfast, Colombo, Dublin, Glasgow, and Helsinki; the general crime rate rose in, among other countries, Denmark, Finland, Norway, and Sweden.

Crime rates are less in underdeveloped nations than in developed ones, although the rate of crimes against persons is higher in the former than in the latter. As a nation progresses economically, the total crime rate increases, but the fraction of those crimes that are violent ones decreases.

One obvious, but partial, explanation for the difference between these two centuries is the age structure of the population. In the second half of the nineteenth century, in both the United States and much of Europe, the proportion of young persons in the population declined as life expectancy increased. During the 1960s and 1970s the proportion of youngsters in the population increased as the baby-boom generation came of age.

But age cannot be the whole story. In Roger Lane's study of Philadelphia, the increase in the median age of that city's residents was not enough to explain all of the decrease in homicide rates during the nineteenth century. Scholars who have examined the upsurge in American crime during the 1960s and 1970s have concluded that the shift in age composition explained no more than half the increase, and probably less.

We have quite clear evidence that much of the recent increase in crime is the result of the greater rate at which young people commit crimes. Marvin Wolfgang and his associates at the University of Pennsylvania followed the criminal careers of two groups of boys, those born in Philadelphia in 1945 (and who remained in that city until they were 18) and those born in Philadelphia in 1958 (and also remained in that city for at least 18 years). Although roughly the same percentage (about one-third) of each cohort had at least one arrest, the number of arrests of those boys in the second cohort who had committed at least one crime was much higher than of the members of the first cohort. The boys who grew up during the 1960s and who had started on a life of crime committed twice as many burglaries, three times as many homicides, and five times as many robberies as the boys who grew up in the 1950s. To put it in technical language, the age-specific arrest rate (and thus presumably the age-specific crime rate) of the newer cohort was much higher than that of the older cohort. The evidence we have from the nation as a whole confirms the Philadelphia data. The probability that a person aged 15 to 29 would commit a murder in the United States increased by nearly 50 percent between 1955 and 1972.

Urbanization also tends to increase crime by increasing the frequency with which persons encounter criminal opportunities (goods to be stolen or persons to be assaulted) and criminal associates (gangs and criminal subcultures that one can join) and by increasing the chances of evading social sanctions by virtue of the anonymity that cities tend to confer. There is no doubt that violent crime is more common in big cities than in small ones. But Philadelphia was not a bigger city in the 1960s than it had been in the 1950s (in fact it was smaller). Yet young boys growing up there were more criminal, and more violently criminal, in the 1960s than they had been in the 1950s. Moreover, in the 1890s, more than a million Philadelphians went about their daily business in an environment so orderly that a present-day resident of that city who was transported back a century in time could be pardoned for thinking he had entered Arcadia. While New York City, Istanbul, Manila, and Calcutta all experienced increases in the homicide rate as they grew in population during the first half of the twentieth century, Bombay, Helsinki, Tokyo, Madrid, Belfast, and Nairobi had murder rates that declined as their populations grew during this same period. And in the nineteenth century's second half, urbanization was associated with declining crime rates.

Perhaps the economic cycle has affected crime rates in a way that might explain the differences between this century and the last. There is some evidence that in the nineteenth century property crimes increased during periods of recession and decreased during times of affluence. But that connection between economic conditions and criminality no longer seems to exist, or to exist to the same degree. In the United States crime rates drifted down between 1933 and 1960, although the first part of this era included a severe depression (1933-1940) and the second part was one of reasonable prosperity (1941-1960). And the most recent increase in crime (and in age-specific crime rates) occurred during a period of unparalleled prosperity (1960-1980). Even the scholars who find evidence that economic factors have some effect on contemporary crime rates concede that "the major movements in crime rates during the last half century cannot be attributed to the business cycle."

One can perhaps put the matter even more strongly: whereas in the nineteenth century property crime was linked to the business cycle, today it is not. If true, that represents a profound change in the relationship between human behavior and historical forces. Criminality has been decoupled from the economy. If the prototypal novel of crime in the nineteenth century was written by Charles Dickens or Victor Hugo, today it would have to be written by whom? Someone, I conjecture, attuned to the effect, not of the economy, but of culture. Tom Wolfe comes to mind.

THE CHARACTER-SHAPING PROCESS

Not having written or read the definitive novel, I offer instead an argument, one that I have advanced before. In the mid-nineteenth century England and America reacted to the consequences of industrialization, urbanization, immigration, and affluence by asserting an ethos of self-control, whereas in the late twentieth century they reacted to many of the same forces by asserting an ethos of self-expression. In the former period big cities were regarded as threats to social well-being that had to be countered by social indoctrination; in the latter period cities were seen as places in which personal freedom could be made secure. The animating source of the ethos of self-control was religion and the voluntary associations inspired by religious life, but religion itself did not produce the resulting social control; rather the processes of habituation in the family, the schools, the neighborhood, and the workplace produced it. The ethos of self-expression was secular, but it was not secularism itself that led to the excesses of self-expression; rather it was the unwillingness of certain elites to support those processes of habituation that even in the absence of religious commitment lead to temperance, fidelity, moderation, and the acceptance of personal responsibility.

Gurr, following the lead of the German sociologist Norbert Elias, suggested that the nineteenth century witnessed the full flowering of the civilizing process, that is, the acceptance of an ethos that attached great importance to the control of self-indulgent impulses. Eric Monkkonen said much the same thing when he observed that from about 1840 into the early decades of the twentieth century a set of Victorian values acquired a remarkable hegemony in England and America, concurrent with the advent of industrialization. Martin J. Wiener has argued that this was more than mere coincidence. The British middle classes, who had invented industrialization and benefited enormously from it, viewed the resulting economic and urban growth with suspicion and disdain. Educated opinion placed industrialism into a kind of "mental quarantine," elevating in its place a conception of the "English way of life" that glorified the countryside—"ancient, slow-moving, stable, cozy, conservative," and its greatest task lay in "taming and 'civilizing' the dangerous engines of progress it had unwittingly unleashed." Bertrand Russell would later sneer that "the concept of the gentleman was invented by the aristocracy to keep the middle classes in order," but in truth the concept of the gentleman enabled the middle classes to supplant the aristocracy. The landed elite gave way to the industrialists on its own cultural terms: the former ceded power to the latter on condition the latter become as much like the former as possible.

In the United States there was no aristocracy that the members of the new bourgeois might ape; in its place was evangelical religion. The first few decades of the nineteenth century witnessed a series of religious revivals that later became known as the Second Great Awakening. Those revivals involved an intense debate over the meaning of the Bible and how man might enter into the right relationship with God. Whatever spiritual effect they may have had, their social effect was enormous. People caught up in them created or joined a host of voluntary associations designed to improve society by improving the character of its members.

Those associations included temperance societies, antislavery movements, Sunday schools, children's aid groups, and the Young Men's Christian Association. The reach of these organizations was remarkable. In 1820 fewer than 5 percent of the adult males in New York City belonged to the lay boards of Protestant organizations; by 1869, 20 percent did. In that latter year something approaching half of all adult Protestant males were members of at least one church-related association. In 1825 the American Sunday School Union claimed that it enrolled one-third of all the children in Philadelphia between the ages of 6 and 15. In 1829 more than 40 percent of the children in New York City were said to attend Sunday school. Within 10 years after its introduction into the United States, the YMCA enrolled more than 25,000 young men.

But the temperance movement had the most far-reaching effects. In the decades leading up to the 1830s, the consumption of alcohol rose sharply. By one estimate the annual per capita consumption of alcohol was 10 gallons in 1829, up from 2.5 gallons in 1790. Respectable Americans were appalled by the results: rowdy urban streets, saloons on every corner, young men showing up for work drunk. In 1829 there was one saloon for every 28 adult males in Rochester, New York, and that city was not atypical.

The temperance movement meant different things to different people. To some it meant moderation, to others total abstinence. Some wanted legal compulsion, others preferred moral suasion. But taken as a whole, the movement embraced almost every strata of society, including the intelligentsia. By the thousands, men were induced to sign temperance pledges and boys were recruited into the Cadets of Temperance and the Cold Water Army. By 1855, 13 states had passed laws that banned the manufacture and sale of liquor statewide or at the option of cities and counties.

The effect of this effort was dramatic. Between 1830 and 1850 annual per capita alcohol consumption for persons aged 15 and older fell from 7.1 gallons to 1.8 gallons. What effect this had on behavior, especially criminal behavior, is impossible to say, but most people at the time believed that it made a difference for the better. And in retrospect we know that crime rates declined far faster than one would have predicted by knowing only the aging of the population. Some places were unaffected, of course. The Tenderloin district of New York and other big cities remained riotous, boozy neighborhoods. But social pressure, police enforcement, and the absence of cheap and convenient transportation kept the rioters and the boozers in their place, a place that respectable folk rarely visited except on missionary errands.

Whatever effect these associational activities had, it was as much from the routine moral training and social pressure they produced as from the religious convictions they imparted. This is pure conjecture since we do not have—and can never have—any measure of either religiosity or habituation. But the conjecture is consistent with what we know about the development of character in people. Aristotle argued that the moral virtues, unlike the intellectual ones, are the product of the regular repetition of right actions. We are habituated to temperate and moderate behavior by routinely acting in temperate and moderate ways. Developmental psychology has confirmed this insight by showing through countless studies how children who are the object of regular, consistent, and appropriate discipline acquire an habitual tendency to control their impulses, take into account the distant consequences of present acts, and attend to the feelings of others.

Both the public schools and the Sunday schools had a moral object: the production of better children. The object was sought by precept as well as practice, but from everything we now know of childrearing, practice is more important than precept. In England and the United States the Sunday schools were staffed by working-class teachers who sought to inculcate values as well as to increase literacy. Both were achieved by rote, that is, by the steady repetition of exercises designed to make habitual behavior that would otherwise be episodic, whether the behavior was recitation of the alphabet and biblical verses or the observance of the rules of punctuality and good order. By these means, as Thomas W. Laqueur was later to write, "the bourgeois world view triumphed in the nineteenth century largely through consent, not through force." The middle class established a "moral hegemony."

Religion played a role in this but more as an animating force than as a moralizing precept. Religious sentiments inspired many of these social movements; churches supplied the institutional catalyst for many of these voluntary associations; church-related societies provided the continual social reinforcement necessary to sustain participation in the movements and associations. But the associations outlasted their religious inspiration. A spiritual awakening tends to be evanescent, organizations tend to be immortal. The Sunday school, the YMCA, the temperance society—these endured for decades, long after the Great Awakening was but a memory. The Victorians, whether in the United States or England, lived off their capital in more ways than one. They retained "a strong moral consensus long after the decline of the religious faith that had originally sustained that morality."

What was decisive about the religiously inspired movements of the nineteenth century was that they were endorsed and often led by the upper classes. In this respect the American experience was like the British one. In both places the "best people" endorsed a view of right conduct and the path to good character that was accepted by almost all classes. Contemporary Marxist historians are correct in asserting that nineteenth-century schools and associations were urged to control the working classes.

They are also correct in suggesting that the requirements of the new industrial workplace rewarded those best able to conform to them and thus encouraged schools to teach those personal traits—order, obedience, punctuality—that would equip people to be successful workers. They are wrong only in suggesting that this was done over the opposition, or contrary to the best interests, of those workers. The working classes not only absorbed those lessons and took those jobs, they taught those lessons and sought those jobs.

CHANGED ATTITUDES

Today matters could scarcely be more different. Beginning in the 1920s and resuming (after time out for a depression and a war) in the 1960s, the best people were at pains to distance themselves from, and even to denounce, what their counterparts a century earlier had taken for granted. Religious revivals, once led by liberal college students (such as Theodore Weld, a founder of the antislavery society), were later scorned by educated people, who saw such enthusiasms as the atavistic rumblings of rural fanatics. Temperance movements were disdained as the domain of elderly women who wished to bring back Prohibition, which "everybody knows" failed. (In fact it did not fail in one regard: Prohibition did result in a reduction in alcohol consumption by at least one-third and perhaps by one-half.) Saloons that were once condemned as dens of iniquity were now called cocktail lounges and hailed as centers of sophisticated sociability. Cities that were once viewed as the breeding ground of vice and disorder were now hailed as indispensable arenas of personal liberty.

The very phrase "middle-class values" became a term of derision rather than pride. Sigmund Freud was interpreted (wrongly) as having blamed mental disease on the suppression of natural human instincts by artificial social conventions. Margaret Mead became a best-selling anthropologist in large measure on the strength of the claim (now much disputed) that Samoans were happy because they enjoyed greater sexual freedom. Schools were criticized for their emphasis on rote learning and moral instruction and urged instead to foster self-discovery and self-directed learning among their pupils.

These changes in attitude probably affected childrearing practices, but not much can be said with confidence on this matter. We can observe how people talked about childrearing; whether what they said mirrored what they did is another matter. In the mid-nineteenth century mothers were advised by the ladies' magazines of the supreme importance of inculcating moral and religious principles. Corporal punishment even then was subject to criticism, but the goal of obedience was not. In 1890, 1900, and 1910, one-third of the childrearing articles published in a sample of articles from the *Ladies Home Journal, Women's Home Companion,* and *Good Housekeeping* were about character development; in 1920 only three percent were. Personality development had taken its place.

When parents in Muncie, Indiana were asked in 1924 what traits they most wanted to see in their children, 45 percent said "strict obedience" and 50 percent said loyalty to the church. When the same question was put to Muncie parents a half century later, 76 percent gave "independence" as the desired quality (47 percent said "tolerance"). Only 17 percent now mentioned obedience.

Today Victorian morality and even the era to which that queen gave her name are known to most of us only as symbols for prudery, hypocrisy, repression, and conformity. There were elements of all of these things in nineteenth-century England and America, but there was something else as well; the maintenance of a reasonable degree of social order, without extensive government repression, in the face of massive economic and demographic changes.

THE INVENTION OF ADOLESCENCE

Between 1860 and 1960 elite opinion underwent a sea change, from advocating self-control to endorsing self-expression (or, as it was quickly understood, self-indulgence). Society's fundamental task has always been to socialize its youth, especially during the tumultuous teenage years. Never an easy task, it was in the nineteenth century easier than it is today because adolescence—that recognized interregnum between childhood and adulthood—did not exist. As soon as children were physically able to work, they worked, usually on the farm but sometimes in grim, satanic mills and mines. Moreover, there was a cultural consensus about what constituted right conduct, a consensus strong enough to follow and to envelop young men and women when they left the farm to work in the growing cities. Today we live in a world in which an intellectual invention—adolescence—has become a practical reality. Large numbers of young people are expected to be free both of close parental control and of the discipline of the market. They live with parents but not under them, they work in the market but not from necessity. They are free to seek mates, not under the old (parent-defined) rules of courtship but under the new (peer-defined) rules of dating. It is obviously a status both privileged and precarious, one that is well managed only by those young people who have already been set on a proper course by virtue of a sound constitution and responsible parents.

What is remarkable about the social invention of adolescence is that by itself it leads to no great harm. The vast majority of teenagers grow up to be perfectly ordinary and respectable adults. A large fraction of the boys (in Philadelphia, London, and Copenhagen, one-third) will be arrested by the police at least once, but the great majority of these will not be arrested again. The reason is that most parents do a very good job of setting their children on the proper course. As Joseph Adelson has reminded us, most adolescents are neither enraged nor disengaged; they are, on the contrary, much like their parents and usually turn out to be something of which their parents approve.

But the existence of adolescence and of a youth culture puts some young people deeply at risk because they have, by virtue of a defective constitution or inadequate parenting, been set on an uncertain or disastrous course. The embarrassment many adults feel at correcting teenagers, the belief inculcated by higher education and the youth culture itself that freedom and self-realization are the supreme goods, the scorn in which Victorian morality is held—all these deprive the at-risk adolescents of the kind of moral instruction the adult world once provided and enforced.

Adolescence by itself is hardly a threatening social invention (Japanese adolescents are not seen as a social problem); the ethos of radical individualism and commitment to self-expression of educated elites is by itself not especially worrisome (nineteenth-century England was filled with the respectable followers of John Stuart Mill). But the two in combination —that is troublesome.

The two coincided in the United States during the 1960s. There ensued a dramatic increase in teenage pathologies: delinquency, drug use, suicide, eating disorders, and teenage pregnancies. The pathologies afflicted only a minority of all adolescents, to be sure, but the minority totaled several million people.

We are not entitled to be surprised. If we set several million teenagers free from direct parental or market supervision, knowing that a fraction of them lack a strong moral compass; if we expect those young people to learn from what they see and hear about them; and if what they hear is a glorification of the virtues of individualism and self-fulfillment, then we ought to be thankful that any adolescents are left intact.

In the 1930s, when marijuana first came to public notice, it was routinely condemned by elites who associated it, often wrongly, with

Mexican immigrants. Marijuana use did not spread widely. When it reappeared in the 1960s, it was praised as a liberating or at least legitimate experience and associated with creativity and musicality; its use spread like wildfire. Peyote and other naturally occurring psychedelics were used by Indians for generations without much notice; when Aldous Huxley, Timothy Leary, and Alan Watts, among others, endorsed the consciousness-expanding properties of LSD, its use spread rapidly. When cocaine was first introduced in this country, it was thought to be a harmless stimulant, and Coca-Cola put it into its soft drink. When elite opinion turned against it, its use shriveled. When cocaine returned to public awareness in the 1970s, it was advertised as being consumed at the best parties attended by the most fashionable people; other people could not wait to try it.

MORAL HABITUATION

I do not wish to blame widespread drug use on the glitterati, but I do wish to point out that all kinds of ideas—not just Marxism or Keynesianism or capitalism—have consequences. Young people do learn from older people; at-risk young people learn from the most self-indulgent older people. As Richard Herrnstein had pointed out, morality must be learned just as surely as the multiplication tables and the rules of grammar. And like multiplication and grammar, morality is largely learned by rote. That form of learning is now in disrepute, partly because rote learning is wrongly seen as the enemy of creativity and individuality and partly because the elites who must inculcate the learning disagree about what is to be inculcated.

This reduction in routinized moral habituation probably affects everyone to some degree, but for most people the effect is minor because their parents and peers have intuitively rewarded decency and punished selfishness and because these people have entered markets and neighborhoods that reinforced the lessons of their early training. But some lack either the earlier training or the later environment, and so become especially vulnerable to the self-indulgent tone of modern elite culture.

Black Americans have been especially vulnerable in this regard. Roger Lane has described how black homicide rates in Philadelphia rose from the mid- to the late-nineteenth century, roughly doubling at a time when, as we have already seen, the overall homicide rate was falling. Other immigrant groups, notably the Irish and the Italians, had high murder rates when first settling in the city, but soon their rates began to fall. Lane attributes the black increase to their systematic exclusion from the economic life of the city, an exclusion that placed the black middle class in a hopeless position: its commitment to respectability was threatened both by whites (who refused to reward respectability with legitimate economic advancement) and by other blacks (who scorned respectability by creating profitable and status-conferring criminal enterprises).

No doubt exclusion is an important part of the story, but it cannot be the whole story because even sharper increases in black crime rates occurred later, in the 1960s, when the barriers to entry into legitimate occupations were falling rapidly. Adult unemployment rates for blacks and whites were declining when age-adjusted crime rates started increasing. The other part of the story, to which Lane's excellent study offers important support, is that the culture of respectability was itself precarious, such that its reach was limited to a minority of the black minority.

William E. DuBois, the leading black scholar of his time, was himself the exemplar of the respectable Negro: intellectual in his manner, puritanical in his views, and reformist in his politics. His book about Philadelphia blacks in the 1890s was at once a revelation of the extent of racism and segregation and a plea for self-help based on a strong family life, steady work habits, and the strict control of crime. But the message was not institutionalized or routinized, and so did not reach those most in need. The folk culture of urban blacks, as observers have noted, was and is aggressive, individualistic, and admiring of semiritualistic insults, sly tricksters, and masculine display. This popular culture may have been a reaction against the repressive and emasculating aspects of slavery; whatever its origin, it was not a culture productive of a moral capital off which people could live when facing either adversity or affluence. The contrast between black popular culture and other repressed minorities—Asian Americans and Hispanic Americans—has often been remarked. This may help explain why, as Lane notes, black crime rates are higher than Hispanic ones, even in cities where black income is significantly higher than Hispanic income. Glenn Loury has complained of the continuing failure of middle-class blacks to provide visible moral leadership on issues such as crime, teenage pregnancy, and single-parent families. While one can appreciate the desire of black leaders to avoid giving ammunition to racists by publicly discussing the moral decay of some parts of the black community, in the long run silence will be self-destructive.

Some critics of liberal democracy argue that the sea change in elite opinion from self-control to self-indulgence was caused by the democratic spirit. I disagree. Nothing in democratic theory leads inevitably to a warped elite ethos. Democracy is, after all, only a system for picking rulers. *Liberal* democracy is a more complicated matter, for "liberal" implies that it will be the goal of democratic rule to enhance liberty. But the liberties the better democracies have secured (and on which their perpetuation depends) are the traditional liberties to life, conscience, and property. The United States functioned democratically (except for the denial of the vote to women and blacks) from about the 1830s on. Removing the barriers to female and black participation did not change matters fundamentally; women, especially, voted much as men had always voted. Yet for about a century after the adult white male franchise was universal, after virtually every office one can imagine was placed under popular control, and after a Civil War had begun the emancipation of blacks, the United States did not experience, on an age-adjusted basis, a sharp increase in criminality during times of prosperity—until the 1960s.

CHANGES IN CULTURE

Some may argue that the extension (in my view the bending) of the constitutionally protected freedom of expression to include not merely political and artistic speech but also pornography and nude dancing has fostered an ethos that harms youthful socialization, but I am not convinced. Scarcely any society consumes more prurient material than does Japan, yet this has not worked any obvious corruption of Japanese character. One might also argue—with considerably more force—that the multiplication of restrictions on the police has made certain aspects of the culture of self-indulgence, notably drug use, harder to bring under control. That is true up to a point. But it is not yet clear how much would be gained by reducing the constraints on the police. In New York City, they made 90,000 drug arrests in 1988; in Washington, D.C., nearly 13,000; yet only a small fraction of these arrests resulted in a jail term. Whether the fallout is the result chiefly of legal barriers to conviction or of a public unwillingness to pay for prison space, I do not know.

If not liberal democracy, what is the culprit? One possible answer is affluence. Only an affluent society can afford an adolescent class; in poorer societies everyone, including the young, must work. Only an affluent society can have a middle class large enough to produce dissidents from the orthodox culture in sufficiently large numbers such that they constitute a critical mass. Only in an affluent society can people afford to buy large quantities of heroin, cocaine, LSD, and crack. Only an affluent society can have enough consumer goods so that feelings of injustice are sufficiently aroused to lead everybody to believe they are entitled to everything and to arouse feelings of injustice if they do not get it.

But we have enjoyed affluence before (though never quite on the scale of the last three decades), yet affluence has not before been associated with so great a commitment to hedonism and self-indulgence. The reason, as I have argued, is that in the past, when freedoms were expanded and economic opportunity enhanced in ways that threatened to free young people from the constraints of conventional morality, the defenders of that morality redoubled their efforts to maintain and extend those constraints. Sometimes, as in the Second Great Awakening, religiosity inspired the effort, but at other times (perhaps one can place the 1890s in this category) the religious impulse was less important. In the contemporary world the adult reaction to enhanced adolescent freedom has not been to control the adolescents but to emulate them. Once upon a time young boys waited impatiently until they were old enough to dress like their fathers; today fathers try to dress like their sons. Today one can imagine the graduates of our best universities leading almost any cause save one designed to instill orthodox morality.

What has changed has been the culture. That change can be described as the working out of the logical consequences of the Enlightenment. The Enlightenment meant the acceptance of skepticism and individualism, coupled with a recurring assertion of the possibility of infinite social progress and human perfectibility. This change brought with it extraordinary social benefits: freedom from religious intolerance and sectarian fanaticism, the development of the scientific method and modern technology, and the intellectual foundation of capitalism and thus of affluence. Man was knowable, authority was suspect, society was malleable.

So summary a statement cannot do justice to the several stages and many variants of Enlightenment thought. The founders of the eighteenth-century Anglo-Scottish Enlightenment—David Hume and Adam Smith—certainly embraced reason over religion (Hume's great *Treatise of Human Nature* was subtitled "An Attempt to Introduce the Experimental Method of Reasoning into Moral Subjects"), but they believed that the scientific study of morality would explain why mankind accepted the same virtues—justice, benevolence, temperance, modesty, chastity—that earlier philosophers derived from natural or divine law. Radical individualism came later and might be thought of as the romantic heresy: reason is an imperfect or wholly unreliable guide to understanding man and the universe.   Virtue, if such there be, can only be apprehended directly, spontaneously, aesthetically, and individually. Reason can at best discover what is useful; only feeling can discover what is beautiful, and beauty is superior to utility. All that is left of the Enlightenment is individualism.

It is another matter for another day to discuss whether the seeds of their own decay were contained in the naturalistic moralities of Hume and Smith, whether, that is, championing reason and science as against revelation and prescription inevitably meant freeing the individual to pursue his own self-expression to the point of self-indulgence. My provisional view is that it was not intellectually inevitable, although it may have been historically so. If an eighteenth-century Scotsman asserts that virtue derives from sentiment, he should not be surprised to discover that an eighteenth-century Frenchman (or a twentieth-century Englishman) concludes that sentiment is more important than virtue—*any* sentiment, so long as it is "authentic" or "natural."

However the Enlightenment may have been altered beyond the intention of its founders, it is clear that wrenched loose from its moorings in the virtuous habits of eighteenth-century Edinburgh or Victorian London, it came to mean the triumph of skepticism and individuality. As received, the Enlightenment that honored freedom contained within it no principle by which to define the limits to freedom. The skeptical reason that challenged religious, scientific, or political orthodoxy challenged every rule by which one could defend moral orthodoxy. The individualism that unleashed the material accomplishments of capitalism was insensitive to the moral preconditions of capitalism.

The Enlightenment has been institutionalized in the university and there has become the public philosophy of the millions of people who each year pass through those ivied halls. Fortunately for most of these people, their philosophy does not much affect their lives. Having been habituated to goodness by those very processes—adult authority, rote learning, and the maintenance of appearances—that the university teaches them to distrust, they absorb the ethos without changing their habits. But their public philosophy alters how they define the proper policy for others. It is an "enlightened" philosophy: people should be left alone to do their own thing, historical lessons should be subordinated to immediate needs, utility should be maximized but authority distrusted.

For two centuries we have been enjoying the benefits of having supplanted revelation with reason. Most of us will continue to enjoy those benefits for centuries to come. But some will know only the costs, costs imposed on them by well-meaning people who want only to do the right thing.

Reprinted with the permission of the American Enterprise Institute for Public Policy Research, Washington, D.C.

Chapter 5

Character and Family

Wade F. Horn

INTRODUCTION

Children are not born with good character. Behaviors such as truthfulness, responsibility, integrity, empathy, and caring are not innate in the human species; they must be developed. So too must brutality, racism, and dishonesty be developed. This simple truth, that whether children grow up to be persons of good character or bad is largely dependent upon learning and experience, reflects the extraordinary responsibility that men and women incur when they become parents. For while it is true that under the best of circumstances all of society's institutions—schools, churches, and neighborhoods—conspire to teach children good character, it is nonetheless also true that *families* are the one indispensable social institution for helping children develop good values and moral behavior.

It is universally recognized that families make two important contributions to society. First, they propagate the human species. Second, they are the primary socializing agent for children. When families fail in either of these tasks, civilization itself is imperiled. How families propagate the species will be left to other texts. This chapter will concentrate on how families socialize children and help them become persons of good character.

SOCIALIZATION AND CHARACTER DEVELOPMENT

We are all born into this world as egocentric and demanding creatures. We are also born helpless. The young of no other animal species is so totally dependent upon others for its survival and for so long as the human infant. It is this extraordinary dependency of the human infant on others that provides the opportunity for socializing children, for it is what motivates children to pay attention to adults and provides adults the leverage for teaching children appropriate behavior.

Socialization can be defined as the process whereby an individual acquires the behaviors, attitudes, values, and customs regarded as desirable and appropriate by society. Proper socialization requires the development of the ability to delay or inhibit impulse gratification in order to follow the rules of society. Well-socialized children have learned not to strike out at others to get what they want; undersocialized children have not. Well-socialized children have learned to listen to and obey the directions of legitimate authority figures, such as parents and teachers; undersocialized children have not. Well-socialized children have learned to cooperate and share with others; undersocialized children have not. In short, well-socialized children have developed the ability to self-regulate impulse gratification; undersocialized children have not.

Much of what is described as good character or virtue reflects this ability to delay or inhibit impulse gratification. When you tell the truth despite the near certainty that in doing so you will be experiencing negative consequences, you are inhibiting the impulse to lie to avoid unpleasantness. When you show charity to others, you are inhibiting the impulse to behave selfishly. When you abstain from sexual intercourse outside of marriage, you are inhibiting the impulse to obtain sexual gratification. Good character reflects a well-socialized individual, and a well-socialized individual is able to inhibit or delay impulse gratification.

A civil society is totally dependent upon most of its adult citizenry having developed this ability to self-regulate impulse gratification. Absent a significant majority of such well-socialized adults, storekeepers would have to post armed guards in front of every display counter; every woman would live in constant fear of being raped by roaming bands of marauding men; and children would be largely left to fend for themselves or be exploited for the gratification of their parents.

Fortunately, well-socialized children generally become well-socialized adults. Unfortunately, undersocialized children often do not. There are few statements one can say with complete certitude; but here is one:

When families fail in their task to socialize children, a civil society is not possible. Herein lies the awesome responsibility of parenting.

Parents socialize children through two mechanisms. First, and most obviously, children learn through direct tuition reinforced by a combination of rewards and punishments for acceptable and unacceptable behavior. Children are first told how they should behave and then reinforced for following the rules and punished for disobedience to the rules. Second, children learn by observing others. Of the two processes, observing others is by far the more important. In fact, most complex human behavior is acquired not through direct instruction, but through observational learning. Children, for example, are much more likely to do as a parent does than what the parent says. This is why parents who lie and cheat invariably have children who lie and cheat, despite any direct instruction to the contrary.

The process of socialization sounds simple enough. Instruct children in the rules of society, reinforce them for following the rules, punish them for disobedience to the rules, and behave well yourself. But the full story is much more complicated. Most importantly, children's cognitive capacities change dramatically over time. Infants do not think in the same way that preschoolers do, preschoolers do not think in the same way that elementary school children do, and elementary school children do not think in the same way that adolescents and adults do. The current cognitive capacities of a child dictate the character lessons a parent can teach them and how such lessons can be taught. What parents must do to instill good character and virtue in their children changes as their children grow older.

Complicating things further is the fact that the age at which the attention of children is most directed toward adults (that is, when children are very young and most dependent upon adults) is the very age at which children are the least cognitively able to understand lessons about character and virtue. As the ability of children to comprehend moral lessons increases (that is, as children grow older) their dependence on adults lessens. Thus, the best time to teach children good character and moral lessons is the time at which children are least likely to understand what you are trying to teach them. But as they grow more cognitively able, they become less dependent upon adults, and hence, less easily malleable by them. As children grow older they also become more oriented toward peers, further reducing the ability of parents to influence their development.

These developmental considerations illustrate two principles. First, parents must alter how they attempt to teach character and moral behavior to their children depending upon their child's age and cognitive capabilities. Second, it is extremely important to begin teaching character early when children are most dependent upon adults, for as children become less dependent upon adults, it is much harder to teach them good character traits. This difficulty in teaching older children good character is illustrated by the increasing use of "boot camps" for violent juvenile offenders[1]—by anyone's standards individuals lacking in good character. In such boot camps, the violent juvenile offender is placed in a highly controlled environment and made dependent upon adults, if not for one's very survival, at least for much of life's comforts. It is only by artificially regressing adolescent violent offenders back to an earlier state of dependency that even a modicum of behavioral change can occur. The lesson for parents: in teaching good character, one must start early, for it becomes much more difficult later on.

THREE GENERAL RULES

Despite the fact that how parents can best teach good character will depend upon the age and cognitive abilities of the child, there are three general parenting rules that increase the probability that children will develop self-regulation and prosocial behaviors. The first rule is that parents must display warmth and affection toward their child. High degrees of parental warmth are associated with self-confident, high-self-esteem children. Parental hostility, on the other hand, is associated with acting-out, aggressive children, and especially with juvenile delinquency. Parental warmth is important, for it enhances children's desire to be like their parents, and to follow and internalize the rules their parents set forth. It also allows parents to use withdrawal of affection as a disciplinary technique in place of harsher, more physical discipline.

The second rule is that parents need to combine high warmth with moderate degrees of control and restrictiveness. Extremes of parental permissiveness or restrictiveness are associated with acting-out children. In contrast, moderate degrees of parental control are associated with high self-esteem, adaptability, competence, internalized control, and popularity with peers. It seems that for children to develop self-control, they first need parents who understand the need to exercise control over them. When a moderate degree of parental control is present and combined with a high degree of warmth, the child is likely to want to internalize the parents' rules about behavior, eventually exchanging self-regulation for regulation by others.

Moderate levels of parental control and restrictiveness are particularly helpful in developing self-control and prosocial behavior in children when combined with explanations for rules and punishments, especially as children grow older. Such explanations help children to understand the rules and to internalize them. For example, parents who use explanations linking punishment of a child's aggressive behavior to its consequences for the victim of the aggression, have children who are more likely to respond in a helpful way when they cause harm to someone else in the future. Explanations for rules and punishment also tend to produce higher levels of empathy and altruism in children.

The third rule is that parents need to be consistent in applying the first two rules. Parental conflict and inconsistency are associated with maladjustment in children, which most often takes the form of aggressive or delinquent behavior. This association between parental inconsistency and conflict and aggressive behavior in children is especially strong for boys. The lowest rates of delinquency are found in homes in which both parents are either consistently controlling or consistently warm.

Figure One
Parental Characteristics and Child Outcomes

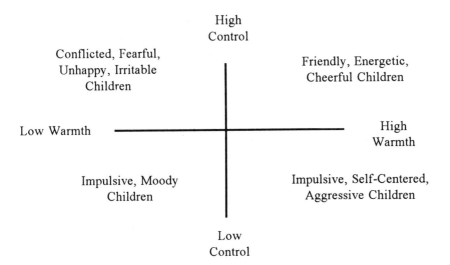

As shown in Figure One, parents who display these three characteristics —high warmth, moderate control, and consistency—tend to have children who are energetic, friendly, cooperative, helpful, and charitable toward others.   In contrast, parents who are low on warmth, but high on restrictiveness, tend to have conflicted, irritable, and passively hostile children frequently lacking in empathy for others.   Parents who display moderate warmth, but low restrictiveness, tend to have children who are impulsive and openly aggressive toward others.   There are exceptions, of course, but these are the rule.[2]

THE IMPORTANCE OF TWO PARENTS

It is now a well-established empirical fact that children who grow up in single-parent households are at-risk for a host of negative outcomes. Such children are, for example, two to three times more likely to experience school failure[3] or to suffer from a serious emotional or behavioral disorder during childhood.[4]   It is also clear that children from single-parent households are less likely than children growing up in a home with two parents to be well socialized and to develop good character traits.   In particular, boys growing up in single-parent households are more likely to engage in aggressive acting out[5] and girls are more likely to engage in promiscuous sexual activity,[6] compared to boys and girls reared in two-parent families.

One reason why children living with a single-parent are more at-risk for negative developmental outcomes is related to the need to be reared with a combination of high warmth and moderate control.   Studies of the differences between the way fathers and mothers parent children indicate that fathers tend to be higher on the control dimension and mothers higher on the warmth dimension.[7]   Whether or not these differences are due to innate or environmental factors is unclear.   What is clear is that for children to develop well, they need a home that is both high in warmth and high in control, and it is more difficult for a single parent to demonstrate high levels on both parenting dimensions.   Thus, children in single-parent households are likely to be exposed to either high levels of warmth, but low control (most common in female-headed, single-parent households), or low levels of warmth and high control (most common in male-headed, single-parent households).   Either way, socialization does not go as well compared to when the parental dimensions of high warmth and high control are both present.

Interestingly, the reason why a parent is absent has a significant impact on the socialization of children. If a parent is absent because of divorce or out-of-wedlock childbearing, socialization is likely to go particularly badly. In such cases, boys experience much greater difficulty developing the capacity to self-regulate aggressive impulses.[8] Girls, on the other hand, when reared without fathers because of divorce or abandonment tend toward sexual promiscuity.[9] But if a parent is absent because of death, the long-term outcome is much better.

The reason death of a parent is less consequential for children than either divorce or abandonment is due, in large part, to the way the surviving spouse treats the memory of the deceased parent. In the case of death, the living parent typically acts to keep the deceased parent's presence felt within the household by invoking positive images of the deceased parent. Although there is little empirical research on this matter, it is my clinical experience that in such situations the memory being invoked often reflects the weaker parenting dimension of the surviving parent. Mothers, for example, typically invoke the memory of a deceased father to encourage achievement in the child (e.g., "Your father would be so proud of you if he were here") or in situations requiring discipline (e.g, "Your father would be so disappointed if he were here today"). Fathers, in contrast, invoke the memory of a deceased mother primarily in situations requiring nurturance (e.g., "That's one of the reasons your mother loved you so very much"). In the case of divorce or out-of-wedlock childbearing, the absent parent, if invoked at all, is usually portrayed in a much more negative manner.

Although the presence of two parents in the home is helpful, it is *not* sufficient to ensure the development of good character in children. Recall that consistency is the third dimension of parenting that predicts the development of well-adjusted, energetic, friendly, and empathetic children, and that inconsistency is associated with aggressive and sexual acting out. The presence of marital discord and hostility between parents is predictive of inconsistency in parenting behavior and child maladjustment.[10] Indeed, there is evidence that in the long run, children in single-parent families are better adjusted than children in conflict-ridden two-parent families[11] (although it is certainly also true that children reared in well-functioning single-parent families do not fare as well as children reared in well-functioning two-parent families). Parents need to understand the critical importance of maintaining a mutually satisfying and respectful marital relationship, both to ensure consistency in parenting and to model such behaviors as caring, cooperation, sharing, effective conflict resolution, and respect for others.

The need for parents to work together and provide consistency in parenting should not be confused with androgenous parenting. As we have seen, mothers and fathers tend to parent children differently, with mothers higher on the affective-warmth dimension and fathers higher on the control-restrictiveness dimension. Gender differences in parental behavior do not need to be minimized for parents to raise well-adjusted and well-socialized children; indeed, it may even be harmful to do so.[12] Rather, parents need to recognize the important, albeit different, contributions each makes to effective parenting and then provide each other with support for those things each does particularly well. The important point is that for children to develop well they need a home high on both warmth and control, not parents that behave exactly the same on these two parenting dimensions.

Exactly how the desired dimensions of high warmth, moderate restrictiveness, and consistency are translated into effective parenting behaviors depends in large part on the child's age and cognitive abilities. This requires that parents have some understanding of child development and children's varying cognitive capacities at different ages.

A DEVELOPMENTAL PERSPECTIVE ON TEACHING CHARACTER

The Infant

Good character development begins at birth. Although infants are quite egocentric and, initially at least, focused on immediate sensory and motor experiences, much important learning is occurring during the first 18 months of life. It is during this period that the infant learns to differentiate himself or herself from other objects, develops an understanding of the concepts of time, causality, and object permanence, and begins to imitate the behavior of others. By the end of this period, labeled the sensorimotor stage by the Swiss psychologist Jean Piaget, the child has shifted his or her focus from immediate internal experiences to the world about him or her.

One of the most important lessons children learn during infancy is whether or not they can trust their environment. In most cases, this translates into can they trust their parents. The reason trust is so important is that it gives children a powerful reason for attending to their parents and to engage the world around them. Babies who learn they can trust their parents are babies who are said to have developed a good attachment to their parents. The quality of early attachment between babies and their parents is the most powerful early predictive of later social adjustment and character development.[13]

Early trust, and hence attachment to one's parents, is developed when parents respond consistently and regularly to their child's needs. When babies cry, it is important that parents attend to their babies' needs. As most parents soon discover, babies have many different types of cries. One kind of cry says, "I'm wet, please change me." Another type of cry says, "I'm hungry, please feed me." Another says, "Something startled me, please comfort me." Parents need to learn what types of cries in their infant transmit which types of messages, and then respond to them.

Learning what each cry signifies is best accomplished when parents have regular and consistent contact with their babies. If the parent does not have regular and consistent contact with the baby, this learning process takes longer or goes largely unaccomplished. This is why research generally shows that babies who are placed in child care before the age of one are less well adjusted later in life than children who are reared in the home by at least one of their parents.[14] Home caretaking allows the adult both to learn the different cries of the infant and to respond more readily. Infant day care, in contrast, rarely offers the kind of staffing needed to ensure such swift attention to the child's cries and needs.

Some parents worry that by responding to the cries of their infants, they will spoil the baby. It is impossible to spoil an infant. It is possible to spoil an older child, but not an infant. The infant's task is to find out whether or not his or her environment will take care of him or her. This extremely important task, whether or not the infant can view his or her environment with trust or mistrust, is largely accomplished by the end of the first year of life.

Because babies are largely preverbal during infancy, many people incorrectly believe that nothing much of significance can be accomplished prior to the development of speech. In point of fact, much of one's character is formed during this period. No less a notable social observer than Alexis de Tocqueville once commented:

When a child is born, his first years pass unnoticed in the toys and activities of infancy. As he grows older and begins to become a man, then the doors of the world open and he comes into touch with his fellows. For the first time notice is taken of him, and people think they can see the germs of the virtues and vices of his maturity taking shape.

That, if I am not mistaken, is a great error.

Go back; look at the baby in this mother's arms; see how the outside world is first reflected in the still hazy mirror of his mind; consider the first examples that strike his attention; listen to the first words which awaken his dormant powers of thought; and finally take notice of the first struggles he has to endure. Only then will you understand the origin of the prejudices, habits, and passions which are to dominate his life. The whole man is there, if one may put it so, in the cradle.[15]

One hundred and fifty years have passed since Tocqueville penned these thoughts, and no one has yet to express it better.

The Toddler

The major cognitive advance made by toddlers is the development of "symbolic functions"—the ability to represent things with symbols, reflected in the use of language to stand for things and events and the emergence of imaginative play. But the thinking of preschoolers is still limited compared to adult standards. For example, the thinking of the preschool child is likely to be animistic, the attributing of life to inanimate objects, and egocentric, the belief that the universe was created and organized for him and is centered on him. The preschool child also continues to find it difficult, although not impossible, to see any point of view but her own.

Despite the continued limitations in the cognitive capacities of preschool children, much character development occurs during this period. The child is now responsive to cultural rules and labels, such as good and bad, and right and wrong but bases these judgments primarily upon the consequences placed on the behavior. Behaviors that are rewarded are good; behaviors that are punished are bad. There is an emerging sense of fairness and sharing, but for reasons like "I'll help you if you help me."

Knowing the degree to which preschool children are oriented toward the consequences of a behavior, parents should be especially vigilant during this period to be consistent in their enforcement of rules and praise for desired behavior. Inconsistency is particularly confusing to the preschool child who sees rules as absolute with few, if any, shades of gray.

Despite preschoolers' essential egocentrism, it is during the preschool period that parents should also begin to emphasize the importance of helping others. This can be accomplished by slowly introducing the notion of chores, not to earn money or an allowance, but to contribute to the family. Beginning when the child is as young as two, parents can begin to encourage a child's sense of community obligation by requesting the child to join in family tasks. A two-year-old can be asked to push the button on the dishwasher to make it go, a three-year-old can be asked to help separate the dirty laundry by color, a four-year-old can be asked to help make their bed, and a five-year-old can be asked to help sweep out the garage. The point is not that the child will make things go easier in the home; indeed, having preschoolers help out around the house often proves more work for the parent than doing it oneself. Rather, the point is to begin to encourage the view that each of us has a responsibility to contribute to the common good, and that things go best when we all pitch in.

During the later part of the preschool period, parents can also help their children develop good character by teaching rudimentary manners. Nothing too severe at first, but by four or five years of age parents can begin to teach children to say "please" when they want something and "thank you" after they receive it. Most importantly, parents should take care to model good manners for their children.

The Elementary School Years

During the elementary school years, children move from obedience for personal rewards to conformity for social approval. Good behavior is that which pleases or is approved of by others. While punishment is certainly still to be avoided, children are increasingly motivated to appear to be a "good boy" or a "nice girl." The elementary school child is now beginning to judge behavior by a person's intentions, excusing negative outcomes, for example, if the person "meant well." At the same time, their cognitive abilities are increasing rapidly, including an increased ability to take the viewpoint of others.

This desire to please others becomes a powerful tool for parents to utilize. Combined with increasing cognitive capacities, the child is now able to benefit from more abstract tuition. For example, it is at this age that fables, myths, and legends can be used to teach moral lessons, thereby enhancing character development. Religious teachings also become more important during this age. This is, therefore, a good time for families to spend time reading together, especially stories with moral implications. William Bennett's Book of Virtues[16] contains an excellent collection of such stories. If one has not done so already, it is also a good time to enroll children in religious classes.

Children during this age are also particularly focused on their parents and look to them as models. Children by now are keen observers of their parents and their desire to emulate them is especially intense at this age. As such, parents should take special care to understand the types of behavior they are modeling for their children.

Adolescence

At about the time children enter junior high school, the desire to please others shifts to a desire to live up to the expectations of one's family, group, community, and nation, oftentimes without regard for immediate or obvious negative consequences. If all has gone well up to this point, younger adolescents tend to follow established rules, to respect authority, and to maintain the social order because they see it as their duty to do so. Thus, younger adolescents tend to identify with the group and try desperately to "fit in."

The group with which the adolescent increasingly identifies, however, is no longer exclusively the family. Adolescents look increasingly toward extrafamilial social groups, and especially peers, for identification and affiliation. This can be an extremely confusing time for adolescents, for they often receive quite conflicting messages about correct behavior and values. Indeed, those behaviors and values taught in the family frequently come into conflict with those valued by peers, the media, and even schools. The result can be great inner tension and conflict as the older adolescent struggles to reconcile these conflicts and settle on a set of personal moral values and principles for living. To whose values should the adolescent be loyal? The family? One's peers? The consumer culture?

If the child has inadequate character development, this period can go quite poorly. There is little parents can do to play "catch up" if they have not attended to character formation and development in the early years. Unfortunately, even if the parents *have* attended to character formation and development during the early years, things can still be confusing and difficult for the adolescent. Parents can help during this period by maintaining clear and consistent rules, offering high levels of warmth and nurturance and acting as a sounding board for the inner conflicts and tension being experienced by the adolescents.

Parents can also help by protecting their children during this period from negative outside influences. Although experts often advise that parents allow their adolescents opportunities to express themselves, unbridled freedom to experiment can be very dangerous during this period. Adolescents need supervision, and only actively involved parents can provide the type of intensive supervision they need. For example, one of the most powerful predictors of teenage sexual activity is the lack of parental supervision after school.[17] Although adolescence can be a difficult time to be a parent, it is no time to capitulate parental responsibility.

CONCLUSION

If all has gone reasonably well, and the parents have attended since birth to the task of character formation and development, children emerge on the other side of adolescence with a well-developed set of personal values and principles for living. Such children become adults to whom we ascribe such character traits as honesty, integrity, trustworthiness, altruism, and caring.

If things have not gone well—if the parents were too busy, too distracted, or simply not presen—children emerge on the other side of adolescence to populate our prisons, psychiatric wards, and homeless shelters, or simply display difficulty in daily living. Poorly socialized adults are those who have difficulty establishing and maintaining intimate relationships, being good workers, cooperating with others, and demonstrating compassion, altruism, and honesty. These are the adults, in other words, we describe as lacking in virtue and character. They are also the inevitable consequence of inadequate parenting. And they are tomorrow's inadequate parents.

For a civil society to exist, the vast majority of its adult citizenry must have developed character and virtue. In order for this to be so, parents must do their job well, for families are the wellspring of character and virtue. There is no more a compelling reason than this, for society to encourage, support, and celebrate the indispensable work of families and parents. Indeed, society's very survival depends upon it.

NOTES

1.   James Austin, Michael Jones, and Melissa Bolyard, *The Growing Use of Jail Boot Camps: The Current State of the Art* (Washington, DC: U.S. Department of Justice, National Institute of Justice, 1993).

2.   For further discussion of parenting practices see: Diana Baumrind, "Child Care Practices Anteceding Three Patterns of Preschool Behavior," *Genetic Psychology Monographs* 75 (1967): 43-88; E. Mavis Hetherington and Ross D. Parke, *Child Psychology: A Contemporary Viewpoint* (New York: McGraw-Hill,

1986); and E. E. Macoby and J. A. Martin, "Socialization in the Context of the Family Parent-Child Interaction," in *Socialization, Personality, and Social Development, Vol. 4, Handbook of Child Psychology* (New York: Wiley, 1983).

3.   Carl Zinsmeister, "Growing Up Scared," *The Atlantic*, June 1990.

4.   Urie Bronfenbrenner, "Discovering What Families Can Do," in David Blankenhorn, Steven Bayme, and Jean Bethke Elshtain, *Rebuilding the Nest: A New Commitment to the American Family* (Milwaukee: Milwaukee Family Service Agenda, 1990); Nicholas Davidson, "Life Without Father," *Policy Review*, Winter 1990; and William Galston and Elaine Kamarck, "A Progressive Family Policy for the 1990s," in *Mandate for Change* (New York: Berkeley Books, 1993).

5.   Nicholas Davidson, "Life Without Father," *Policy Review*, Winter 1990; Carl Zinsmeister, "Growing Up Scared," *The Atlantic*, June 1990; and Robert Rector, "How To Strengthen America's Crumbling Families," Heritage Foundation *Backgrounder* No. 894, 28 April 1992.

6.   Irwin Garfinkel and Sara S. McLanahan, *Single Mothers and Their Children: A New American Dilemma* (Washington, DC: The Urban Institute Press, 1988).

7.   Henry B. Biller and Robert J. Trotter, *The Father Factor: What You Need To Know To Make a Difference* (New York: Pocket Books, 1994); and Henry B. Biller, *Fathers and Families: Paternal Determinants of Personality Development* (Westport, CT: Auburn House, 1993).

8.   J. Perry Guidubaldi, J.D. and H. K. Cleminshaw, "The Legacy of Parental Divorce," *School Psychology Review*, Summer 1983; and N. Zill, *Happy, Healthy and Secure* (New York: Doubleday, 1985).

9.   E. Mavis Hetherington, "Effects of Father Absence on Personality Development in Adolescent Daughters," *Developmental Psychology* 7 (1972): 303-26.

10.   Patrick T. Davies and E. Mark Cummings, "Marital Conflict and Child Adjustment: An Emotional Security Hypothesis," *Psychological Bulletin* 116 (1994): 387-411.

11.   E. Mavis Hetherington, M. Cox, and R. Cox, "Effects of Divorce on Parents and Children," in Michael Lamb, ed., *Nontraditional Families* (Hillsdale, NJ: Erlbaum, 1982).

12.   David Popenoe, "Parental Androgyny," *Society* 30 (1993): 5-11.

13.   John Bowlby, *Maternal Care and Mental Health* (New York: Schocken Books, 1950); M. Lewis, et al., "Predicting Psychopathology in Six-Year-Olds From Early Social Relations," *Child Development* 55 (1984): 123-36; and L. A. Sroufe, "Individual Patterns of Adaptation From Infancy to Preschool," in M. Perlmutter, ed., *Minnesota Symposium on Child Psychology, vol. 16* (Hillsdale, NJ: Erlbaum, 1983).

14.   Jay Belsky, "Parental and Nonparental Child Care and Children's Socioemotional Development: A Decade in Review," in Alan Booth, ed., *Contemporary Families: Looking Forward, Looking Back* (Minneapolis: National

Council on Family Relations, 1991); and Alison Clarke-Stewart, "Infant Day Care: Maligned or Malignant?" *American Psychologist* 44 (1989): 268-69.

15. Alexis de Tocqueville, *Democracy in America: A New Translation by George Lawrence* (Garden City, NY: Anchor Books, 1969).

16. William J. Bennett, *The Book of Virtues* (New York: Simon and Schuster, 1993).

17. John O. G. Billy, Karin I. Brewster, and William R. Grady, "Contextual Effects on the Sexual Behavior of Adolescent Women," *Journal of Marriage and the Family*, 56 (1994): 387-404; and L. Ku, F. L. Sonenstein, and J. H. Pleck, "Factors Influencing First Intercourse for Teenage Men," *Public Health Reports* 108 (1993): 680-94.

Chapter 6

Character, Citizenship, and Constitutional Origins

Charles R. Kesler

INTRODUCTION

The problem of civility and citizenship may be stated succinctly. It is not at all unusual for countries to have citizenship without the restraints of civility; nor is it surprising to find examples of civility among people who are not united by formal ties of citizenship. But how is it possible to combine civility and citizenship in healthy and mutually reinforcing ways?

To be "civil" in ordinary usage means to be polite, respectful, decent. It is not the same thing as warmth and indeed implies a certain coolness: civility helps to cool the too-hot passions of citizenship. When citizens are civil to one another, despite their political disagreement, they reveal that these disagreements are less important than their resolution to remain fellow citizens. They agree on the fundamental political questions, even if they differ on secondary issues. Without this fundamental agreement reflected in civility, citizenship would be self-contradictory and finally self-destructive.

The French Revolution remains the unforgettable modern example of citizenship's self-destruction in the absence of civility. Citizen Brissot, Citizen Danton, Citizen Robespierre—one by one they fell victims to ever more radical and exclusive definitions of the good citizen. Tyranny itself is this process of exclusion carried to its logical extreme, in which a permanent civil war may be said to exist between the tyrant, on the one hand, and his oppressed people, on the other.

Still, it would be a great mistake to believe that the opposite of tyranny or of permanent civil war, whether explicit or implicit, is simply a concord of opinion. Political friendship can be based on better or worse opinions. The criteria for evaluating them must therefore be extrinsic to the opinions themselves. In other words, even as citizenship requires civility, so civility points beyond itself to permanent and objective moral standards—to the nature of "civil government," and higher still, to the moral and theoretical concerns of what is called civilization.

These terms—citizenship, civility, civilization—are cognates, deriving from the Latin *civis* (citizen) and *civitas* (city), which are themselves the Latin equivalents of the Greek family of words stemming from *polis* (city). From the classical point of view, the civilized are those fit to live in cities, fit to bear the burdens and enjoy the fruits of citizenship. Of course "civilization" is a word neither the Greeks nor the Romans used. It arose, and changed the focus of political life, only after the advent of Christianity. As shall be shown, this is important for the case of America, the first republic founded explicitly on the rights of man as man, rights whose title derived from the "Laws of Nature and of Nature's God." Broadly speaking, the Founders thought of themselves as perfecting the tradition of republicanism. Yet in invoking "Nature's God," they acknowledged a world changed, in vital respects, by the presence of Christianity. In these circumstances, the republican cause had to be thought through again in light of the conflicts and potential harmony between reason and biblical revelation.

There is nothing more representative of the Founders' consensus on these difficult questions, nor is there a more reliable guide to civility and citizenship in the American founding, than the words and deeds of General and later President George Washington. Although I have no desire to out-parson Parson Weems, I think it is impossible to understand the founding without coming to grips with the phenomenon of Washington. In what follows I will appeal primarily to his speeches and writings to illustrate my argument.[1]

WASHINGTON'S CHARACTER

Civility in the first place is a matter of shaping young people's moral character. The tools of this art include precepts, examples, exhortation, and shame liberally applied as the case permits or demands. It is not surprising, then, to find that one of the earliest writings of the young Washington, laboriously entered into his copybook, is a set of 110 "Rules of Civility and Decent Behavior in Company and Conversation." For the most part these are useful lessons for reducing any adolescent to a civilized state: "Shake not the head, feet or legs; roll not the eyes; lift not one eyebrow higher than the other; wry not the mouth and bedew no man's face with your spittle by [approaching too near] him [when] you speak." These rules are a playful (although serious) reminder that civility consists first of all in good manners. "Every action done in company," reads the first rule, "ought to be with some sign of respect to those that are present."[2] Good manners are a reminder that one's own interest and happiness are bound up with one's family and friends, and that the authority of such essential social groups is—practically speaking—more obvious than the liberty of their members.

Civility in this sense stands athwart the contemporary ethic of self-expression. Nevertheless, good manners aim not to crush but to form individual character. Washington's list begins with what might be dismissed today as mere social conformity, but it ends: "Labor to keep alive in your breast that little sparkle of celestial fire called conscience."[3] Conformity to social custom is part of good manners but is justified because it frees us to cultivate the distinctions that matter. A serious man does not show his superiority by eating spaghetti with his fingers. Civility allows for, and at its best is, the fanning of that "sparkle of celestial fire" in man to produce a steady blaze of moral seriousness.

Washington's civility is thus a species of honor. Explaining to his wife why he had to accept command of the Continental Army, he wrote:

> It was utterly out of my power to refuse this appointment, without exposing my character to such censures, as would have reflected dishonor upon myself, and given pain to my friends. This, I am sure, could not and ought not to be pleasing to you and must have lessened me considerably in my own esteem.[4]

Washington's consciousness of his own honor, reflected in and reflecting the honorableness of his friends, provided the touchstone of his conduct. At the highest level, his civility was thus a form of magnanimity. As Aristotle explains, the magnanimous man accepts external honors as the greatest tribute that can be paid him but regards all such popular offerings as vastly inferior to his own sense of dignity and propriety.[5]

THE BASIS OF CIVILIAN RULE

One of the most instructive displays of Washington's magnanimity was his response to Colonel Lewis Nicola's letter (22 May 1782) proposing that Washington be made king. "With a mixture of great surprise and astonishment I have read with attention the Sentiments you have submitted to my perusal," he answered Nicola, a loyal and respected officer.

> ...I am much at loss to conceive what part of my conduct could have given encouragement to an address which to me seems big with the greatest mischiefs that can befall my Country. If I am not deceived in the knowledge of myself, you could not have found a person to whom your schemes are more disagreeable.... Let me conjure you then, if you have regard for your country, concern for yourself or posterity, or respect for me, to banish these thoughts from your Mind and never communicate, as from yourself or anyone else, a sentiment of the like nature.[6]

The letter's tone is calculated to shame, and Nicola was so ashamed that he wrote three apologies in as many days. In this short missive Washington refused the honor of being king on the ground that it was beneath him! True honor lay in performing noble deeds for their own sake, not for the sake of extrinsic rewards. And in the most fundamental sense, the letter's tone was "civil"; it was not the voice of a commander upbraiding his inferior officer but of one civilian to another. The foundation of civilian control of the military was the civility of the commanding general—his reasonable control of his militant passions.[7]

Thus did Washington's civility lay the basis and set the standard for republican citizenship in America. His virtues may be considered the final cause of the new regime, even as they played an indispensable role in its efficient causation—the victories won by the Continental Army. Be that as it may, the formal cause of the new order was something different: the great principle proclaimed in the Declaration of Independence, "that all Men are created equal." It is a matter of some academic and political dispute how this was understood at the time. Certainly, however, there should not be any dispute over how Washington understood it.

WASHINGTON'S PRINCIPLES

As opposed to many present-day commentators who emphasize the lowness of "unalienable Rights," reducing them to expressions of the most elemental passions, Washington esteemed them as high and dignified principles. Far from signifying the abandonment of virtue, man's natural rights required the virtues to sustain and justify them. As he put it in his general orders to the army on 1 March 1778, the fortitude of

the virtuous officers and soldiery of this Army... not only under the common hardships incident to a military life, but also under the additional sufferings to which the peculiar situation of these States have exposed them, clearly proves them worthy of the enviable privilege of contending for the rights of human nature, the freedom and independence of their country.[8]

In addition to Washington's own honor, then, there is an honor due to human nature, which honor may be called the rights of man. It is an "enviable privilege" to contend for them because they are based on what is special to man—his rank in creation. Man's possession of reason distinguishes him from the beasts, but his imperfect possession of reason—above all the fact that his passions may cloud his reason—distinguishes him from the divine being, the kind of being whose rationality is perfect and unaffected by desire. As the in-between being, man's dignity derives from his place in this ordered universe.

The rights of man are governed by man's nature, which means man's place in nature, which means the natural law. For man to deserve his rights, he must live up to the law that ordains them: He must act like a man to deserve the rights of man. Writing to the inhabitants of Canada, Washington contrasted "the Blessings of Liberty" with "the Wretchedness of Slavery," warning that to submit slavishly to Great Britain would show their "poverty of Soul and baseness of Spirit." He called upon them to prove "that you are enlightened, generous, and Virtuous; that you will not renounce your own Rights, or serve as Instruments to deprive your Fellow subjects of theirs."[9] Today, unalienable rights are often presented as being a repudiation of the high-minded concern for moral virtue. In fact, in the original American understanding, the rights of man demand an *unprecedented* moralization of politics.

THE THEOLOGICAL-POLITICAL PROBLEM

To grasp the significance of this for American citizenship, it is important to understand the relation between what the Founders called civil and religious liberty. Indeed, Washington expressed the whole purpose of the Revolution in these words: "The establishment of Civil and Religious Liberty was the motive which induced me to the Field...."[10] This motive takes us to the heart of problem—the theological-political problem, as Benedict de Spinoza called it—confronting the Founders.

In the ancient world, this problem did not exist. Every city had its own gods and understood itself either to have been founded by these gods or to have been founded by mortals who were later taken up into heaven as gods. The "constitutional" law of every ancient city was therefore divine law. Ancient cities as such had no "religion." They had only their gods, law-giving gods, who were perforce jealous gods. To be sure, some cities held some gods in common, most notably the Olympian deities among the Greek cities. But these gods commanded different things to different cities, and at any rate were only part of the elaborate structure of local and ancestral gods that cumulatively distinguished each city.[11] The city was the work of its gods, who in return demanded not so much faith but obedience to the city's laws. Indeed, if the city was defeated in battle, its gods were also considered losers; and it was not thought craven or impious for the vanquished (if their lives were spared) to transfer their allegiance to the gods of their conquerors.

When Christianity conquered Rome, however, the nature of political life in the West was profoundly changed. In the place of the city gods rose the Christian God, knowable only through His revelations, the God of all men everywhere but of no city in particular. Now it was that the idea of "religion" was born, for men's civic and divine loyalties were no longer identical. Under the Christian dispensation, the City of God was not a human municipality. Divine law no longer constituted particular polities; rather it offered the means of salvation to individual souls in every city. Hence the problem: If the principle of civic obligation was obedience to the divine law, and cities were no longer thought to have divine lawgivers, what principle was to oblige citizens to obedience?

The political history of the West after the establishment of the Holy Roman Empire consisted of a series of attempts to answer this fundamental question—to find a new ground for political right. Each attempt ultimately unraveled, partly because Christians fell to fighting among themselves over the exact definition of Christianity but more profoundly because of the conflict between revelation as such and reason. This conflict underlies the battles between theological and secular authorities during the Holy Roman Empire and during and after the Reformation.[12]

In the face of this theological-political problem, citizenship and civility were both endangered. Christianity, when established by temporal authorities, had the distressing if somewhat paradoxical tendency both to sap obedience to civil laws and to invite civil coercion in matters of faith. By virtue of the first tendency, citizenship became particularly problematic. By virtue of the second, civility became swamped by fanaticism and hypocrisy.

THE AMERICAN ANSWER

Restoring the foundations of civility and citizenship in the Christian West was the great accomplishment of the American founding. It did this in the name of civil and religious liberty, not explicitly of virtue, for the deepest cause of the civil war in the West was the dispute over the ultimate meaning of virtue—whether it consisted in following Athens or Jerusalem, in skeptical reasoning or faithful obedience. But this was a debate that had precisely to be carried on at the highest intellectual and spiritual levels, in conversations among friends who are disposed to seek the truth. It could not be conducted politically, and any attempt to decide it politically was bound to be tyrannical. This had been the cause of the holocausts of the Old World. In America, people would have the liberty to carry on this transpolitical debate while cultivating the civic and religious friendship that was its precondition and product.

Two principles were required: a ground of citizenship and a ground for separating citizenship from church membership. Both were found in the doctrine of the rights of man. In the first place, the basis of political obligation was found in the consent of individuals, premised on the grounds of their natural freedom and equality. At the same time, religious liberty was secured by the limited nature of the social contract. By virtue of these principles, men may be good citizens of the City of God and good citizens of their earthly city without prejudice to either. "Civil government" and "civil liberties" are made possible by excluding questions of revealed truth from determination by political majorities. Majority rule and minority rights can be made consistent only on this basis. Under modern conditions, limited government is thus essential to the rule of law. But the justice of limited government for all times and places depends upon the limits of human knowledge, whether viewed in terms of Socratic ignorance or of man's inferiority to God. In light of these limits, the separation of church and state means that revelation is not forced to overrule human reason, nor reason compelled to pass judgment on the claims of revelation. The limits of human wisdom from every point of view thus affirm the justice of limited government and of citizenship governed by civility.

RIGHTS AND DUTIES

Although church and state must be separated, this is not true for religion and politics more generally, or for religion and morality. Today, the separation of church and state is often regarded as the beginning of the divorce between morals and politics or between values and facts. What this interpretation overlooks is that separation was intended to *unite* civic morality and the *moral* teaching of religion: disestablishment was meant to *establish* common standards of morality to guide political life. The point is well illustrated in the Founders' use of the term "conscience." In general, conscience is the knowledge of right and wrong that men share with one another and with their Creator. It comprises the duties men owe to their Creator, especially the duty of worshiping Him according to the modes they think He finds agreeable—hence the "right of conscience." Writing in 1789 to a group of Quakers, Washington expressed the idea in these words: "The liberty enjoyed by the people of these States, of worshipping Almighty God agreeably to their consciences, is not only among the choicest of their *blessings*, but also of their *rights*."[13]

That is, religious freedom is not only a dispensation of a loving God who abhors persecution, but also of the fallible human reason that admits it cannot penetrate the highest mysteries of faith.

But conscience comprises also the duties men owe to themselves and to others. Yet the Founders distinguished these commands of conscience from the "right" of conscience grounded in the limits of human reason. Our duties to our fellow man depend not upon a right to interpret private or revealed wisdom but upon our duty to acknowledge the "self-evident" truths of human nature—the special status of man in the universe, whether that universe is thought to be ordered by the inherent power of nature or by the will of the Living God. In short, the fact that human knowledge of the highest things is limited does not mean that we know nothing at all: We know, for instance, that there is an essential difference between a man and a dog. Such fundamental distinctions must be knowable if revelation itself is to make sense—in order to understand, e.g., that "love thy neighbor as thyself" applies to neighboring human beings but not cows or horses. This broad morality built on the common sense of revelation and reason—on "the Laws of Nature and of Nature's God"—was what the Founders meant to inculcate as America's public orthodoxy.

One of Washington's most famous letters, composed during his first term as president, was to the Hebrew Congregation in Newport. "All Americans," he wrote,

> possess alike the liberty of conscience and immunities of citizenship. It is now no more that toleration is spoken of as if it were the indulgence of one class of people that another enjoyed the exercise of their inherent natural rights, for, happily, the Government of the United States, which gives to bigotry no sanctions, to persecution no assistance, requires only that they who live under its protection should demean themselves as good citizens in giving it on all occasions their effectual support.[14]

But good citizenship involves more than simply a quid pro quo for the state's protection. It requires that those whose citizenship depends on the rights of man conduct themselves as *human beings*. In other words, to be worthy of the rights of self-government they must show themselves capable of governing themselves and their passions. Despite reason and revelation's disagreements about the ultimate basis of morality—whether nature or God is the highest principle—they agree substantially on the definition of morality. The moral virtues provide a touchstone to help distinguish good from bad citizenship and true from false prophecy. As Washington puts it in a letter to the General Assembly of Presbyterian Churches:

> While all men within our territories are protected in worshipping the deity according to the dictates of their consciences, it is rationally to be expected from them in return that they will be emulous of evincing the sanctity of their professions by the innocence of their own lives and the beneficence of their actions; for no man, who is profligate in his morals, or a bad member of the civil community, can possibly be a true Christian, or a credit to his own religious society.[15]

Washington's point is that the "right of conscience" cannot command anything contrary to the natural law. The right of conscience itself being one of man's natural rights, it has to be exercised consistently with the rest of them. The same point may be expressed in religious terms: New revelations cannot repeal or contradict the basic moral commandments of the Bible.

ESTABLISHING THE AMERICAN CHARACTER

It is common in the Founders' writings to come across the distinction between public and private happiness. The innermost core of the distinction is the profoundly private relationship between the individual soul and its Creator, which ultimately involves the destiny of that soul in the life to come. In this world, however, public and private happiness are aspects of the same reality. Above all, both public and private happiness are connected to moral virtue. "The foundation of our national policy," Washington urged in his First Inaugural Speech, should be "laid in the pure and immutable principles of private morality."[16] In his Farewell Address he proclaimed, "Of all the dispositions and habits which lead to political prosperity, Religion and morality are indispensable supports. In vain would that man claim the tribute of Patriotism, who should labor to subvert these great Pillars of human happiness, these firmest props of the duties of men and citizens."[17]

In his First Inaugural, Washington had emphasized the same point: "there is no truth more thoroughly established," he declared, "than that there exists an indissoluble union between virtue and happiness...."[18] Morality, or morality and religion, were therefore indispensably necessary to the happiness of the American people. Accordingly, the line dividing church and state or private and public did not run, as John Locke has seemed to argue, between the soul and the body.[19] It ran *within the soul*, distinguishing the exercise of the right of conscience, with its concern for revealed religion, from the consciousness of moral right.[20] The political effects were striking. With the doctrines of theology now free to be expounded and contested in the churches, uncontaminated by the secular pursuit of power, morality and the moral teachings of religion were free to wield an unprecedented influence over public and private opinion. This *moralization* of politics gave an unprecedented scope for civility.[21]

It was the statesmanship of the Founders, and above all of Washington, that secured this realm of civility for the United States. "We are a young nation and have a character to establish," Washington wrote candidly in 1783.[22] The founding properly so-called was this great act of establishing the American character. To do justice to Washington's role would require a biography, not a chapter, but the core of his genius was always to recognize the moral implications and consequences of human action. He knew when and how to conciliate opinions—on the democratic character of the House of Representatives (the subject of his sole intervention in the debates of the Constitutional Convention), on the Bill of Rights, even among party factions in his own cabinet—so that his countrymen might join hands as fellow citizens. Most importantly, he knew the power of his own example. During the ratification debates he wrote confidently of the historic role that the first officers elected under the Constitution would be called upon to play.

> I have no doubt but...those persons who are chosen to administer it will have wisdom enough to discern the influence which their example as rulers and legislators may have on the body of the people, and will have virtue enough to pursue that line of conduct which will most conduce to the happiness of their Country; as the first transactions of a nation, like those of an individual upon his first entrance into life, make the deepest impression, and are to form the leading traits in his character....[23]

CONCLUSION

In the Founders' view, American citizenship and civility were distinguished by their dedication to the common purpose of Western civilization. Neither the best city of the classics nor the holy city of the Church was what the Founders sought but a polity that for the first time in history would seek to do justice to both without establishing either at the expense of the other, a polity dedicated to "protecting the rights of human nature and establishing an Asylum for the poor and oppressed of all nations and religions."[24] This was the *novus ordo seclorum* they proclaimed.

To Washington belongs perhaps the most striking statement of the Founders' consciousness of the West as a civilization. It occurs in his famous Circular Letter of 14 June 1783.

> The foundation of our empire was not laid in the gloomy age of Ignorance and Superstition, but at an Epocha in which the rights of mankind were better understood and more clearly defined, than at any former period; the researches of the human kind, after social happiness, have been carried to a great extent; the Treasures of knowledge, acquired through a long succession of years, by the labours of Philosophers, Sages and Legislatures, are laid open for our use, and their collected wisdom may be happily applied in the Establishment of our forms of Government; the free cultivation of Letters, the unbounded extension of Commerce, the progressive refinement of manners, the growing liberality of sentiment, and above all, the pure and benign light

of Revelation, have had a meliorating influence on mankind and increased the blessings of Society. At this auspicious period, the United States came into being as a Nation, and if their Citizens should not be completely free and happy, the fault will be entirely their own.[25]

The auspices could not be more favorable, but the political lesson is that the freedom and happiness of the American people, and the destiny of the civilization they represent, depend on their conduct. "This is the time of their political probation," Washington adds in the next paragraph, "...the moment to establish or ruin their national Character forever...."[26]

The civility of the American founding connects American citizenship to the civilization of which it is an illustrious part and looks to the other part of the civilized world as a kind of community of like-minded nations. Thus the Declaration of Independence pays "a decent Respect to the Opinions of Mankind," presupposing that those opinions are at least decent enough to merit respect. But Washington and the signers of the Declaration were well aware that "Cruelty and Perfidy, scarcely paralleled in the most barbarous Ages" could be committed by "the Head of a civilized Nation"—were aware more generally that ages of science and commerce could be as barbarous, in some respects more barbarous, than ages of "Ignorance and Superstition."

It was precisely such a threat from within that faced the United States less than 75 years later in the Civil War, when civility and citizenship were rent in two by the controversy over slavery. It was in the midst of this crisis that Abraham Lincoln, leaving Springfield for the nation's capital, declared somberly that he went "with a task before me greater than which rested upon Washington." In contemplating the future of American citizenship and civility, in contemplating the future of the West, we ought to remember how Lincoln bore the task—and what he may have learned to help him bear it, as an avid young reader of Parson Weems's *Life of Washington*.

NOTES

1. In fairness to Parson Weems, his famous, heroic nineteenth-century biography of Washington has not been read lately with the political sophistication it deserves. For the beginning of a correction, see Garry Wills, *Cinncinatus: George Washington and the Enlightenment* (Garden City, NY: Doubleday, 1984), chapters 3-4.

2. W. B. Allen, ed., *George Washington: A Collection* (Indianapolis: Liberty Classics, 1988), 6.

3. Allen, *Washington: A Collection*, 13.

4. Allen, *Washington: A Collection*, 41; cf. 57-58, 65, 83.

5. Aristotle, *Nicomachean Ethics*, 1123b17-1124a19.

6. Allen, *Washington: A Collection*, 203-4.

7. Gouverneur Morris, *Eulogies and Orations on the Life and Death of General Washington* (Boston, 1800), 44-45, quoted in Wills, *Cincinnatus*, xxiii-xxiv.

8. Allen, *Washington: A Collection*, 95; cf. 220, 222, 237.

9. Allen, *Washington: A Collection*, 47.

10. Allen, *Washington: A Collection*, 271.

11. Fustel de Coulanges has given the clearest picture of this in his classic book, *The Ancient City* (Garden City, NY: Doubleday Anchor, n.d.; orig. pub. 1864).

12. See the important discussion in Harry V. Jaffa, "Equality, Liberty, Wisdom, Morality, and Consent in the Idea of Political Freedom," *Interpretation*, vol. 15 (January 1987), 24-28.

13. Allen, *Washington: A Collection*, 533.

14. Allen, *Washington: A Collection*, 548.

15. Allen, *Washington: A Collection*, 533.

16. Allen, *Washington: A Collection*, 462.

17. Allen, *Washington: A Collection*, 521.

18. Allen, *Washington: A Collection*, 462.

19. John Locke, "A Letter Concerning Toleration," in *The Works of John Locke*, vol. 6 (London, 1823), 9-13.

20. For a fine account of how this principle was translated into legal and constitutional practice, see Michael W. McConnell, "The Origins and Historical Understanding of Free Exercise of Religion," *Harvard Law Review*, May 1990, 1409-517.

21. Thus Washington suggested that in America, on the basis of religious freedom, Christianity could achieve a purity and power it had never enjoyed before. "The consideration that human happiness and moral duty are inseparably connected, will always continue to prompt me to progress of the former, by inculcating the practice of the latter," he wrote to the Protestant Episcopal Church in 1789. In W. W. Abbot, gen. ed., *The Papers of George Washington*, Presidential Series, vol. 3 (Charlottesville: University Press of Virginia, 1989), 497.

22. Allen, *Washington: A Collection*, 246.

23. Allen, *Washington: A Collection*, 387.

24. Allen, *Washington: A Collection*, 237.

25. Allen, *Washington: A Collection*, 240-41.

26. Allen, *Washington: A Collection*, 241.

Chapter 7

The Roots of Character in Civil Society

Charles L. Glenn

> Where do citizens acquire the capacity to care about the common good? Where do people learn to view others with respect and concern, rather than to regard them as objects, means, or obstacles?
>
> Mary Ann Glendon[1]

INTRODUCTION

It seems as though almost everyone these days agrees that families play the primary role in making us the sorts of people we are and thus in shaping our society as well. As Samuel Smiles wrote in one of his many Victorian bestsellers, "it is mainly in the home that the heart is opened, the habits are formed, the intellect is awakened, and character moulded for good or for evil."[2] Of course, the conclusions to be drawn from this commonplace observation differ widely among contemporary observers.

Some argue that the contribution of the family to the formation of character is more than a matter-of-fact observation based upon its predominant role in the earliest years of a child's life, subject to some limitation by the growing use of infant day care. They insist that the family is primary also *in principle*, and that this primacy should extend well beyond what occurs in the home. They draw support from the Supreme Court's observation in 1923, that "The child is not the mere creature of the state; those who nurture him and direct his destiny have the right, coupled with the high duty, to recognize and prepare him for additional obligations."[3]

They could also claim the support of various international conventions protecting human rights.[4] For example, the *Universal Declaration of Human Rights* states that "parents have a prior right to choose the kind of education that shall be given to their children" (article 26, 3). According to the *International Covenant on Economic, Social and Cultural Rights*,

> the States Parties to the present Covenant undertake to have respect for the liberty of parents...to choose for their children schools, other than those established by public authorities, which conform to such minimum educational standards as may be laid down or approved by the State and to ensure the religious and moral education of their children in conformity with their own convictions. (article 13, 3)

Similarly, the First Protocol to the *European Convention for the Protection of Human Rights and Fundamental Freedoms* provides that in the exercise of any functions which it assumes in relation to education and teaching, the State shall respect the right of parents to ensure such education and teaching in conformity with their own religious and philosophical convictions (article 2).

Those who hold this "strong" position on the conclusions to be drawn from the primacy of the family argue, to take one example, that government should confine its role in education to making it financially possible for parents to select schools that correspond to their own convictions about what will be in each child's best interests, just as they can decide what their children will eat and what they will wear and to providing general consumer protection of the sort necessary in a complex society. Government, in this view, should arrange for a nonintrusive supervision of the overall provision of schooling, but should overrule the decisions of parents about schooling, as about other spheres of their responsibility, only in the most egregious cases of child abuse or neglect.

The case for supporting parent choice is only one of an assortment of policy prescriptions intended to strengthen the scope and ability of families to take responsibility for their members, from the youngest to the oldest.

Others contend that such policies, while fine in theory, are unworkable because "the family" has almost entirely collapsed or—perhaps worse—has been revealed to be dysfunctional and abusive even in its apparently solid forms. The only remedy is an ever expanding role for government. Professional interventions—by educators, day-care specialists, social workers, therapists, and other members of the "New Class"—must be substituted for the ineffectual and often damaging efforts of families to give their children the right start in life.

IS THERE AN IDEAL MODEL OF FAMILY?

Elite opinion in the United States was dominated for several decades by the contention that there is no ideal model of family life; there are only "families" in endlessly different, equally valid (or invalid, dysfunctional) forms. The assumption that marriage is the normative basis for family life and for raising children has increasingly retreated, at least in the media and professional circles of American society, in response to claims that the "traditional" family is a vanishing species in American life. This contention has been repeated so frequently and in such an apparently authoritative display of census data that it has been widely accepted, though a visit to any suburban mall on a Saturday—or to any church on a Sunday—would call it seriously into question.

Claims that the traditional family has collapsed rest upon extensive manipulation of the data. For example, it is commonly stated that "fewer than 10 percent of families today fit the old model of homemaker mother and breadwinner father," but this result is arrived at by counting as "families" every household in the nation, including old people and students living alone, and then denying the "traditional" label to any family in which the mother works for any amount of time at any point in the year, or in which there are less than or more than two children! Actually, in 1987 only 28.8 percent of families with preschool children had both parents working full-time; in 33.3 percent of these families, the mother did not have any paid employment and in 15.8 percent the mother had part-time employment. Employed single mothers headed 10.1 percent of all families with preschool children.[5]

To take a personal example, my own family would count as "untraditional" in several respects: we have too many children, my wife works part-time, we often invite other adults (graduate students or visiting scholars in my university department) to share our house for a time. None of these seem to us danger signals of social collapse!

To assert that the traditional family is not on its last legs is not to deny the seriousness of the current high rates of illegitimacy and family break-up and of the stresses experienced by many intact families in which both parents have highly demanding jobs and devote inadequate time and energy to their children. It seems unlikely that a solution can be found short of a national "change of heart" (starting with the media) about what matters in life and how it should be lived, but the policy measures proposed in recognition of the contribution of effective families to the health of society, such as family leave, tax credits or increased tax deductions for dependent children, disincentives for teenage pregnancy, and subsidized parent choice of schools, are worthy of support. After all,

> the public has a much greater interest in the conditions under which children are being raised than in the ways that adults generally choose to arrange their lives. European laws and policies...routinely distinguish for many purposes ...between households that are engaged in child rearing and other types of living arrangements.[6]

American public policy can and should do as much.

WHAT GOVERNMENT SHOULD AND SHOULD NOT DO

While there are measures that government can take—or stop taking—that would tend to strengthen families and expand their scope to nurture, in their children, the habits of a virtuous life, it would be a mistake to accept the simple family/government dichotomy (fated, like the gingham dog and the calico cat, to fight forever) of much current political discourse. Government oversteps its appropriate limits when it seeks to use schooling to shape the character of its citizens. The Founders considered but did not adopt proposals for a national system of education for that very purpose, and recent attempts to include aspects of character in state-mandated assessments of educational outcomes have been defeated by the bitter resistance of parents who rightly perceive the potential for abuse of such an effort.[7] In the words of former Justice William Brennan, "In *The Republic* and in *The Laws*, Plato offered a vision of a unified society, where the needs of children are met not by parents but by the Government, and where no intermediate forms of association stand between the individual and the State. The vision is a brilliant one, but it is not our own."[8]

Government's role is essential: it is, as Luther wrote, to restrain evil-doers and to maintain justice. What government does not do well and should not do at all is to take up the task of education beyond (though not in necessary opposition to) where the family's formative influence can go, teaching the child, the youth, even the adult the broader sympathies and modes of relating which the family cannot teach. Political scientist James Q. Wilson asks us to

> imagine a world in which people attached no significance to any larger social entity than themselves, and their immediate families. Can we suppose that in such a world there would be any enlarged sense of duty, any willingness to sacrifice oneself for the benefit of others, or even much willingness to cooperate...?[9]

No, we need a context for the development and exercise of character which is wider than the family, and we find this in that intermediate sphere which social scientists often call the "civil society." Michael Walzer has defined this as "the space of uncoerced human association and also the set of relational networks—formed for the sake of family, faith, interest, and ideology—that fill this space."[10] Zbigniew Rau writes of a

> historically evolved form of society that presupposes the existence of a space in which individuals and their associations compete with each other in the pursuit of their values. This space lies between those relationships which result from family commitments and those which involve the individual's obligations toward the state. Civil society is therefore a space free from both family influence and state power.[11]

As such, civil society has an indispensable role to play in the lifelong development of character. Alexis de Tocqueville asked,

> what political power could ever carry on the vast multitude of lesser undertakings which associations daily enable American citizens to control? ...The more government takes the place of associations, the more will individuals lose the idea of forming associations and need the government to come to their help. That is a vicious circle of cause and effect.... The morals and intelligence of a democratic people would be in as much danger as its commerce and industry if ever a government wholly usurped the place of private associations. Feelings and ideas are renewed, the heart enlarged, and the understanding developed only by the reciprocal action of men one upon another.[12]

If early family experience forges the blade of character, it is in transactions with society that the blade is sharpened. The family is primary for good or ill in the formation of character as in other aspects of nurturance, but it does not and cannot stand alone like the Swiss Family

Robinson. Anyone who has raised children to adolescence is familiar with the ever increasing influence of the social and cultural environment in which that is done.

> We should not have to apologize for defining our society as one that relies heavily on families to socialize its young citizens, and that encourages, aids and rewards persons who perform family obligations. But an indispensable element of any such efforts to improve conditions for the nurture of citizens must be to attend more closely to the structures of civil society with which families are in a symbiotic relationship.[13]

If there has been a certain neglect of the role of the civil society among opinion-makers, this may be because it is of the very nature of society to be unpredictably responsive to government interventions. Not *un*responsive; the capacity of civil society to do its civilizing and regulating work can be gravely injured by the actions of government, or (less commonly) strengthened thereby. But the law of unanticipated consequences prevails, and that is something which most policy-makers detest.

There may also be a lingering sense among policy elites that the effects of civil society are of a lower order of dignity and worth than those of the state;[14] they are the stubbornly resistant stuff, the sow's ear out of which wise state action can perhaps make a silk purse of sorts. While the unavoidable context of policy, the civil society is (in this view) frustratingly arbitrary, complex, and ill-assorted, as if it were a box of jumbled pieces from different construction sets that a family might put away in the attic and bring out to baffle the grandchildren.

A further source of resistance to recognizing the centrality of civil society may be that, for many who become shapers of opinion, it is made up of organizations and institutions against which they themselves have been in rebellion: religious institutions, ethnic neighborhoods, extended families, and other embodiments of traditional habits and ways of understanding the world. The civil society is, from this perspective, the source of superstition, hypocrisy, conventionality, sex-role stereotyping, and much else assumed to be evil or at least outmoded.

All three are bad reasons for neglecting the centrality of civil society in shaping character, the character of women and men upon which society itself, and all else, depend. This is all the more the case today, when the permanence of this environing moral and social order can no longer be taken comfortably for granted. We see the results in America's inner cities, and we see it—though for quite other reasons—in Moscow.

THE RENEWAL OF CIVIL SOCIETY IN EASTERN EUROPE

A primary strategy of communist regimes was to eliminate or subordinate all expressions of the civil society to its direct control: "the state dissolved the institutions of civil society and replaced the normative order of that society with one of its own making.... Political parties, business associations, trade unions, learned societies, religious organizations, and publishing houses were abolished or put under the control of the state."[15] The fall of those regimes has not led automatically to a restoration of social self-organization, and the conviction has grown that economic and political reforms in the nations of the former Soviet bloc will not be successful without such a continuing revival of this civil society, of habits of association and grassroots initiative and the cultural norms that make them possible. Efforts from the center, during Mikhail Gorbachev's campaign of perestroika, to insist upon new forms of behavior at the periphery of Soviet life—harder work, less abuse of alcohol, more economic initiative—within a system that was fundamentally unchanged proved largely incapable of reaching the desired results, confirming Martin Malia's insistence upon "the intrinsic irreformability of communism."[16] Or, as Victor Zaslavsky put it, *"Perestroika* was essentially a political revolution that destroyed the old political order but neither shattered the institutional structure of the economy nor changed the state-dependent mentality of the population."[17]

The situation has grown worse as imposed constraints have been lifted and democracy and free markets put in place without the social habits and attitudes essential to sustain their functioning. A collapse of moral order is painfully evident in reports from Russia, and there is no remedy apart from the slow self-restoration of the civil society.

Long before the "velvet revolution," Václav Havel saw how essential this autonomous process in the society was to freedom itself. He wrote in a 1978 essay that "the attempt at political reform [in the Prague Spring of 1968] was not the cause of society's reawakening, but rather the final outcome of that reawakening." Fundamentally disagreeing with the Marxist/Leninist assumption that human nature would change in response to changes in the economic and political order, Havel insisted that political and economic reform could only occur through "profound existential and moral changes in society."[18] Through initiatives independent of state and party control, those determined to reject the lies imposed upon them by ideology would begin to recreate a social space within which it would be possible to "live within the truth," and not only for themselves, but ultimately for the entire society.

> What else are those initial attempts at social self-organization than the efforts of a certain part of society to live—as a society—within the truth, to rid itself of the self-sustaining aspects of totalitarianism and, thus, to extricate itself radically from its involvement in the post-totalitarian system? What else is it but a non-violent attempt by people to negate the system within themselves and to establish their lives on a new basis, that of their own proper identity? ...it would be quite wrong to understand the parallel structures and the parallel *polis* as a retreat into a ghetto and as an act of isolation, addressing itself only to those who had decided on such a course, and who are indifferent to the rest...the parallel *polis* points beyond itself and only makes sense as an act of deepening one's responsibility to and for the whole.... Independent initiatives ...demonstrate that living within the truth is a human and social alternative and they struggle to expand the space available for that life....[19]

This phenomenon of a gradual reanimation and organization of civil society by voluntary efforts from below has been described "as 'the social self-organization of society' in Poland, a 'parallel' or 'independent society' in Czechoslovakia, or a 'second society' in Hungary."[20]

Just as educational systems were for several generations deeply implicated in efforts to reshape human nature into obedience to central direction by the Communist party/state by eliminating all forms of independent thinking and all competing loyalties, so today the same systems are on the front lines of the revival of civil society in Eastern and Central Europe.[21] Havel predicted accurately that

> the official structures—as agencies of the post-totalitarian system, existing only to serve its automatism and constructed in the spirit of that role—[would] simply begin withering away and dying off, to be replaced by new structures that have evolved from "below" and are put together in a fundamentally different way.

These new structures would be

> held together more by a commonly shared feeling of the importance of certain communities than by commonly shared expansionist ambitions directed "outward." There can and must be structures that are open, dynamic and small; beyond a certain point, human ties like personal trust and personal responsibility cannot work.[22]

Havel was not referring primarily to schools in his 1978 essay (though he mentions, as an example of the "independent life of society," "teachers who privately teach young people things that are kept from them in the state schools"[23]), but in fact new and transformed schools have been among the most common "new structures" emerging during the last years of Communist rule and in a flood since its collapse.   Groups of parents and teachers have begun to recreate education through school-level initiatives to serve their children more honestly and more effectively, and education policy debates have focused on whether such initiatives should be merely tolerated as an expression of freedom or welcomed and supported in the interest of society as a whole.

Even more than in the West, such initiatives are an essential aspect of educational reform in the formerly Communist nations, where

> a rich network of independent institutions and organizations has to be formed, that are neither state-directed nor state-controlled, that are autonomous social, political, and cultural entities.... Seeking and constituting such social, cultural, political forces, capable of attaining such independence and balance, is the process which will decide whether a postcommunist regime is successful in its efforts to achieve democracy.[24]

Schools are ideally situated to serve as the occasion for new habits of cooperation, for the development of trust as adults work together in the interest of their children.

The hundreds of new school initiatives—up to 2,000, by my estimate—and of schools fundamentally transformed through school-level decisions, are highly promising for the growth of the habits of responsible freedom.

> Restoring the civil society entails...a moral rebuilding: the reconstruction of the sense of solidarity which has been undermined by the system; the reassertion of the dignity of politics, the rehabilitation of the individual against the officially sanctioned cult of the collectivity; and the identification of niches where autonomous actions and initiatives could develop.[25]

As Zbigniew Rau puts it, "the moral character of the individual's decision to leave the structure of the state gives the newly emerged civil society its moral dimension."[26]   Teachers and parents who associate together freely to educate a group of children are making a commitment of far deeper moral significance than teachers who take a job in a state system or parents who send their children off to the nearest public school.[27]   They have engaged themselves in one of the "little platoons" that, in Edmund

Burke's celebrated image, are the first link in responsible citizenship.

Freedom won must always be sustained by virtue, or it ceases to be freedom and falls away into some new tyranny. The freedom that has come almost miraculously to the peoples of Eastern Europe will not continue to be a blessing to them unless they learn how to live as free women and men. That is a lesson not to be learned through voting in elections alone but by sustaining the voluntary associations and institutions that make up a healthy civil society. After all, politics truly understood is about more than the balancing of diverse interests; it is also an "ongoing and public deliberation about the good man and the good society,"[28] and it abhors a vacuum of ideas and convictions.

Political life in a free society does *not* depend upon a society-wide consensus upon the ideas and convictions which will prevail; that premise, indeed, was the central unfreedom of the Communist systems. The liberal "public square" of debate welcomes the presence of a diversity of views but—rightly understood—it does not privilege rootless opinions over convictions rooted in communities of shared belief and responsibility.[29]

In the Communist systems, according to Rau, there was "a complete lack of personal responsibility for the public good," no "community united around commonly accepted values and shared obligations for implementing them."[30] Free schools, because they are such communities, can teach the adults who work in and support them as much as they teach the children who attend them about what it means to be a person worthy of trust. To quote Havel once more, they are a part of that "parallel *polis*," that social and political and, ultimately, moral order that "points beyond itself and only makes sense as an act of deepening one's responsibility to and for the whole.... Independent initiatives...demonstrate that living within the truth is a human and social alternative and they struggle to expand the space available for that life...."[31]

SUSTAINING CIVIL SOCIETY IN OUR SCHOOLS

Just as free schools provide an occasion for a kind of social relearning in the countries whose civil society was devastated by totalitarian rule, they can also play an important role in sustaining civil society in Western democracies like the United States, where the rich associational life described by Tocqueville has weakened significantly in recent decades. Owners of bowling alleys complain, it was reported recently, that patrons come in to bowl alone, rather than as members of leagues, and thus do not linger for beer and conversation, the Red Cross has fewer volunteers, and public school parent-teacher associations have experienced a devastating loss of membership. Each of these declines in participation represents also a decline in the lifelong character-formation that voluntary association can provide for parents and thus, through example, for their children.

Schools, if they are an expression of the civil society rather than of the state, can be one of the settings within which adults and children cooperate to make decisions about and to sustain a common enterprise, and thus can be important character-forming institutions. It seems likely that public schools in small towns often have something of this nature as well, though the combined effects of state regulation and of the professional socialization of teachers place it under threat.

Public schools that are enmeshed in large and bureaucratized systems, by contrast, provide little scope for parents or indeed teachers to act as responsible adults, and thus to model that behavior for children. Despite much talk in recent years about "school-based management" and "shared decision-making," reports from the field indicate that actual results have been disappointing. Not only is the scope for decision by teachers and for participation by parents generally limited, but the reality of these limits can encourage factionalism and irresponsibility. After all, if little is really at stake in decisions, those making them can indulge themselves in behaviors that are the opposite of the principled responsibility and mutual accommodation which they should be modeling.

Most free schools, by contrast, have no assurance of survival if those who are directly involved fail to act responsibly, not just from time to time but consistently over the course of years. This necessarily concentrates the minds of teachers and parents and encourages the development of that settled disposition to act virtuously that is the essence of character.

Of course, the explicit curriculum of schools, and the way it is taught, can and should also contribute powerfully to the formation of character through guided reflection on stories (both fictional and historical) and through the daily classroom and schoolyard habits which, for children, are a primary opportunity to acquire the settled disposition to do what is right.[32] In this respect, as well as in their organizational context, public schools are often at a disadvantage. Controversy almost invariably surrounds efforts to introduce questions of "values" in schools operated by government and backed by mandatory attendance laws; the almost invariable result is a kind of "defensive teaching" which seeks by all means to avoid controversy, and thus fails to engage the ultimate—or even the antepenultimate—questions of life. Schools that are morally incoherent, as too many American schools are, cannot help their pupils to acquire the inner consistency of sentiment and outer consistency of behavior that are worthy of free women and men.[33]

CONCLUSION

If my comments have focused upon schools as an expression of and support for the civil society—when they are not made to serve the state—that is because schools are my business. Many other institutions and associations are capable of playing the same role, both as occasions for cooperation and as bearers of explicit messages about the good life and why and how it should be lived. Churches, of course, but also summer camps and scouts, sports leagues, and other organizations that serve youth. Producer and consumer cooperatives can—indeed must—insist upon a settled disposition to do right, as do many employment settings. Significantly, the larger and more bureaucratized the latter become, the higher their rate of staff alienation and dishonesty tends to become.

Just as schools are threatened in their ability to serve as character-forming institutions by external constraints and criticism (as well as by a loss of nerve on the part of many of their leaders), so the other institutions of the civil society are under assault by what Richard Bernstein has called a "dictatorship of virtue."[34] The demand increasingly heard, that nongovernmental organizations serving the public and supported by private donations or by public fees for service give up their distinctive convictions in order to conform to current elite opinion, is all too likely to lead to weakening their ability to do what they do best: setting clear expectations and enforcing them through example and noncoercive influence. The irreplaceable contribution of these "third sector organizations," as David Osborne and Ted Gaebler have pointed out in an influential book, is that they are "best at performing tasks that generate little or no profit, demand compassion and commitment to individuals, require extensive trust on the part of customers or clients, need hands-on, personal attention...and involve the enforcement of moral codes and individual responsibility for behavior."[35] Vendettas by the politically correct against the Salvation Army or the Boy Scouts can only contribute to a further degeneration of the capacity of American civil society to contribute to the development of the character that a free society requires of its citizens.

If we wish to ensure that the American people are capable of sustaining a free and just society—and if they are not, the American experiment will come to an inglorious end—we must do what is necessary to allow the civil society to flourish in all its diversity. Perhaps it is fortunate that the

United States continues to welcome nearly a million legal immigrants a year (37 percent of our current population growth), for there is every indication that many of them possess the qualities of character that no government can supply, the habits of association, discipline, and self-sacrifice that too many native-born Americans have lost along the way to Nirvana.

A healthy civil society depends upon the virtue of citizens, but it also serves as the training field where that virtue is developed. Through wise public policy (and wisdom calls for both restraint and, when appropriate, boldness) and through renewed personal commitment to the public life of the *polis*, we can renew our American civil society, and allow it to renew us.

NOTES

1. Mary Ann Glendon, *Rights Talk* (New York: Free Press, 1991), 129.
2. Samuel Smiles, *Character* (New York: Harper & Brothers, no date).
3. *Pierce v. Society of the Sisters of the Holy Names of Jesus and Mary*, 268 U.S. 510 (1 June 1923).
4. The passages that follow are taken from the very useful collection entitled *Liberté d'enseignement. Les textes* (Geneva: Organisation internationale pour le développement de la liberté d'enseignement, no date); texts are provided in French, English, and Spanish.
5. David Blankenhorn, "Ozzie and Harriet: Have Reports of Their Death Been Greatly Exaggerated?" *Family Affairs*, Summer/Fall 1989, 10.
6. Glendon, *Rights Talk*, 125.
7. Charles L. Glenn, *The Myth of the Common School* (Amherst: University of Massachusetts Press, 1988); Glenn, "Outcome-based Education: Can It Be Redeemed?" in James Sears and James Carper, eds., *Public Education and Religion* (New York: Teachers College Press, forthcoming).
8. *Bowen v. Gilliard*, 483 U.S. 587, 632 (1987) (Brennan, J., dissenting).
9. James Q. Wilson, *The Moral Sense* (New York: Free Press, 1993), 228.
10. Michael Walzer, "The Idea of Civil Society," *Dissent,* Spring 1991, 293.
11. Zbigniew Rau, "Introduction," in Zbigniew Rau, ed., *The Reemergence of Civil Society in Eastern Europe and the Soviet Union* (Boulder: Westview Press, 1991), 2.
12. Alexis de Tocqueville, *Democracy in America*, trans. George Lawrence and ed. J. P. Mayer (New York: Harper & Row, 1988), 515.
13. Glendon, *Rights Talk*, 135.
14. An idea derived, ultimately, from G. W. F. Hegel.

15. Zbigniew Rau, "Introduction," in *The Reemergence of Civil Society in Eastern Europe and the Soviet Union*, 9-10.

16. Martin Malia, "Leninist Endgame," *Daedalus: The Exit from Communism*, Spring 1992, 60.

17. Victor Zaslavsky, "Nationalism and Democratic Transition in Postcommunist Societies," *Daedalus: The Exit from Communism*, Spring 1992, 116.

18. Václav Havel, *Living in Truth* (London: Faber and Faber, 1987), 60, 71.

19. Havel, *Living in Truth*, 102-6.

20. Václav Benda, Milan Šimečka, Ivan M. Jirous, Jiří Dienstbier, Václav Havel, Ladislav Hejdánek and Jan Šimsa, "Parallel Polis, or An Independent Society in Central and Eastern Europe: An Inquiry," *Social Research*, Spring/Summer 1988, 211.

21. Charles L. Glenn, *Educational Freedom in Eastern Europe* (Washington, DC: Cato Institute), 1995.

22. Havel, *Living in Truth*, 108, 118.

23. Havel, *Living in Truth*, 87.

24. Jiří Musil, "Czechoslovakia in the Middle of Transition," *Daedalus: The Exit from Communism*, Spring 1992, 189-90.

25. Vladimir Tismaneanu, "Unofficial Peace Activism in the Soviet Union and East-Central Europe," in Vladimir Tismaneanu, ed., *In Search of Civil Society* (New York and London: Routledge, 1990), 5.

26. Zbigniew Rau, "The State of Enslavement: The East European Substitute for the State of Nature," *Political Studies* 39 (1991): 258.

27. Polish sociologists have found that both pupils in nonstate schools and their parents are three times as likely as their counterparts in state schools to report that they have real influence in and responsibility for their schools. Seventy percent of teachers in state elementary schools believe that parents have quite enough influence. Malgorzata Kopcynska, "Kto na kogo wplywa?" (who is influencing whom?), *Edukacja i Dialog* 4 (1992): 10-11, summarized by Malgorzata Radziszewska-Hedderick.

28. George Weigel, "Death of a Heresy," *National Review*, 20 January 1992, 46.

29. Richard John Neuhaus, *The Naked Public Square* (Grand Rapids, MI: Eerdmans, 1984).

30. Zbigniew Rau, "Human Nature, Social Engineering, and the Reemergence of Civil Society," in *The Reemergence of Civil Society in Eastern Europe and the Soviet Union*, 42.

31. Havel, *Living in Truth*, 102-6.

32. To discuss the role of school curriculum and teaching in the development of character would go well beyond the scope of this chapter; fortunately, a splendid collection of papers on this topic has been published in the *Journal of Education* (Boston University) 2 (1993).

33.   Charles L. Glenn, "Religion, Textbooks, and the Common School," *The Public Interest*, Summer 1987.

34.   Richard Bernstein, *Dictatorship of Virtue: Multiculturalism and the Battle for America's Future* (New York: Alfred A. Knopf, 1994).

35.   David Osborne and Ted Gaebler, *Reinventing Government* (Reading, MA: Addison-Wesley, 1992), 45-46.

Chapter 8

The Religious Roots of Character

Keith J. Pavlischek

INTRODUCTION

To get a grip on a subject as diverse and complex as the religious roots of the American character is no easy task. Indeed, one might be tempted to say that given the pluralistic nature of contemporary American society, it would be foolish to speak of "the" religious roots of the American character. But one has to start somewhere. Since "outsiders" often see what "insiders" miss by taking for granted what is too familiar, we might start by comparing and contrasting what two foreigners, Alexis de Tocqueville and Alexander Solzhenitsyn, writing a century and a half apart, have to tell us about the religious character of the American people. We can learn a good deal from what they have to tell us about who we Americans are, where we have come from and why, for better or worse, we are not what we used to be.

TOCQUEVILLE AND THE NOVEL ROLE OF RELIGION IN AMERICA

Tocqueville's reflections on religion in his famous *Democracy in America*[1] are found, significantly, as part of a chapter in which he is discussing the main causes tending to maintain a democratic republic in the United States. "The religious atmosphere of the country was the first thing that struck me on arrival in the United States," states Tocqueville, and the longer he stayed in the country the more impressed he became with "the important political consequences resulting from this novel situation."

Tocqueville was particularly struck by the "*indirect* influence of religious beliefs upon political society." He seemed fascinated by the irony that "it is just when it [religion] is not speaking of freedom at all that it best teaches the Americans the art of being free" (290). The "mores" of the American people, what Tocqueville called "habits of the heart" (287), were "controlled by religion" (292), and the mores indirectly influenced the political order. "One cannot therefore say that in the United States religion influences the laws or political opinions in detail, but it does direct mores, and by regulating domestic life it helps to regulate the state" (291).

While the law "allows the American people to do everything," nevertheless, he observed with less exaggeration, "there are things which religion prevents them from imagining and forbids them to dare." Thus, while religion "never intervenes directly in the government of American society," it should still be considered as "the first of their political institutions" (292).

While Tocqueville was astonished at the "innumerable multitude of sects," he was equally impressed with the unity amidst this diversity since "the sects in the United States belong to the great unity of Christendom, and Christian morality is everywhere the same" (290). Although he acknowledges that in their worship, a certain amount of Americans may be "following their habits rather than their convictions," America is nonetheless "the place where the Christian religion has kept the greatest real power over men's souls; and nothing better demonstrates how useful and natural it is to man, since the country where it now has widest sway is both the most enlightened and the freest" (291). Perhaps the most important implication of this was the extent to which the American understanding of liberty was colored by this widely held common morality. For Tocqueville, Christianity provided America the moral character without which, he believed, democracy and liberty could not function. Certain "habits of restraint" were found in American political society which "singularly favor the tranquillity of the people as well as the durability of the institutions they have adopted." Even "American revolutionaries," Tocqueville observed, "are obliged ostensibly to profess a certain respect for Christian morality and equity, and that does not allow them easily to break the laws when those are opposed to the executions of their designs." No one in the United States had yet dared to "profess the maxim that everything is allowed in the interests of society," a view Tocqueville thought was "impious."

When Tocqueville takes up the subject of the main causes that make religion powerful in America, he sought to account for what struck him as a "novel situation." In France, Tocqueville had seen "the spirits of religion and of freedom almost always marching in opposite directions." But in America he found them "intimately linked together in joint reign over the same land" (295). To discover why this was so, Tocqueville went to the clergy, especially those "who are the depositories of the various creeds and have a personal interest in their survival" (295). Tocqueville found among the Catholic clergy almost unanimous agreement: "All thought that the main reason for the quiet sway of religion over their country was the complete separation of church and state. I have no hesitation in stating that throughout my stay in America I met nobody, lay or cleric, who did not agree about that" (295).

Lest we too hastily read this comment through the lens of late twentieth-century "strict separationist" ideology and make Tocqueville an early candidate for organizations like Americans United for the Separation of Church and State, it should be observed that what Tocqueville meant by the "complete separation of church and state" is revealed in what immediately follows. He was surprised to find that American priests "held no public appointments," unless of course, he observes incidentally, one counted their work in schools where the greater part of education is entrusted to the clergy. They were not to be found in the administration and were not even represented in state assemblies. In fact, he observed, in several states the law and in others, public opinion, excluded them from a career in politics. And Tocqueville found that clergy seemed voluntarily to steer clear of political power and even took "a sort of professional pride in claiming that it was no concern of theirs" (296). The clergy "were careful to keep clear of all parties, shunning contact with them with all the anxiety attendant upon personal interest" (296). For Tocqueville, the separation of church and state referred to the separation of the clergy from politics.

Convinced that he had been told the truth about why religion in America was strong, Tocqueville wondered "how it could come to be that by diminishing the apparent power of religion one increased its real strength." Before looking at Tocqueville's attempt to account for what to him seemed the height of irony, however, let's first turn to the contrast offered by the great Russian novelist Solzhenitsyn.

HAPPINESS AS AN END IN ITSELF

In his famous Harvard address in 1978, Solzhenitsyn reported that in his own country, "Life's complexity and mortal weight have produced stronger, deeper, and more interesting characters than those generated by the standardized Western well-being." While a society could not "remain in an abyss of lawlessness, as in our country," it would be "demeaning for it to elect such mechanical legalistic smoothness as you have." Solzhenitsyn found it impossible to recommend the American character to his native Russians: "After the suffering of decades of violence and oppression, the human soul longs for things, higher, warmer, and purer than those offered by today's mass living habits, introduced by the revolting invasion of publicity, by TV stupor, and by intolerable music."[2]

While Tocqueville in the 1830s could praise the role religion played in stemming the excesses of liberty, Solzhenitsyn could not do the same. The virtues that Tocqueville believed kept freedom from turning into license were no longer widely extant in American society. The "pursuit of happiness" had become an end in itself.

> Every citizen has been granted the desired freedom and material goods in such quantity and of such quality as to guarantee in theory the achievement of happiness. In the process, however, one psychological detail has been overlooked: the constant desire to have still more things and a still better life and the struggle to maintain them imprints many Western faces with worry and even depression, though it is customary to conceal such feelings. Active and tense competition permeates all human thoughts without opening a way to free spiritual development.[3]

Needless to say, a lot of water passed under the bridge between the 1830s and the 1970s. A full discussion would require volumes addressing the role of industrialization, immigration, urbanization, the impact of slavery and the rise of the civil rights movement, the role of America in foreign affairs, the impact of biological and social Darwinism, and the growth of the bureaucratic state on the religious character of the American people. But I am not particularly interested in addressing that development. Rather, I want to suggest that by juxtaposing Tocqueville's and Solzhenitsyn's commentary on the state of affairs they found, we can illuminate something of the ambivalent relationship between the American regime and those citizens with strong religious convictions.

RELIGIOUS CONVICTIONS AND CITIZENSHIP

Tocqueville wondered "how it could come to [be] that by diminishing the apparent power of religion one increased its real strength." His observations on the state of religion in America led him to conclude that "when a religion chooses to rely on the interests of this world, it becomes almost as fragile as all earthly powers" (298). By becoming "linked to ephemeral powers, it follows their fortunes and often falls together with the passions of a day sustaining them" (298). It is particularly dangerous for religion to ally itself with authority when "a nation adopts a democratic social state and communities show republican inclinations." While "immobility and somnolence" may be the rule in absolute monarchies, "agitation and instability are natural elements in democratic republics." The American clergy, Tocqueville saw, "were first to see that if they wanted to acquire political power, they would have to give up religious influence." They preferred to lose the support of political authority "rather than share its vicissitudes" (299). The problem of European Christianity, on the other hand, was that it "allowed itself to be intimately united with the powers of this world." Since these political powers were falling, "it is as if religion was being buried under their ruins." "A living being has been tied to the dead," Tocqueville said of European religion, "cut the bonds holding it and it will arise" (301).

Solzhenitsyn, surveying the American landscape a century and a half later, is not so sure. In fact, what Tocqueville could see as the solution Solzhenitsyn suggests is the problem. Solzhenitsyn argues that the current state of American society is the inevitable result of a social order premised on an Enlightenment humanism which presumed that intrinsic evil did not exist and which assumed that man had no higher task than the attainment of his own happiness. "Everything beyond physical well-being and accumulation of material goods, all other human requirements and characteristics of a subtler and higher nature, were left outside the area of attention of state and social system, as if human life did not have any superior sense." A political and social order founded on the false presumption of the irrelevance of the spiritual could only lead to destruction. "If humanism were right in declaring that man is born to be happy," argued Solzhenitsyn, "he would not be born to die." However:

> Since his body is doomed to die, his task on earth must be of a more spiritual nature. It cannot be unrestrained enjoyment of everyday life. It cannot be the search for the best ways to obtain material goods and then cheerfully get the most out of them. It has to be the fulfillment of a permanent, earnest duty so that one's life journey may become an experience of moral growth, so that one may leave life a better human being than one started it.[4]

Solzhenitsyn's criticism cuts deeper than just a mere complaint about American culture. He links the depressing state of the American character and its lack of spiritual depth to the very foundation of the American political order. While Tocqueville saw the separation of politics and religion to be the genius of the American founding, Solzhenitsyn sees in it the weakness. How should we evaluate their respective assessments?

The difference between what Tocqueville saw, and believed was working well, and what Solzhenitsyn saw, and believed was corrupting, was that in the 1830s the moral and religious views of the American people still had a felicitous *indirect* public impact. The American pursuit of their own "self-interest," which Tocqueville observed was such a powerful force, was held in check by the widely shared Christian moral consensus. By 1978 Solzhenitsyn could not be so optimistic about the *indirect* effects of religion on American public life. In fact, according to Solzhenitsyn, rather than religion mitigating the effects of self-interest, materialism, and individualism, self-interest and individualism were mitigating the effects of religion. And because Solzhenitsyn holds to a more or less classical conception of the role of the polity, insisting that the task of a well-organized political community is to direct them to the good, the America polity could be measured and could be held accountable for creating a spiritually bankrupt people. What are we to think of this?

Apart from the belief that a polity founded on the basis of Enlightenment humanism and the "pursuit of happiness" is flawed from the beginning, what Solzhenitsyn and others who hold to this more classical conception are likely to find objectionable in the American founding is the purely procedural and formal status given to religion in the nation's founding document. The Constitution had no substantive religion, no reference to "Providence," to the "Creator," to "Nature or Nature's God," or to the "Supreme Being" let alone to God or Christ. The body of the Constitution contains only three references to religion. It exempts

Sundays from the days to be counted in the countdown for a presidential pocket veto; at the end of the document it gives as its date "in the year of our Lord one thousand seven hundred and eighty-seven, and of the Independence of the United States of America the twelfth;" and in Article VI, the Founders wrote into the body of the Constitution a prohibition of religious tests. Of course, the First Amendment to the Constitution prohibits the establishment of religion and guarantees its free exercise.

THE *FEDERALIST* ON MATTERS RELIGIOUS

One is also struck by the near silence of The Federalist on matters religious. Strikingly absent from its eighty-five essays is any extended discussion of religion and its place within the social order. But the question of religion does receive brief, almost incidental, mention in two of the most important and studied essays: *Federalist 10* and *51*. Those references, however, give a significant clue to what was implicitly held by James Madison and other Founders.

As we all know, *The Federalist Papers*, the work of Alexander Hamilton, John Jay, and James Madison, were articles written in New York newspapers defending the federal Constitution to the voters of New York and other states. At the heart of Madison's defense of the Constitution is what is commonly called a "realistic" defense of liberty, that is, liberty defended not only by "ingrained principle and constitutional fiat"[5] but also by what we would call today "pluralism." Madison was, of course, countering the Antifederalist arguments that "republican government" only works in small-scale communities and that the new powerful central government would dominate and almost obliterate the states, towns, and small units in which liberty and true democracy could flourish. His strategy was to turn that argument on its head, insisting that only in an "extended Republic" under this Constitution would liberty be protected. By joining together the states with all their diversities, the new nation would encompass a sufficiently complex variety of "factions"—"a number of citizens, whether amounting to a majority or minority of the whole, who are united and actuated by some common impulse of passion, or of interest, adverse to the rights of other citizens, or to the permanent and aggregate interests of the community"—to prevent any one from dominating.

In *Federalist 10*, Madison develops his argument about the "latent causes of faction" which are "sown in the nature of man," the most common and durable of which is "the various and unequal distribution of common and durable of which is "the various and unequal distribution of property." But first on his list of the causes of factions, he mentions "a zeal for different opinions concerning religion." So, also in *Federalist 51*, Madison applies his "realism" about human nature to the separation of powers in the federal government, and, more specifically to the legislative branch. Madison argues that by dividing, separating, and limiting power the Constitution provides security of the rights of the people against their rulers. However, there is another requirement to guard society not only against their rulers but also to "guard one part of the society against the other part." That is done "by comprehending in the society so many separate descriptions of citizens as will render an unjust combination of the majority of the whole very improbable, if not impracticable." That, says Madison, is what "the Federal republic of the United States" proposes to do:

> Whilst all authority in it will be derived from and dependent on the society, the society itself will be broken into so many parts, interests, and classes of citizens, that the rights of individuals, or of the minority, will be in little danger from interested combinations of the majority.

And then Madison, significantly, chose an analogy to support his broader claim.

> In a free government the security for civil rights must be the same as that for religious rights. It consists in the one case in the multiplicity of interests, and in the other in the multiplicity of sects. The degrees of security in both cases will depend on the number of interests and sects....In the extended republic of the United States, and among the great variety of interests, parties, and sects which it embraces, a coalition of a majority of the whole society could seldom take place on any other principles than those of justice and the general good.

To put matters rather bluntly, Madison understood religious groups to be analogous to economic interests. As far as the federal Constitution was concerned, religion was just another interest group. Religion was in a sense a "commodity" and by enacting the First Amendment and (later) by ending established churches in the states, the Founders "deregulated the religion market."[6] For Solzhenitsyn and others who believe that statecraft must be to some extent soulcraft this is shallow and ultimately pernicious.

JUDEO-CHRISTIAN MORALITY AND THE FOUNDERS

In one sense, of course, the American Founders were in agreement with Solzhenitsyn. It was precisely because America's Founders, irrespective of their own personal religiosity, could presuppose a broadly based Christian morality, that they thought all they needed to provide was a framework, a constitution, for American society to work well. Almost without exception our Founders recognized that the system of competing factions would only work well to the extent that people continued to be virtuous. That is, only to the extent that the people did not understand religion to be what Madison understood it to be—just like other "interests"—could their approach work. They knew that the Constitution and laws and all the institutionalized checks on the accumulation of power could not supply all the conditions required for the success of the new regime. As Madison put it in *Federalist 55*:

> As there is a degree of depravity in mankind which requires a certain degree of circumspection and distrust, so there are other qualities in human nature which justify a certain portion of esteem and confidence. Republican government presupposes the existence of these qualities in a higher degree than any other form.

Shortly after the Constitution was ratified Vice President John Adams was even more explicit: "We have no government armed with power capable of contending with human passions unbridled by morality and religion. Our constitution was made only for a moral and religious people. It is wholly inadequate for the government of any other."

And, in what became known as his Farewell Address, George Washington said, "Of all the dispositions and habits which lead to political prosperity, religion and morality are indispensable supports. In vain would that man claim the tribute of patriotism who should labor to subvert these great pillars of human happiness—these firmest props of the duties of men and citizens...."

And then Washington adds the familiar view that morality requires religion, at least for the most part. "And let us with caution indulge the supposition that morality can be maintained without religion. What ever may be conceded to the influence of refined education on minds of peculiar structure, reason and experience both forbid us to expect that national morality can prevail in exclusion of religious principle."[7]

There were Americans surrounding the period of the founding that aggressively argued against "revealed religion," and who took their opposition aggressively into the public forum. These included Ethan Allen, Joel Barlow, Elihu Palmer, and Thomas Paine. But the major political leaders—Benjamin Franklin, Thomas Jefferson, John Adams, and George Washington—whose own personal religious views were similar to those of the aggressive deists, disapproved of their attacks against the religious beliefs of the orthodox. Either out of solid private convictions (Adams and Washington), or simply strategically (Jefferson and Franklin) these "moderate" Enlightenment rationalists refused to join in the Enlightenment's project to show that religion was not indispensable to morality.

FREE MARKET IN RELIGION

This general outlook was still the order of the day—in spades—when Tocqueville visited America in the 1830s. The resulting free market in religion, as William Miller has observed, was not really neutral among competitors but rather favored those in a position to take advantage of its particular conditions. These well-positioned "entrepreneurs," to continue the metaphor, were the evangelicals, the revivalists, the pietists, the free churches, and the churches of the common man. These groups were "well positioned to take advantage of the new 'market' because the 'voluntary way,' to which the new nation was now committed was their metier; because the method most of them used—their emotion-laden revival their marketing tool, as it were—fit the situation, especially the opening of the vast territory to the west." In addition, Miller observes, "the comparative lack of emphasis on an educated ministry made it easier to open new franchises, so to speak, more quickly; because their creedal requirements came after a time not to be particularly exacting." The aristocratic deists were not "going to send circuit riders out West to hold enthusiastic jumping-up-and-down camp meetings to convert people," and neither were "the staid old orthodox churches, with their formal creeds and rituals and their educated ministry." Revivalistic evangelical Protestantism did so and did it, notes Miller, "at a time when the West was being settled and the nation was taking form."[8] That is what Tocqueville found, and significantly he could find no American who rejected the "voluntary way" in religion.

CULTURAL CAPITAL

But by 1798 the social and moral presuppositions supplied by "revealed religion" had long lost its hegemony, and Madison's framework of factions and counteracting factions became what it was never meant to be—an end in itself. While the Founders relied upon traditional, largely Christian views as they established the Constitution, they did not, however, address the question of how the Constitution was to function if the supporting culture changed. By their own admission the Constitution possessed little means to hold in check the negative consequences within a society in which those assumptions were no longer broadly extant, when the morals market, as it were, became as diverse as the religion market.

As Francis Canavan has argued, liberal democracies can only function well to the extent that they live off (to continue the metaphor) borrowed capital. The Madisonian strategy of bracketing or withdrawing contentious areas from public life precisely because they are contentious is less successful once that capital has been spent.

> Liberal democracy has worked well as well as it has and as long as it has because it has been able to trade on something it did not create which it tends on the whole to undermine. That is the moral tradition that prevailed among the greater part of the people. It is not necessary to pretend that most Americans in the past kept the Ten Commandments, certainly not that they kept them all the time. It is enough that by and large Americans agreed that there were Ten Commandments and that in principle they ought to be kept. The pluralist solution of withdrawing certain areas of life from legal control worked precisely because American pluralism was not all that pronounced. In consequence, many important areas of life were not withdrawn from the reach of law and public policy and were governed by a quasi-official public ethos.[9]

This "quasi-official public ethos" was so pervasive that Tocqueville understated the extent to which law and public policy incorporated Christian morals. The law and legal system was more than "indirectly" affected by the mores of the American people. The religious and moral consensus was, in fact, reflected in law and assumed by the legal system. The views of Justice Joseph Story were common throughout the nineteenth century:

> the promulgation of the great doctrines of religion...can never be a matter of indifference to any well ordered community....Indeed, in a republic, there

would seem to be a peculiar propriety in viewing the Christian religion, as the great basis, on which it must rest for its support and permanence, if it be, what it has been deemed by its truest friends to be, the religion of liberty.[10]

One of the reasons for the recent resurgence in the ethics of virtue and the focus on the character of the people is the growing conviction that the religious and moral consensus that once held sway has disintegrated and that the legal system cannot function well without it. Many are questioning whether the liberal idea of Madison and others that government should be neutral on the very subjects that matter most to people, precisely because they matter the most, is any longer adequate. Again, Francis Canavan:

> At this point, it is doubtful whether the typical response of the liberal pluralist society is any longer adequate, that is, to take the dangerously controversial matters out of politics and relegate them to the conscience of individuals. For this way of eliminating controversy in fact does much more. Intentionally or not, it contributes to the reshaping of basic social institutions and a revision of the moral beliefs of multitudes of individuals beyond those directly concerned. It turns into a process by which one ethos, with its reflection in law and public policy, is replaced by another. Liberal pluralism then becomes a sort of confidence game in which, in the guise of showing respect for individual rights, we are in reality asked to consent to a new kind of society based on a new set of beliefs and values.[11]

This bait and switch is nowhere more evident than in the way the predominant legal culture understands religion. This "new set of beliefs and values" is at times, of course, openly and aggressively hostile to religion. The village atheist, like death and taxes, will always be with us. But this new view, which has gained as wide a cultural hegemony as Christian morality had in Tocqueville's day, is perhaps even more pernicious. That view, as Stephen Carter writes in his *The Culture of Disbelief*[12] tends to treat religion as something like a hobby, somewhat akin to building model airplanes. Carter's claims are as powerful as they are sweeping:

> One sees a trend in our political and legal cultures toward treating religious beliefs as arbitrary and unimportant, a trend supported by rhetoric that implies that there is something wrong with religious devotion. More and more, our culture seems to take the position that believing deeply in the tenets of one's faith represents a kind of mystical irrationality, something that thoughtful, public-spirited American citizens would do better to avoid. (7)

A strong undercurrent of contemporary American politics holds that religion must be kept in its proper place and, still more, in proper perspective. There are, we are taught by our opinion leaders, religious matters and important matters, and disaster arises when we confuse the two. Rationality, it seems, consists in getting one's priorities straight. (7-8)

In contemporary American culture, the religions are more and more treated as just passing beliefs—almost as fads, older, stuffier, less liberal versions of so-called New Age—rather than as the fundaments upon which the devout build their lives. (14)

The message of contemporary culture seems to be that it is perfectly all right to *believe* that stuff—we have freedom of conscience, folks can believe what they like—but you really ought to keep it to yourself, especially if your beliefs are the sort that cause you to act in ways that are...well...a bit unorthodox. (25)

If Carter is right about this, and I have no doubt that he is, then, in a sense, the Madisonian idea of religion as a "faction" has gone to seed. Except that in contemporary American culture, religion does not even rise to the level of a marketable commodity, at least not in the minds of some of its most prominent cultural despisers.

CONCLUSION

Of course, a significant portion of the American public dissents from this view. Religious conviction continues to shape their lives and they are increasingly alienated from a legal and political system that trivializes those convictions. Over the next several decades Americans will be forced to reflect seriously on the words of Joseph Story: "the promulgation of the great doctrines of religion...can never be a matter of indifference to any well ordered community." Indeed, we may ask whether the real question is not if we will have a community that is well ordered, but, given the lack of a broad-based moral consensus, whether we can have any community at all.

NOTES

1.   Alexis de Tocqueville, *Democracy in America*, trans. George Lawrence and ed. J. P. Mayer, Perennial Library Edition (New York: Harper and Row, 1988). Pages references have been inserted into the text.

2.   Alexander Solzhenitsyn, An address given at Harvard University, reported in the *Harvard Gazette*, June 1978, 2.

3.   *Harvard Gazette*, 1.

4.   *Harvard Gazette*, 3.

5.   See William Lee Miller, *The First Liberty: Religion and the American Republic* (New York: Alfred A. Knopf, 1987), 114.

6.   Miller, *First Liberty*, 251.

7.   Miller, *First Liberty*, 244-45.

8.   Miller, *First Liberty*, 252.

9.   Francis Canavan, "The Dilemma of Liberal Pluralism," *The Human Life Review* 5, Summer 1979, 14.

10.   Mark Noll, *One Nation Under God?: Christian Faith and Political Action in America* (San Francisco: Harper and Row, 1988), 74.

11.   Canavan, "The Dilemma," 15.

12.   Stephen L. Carter, *The Culture of Disbelief: How American Law and Politics Trivialize Religious Devotion* (New York: Basic Books, 1993).

III. Educating for Character

Chapter 9

A Comprehensive Approach to Character Education

Thomas Lickona

To educate a person in mind and not in morals is to educate a menace to society.

Theodore Roosevelt

INTRODUCTION

Moral or character education is a universal and age-old concern. In the United States, as in countries around the world, education was from the outset seen as having two great goals: helping people become smart and helping them become good.

In the United States, the 1990s are witnessing renewed attention to character education in the schools. One cause of this is the widespread breakdown of the family. Another is problems in youth character as indicated by these troubling trends:

1. Rising youth violence
2. Increasing dishonesty (lying, cheating, and stealing)
3. Growing disrespect for parents, teachers, and other legitimate authority figures
4. Peer cruelty

5. A rise in bigotry and hate crimes
6. The deterioration of language
7. A decline in the work ethic
8. Declining personal and civic responsibility
9. A rise in self-destructive behaviors such as premature sexual activity, drug and alcohol abuse, and suicide
10. Ethical illiteracy, including ignorance of moral knowledge as basic as the Golden Rule and the tendency to engage in behaviors harmful to self or others without thinking it wrong.

A COMPREHENSIVE APPROACH TO CHARACTER EDUCATION

This chapter describes a comprehensive approach to character education. This approach seeks to teach moral values directly and indirectly and to develop the kind of character that puts those values into practice. The following are the "big ideas" that define this approach:

1. "Good" can be defined in terms of moral values that have objective worth—values that affirm our human dignity and promote the good of the individual and society.

2. Two universal values form the core of a public, teachable morality: respect and responsibility.

3. *Respect* means showing regard for the worth of someone or something. It includes respect for self, respect for the rights and dignity of all persons, and respect for the environment that sustains all life. Respect is the restraining side of morality; it keeps us from hurting what we ought to value.

Responsibility is the active side of our morality. It includes taking care of self and others, fulfilling our obligations, working to improve the human condition, and taking responsibility for our actions.

Other moral values can be derived from respect and responsibility. Honesty, civility, and fairness, for example, can be seen as forms of respect. Similarly, caring, cooperation, fulfilling obligations, and moral courage are forms of responsibility.

4. If schools wish to make respect and responsibility operative values in the lives of students, they must educate for *character*.

Good character can be defined as having three interrelated parts: moral knowing, moral feeling, and moral action. Good character consists of knowing the good, desiring the good, and doing the good.

Moral knowing, or cognitive side of character, includes at least six specific moral qualities: *awareness of the moral dimensions of a situation, knowing moral values and what they require of us in concrete cases, perspective-taking, moral reasoning, thoughtful decision-making,* and *moral self-knowledge.*

The emotional side of character includes at least the following six moral qualities: *conscience* (the felt obligation to do what one judges to be right), *self-respect, empathy, loving the good, self-control,* and *humility* (a willingness to both recognize and correct our moral failings).

There are times when we know what we should do, feel strongly that we should do it, yet still fail to translate moral judgment and feeling into effective moral behavior. Moral action, the third part of character, draws upon three additional moral qualities: *competence* (moral skills such as being able to solve conflicts), *will* (which mobilizes our moral judgment and feeling), and *moral habit* (which exists when a value becomes a virtue, a reliable inner disposition to respond to situations in a morally good way).

5. If schools wish to maximize their positive impact in the face of powerful negative influences outside the school, and if they wish to develop all three parts of character, they must take a comprehensive approach—one that uses all phases of school life as deliberate opportunities for character development.

My work with teachers and schools over the past 25 years has helped me to develop a model of comprehensive character education that includes 12 strategies, nine for the classroom and three schoolwide strategies. Let me define and briefly illustrate each of these.

CLASSROOM STRATEGIES

The Teacher as Caregiver, Moral Model, and Moral Mentor

Students of all ages need to form caring attachments to adults that will motivate them to learn and to want to be good persons. This first strategy calls upon the teacher to foster such attachments by treating students with love and respect. It also calls up the teacher to set a good example, directly teach and encourage moral behavior, and correct disrespectful or irresponsible actions through individual guidance and group discussion.

For example, teacher Molly Angelini makes courtesy an important value in her fifth-grade classroom. She models courtesy in how she speaks to her students. She requires students to apologize in writing if they call a classmate a name. She teaches them to say "Pardon me?" instead of "What?" when they wish something repeated. When they go to lunch, she teaches them to greet the cafeteria workers by name and thank them when they put the food on their tray. And she teaches her children that all these behaviors are not mechanical gestures but meaningful ways of respecting other people.

Creating a Moral Community

Students need caring relationships with adults, but they also need caring relationships with each other. When they are part of a caring classroom community, they feel valued as persons. When they are challenged to practice respect and care in their everyday peer relations, these values begin to become part of their characters.

For example, Hal Urban, who teaches history and psychology at Woodside High School, California, does three simple things at the start of each class that take only five minutes but go a long way toward developing a sense of community. First, he asks, "Who has good news?" After the sharing of good news, he asks, "Would anyone like to affirm anyone else?" Students gradually become comfortable doing that. Finally, he asks students to take a seat different from the one they had in the previous class and take a minute to get to know their new neighbor. At the end of the semester, on course evaluations, students say that one thing they will remember about the course ten years from now is the way Mr. Urban began each class.

Moral Discipline

Moral discipline means using the creation and enforcement of rules as opportunities to foster moral reasoning, self-control, voluntary compliance with rules, and a generalized respect for others.

For example, Kim McConnel, on the first day of school, puts her sixth-graders in groups of four. She asks each group to write down, on a large sheet of paper, classroom rules that will help them: get our work done; feel safe; and be glad we're here.

When they are finished, the small groups tape their lists of suggested rules on the blackboard. Drawing from all the lists, the teacher helps the class come up a list that will serve as "our class rules."

Regardless of whether students help to create the rules, the teacher using moral discipline ensures that students understand the moral basis of the classroom rules. A high school mathematics teacher explains his approach:

> I tell my students that I have only two rules: 1) Everybody respects each other; and 2) Come prepared for class every day—which is a form of respect for me, your classmates, and yourself. If you violate one of these rules, I will stop and point out the rule. If you have been disrespectful toward someone, I'll wait for you to apologize.

With moral discipline, consequences for rule-breaking seek to teach a moral lesson (for example, why the offense was wrong); require the student, whenever possible, to make reparation; and develop the student's self-control and willingness to follow the rule in the future.

Creating a Democratic Classroom Environment

This means involving students, on a regular basis, in shared decision-making that increases their responsibility for making the class a good place to be and to learn. The chief means of creating a democratic classroom is the class meeting. This is a meeting of the whole class emphasizing interactive discussion and problem-solving. The class meeting contributes to character development by providing a forum where students' thoughts are heard and valued and by providing a support structure for understanding, internalizing, and practicing respect and responsibility.

For example, Carl Fospero, a 20-year-old graduate student in education, was called to take over an unruly class (Introductory Spanish) of high school students whose regular teacher had suddenly died. In the month that followed the teacher's death, the students—a low-achieving group with a history of behavior problems—had become uncontrollable. They went through four substitute teachers in four weeks.

When Carl Fospero came into the class, the first thing he did was to ask every student to take out a sheet of paper and write him a letter, responding to two questions: "What are your feelings about the class? How can we make it better?"

Students complained that other substitute teachers had been "throwing worksheets at them"; they could not keep up with the material; they did not understand Spanish; they often felt embarrassed when they did not know an answer, and so on.

Carl Fospero read portions of the students' letters aloud, using them as a springboard for a discussion of how to improve the course. They decided to slow down the pace of instruction to make sure no one got lost. They decided to make time during each class for cooperative learning—such as conversational Spanish between partners—which students found less threatening. Teacher Fospero said he also wanted to try some new things they had not done before, such as writing a play in Spanish and performing and videotaping it. The class also started to write and publish a class newspaper—in Spanish. They used their class meetings to plan these new projects, assign responsibilities, and monitor progress and problems.

Students' behavior and learning improved dramatically. Teacher Fospero had achieved this by applying a widely known but much-neglected educational principle: Involve students in making decisions about—and sharing responsibility for—the life of the classroom.

Teaching Values Through the Curriculum

There are countless opportunities for teachers to use the ethically rich content of academic subjects—such as literature, history, and science—as a vehicle for teaching values and examining moral questions. Here the teacher's question is, what are the natural intersections between the curriculum I wish to cover and the values I wish to teach?

There are outstanding published programs that illustrate how to do this. One is the Heartwood Ethics Curriculum for Children.[1] This award-winning program uses multicultural children's literature to foster seven character attributes affirmed by cultures around the world: courage, loyalty, justice, respect, hope, honesty, and love.

For each of these seven attributes, the Heartwood program provides six children's books (folk tales, hero stories, legends, and modern classics from different cultures) along with interdisciplinary activities that develop children's understanding of the particular value and how to apply it.

When the class finishes studying a particular character attribute, all the children, at a moment of their own choosing, look in the classroom mirror and ask themselves if they have shown that attribute (for example, "How have I shown courage?"; "How have I been a respectful person?"). Then the child goes to his or her Heartwood Journal and writes a personal answer to that question. This encourages children to act upon the ethical insights emerging from their reading and discussion of the value-laden literature. *Facing History and Ourselves*[2] is another much-acclaimed curriculum, initially developed for eighth-graders and later adapted to high school and college levels as well.   This eight-week social studies curriculum uses history, films, and guest lectures (including talks by death camp survivors) to investigate the Nazi and Armenian Holocausts. Along the way, it has students look within themselves to examine the universal human tendency toward prejudice and scapegoating.

An experimental study of this curriculum found that *Facing History* students were significantly superior in their understanding of how individuals' decisions are affected by their society and in the complexity of their reasoning about issues such as leadership, exclusion, and conflict resolution.

Cooperative Learning

Whereas curriculum-based values education teaches values and develops character through the subject matter content, cooperative learning does this through the *instructional process*. It says to the teacher: "Take what you would normally teach, teach it through cooperative learning for at least part of every day, and you will be teaching values and academics at the same time."

Cooperative learning, which can be done in pairs or small groups, contributes to character in many ways. It teaches students the value of cooperation; builds community in the classroom (reducing conflict, the research shows, and fostering friendships across racial and ethnic lines); and teaches basic life skills such as communicating and working together.

For example, in a sixth-grade classroom in Montreal, Quebec, a teacher faced the most divisive group she had ever taught. The class was torn apart by racial conflict; blacks and whites exchanged insults and physically assaulted each other during recess and after school.

The school psychologist observed the class and recommended that the teacher set up structured cooperative learning groups. Put together children who have trouble getting along, he said. Give them joint assignments and projects with roles for all members. Monitor them closely. Most important, stick with the groups even if they do not seem to be working in the beginning.

The teacher started having students work together—usually in threes or fours—in all subjects for part of each day. They worked on math problems in groups, researched social studies questions in groups, practiced reading to each other in groups, and so on.

"It took them two months to really make this work," the teacher said, "but they finally got it together. Moreover, their test scores went up." Mastering the skills of cooperative learning is a gradual, developmental process for both teacher and students, but the academic and character development benefits—documented at all grade levels—justify the effort.

Develop the "Conscience of Craft"

The literature on moral and character education often treats moral learning and academic learning as separate spheres. But academic work and learning have moral meaning for at least three reasons:

1. Learning increases, and ignorance reduces, our ability to make informed moral judgments and participate as citizens in a complex world.

2. Work is one of the most basic ways we affect the lives of others and contribute to the human community.

3. It is a mark of people's character when they take care to perform their jobs and other tasks well. Syracuse University professor Tom Green calls this a "conscience of craft"—the capacity to feel satisfaction at a job well done and to be ashamed of slovenly work. If people lack this kind of conscience, and do not feel obligated to do good work, something basic is missing in their moral make-up.

Specific character development objectives in the realm of work include self-discipline; the ability to delay gratification; persistence in the face of discouragement; a public sense of work as affecting the lives of others; and Green's conscience of craft.

Teachers who develop these character qualities typically combine high expectations and high support. For example, Anne Ritter is the kind of teacher who believes that every child can learn. As a new teacher in her school, she taught a class of first-graders, 85 percent of whom came from families below the poverty line. She astonished fellow teachers by getting 90 percent of her class up to grade level in reading and math. Her comment: "It's the job."

When I visited her classroom, a list of classroom rules was written large and posted in the front. The first rule was: "Always do your best in everything." On the wall was a sign: A PERSON WILL SELF-DESTRUCT WITHOUT A GOAL. The "value of the month," featured on the class bulletin board, was AMBITION, defined as "hard work directed toward a worthwhile goal."

Encouraging Moral Reflection

This strategy focuses on developing the several qualities that make up the cognitive side of character: being morally aware; understanding objectively worthwhile moral values; being able to take the perspective of others; being able to reason morally; being able to make thoughtful moral decisions; and having moral self-knowledge, including the capacity for self-criticism.

Bringing this knowing side of character to maturity is one of the most difficult challenges of character education. It requires clear ethical thinking by the teacher as well as a sophisticated set of teaching skills.

Teachers can foster moral reflection through reading, research, essay writing, journal-keeping, discussion, and debate. At the secondary level, a promising approach to developing moral reflection through controversial issues is called "structured academic controversy." Developed by cooperative learning experts David and Roger Johnson, this approach defines controversies as "problems to be solved rather than win-lose situations."

The teacher assigns students to groups of four, composed of two, two-person "advocacy teams." Within each group, one team is assigned the responsibility of advocating one position (for example, that there should be more government regulation of hazardous waste disposal), the other team the task of arguing the opposite position (that there should be less regulation), both teams using background information supplied by the teacher.

In the course of the week, each team must do a position-switch and argue *for* the position it originally opposed. Finally, the four group members synthesize what they see as the best information and reasoning from both sides into a consensus solution and write and submit a group report. Following that, each student takes an individual test, which holds everyone accountable for learning the information and arguments on both sides of the issue.

Ten years of research on the academic controversy process finds that students:

1. Gain in their perspective-taking abilities;
2. Demonstrate greater mastery of the subject matter than is true with either debate or individualistic learning formats;
3. Show greater liking of other student participants and higher academic self-esteem.[3]

Some controversial issues—abortion, for example—may not lend themselves to a discussion format which has the goal of arriving at a "consensual solution." In such cases, the more conventional debate format, ensuring full and balanced presentation of both sides, may be preferable. At my state university, for example, the Collegians for Life group for which I serve as adviser wanted to have the student body and the community consider the claims of what is called the "consistent life ethic" (sometimes known as the "seamless garment ethic"). The consistent life ethic argues that abortion, like economic injustice and unjust war, violates social justice and respect for the value and dignity of every individual life at every stage of development. Groups such as Feminists for Life promote a consistent life ethic.

To present this underrepresented perspective on the abortion controversy, we sponsored a two-hour public debate between two women, one a pro-choice feminist, the other a pro-life feminist. The pro-choice feminist argued that a woman has a right of self-determination to control her own body and therefore to abort an unwanted baby. The pro-life feminist argued that the most basic human right—more basic than privacy —is the right not to be killed; that the pregnant woman alone has the power to sustain the life in her womb; and that she therefore has a corresponding moral obligation to protect and nurture it—as well as a claim to far more societal support than women currently receive for childrearing. We sought to enhance the moral education value of this debate format by having the two speakers, after their initial presentations, engage in direct, face-to-face dialogue as well as respond to audience questions.

Teaching Conflict Resolution

Teaching students how to resolve conflicts without force or intimidation is a vitally important part of character education for two reasons: 1) conflicts not settled fairly will prevent or erode a moral community in the classroom; and 2) without conflict resolution skills, students will be morally handicapped in their interpersonal relationships now and later in life, and may end up contributing to violence in school and society.

Growing numbers of schools are training students to serve as official "conflict mediators." For example, in one elementary school a student from each fourth-, fifth-, and sixth-grade homeroom is chosen to be the conflict mediator for that day. Chosen students wear a hat, a vest, a T-shirt, or a button to identify themselves as official mediators.

If there is a conflict—in a classroom or on the playground—the student mediator is trained to step between the disputants. (All students, of course, must be coached in advance to prepare them to accept this kind of peer intervention.) The dialogue then unfolds as follows:

Mediator: My name is Sara. I'm a conflict mediator today. Would you like me to help you solve this problem?

Disputants: Okay.

Sara: There are four rules you must agree to: No blaming, no name-calling, no interrupting, and you must agree to try to solve the problem so you both feel okay. Do you agree to these rules?

Disputants: Yes.

Mediator: Okay, each tell your side of the story. Who wants to go first? Remember, no interrupting.

After each person tells his or her side of the story, the mediator paraphrases the account back to that person. She then asks, "Okay, how can you solve this problem in a way that's fair to both of you?" When a solution is arrived at, the mediator concludes, "Congratulations, you've solved your problem!" and asks them to "shake on it."

These behavior patterns have the best chance of becoming part of a child's character when they are learned early and practiced often. But effective training is still possible at the adolescent level, where the stakes are even higher because conflicts more easily explode into deadly violence.

Dr. Deborah Prothrow-Smith, a Harvard professor and physician, has developed a 10-week mini-course that teaches teenagers what causes violent conflict and how to avoid it. Says one 18-year-old who took the course at a Boston high school: "I had my share of fights, and I learned how to avoid them by talking things out. Otherwise I could lose my life over something really stupid like stepping on someone's shoe and not wanting to say 'Excuse me.'"

SCHOOLWIDE STRATEGIES FOR CHARACTER EDUCATION

The preceding examples demonstrate that it is clearly possible for the individual teacher, acting within the classroom, to contribute to the moral growth of students. But teachers feel more secure, and their efforts are greatly enhanced, if the whole school—and ideally the community as well

—is working to promulgate, model, teach, celebrate, and enforce high standards of respect and responsibility.

A comprehensive approach therefore calls upon schools to implement three schoolwide strategies. These strategies are:

1. Creating a positive moral culture in the school—developing a total moral environment or schoolwide ethos (through the leadership of the principal, schoolwide discipline, a schoolwide sense of community, meaningful student government, a respectful and cooperative moral community among adults, and making time at all levels to discuss moral concerns) that supports the values taught in classrooms;

2. Fostering caring beyond the classroom—including using positive role models to inspire altruistic behavior and providing opportunities at every grade level to perform acts of school and community service; and

3. Recruiting parents and the community as partners in character—educationletting parents know that the school considers them their child's first and most important moral teacher; giving parents specific ways they can support the values the school is trying to teach; and seeking the help of the community (including churches, businesses, local government, and the media) in promoting respect and responsibility.

Let me offer several examples of schoolwide approaches to character education that contain one or more of these three strategies.

"Let's Be Courteous, Let's Be Caring"

Several years ago, Winkelman Elementary School, which serves a diverse community north of Chicago (some children are from welfare families, others come to school in limos), found itself increasingly unhappy with student attitudes and behavior. Fights and put-downs among children were common. Students would frequently "smart-off" ("I don't have to listen to you!") to teachers and other adults in the building.

To address this problem effectively, Winkelman's principal and faculty decided they needed a schoolwide approach. They launched a project called Let's Be Courteous, Let's Be Caring. The project emphasized the values of courtesy and caring at every opportunity: through photo displays in the corridors, discussions in classrooms, one-to-one conversations between teachers and children, school assemblies, citizenship awards, parent-teacher conferences, and service projects in the community.

A giant display inside the school entrance defined "courtesy" as saying please, thank you, you're welcome, and excuse me; being a good listener; waiting your turn; acting politely everywhere; and discussing problems.

"Caring" was defined as sharing; respecting others' feelings; following rules; working cooperatively; and being a good friend.

The moral environment at Winkelman steadily improved. When I visited the school, parents said fights are now very rare; children said that if you forgot your lunch, you could always count on somebody to give you some of theirs; and a veteran teacher who had taught in several other schools said that Winkelman students showed an unusually high level of respect for adults and each other. Three years after beginning its character education project, Winkelman was recognized in a Chicago-area competition for excellence in both academic achievement and character development.

Value of the Month

Carl Campbell is principal at Dry Creek Elementary School in Clovis, California. He explains that the school's mission is to help students develop their potential in five areas: academics, athletics, performing arts, citizenship in the school, and citizenship in the community. And that commitment, he says, goes for *every* student:

> Our philosophy is that we do everything we can do while we've got a kid. When he walks through that door, we're responsible for the quality of his experience. We may not be able to control his environment elsewhere, but we can control the environment here.

Dry Creek has a Value of the Month program. For an entire month, the whole school—every teacher at every grade level—focuses on the same value (e.g., honesty, cooperation, self-control, ambition). Teachers talk to their students about the value of the month—making connections, for example, with classroom incidents that arise. They work it into the writing assignments. They do special projects and displays related to the value. Students also bring in books or articles that tell about a person or incident that exemplifies the value.

Teachers take heart from the fact that they are all working together on the same value, something that is becoming part of the shared moral vocabulary that defines the common moral culture of their school.

Principal Campbell spoke about the impact this Value of the Month program had in a previous district where he worked:

Before coming to Clovis, I was principal in a school where stealing was an everyday occurrence when I first arrived. The attitude among students was that it was okay to steal as long as you did not get caught. There was also a problem of kids being intimidated for their lunch money.

I said to the faculty, "How can we change this?" We selected basic values to teach, one each month. We started with honesty. As time went on, kids started turning in money they found on the playground. Intimidation became less and less of a problem. By the end of our second year with the program, stealing was a very rare event at this school.

The lesson here: Even when there is not a positive moral culture outside the school, it is still possible to create one within the school. If teachers at every grade level are simultaneously teaching the same moral value, doing so in different and creative ways, and doing so all school year long, year after year, the school has a cumulative effect with the power to change students' moral behavior.

A Five-Year Plan: A Middle-School Success Story

Vera White is an African American principal working with an African American, inner-city community. Principal White came to Washington, D.C.'s Jefferson Junior High School nine years ago. She comments:

Ninety percent of our students come from single-parent homes. When I arrived, parents and the community felt they were losing the children.

We met—administration, faculty, and parents—for a full year to prioritize our goals. We decided we needed a five-year plan. Each year would have a special theme.

Year one of the new effort focused on planning the objectives and strategies of the new character education program. Year two had the theme "Attitude Counts." Principal White explains: "We wanted students to have the idea that wherever you are—in school, at home, at the mall—your attitude makes a difference."

Year three focused on conflict resolution training. Year four's theme was community service. "Our kids had been destroying the high-rise projects," Principal White says. "Now every student does community service."

Our overall theme has been "how to be responsible." We stress and teach responsibility throughout the day. For example, our students have to have assignment notebooks and use them in *every* class.

We also set high expectations for our parents. Our parents *must* come to school for Back to School Night and for teacher-parent conferences during the year.

Jefferson Junior High School now has a waiting list of 400 to 500 students. It has won two U.S. Department of Education awards. In the city of Washington, D.C., it has been recognized for having the highest student academic achievement, the greatest academic improvement, and the highest attendance rate (its attendance rate used to be one of the worst). There have been no student pregnancies during the past five years.

The No Putdowns Project

The No Putdowns Project, based in Syracuse, New York, is a response to rising school violence and racial and ethnic intolerance. It has three goals: to create a school and home environment that recognizes the destructive effects of putdowns; to reject the use of putdowns in all interpersonal interactions; and to replace putdowns with healthy communication skills.

A five-week curriculum, developed by classroom teachers, uses videos, posters, contests, role-playing, and other activities to achieve these goals. The curriculum is reinforced throughout the school year.

One participating parent commented: "I see a noticeable difference in how much my child enjoys school." Other parents report that family members now catch each other ("Hey, Mom, that's a putdown!") when they slip.

Twenty-five elementary and middle schools in central New York are now implementing the No Putdowns Project. Several have already reported that discipline referrals and student fights are down for the first time in many years.

Participatory School Democracy

Another schoolwide character development strategy, greatly underused, challenges students to help govern the life of their school.

One of my favorite examples of this strategy comes from a school action project carried out by teacher Mary Ann Taylor when she took my graduate course, Teaching Moral Values. With some trepidation, she tackled the problem of her school cafeteria. She described it as "a war zone" where teacher aides yelled at children, students yelled at each other, food fights were common, and the place was a mess when students left.

Teacher Taylor set up a Cafeteria Council with student delegates elected from each classroom. Being an elected delegate meant you had to *represent* your constituency's ideas, as expressed in class meetings.

At every grade level, classes held discussions: What are the characteristics of an ideal cafeteria? What should be rules for cafeteria manners? Delegates carried their classrooms' views into the Cafeteria Council's weekly meetings, where they discussed these ideas with teacher Taylor and the school's principal and shaped them into action proposals.

The Council also conducted a survey of all students, staff, and parents on how to improve the cafeteria. It solicited everyone's ideas through a suggestion box. It published a monthly newsletter reporting progress.

The positive outcomes of all this effort were many: student cafeteria behavior improved greatly; students were enthusiastic about improvements in the cafeteria; parent feedback was positive; a recycling project was begun; and, most important, the school decided to keep its new delegate system of democratic student government as a way to deal with other problems in the school environment.

Similar student government efforts have been carried out at the high school level to bring students into a larger role of responsibility for solving school problems. In the process, students are provided with the kind of opportunities for real-life moral action that develop the action side of character. *Preparing for Citizenship: Teaching Youth to Live Democratically* by Ralph Mosher et al. tells the story of several high schools that have effectively used participatory school democracy to foster their students' political and moral development.[4]

A High School That Turned Around

St. Benedict's is a Catholic urban school, located in downtown Newark, New Jersey, that serves poor black and Hispanic teenage boys. It produces exceptional results, breaking for many of its students the vicious cycle of poverty into which they were born. It has a waiting list, with many students from the affluent suburbs seeking admission.

It was not always so. Twenty years ago St. Benedict's was on the verge of closing. Enrollment was steadily declining, student achievement discouragingly low.

St. Benedict's achieved this turnaround through high moral and academic expectations. The school insists on good manners and restrained behavior. Noise, bad language, and rowdiness are not tolerated. The halls are safe and free of graffiti. Strict standards of discipline and responsibility are reinforced in the classroom. Students are taught how to take notes and use their notebooks in all classes.

Strenuous athletic and extracurricular activity is also encouraged. A high level of peer support is encouraged in all areas of school life. During the early and continuing initiation into the school's curriculum and code of conduct, each student is assisted by fellow students who have mastered the school's standards and who help younger boys succeed.

A CHARACTER-BASED APPROACH TO SEX EDUCATION

No discussion of moral and character education can exclude sex education. More young people, I believe, are at risk from the destructive consequences of premature, uncommitted sex than from any other single threat to their healthy physical, emotional, and moral development.

To consider just one dimension of the physical dangers: In the United States, according to the Medical Institute for Sexual Health, about a third of sexually active teenage girls are now infected with human papilloma virus (the leading cause of cervical cancer) and/or chlamydia (the leading cause of infertility).[5] Recent medical studies show that condoms provide virtually no protection against either human papilloma virus or chlamydia, both of which can be transmitted by skin-to-skin contact in the entire genital region, only a small part of which is covered by the condom.

Unfortunately, young persons are growing up in what Boston University's Kevin Ryan calls a "sexually toxic" environment. This environment trivializes and debases sex and leads them into a pattern of short-lived sexual relationships that undermine self-respect and corrupt character.

There is fortunately now a growing effort to bring sex education into line with the principles of good character education.[6] That means adopting an approach to sex education that develops character traits of good judgment and self-control, and guides young people toward morally sound conclusions about how to apply the values of respect and responsibility to sexual behavior. And this means helping students understand all the reasons why sexual abstinence is the *only* medically safe and morally responsible choice for an unmarried teenager.

An exemplary character-based program in sex education is *Decision-Making: Keys to Total Success*, developed by the San Marcos, California school district. San Marcos faced a serious teen pregnancy problem—147 high school girls known to be pregnant during the 1984-85 school year. Its program included the following elements: daily 10-minute lessons for junior high school students on "how to be successful" (using materials from the Jefferson Center for Character Education[7]); a six-week course for seventh-graders on self-esteem and positive moral values; and a six-week pro-abstinence course for eighth-graders, "Sexuality, Commitment, and the Family."

The "Sexuality, Commitment, and the Family" course, created by Teen Aid, conveys the message that the only truly safe sex is having sex *only* with your marriage partner who is having sex *only* with you. Teen Aid's program also sends summaries of all lessons to parents and holds a workshop for parents on how to talk to teens about sex.

San Marcos reports that two years after implementing its Keys to Total Success program, known pregnancies in the school dropped from 147 to only 20—and have continued to remain far lower than they were before the program. There were other positive outcomes as well: drug referrals, grade point averages, standardized test scores, and attendance rates also showed marked improvement. The San Marcos character-building program won a California state award for excellence in education.

THE EVALUATION OF CHARACTER EDUCATION PROGRAMS

As the character education movement gains momentum, questions of evaluation loom larger. In thinking about evaluation, it is helpful to identify three kinds of results schools hope for when they undertake character education.

Documented Improvements Within the School Environment

Schools often begin character education programs because they hope to make the school a better place by effecting a positive change in student attitudes and behavior. Evaluation in this area asks questions such as: Has student attendance gone up? Fights and suspensions gone down? Vandalism declined? Drug incidents diminished? Attitudes toward cheating, and self-reported frequency of cheating, improved? One can assess such before-and-after-the-program differences by keeping records of observable behavior and by anonymous questionnaires that measure student moral judgment (for example, "Is cheating on a test wrong?"), moral commitment ("Would you cheat if you were sure you would not get caught?") and self-reported moral behavior ("How many times have you cheated on a test in the past year?").

Character Effects Beyond the School Environment

This is a measure of generalization. Here evaluation asks, to what extent do students, when they are outside the school, engage in prosocial behaviors such as helping others in need? Stand up for a moral value they believe in? Refrain from antisocial behaviors such as shoplifting? Refrain from high-risk behaviors such as drinking and driving and sexual intercourse? These behaviors outside the school environment, like in-school behaviors, can be assessed through anonymous self-report surveys. (The California-based Josephson Institute for Ethics has developed one such survey for use at the high school level.[8])

Life Outcomes After Graduation

This is a measure of the school's enduring effects on character. To what extent do graduates become faithful spouses and responsible parents? Law-abiding citizens? Productive and contributing members of their communities? This third area—which reflects what Henry Huffman calls character education's "future orientation"—can be assessed only through longitudinal research typically beyond the capacity of schools themselves. Other agencies can and must undertake such evaluations.

What does the available research tell us about the effectiveness of character education? The best of the evaluation research has sought to measure all three facets of character—cognitive, attitudinal, and behavioral outcomes.

For example, the Child Development Project in California has conducted a longitudinal experimental study of a character program that combines cooperative learning, teaching empathy through literature, positive role models, developmental discipline, involving students in helping relationships, and parent involvement. By the end of elementary school, students who experienced the program, compared to those who did not:

1. Showed more spontaneous acts of helping and encouraging their classmates (a measure of the behavioral side of character);
2. Were better at thinking of prosocial solutions to hypothetical social conflicts (a measure of the cognitive side of character);
3. Were more committed to democratic values such as the belief that all members of a group have a right to participate in decisions affecting the

group (a measure of the affective or attitudinal side of character.[9])

Recent research also supports the effectiveness of school, family, and community partnerships—as opposed to only school-based efforts—in one of the most challenging areas: changing student attitudes toward and use of drugs and alcohol. In June 1989, for example, the *Journal of the American Medical Association* reported a major intervention study of 20,000 sixth- and seventh-graders. The study compared a well-regarded school-based drug education curriculum with a program that combined the school curriculum with family involvement (students interviewed their parents and role-played refusal skills at home) and community involvement (extensive media support). The more comprehensive approach was significantly superior in slowing adolescent use of marijuana, cigarettes, and alcohol.

The greatest danger facing character education, as educational researchers David and Cheryl Aspy observe, is that severe social problems will be met with only weak educational efforts. When weak efforts fail to ameliorate the problems significantly, people will say, "We tried character education, and it failed." The scale of our character education efforts must therefore be commensurate with the seriousness of the moral problems that confront us. In the long run, this means that all groups— schools, families, communities, churches, youth organizations, government, and the media—that touch the values and character of the young must come together in common cause. As we seek to secure a future for our children in the next century, educating for character is a moral imperative for us all.

NOTES

1. For information, write: Heartwood Institute, 12300 Perry Highway, Wexford, PA 15090.

2. For information write: Facing History and Ourselves National Foundation, 25 Kennard Rd., Brookline, MA 02146.

3. David W. Johnson and Roger T. Johnson, "Critical Thinking Through Structured Controversy," *Educational Leadership*, May 1988.

4. R. Mosher, et al., *Preparing for Citizenship: Teaching Youth to Live Democratically* (Westport, CT: Praeger, 1994).

5. For medical studies on these and other STDs, write for Sexual Health Update, published by the Medical Institute for Sexual Health, P.O. Box 4919, Austin, TX 78765.

6.   Write the Medical Institute for Sexual Health for the forthcoming National Guidelines for Comprehensive Sexuality and Character Education.

7.   For more information contact the Jefferson Center for Character Education, Suite 240, 202 South Lake Avenue, Pasadena, CA 91101.

8.   For a copy of the High School Values Survey, write: The Josephson Institute of Ethics, 310 Washington Boulevard, Suite 104, Marina del Rey, CA, 90292.

9.   For a research report on the Child Development Project, write: The Child Development Project, 200 Embarcadero, Suite 305, Oakland, CA 94606-5300.

Chapter 10

Ethical Relativism: Teaching the Virtues

Christina Hoff Sommers

INTRODUCTION

What do students in our nation's schools do all day? Most of them are clearly not spending their time reading the classics, learning math, or studying the physical sciences. It is likely that, along with photography workshops, keeping journals, and perhaps learning about computers, students spend part of their day in moral education classes. But these classes are not, as one might expect, designed to acquaint students with the Western moral tradition. Professional theorists in schools of education have found that tradition wanting and have devised an alternative, one they have marketed in public schools with notable success.

The opening paragraph is taken from an article I wrote some time ago, titled "Ethics without Virtue," in which I criticized the way ethics is being taught in American colleges. I pointed out that there is an overemphasis on social policy questions, with little or no attention being paid to private morality. I noted that students taking college ethics are debating abortion, euthanasia, capital punishment, DNA research, and the ethics of transplant surgery while they learn almost nothing about private decency, honesty, personal responsibility, or honor. Topics such as hypocrisy, self-deception, cruelty, or selfishness rarely come up. I argued that the current style of ethics teaching, which concentrates so much on social policy, is giving students the wrong ideas about ethics. Social morality is only half of the moral life; the other half is private morality. I urged that we attend to both.

A colleague of mine did not like what I said. She told me that in her classroom she would continue to focus on issues of social injustice. She taught about women's oppression, corruption in big business, multinational corporations and their transgressions in the Third World—that sort of thing. She said to me, "You are not going to have moral people until you have moral institutions. You will not have moral citizens until you have a moral government." She made it clear that I was wasting time and even doing harm by promoting bourgeois virtues instead of awakening the social conscience of my students.

At the end of the semester, she came into my office carrying a stack of exams and looking very upset.

"What's wrong?" I asked.

"They cheated on their social justice take-home finals. They plagiarized!" More than half of the students in her ethics class had copied long passages from the secondary literature. "What are you going to do?" I asked her. She gave me a self-mocking smile and said, "I'd like to borrow a copy of that article you wrote on ethics without virtue."

There have been major cheating scandals at many of our best universities. A recent survey reported in the *Boston Globe* says that 75 percent of all high school students admit to cheating; for college students the figure is 50 percent. A *U.S. News and World Report* survey asked college-age students if they would steal from an employer. Thirty-four percent said they would. Of people 45 and over, six percent responded in the affirmative.

Part of the problem is that so many students come to college dogmatically committed to a moral relativism that offers them no grounds to think that cheating is just wrong. I sometimes play a macabre game with first-year students, trying to find some act they will condemn as morally wrong: Torturing a child. Starving someone to death. Humiliating an invalid in a nursing home. The reply is often, "Torture, starvation, and humiliation may be bad for you or me, but who are we to say they are bad for someone else?"

Not all students are dogmatic relativists, nor are they all cheaters and liars. Even so, it is impossible to deny that there is a great deal of moral drift. Students' ability to arrive at reasonable moral judgments is severely, even bizarrely, affected. A Harvard University professor annually offers a large history class on the Second World War and the rise of the Nazis. Some years back, he was stunned to learn from his teaching assistant that the majority of students did not believe that anyone was really to blame for the Holocaust. In the students' minds the Holocaust was like a natural cataclysm: It was inevitable and unavoidable. The professor refers to his students' attitude about the past as "no-fault history."

One philosopher, Alasdair MacIntyre, has said that we may be raising a generation of "moral stutterers." Others call it moral illiteracy. Education consultant Michael Josephson says "there is a hole in the moral ozone." Well, what should the schools be doing to make children morally literate, to put fault back into no-fault history, to mend the hole in the moral ozone?

THE NEW ETHICS

First, a bit of history. Let me remind you of how ethics was once taught in American colleges. In the nineteenth century, the ethics course was a high point of college life. It was taken in the senior year, and was usually taught by the president of the college, who would uninhibitedly urge the students to become morally better and stronger. The senior ethics course was in fact the culmination of the students' college experience. But as the social sciences began to flourish in the early twentieth century, ethics courses gradually lost prominence until they became just one of several electives offered by philosophy departments. By the mid-1960s, enrollment in courses on moral philosophy reached an all-time low and, as one historian of higher education put it, "college ethics was in deep trouble."

At the end of the 1960s, there was a rapid turnaround. To the surprise of many a department chair, applied ethics courses suddenly proved to be very popular. Philosophy departments began to attract unprecedented numbers of students to courses in medical ethics, business ethics, ethics for everyday life, ethics for lawyers, for social workers, for nurses, for journalists. More recently, the dubious behavior of some politicians and financiers has added to public concern over ethical standards, which in turn has contributed to the feeling that college ethics is needed. Today American colleges and universities are offering thousands of well-attended courses in applied ethics.

I too have been teaching applied ethics courses for several years. Yet my enthusiasm tapered off when I saw how the students reacted. I was especially disturbed by comments students made again and again on the course evaluation forms: "I learned there was no such thing as right or wrong, just good or bad arguments." Or, "I learned there is no such thing as morality." I asked myself what it was about these classes that was fostering this sort of moral agnosticism and skepticism. Perhaps the students themselves were part of the problem. Perhaps it was their high school experience that led them to become moral agnostics. Even so, I felt that my classes were doing nothing to change them.

The course I had been giving was altogether typical. At the beginning of the semester we studied a bit of moral theory, going over the strengths and weaknesses of Kantianism, utilitarianism, social contract theory, and relativism. We then took up topical moral issues such as abortion, censorship, capital punishment, world hunger, and affirmative action. Naturally, I felt it my job to present careful and well-argued positions on all sides of these popular issues. But this atmosphere of argument and counterargument was reinforcing the idea that all moral questions have at least two sides (i.e., that all of ethics is controversial).

Perhaps this reaction is to be expected in any ethics course primarily devoted to issues on which it is natural to have a wide range of disagreement. In a course specifically devoted to dilemmas and hard cases, it is almost impossible not to give the student the impression that ethics itself has no solid foundation.

UNCONTROVERSIAL TRUTHS

The relevant distinction here is between "basic" ethics and "dilemma" ethics. It is basic ethics that G. J. Warnock has in mind when he warns his fellow moral philosophers not to be bullied out of holding fast to the "plain moral facts." Because the typical course in applied ethics concentrates on problems and dilemmas, the students may easily lose sight of the fact that some things are clearly right and some are clearly wrong, that some ethical truths are not subject to serious debate.

I recently said something to this effect during a television interview in Boston, and the skeptical interviewer immediately asked me to name some uncontroversial ethical truths. After stammering for a moment I found myself rattling off several that I hold to be uncontroversial:

It is wrong to mistreat a child, to humiliate someone, to torment an animal. To think only of yourself, to steal, to lie, to break promises. And on the positive side: It is right to be considerate and respectful of others, to be charitable and generous.

Reflecting again on that extemporaneous response, I am aware that not everyone will agree that all of these are plain moral facts. But teachers of ethics are free to give their own list or to pare down mine. In teaching ethics, one thing should be made central and prominent: Right and wrong do exist. This should be laid down as uncontroversial lest one leaves an altogether false impression that *everything* is up for grabs.

It will, I think, be granted that the average student today does not come to college steeped in a religious or ethical tradition in which he or she has uncritical confidence. In the atmosphere of a course dealing with hard and controversial cases, the contemporary student may easily find the very idea of a stable moral tradition to be an archaic illusion. I am suggesting that we may have some responsibility here for providing the student with what the philosopher Henry Sidgwick called "moral common sense." More generally, I am suggesting that we should assess some of the courses we teach for their *edificatory* effect. Our responsibility as teachers goes beyond purveying information about the leading ethical theories and developing dialectical skills. I have come to see that dilemma ethics is especially lacking in edificatory force, and indeed that it may even be a significant factor in encouraging a superficial moral relativism or agnosticism.

I shall not really argue the case for seeing the responsibility of the teacher of ethics in traditional terms. It would seem to me that the burden of argument is on those who would maintain that modern teachers of ethics should abjure the teacher's traditional concern with edification. Moreover, it seems to me that the hands-off posture is not really as neutral as it professes to be. (Author Samuel Blumenfeld is even firmer on this point. He says, "You have to be dead to be value-neutral.") One could also make a case that the new attitude of disowning responsibility probably contributes to the student's belief in the false and debilitating doctrine that there are no "plain moral facts" after all. In tacitly or explicitly promoting that doctrine, the teacher contributes to the student's lack of confidence in a moral life that could be grounded in something more than personal disposition or political fashion. I am convinced that we could be doing a far better job of moral education.

HOW TO TEACH ETHICS

If one accepts the idea that moral edification is not an improper desideratum in the teaching of ethics, then the question arises: What sort of course in ethics is effective? What ethical teachings are naturally edificatory? My own experience leads me to recommend a course on the philosophy of virtue. Here, Aristotle is the best place to begin. Philosophers as diverse as Plato, Augustine, Kant, and even Mill wrote about vice and virtue. And there is an impressive contemporary literature on the subject. But the *locus classicus* is Aristotle.

Students find a great deal of plausibility in Aristotle's theory of moral education, as well as personal relevance in what he says about courage, generosity, temperance, and other virtues. I have found that an exposure to Aristotle makes an immediate inroad on dogmatic relativism; indeed, the tendency to discuss morality as relative to taste or social fashion rapidly diminishes and may vanish altogether. Most students find the idea of developing virtuous character traits naturally appealing.

Once the student becomes engaged with the problem of what kind of person to be, and how to *become* that kind of person, the problems of ethics become concrete and practical and, for many a student, moral development is thereafter looked on as a natural and even inescapable undertaking. I have not come across students who have taken a course in the philosophy of virtue saying that they have learned there is no such thing as morality. The writings of Aristotle and of other philosophers of virtue are full of argument and controversy, but students who read them with care are not tempted to say they learned "there is no right or wrong, only good or bad arguments."

At the elementary and secondary level students may be too young to study the philosophy of virtue, but they certainly are capable of reading stories and biographies about great men and women. Unfortunately, today's primary school teachers, many of whom are heavily influenced by what they were taught in trendy schools of education, make little use of the time-honored techniques of telling a story to young children and driving home "the moral of the story." What are they doing?

HOW *NOT* TO TEACH ETHICS

One favored method of moral education that has been popular for the past 20 years is called "values clarification," which maintains the principle that the teacher should never directly tell students about right and wrong; instead the students must be left to discover "values" on their own. One favored values clarification technique is to ask children about their likes and dislikes: to help them become acquainted with their personal preferences. The teacher asks the students, "How do feel about homemade birthday presents? Do you like wall-to-wall carpeting? What is your favorite color? Which flavor of ice cream do you prefer? How do you feel about hit-and-run drivers? What are your feelings on the abortion question?" The reaction to these questions—from wall-to-wall carpeting to hit-and-run drivers—is elicited from the student in the same tone of voice, as if one's personal preferences in both instances are all that matter.

One of my favorite anecdotes concerns a teacher in Massachusetts who had attended numerous values clarification workshops and was assiduously applying their techniques in her class. The day came when her class of sixth-graders announced that they valued cheating and wanted to be free to do it on their tests. The teacher was very uncomfortable. Her solution? She told the children that since it was *her* class, and since she was opposed to cheating, they were not free to cheat. "I personally value honesty; although you may choose to be dishonest, I shall insist that we be honest on our tests here. In other areas of your life, you may have more freedom to be dishonest...."

Now this fine and sincere teacher was doing her best not to indoctrinate her students. But what she was telling them is that cheating is not wrong if you can get away with it. Good values are "what one values." She valued the norm of not cheating. That made this value binding on her, and gave her the moral authority to enforce it in her classroom: others, including the students, were free to choose other values "in other areas." The teacher thought she had no right to intrude by giving the students moral direction. Of course, the price for her failure to do her job of inculcating moral principles is going to be paid by her bewildered students. They are being denied a structured way to develop values. Their teacher is not about to give it to them lest she interfere with their freedom to work out their own value systems.

This Massachusetts teacher values honesty, but her educational theory does not allow her the freedom to take a strong stand on honesty as a moral principle. Her training has led her to treat her "preference" for honesty as she treats her preference for vanilla over chocolate flavored ice cream. It is not hard to see how this doctrine is an egoistic variant of ethical relativism. For most ethical relativists, public opinion is the final court of ethical appeal; for the proponent of values clarification, the locus of moral authority is found in the individual's private tastes and preferences.

How sad that so many teachers feel intellectually and "morally" unable to justify their own belief that cheating is wrong. It is obvious that our schools must have clear behavior codes and high expectations for their students. Civility, honesty, and considerate behavior must be recognized, encouraged, and rewarded. That means that moral education must have as its *explicit* aim the moral betterment of the student. If that be indoctrination, so be it. How can we hope to equip students to face the challenge of moral responsibility in their lives if we studiously avoid telling them what is right and what is wrong?

The elementary schools of Amherst, New York provide good examples of an unabashedly directive moral education. Posters are placed around the school extolling kindness and helpfulness. Good behavior in the cafeteria is rewarded with a seat at a "high table" with tablecloth and flowers. One kindergarten student was given a special award for having taken a new Korean student under her wing. But such simple and reasonable methods as those practiced in Amherst are rare. Many school systems have given up entirely the task of character education. Children are left to fend for themselves. To my mind, leaving children alone to discover their own values is a little like putting them in a chemistry lab and saying, "Discover your own compounds, kids." If they blow themselves up, at least they have engaged in an authentic search for the self.

Ah, you may say, we do not let children fend for themselves in chemistry laboratories because we have *knowledge* about chemistry. But is there really such a thing as *moral* knowledge? The reply to that is an emphatic "Yes." Have we not learned a thing or two over the past several thousand years of civilization? To pretend we know nothing about basic decency, about human rights, about vice and virtue, is fatuous or disingenuous. Of course we know that gratuitous cruelty and political repression are wrong, that kindness and political freedom are right and good. Why should we be the first society in history that finds itself hamstrung in the vital task of passing along its moral tradition to the next generation?

Some opponents of directive moral education argue that it could be a form of brainwashing. That is a pernicious confusion. To brainwash is to diminish someone's capacity for reasoned judgment. It is perversely misleading to say that helping children to develop habits of truth telling or fair play threatens their ability to make reasoned choices. Quite the contrary: Good moral habits enhance one's capacity for rational judgments.

The paralyzing fear of indoctrinating children is even greater in high schools than it is in elementary schools. One favored teaching technique that allegedly avoids indoctrination of children—as it allegedly avoids indoctrination of college students—is dilemma ethics. Children are presented with abstract moral dilemmas: Seven people are in a lifeboat with provisions for four—what should they do? Or Lawrence Kohlberg's famous case of Heinz and the stolen drug. Should the indigent Heinz, whose dying wife needs medicine, steal it? When high school students study ethics at all, it is usually in the form of pondering such dilemmas or in the form of debates on social issues: abortion, euthanasia, capital punishment, and the like. Directive moral education is out of favor. Storytelling is out of fashion.

TELLING STORIES

Let's consider for a moment just how the current fashion in dilemmas differs from the older approach to moral education, which often used tales and parables to instill moral principles. Saul Bellow, for example, asserts that the survival of Jewish culture would be inconceivable without the stories that give point and meaning to the Jewish moral tradition. One such story, included in a collection of traditional Jewish tales that Bellow edited, is called "If Not Higher." I sketch it here to contrast the story approach with the dilemma approach in primary and secondary education, but the moral of the contrast applies to the teaching of ethics at the college level as well:

There was once a rabbi in a small Jewish village in Russia who vanished every Friday for several hours. The devoted villagers boasted that during these hours their rabbi ascended to Heaven to talk with God. A skeptical newcomer arrived in town, determined to discover where the rabbi really was.

One Friday morning the newcomer hid near the rabbi's house, watched him rise, say his prayers, and put on the clothes of a peasant. He saw him take an ax and go into the forest, chop down a tree, and gather a large bundle of wood. Next the rabbi proceeded to a shack in the poorest section of the village in which lived an old woman. He left her the wood, which was enough for the week. The rabbi then quietly returned to his own house.

The story concludes that the newcomer stayed on in the village and became a disciple of the rabbi. And whenever he hears one of his villagers say, "On Friday morning our rabbi ascends all the way to Heaven," the newcomer quietly adds, "If not higher."

In a moral dilemma such as Kohlberg's Heinz stealing the drug, or the lifeboat case, there are no obvious heroes or villains. Not only do the characters lack moral personality, but they exist in a vacuum outside of traditions and social arrangements that shape their conduct in the problematic situations confronting them. In a dilemma there is no obvious right and wrong, no clear vice and virtue. The dilemma may engage the students' minds; it only marginally engages their emotions, their moral sensibilities. The issues are finely balanced, listeners are on their own and they individually decide for themselves. As one critic of dilemma ethics has observed, one cannot imagine parents passing down to their children the tale of Heinz and the stolen drug. By contrast, in the story of the rabbi and the skeptical outsider, it is not up to the listener to decide whether or not the rabbi did the right thing. The moral message is clear: "Here is a good man—merciful, compassionate, and actively helping someone weak and vulnerable. Be like that person." The message is contagious. Even the skeptic gets the point.

Stories and parables are not always appropriate for high school or college ethics courses, but the literary classics certainly are. To understand *King Lear*, *Oliver Twist*, *Huckleberry Finn*, or *Middlemarch* requires that the reader have some understanding of (and sympathy with) what the author is saying about the moral ties that bind the characters and that hold in place the social fabric in which they play their roles. Take something like filial obligation. One moral of *King Lear* is that society cannot survive when filial contempt becomes the norm. Literary figures can thus provide students with the moral paradigms that Aristotle thought were essential to moral education.

WHAT TO DO

I am not suggesting that moral puzzles and dilemmas have no place in the ethics curriculum. To teach something about the logic of moral discourse and the practice of moral reasoning in resolving conflicts of principles is clearly important. But casuistry is not the place to *start*, and, taken by itself, dilemma ethics provides little or no moral sustenance. Moreover, an exclusive diet of dilemma ethics tends to give the student the impression that ethical thinking is a lawyer's game.

If I were an educational entrepreneur I might offer you a four- or five-stage program in the manner of some of the popular educational consultants. I would have brochures, audio-visual materials. There would be workshops. But there is no need for brochures, nor for special equipment, nor for workshops. What I am recommending is not new, has worked before, and is simple:

1.   Schools should have behavior codes that emphasize civility, kindness, self-discipline, and honesty.
2.   Teachers should not be accused of brainwashing children when they insist on basic decency, honesty, and fairness.
3.   Children should be told stories that reinforce goodness. In high school and college, students should be reading, studying, and discussing the moral classics.

I am suggesting that teachers must help children become acquainted with their moral heritage in literature, in religion, and in philosophy. I am suggesting that virtue can be taught, and that effective moral education appeals to the emotions as well as to the mind. The best moral teaching inspires students by making them keenly aware that their own character is at stake.

Reprinted with permission of the author and The Public Interest, Number 111, Spring 1993, pp. 3-13 © 1993 by National Affairs, Inc.

Chapter 11

The Parent-School Connection

Eric R. Ebeling

INTRODUCTION

In the United States, moral education has been getting a lot of attention recently. As one measure of national interest, the White House itself hosted a conference on the subject in the summer of 1994, assembling representatives from government and education groups to deliberate for two days.[1] In addition, a number of books and articles have appeared on various aspects of virtue and character development. No doubt increasing rates of crime, illegitimacy, and other antisocial acts among the young have prompted discussions about moral education in the hopes that it can do something to reverse these trends.

What is noteworthy amid the diversity of thought about moral education is the conformity of opinion about where it should take place. Predictably, the recent White House conference focused on how the nation's schools should instill character traits such as self-discipline and empathy in students. Indeed, many discussions of moral education today seem predicated on the assumption that schools are the best or only settings for the project. This assumption may stem from modern tendencies to equate education with schooling and to charge the educational system with societal reform. If education occurs in schools and if schools are responsible for curing social ills, then moral education must be a scholastic affair, so the thinking goes.

These premises deserve some scrutiny. After all, learning is not limited to school environments and rescuing society is not necessarily the job of teachers and administrators. In addition, the potential efficacy of school-based programs of moral education is uncertain given the failure of similar efforts in the past to affect student behavior. For example, sex education classes have done little to stem the tide of teenage pregnancy in this country.[2] The fact that the rectitude of young people over the past three decades has generally decreased while most of them have been enrolled in academic institutions raises some disturbing questions about whether schools have unwittingly aggravated the problem and, if so, whether they can really alleviate it.

The purpose of this chapter is to explore the problems and possibilities of moral education in schools. It begins with a brief history of the subject, focusing in turn on the initial role of schools as religious and ancillary agencies, their subsequent transformation into civil institutions to teach a secular ethic, and their ultimate abandonment of moral education in the public sector. There follows a critique of schools in terms of their current influence on the character of their students. Next is an examination of the theories of John Dewey who probably best envisioned how schools could serve as settings for character development. Finally, building on Dewey's ideas, the chapter concludes by considering some possibilities for effective moral education today both inside and outside school environments.

ORIGINS OF MORAL EDUCATION

Moral education as a philosophical topic emerges in the dialogues of Socrates, the social theorist of ancient Greece. As a religious matter, however, it dates back to the dawn of civilization, a concern of the major religions in both the Eastern and Western worlds. Of course, teaching children codes of conduct has always been an important aspect of inducting them into society, whether that society takes the form of a city-state, a community of believers, or some other cultural cluster of people.

The homogeneity of early societies greatly facilitated the processes of moral training within them. In these settings, consensus about the ends of education prompted cooperation about the means. In other words, inculcating proper values in the young was a responsibility which everyone in the group shared. Although parents may have been expected to shoulder most of the duty, they were assisted formally and informally by other parties. In addition, simply by participating in the day-to-day life of the society and interacting with its members, children acquired a sense of virtue and propriety.

The historical roles of the community and family in moral education are significant because they predate and overshadow the role of the school in the enterprise. The fact that schools are prevalent today in the United States should not obscure the fact that before the nineteenth century they were rare and accessible to only a small and often elite fraction of the total population of children. In addition, the school day and year were usually short and attendance was frequently intermittent. Consequently, the impact of the school, both moral and intellectual, was limited.

The minor influence of the school was not a problem, however, given its auxiliary function in early American society to buttress other institutions. Initially, many schools were established as extensions of a church, and the master was often the minister. As the instructional arm of a parish, these educational agencies provided formal religious training for the young and complemented the efforts of the home and the community to instill proper values. This adjunct role for schooling is especially apparent in colonial Massachusetts, which stands out in American history for its preoccupation with both religion and education. That these two spheres were intimately connected in the minds of New Englanders is manifest in their desire to become literate so they could personally acquire gospel knowledge and in their use of the Bible as an academic as well as an ecclesiastical textbook.

During the Enlightenment, schools assumed a distinctive role in character development as the notion of a secular morality surfaced. Championed by social theorists such as Emile Durkheim, the new standard for conduct no longer required a religious foundation. This development coincided with the emergence of the state as the political organization of modern society. The state had a vested interest in the good behavior of its citizens just as the church had of its parishioners, and the separation of the two necessitated both a new basis for morality and a new means for inculcating it. As a result, the public school eventually became the agency to teach the secular ethic. In effect, the state superseded the church as the governing authority, and schools evolved from ecclesiastical into civil institutions.

Thomas Jefferson and other Revolutionary figures were the first to push formal education in this direction with their reasoning about the need for an enlightened citizenry in a democracy. However, it was Horace Mann and his allies two generations later who made the most extensive case for schooling as a prerequisite for civic order. What impelled them in their mission was the apparent disintegration of society during the Jacksonian period in which they lived. A purported epidemic of crime, insanity, and poverty prompted reformers to build prisons, asylums, and almshouses to deal with these problems.[3] Public schools became another institutional solution in the effort to buttress society with the demise of the community, home, and church of the early American past.

Horace Mann especially emphasized the importance of the moral component in his arguments for popular education. As he maintained, "No idea can be more erroneous than that children go to school to learn the rudiments of knowledge only, and not to form character."[4] Although sectarian institutions understood this priority during the colonial period, district schools had lost sight of it in the new republic. Indeed, the impact of the separation of church and state on the public school curriculum left a void that had to be filled. "This entire exclusion of religious teaching, though justifiable under the circumstances, enhances and magnifies, a thousand fold, the indispensableness of moral instruction and training."[5]

Although the formation of good character in school was vitally necessary, in Mann's opinion it was sadly neglected.

> For one man who has been ruined for want of intellect or attainment hundreds have perished for want of morals. And yet, with this disproportion between the causes of human ruin, we go on, bestowing at least a hundred times more care and pains and cost in the education of the intellect, than in the cultivation of the moral sentiments, and in the establishment of moral principles.[6]

Accordingly, character education had to be enthroned as the priority in schooling. What did this require? Probably the most important implication had to do with instructors. "Is not the importance immeasurably augmented of employing teachers," Mann asked, "who will, themselves, be a living lesson to their pupils, of decorous behaviour, of order, of magnanimity, of justice, of affection; and who, if they do not directly teach the principles, will still, by their example, transfuse and instill something of the sentiment of virtue?"[7] For this assignment, Mann especially esteemed women "who are incomparably better teachers for young children than males" because they naturally possessed "purer morals" and exerted a virtuous influence. In addition, they could be employed at two-thirds the expense of men.[8]

With a predominantly female teaching corps and an overtly moral focus, the public school promised to be the panacea of society. In 1847, Mann wrote to several distinguished teachers, asking them about the potential impact of the school upon the moral problems of the day. He summarized their consensus the following year in his twelfth and final annual report to the Massachusetts Board of Education:

> If all the children in the community, from the age of four years to that of sixteen, could be brought within the reformatory and elevating influences of good schools, the dark host of private vices and public crimes, which now embitter domestic peace and stain the civilization of the age, might, in 99 cases in every 100, be banished from the world.[9]

As it turned out, Mann's vision was quixotic. Although he succeeded in launching a system of public schooling that would accept all children, he failed in establishing a program of moral education that would accommodate all values. To his credit, Mann recognized one obstacle to his plans: "But while there is such a practical diversity of opinion, in regard to what constitutes the highest destination of our nature, even in a worldly point of view, we cannot expect a general concurrence of opinion as to the influences under which the youthful character should be formed."[10] However, he was not attentive to the sharp disagreements of his time about this matter, and he did not foresee how divisive an issue the moral training of the young would become. For example, Mann was apparently unconscious of the Protestant nature of the common schools he supported, a fact not lost on Catholics who started their own parochial institutions after repeated attempts to point out the problem over the nineteenth century.

Eventually, even the pan-Protestant tone of public education disappeared as all vestiges of religion such as Bible reading and prayer became casualties of a narrow interpretation of the separation of church and state. This has resulted in a moral vacuum, because deciding whose values to teach to replace the former Protestant ones has been difficult. As an institution open to all members of society, the public school must not discriminate against particular segments of society in imposing a certain morality on students. The effort to identify common values that everyone would share, while possible in theory, is problematic in practice. Consequently, the solution by default has been to avoid any overt program of moral education and assign parents and other private parties and agencies the responsibility for this endeavor.

In summary, despite the original moral role of schools and Horace Mann's subsequent hopes, nothing has really filled the void for character development. Consequently, moral education is generally neglected in public schools across the United States today. From the perspective of educational history, it is ironic that education is so often considered an academic or vocational enterprise now when it was so thoroughly regarded as a moral one in the not-too-distant past.

THE INFLUENCE OF SCHOOLS ON CHARACTER TODAY

The absence of any formal moral program in public schools does not mean that an informal one is not going on, however. Education is inherently and therefore inescapably a value-laden enterprise, despite the claims of proponents of "value-free" schooling. Consequently, the character of children is being shaped simply by their attendance at school. In fact, there are at least three ways in which this happens. The ideology, method, and social milieu of schools each contribute to character development, and while some schools exert a positive influence, many other schools unfortunately exert a negative one.

As many critics of public schooling have observed, a particular worldview obtains in public schools the effort to keep them religion-free. Known by terms such as "secular humanism," this ideology promotes reliance on science, and, some would argue, denigrates religious faith. The attendant lessons for moral education are significant. For example, children learn to seek the technological fix instead of the ethical resolution of social problems. In the recent past, some groups such as fundamentalist Christians have left the public school system to start their own private institutions because of this repudiation of religion. In the private sector they at least have the opportunity to deliberately and formally instill desirable values in their young.

Although private schools generally avoid debate about what values to teach, they do not necessarily escape other problems with moral education. In addition to ideology, the method of schooling also has implications for character development. For example, the focus on individual achievement often engenders a competitive and selfish atmosphere in schools. The passivity of students in classes where they sit and receive information does little to engender character traits of initiative and self-direction. In addition, the emphasis on short-term memorization to pass tests does not encourage habits of hard work and sacrifice.

More significantly, beyond the content and method of schooling there is the social milieu in which it takes place. As Ralph Waldo Emerson observed, "You send your child to the schoolmaster, but 'tis the schoolboys who educate him."[11] The pervasive youth culture in society today which has such an impact on the opinions of teenagers is based largely in schools where they congregate. The influence of peers on behavior is also astounding, as anyone in the fashion or entertainment world knows. One of the greatest obstacles to academic success is the belief among some students in schools that working hard or succeeding in class is not "cool." Perhaps more serious is the fact that schools are the settings in which drugs are passed as well as attitudes. These realities raise questions about the role of schools as nurseries for vice rather than virtue.

JOHN DEWEY ON MORAL EDUCATION

Although many schools have a negative influence on the character of their students, they could be organized to have a positive impact instead. In support of this possibility, John Dewey offered what is arguably the best blueprint for schools as agencies of moral education. What makes his ideas so insightful regarding this matter is his understanding of the social aspects of schooling which represent the working conditions for character development.

Dewey's theory rests on an expansive notion of morality. In discussing the topic, he stated that "morals are as broad as acts which concern our relationships with others."[12] In addition, he did not view character formation as a piecemeal process: "To possess virtue does not signify to have cultivated a few nameable and exclusive traits; it means to be fully and adequately what one is capable of becoming through association with others in all the offices of life."[13] The overarching social dimension of Dewey's thought is evident in these definitions.

Since virtue stems from human interaction, Dewey believed it could be engendered in particular social settings. In his mind, the environment was more important than the instructional program: "This right character is not to be formed by merely individual precept, example, or exhortation, but rather by the influence of a certain form of institutional or community life upon the individual."[14] In other words, Dewey was convinced that moral education must be a collective enterprise.

Where should such an enterprise take place? Dewey argued that if schools were run as miniature communities, they could foster moral and social sensitivities among the young by bringing them into positive interaction with each other in educational pursuits. This understanding of schooling forms an important plank of his pedagogic creed: "I believe that the moral education centers upon this conception of the school as a mode of social life, that the best and deepest moral training is precisely that which one gets through having to enter into proper relations with others in a unity of work and thought."[15] Carried out effectively, this approach has great promise: "When the school introduces and trains each child of society into membership within such a little community, saturating him with the spirit of service, and providing him with the instruments of effective self-direction, we shall have the deepest and best guarantee of a larger society which is worthy, lovely, and harmonious."[16]

Implementing this vision is not an easy task, however. Dewey himself recognized that traditional approaches to instill virtue would not work:

> Moral education in school is practically hopeless when we set up the development of character as a supreme end, and at the same time treat the acquiring of knowledge and the development of understanding, which of necessity occupy the chief part of school time, as having nothing to do with character. On such a basis, moral education is inevitably reduced to some kind of catechetical instruction, or lessons about morals. Lessons "about morals" signify as matter of course lessons in what other people think about virtues and duties. It amounts to something only in the degree in which pupils happen to be already animated by a sympathetic and dignified regard for the sentiments of others. Without such a regard, it has no more influence on character than information about the mountains of Asia.[17]

Thus, the unified school experience and attendant social spirit are essential to moral education. These requirements are dependent on two conditions. First, "the school must itself be a community life in all which that implies," and second, "the learning in school should be continuous with that out of school."[18] Much of Dewey's work was an exposition on how schools could meet these two conditions. The first requires a realignment of schooling for the purposes of social interaction. The second necessitates a reorganization of schooling around the life of the child instead of the tradition of the curriculum, a reorganization that connects his or her experiences in school with those in the home and community.

POSSIBILITIES FOR EFFECTIVE MORAL EDUCATION TODAY

The disparity between how Dewey envisioned schools and how most of them operate today is quite large. Although Dewey is often extolled (or blamed) for having the most impact on public schooling in the United States, in terms of his social vision of education he really had very little lasting effect. In fact, neither of the two essential conditions mentioned is evident in many scholastic settings. Regarding the first one about schools operating as communities themselves, the overwhelming emphasis on academic subjects leaves little room for engendering a sense of association or cooperation. In their efforts to secure good grades for individual advancement, students have little commitment to the notion that schooling is a collective enterprise to which they can each contribute for the betterment of all. Instead, they view it as an individual experience for themselves.

Regarding the second condition about a continuity of learning inside and outside of schools, most things that are taught have little immediate relevance in the lives of students. In addition, educators tend to work in isolation from the larger society in which the school is situated. Consequently, school is largely an artificial experience for young people, a separate component of their lives.

How could Dewey's vision about schools as settings for effective moral education be realized today? Perhaps the past offers some ideas in answer to this question. The small-scale constellation of community, home, church, and school of the early American era may provide something of a model. While it may not be possible or even desirable to reconstruct this arrangement, there may be a part of it that could be resurrected. Certainly, the family deserves some attention as an agency that could contribute to character formation.

The Family and Moral Education

Although John Dewey emphasized the function of the school in moral education, he did not overlook the effect of the home in the endeavor. In fact, he viewed the home as a point of departure for the school, deriving the latter as an extension and enlargement of the former.[19] As the first and perhaps the most influential social institution for the child, the family played a significant role in his theory.

In devising an educational setting that would promote the development of character, Dewey cited the former household in agrarian society as an ideal prototype. The demands of farming life exerted a natural moral influence on the young which he acknowledged and appreciated:

> We cannot overlook the factors of discipline and of character-building involved in this: training in habits of order and of industry, and in the idea of responsibility, of obligation to do something, to produce something, in the world. There was always something which really needed to be done and a real necessity that each member of the household should do his own part

faithfully and in cooperation with others.[20]

Although the industrial revolution, by displacing families from farms, eliminated this type of experience for many young people, Dewey argued that it could be reconstituted to some degree in schools. By providing opportunities for children to participate in meaningful group activities, educational environments could engender the same character traits that domestic ones had in the past. In fact, Dewey almost suggested that schools could do a better job because they could be organized deliberately to achieve these objectives.

In advancing this role for schools, however, Dewey never implied that they could or should take on the responsibility for moral education alone. Rather, he indicated that families were an essential part of the enterprise, and he expected teachers to work in conjunction with parents in forming the character of their children.

Dewey, of course, was sensitive to the moral influence of the older generation on the younger one in the home. Fathers and mothers, perhaps in both similar and distinctive ways, convey values to their children. Obviously, they do so directly with the instruction and discipline they give, but they also do so indirectly with the models they provide. The natural admiration of young children for their parents and their desire to emulate them are testimony to the efficacy of the latter approach. In moral education, teaching by example usually has a more powerful and lasting impact than teaching by precept.

In addition to the social influence they have on their sons and daughters, parents may have a genetic one as well. One of the historical and philosophical issues regarding moral education has been to what extent character is a product of nurture or nature. Generally, the word character refers to the sum of moral qualities or the ethical strength of an individual, a dimension of personality that is formed after birth. Since education in a broad sense is usually considered an enterprise in nurturing, many educators work under the premise that anyone can be molded in a moral way.

Although this belief may have currency among educational theorists, it may be controversial among educational practitioners. In working on a close and daily basis with recalcitrant and rebellious youngsters, teachers may unsurprisingly come to accept the notion of natural depravity proposed by John Calvin. Some instructors, no doubt, may even be tempted to beat this condition out of their students as their predecessors did in early America.

Recent research about the inherited aspects of personality adds supporting evidence to the intuition of frustrated teachers. In other words, there may be a scientific argument as well as a religious one that character is partly a result of nature. Interestingly, in the field of genetics, character is already an established term which refers to an attribute or structure determined by genes.

If children acquire traits or tendencies related to moral development from their progenitors, then character formation may begin at conception, and parents may be unwitting contributors to the project before they even set eyes on their offspring. Even if scientists fail to conclusively link chromosomes to conduct, moral education will still have an inherited component to the extent that childrearing practices may be passed from one generation to the next.

In summary, since character is definitely a product of nurture and possibly a product of nature, the intersection of these two dimensions in the home makes it an important setting for moral education. In that influential environment, parents play especially significant roles because they intentionally or unintentionally contribute in at least one and possibly both ways to the enterprise.

Home and School Partnerships

To recognize the effect of the family on character development is to realize that the school must support and not supplant the home if it is to be an effective agency of moral education. Some educators are beginning to reach this conclusion, understanding that although teachers and parents may work in a parallel fashion to instill particular virtues, they may work at cross purposes as well. Obviously, the best results occur when they cooperate and coordinate their efforts.[21]

What is the possibility for partnerships between homes and schools in moral education? Unfortunately, the established routine and independence of professional educators in doing their job impede such an alliance. In addition, many teachers and administrators seem to have a low opinion of parents, believing they do not care or have misplaced concerns about their children. This attitude has fueled the arrogation of educational authority by schools, and it must be dispelled for a united effort to occur.

Perhaps families need to take the initiative to form partnerships with professional educators. The potential for effective associations seems to be greater in the private sector where schools are usually more receptive to parental wishes and participation. From another perspective, homeschoolers may have the best approach for instilling values in the young in using the home as a base for moral education. The growing body of evidence testifying to their success raises the question of whether their children miss anything in character development by not going to school outside the home.

Homeschoolers are a minority in this country, however, and they probably will always be. Some other plan is necessary, then, for the vast majority of children, especially for those whose parents are indeed negligent or even abusive. Whatever the arrangement, families must be involved in a much more meaningful way than they currently are if the desired ends of moral education are to be realized.

CONCLUSION

In short, moral education in schools is problematic today. As accessories to churches, communities, and families in early America, schools initially exerted a positive influence on the character of their students. However, over time that influence waned as teaching subjects became more important and teaching values became more controversial in public institutions. During the past three decades the impact has even become negative with the denigration of religious faith, the dehumanization of educational practice, and the degeneration of youth culture in many school settings.

Although John Dewey offers a blueprint for schools as moral agencies in modern society, realizing his plan would be a formidable task today. It would require the operation of schools as miniature communities and as integrated components of a larger social network of organizations concerned about rearing the young. The current internal detachment and external isolation of most schools would be serious obstacles, not to mention the traditional resistance of educational institutions to change. Because of these problems, parents may decide that the private and homeschooling sectors offer the brightest promise of effective moral education as Dewey envisioned it.

Wherever the formation of character is attempted, it is important to recognize the distinction between teaching and learning in the process. The goal of moral education is to prompt students to incorporate values in their lives, not to amass facts in their minds. The enterprise is concerned about who people are and how and why they act rather than just what they know. Consequently, it is hardly fair or reasonable to expect schools alone to fulfill so vital and complex a mission.

NOTES

1. "White House Puts Accent on Duties Instead of Rights," *Christian Science Monitor*, 29 July 1994.

2. See Barbara Dafoe Whitehead, "The Failure of Sex Education," *The Atlantic Monthly*, October 1994, 55-80.

3. See David Rothman, *The Discovery of the Asylum: Social Order and Disorder in the New Republic* (Boston: Little, Brown, 1990).

4. Horace Mann, *Lectures on Education* (New York: Arno Press, 1969), 93.

5. Horace Mann, *First Annual Report of the Board of Education together with the First Annual Report of the Secretary of the Board of Education* (Boston: Dutton and Wentworth, 1838), 62. Hereafter, only the number and year of Mann's reports will be given in citations.

6. Mann, *Lectures on Education*, 330-31.

7. Mann, *First Annual Report* (1838), 63.

8. Mann, *Fourth Annual Report* (1841), 45-46.

9. Mann, *Twelfth Annual Report* (1849), 96.

10. Mann, *Ninth Annual Report* (1846), 144.

11. Ralph Waldo Emerson, "Culture," in *The Complete Writings of Ralph Waldo Emerson*, vol. I (New York: Wise, 1929), 562.

12. John Dewey, *Democracy and Education* (New York: Free Press, 1916), 357.

13. Dewey, *Democracy and Education,* 358.

14. Martin S. Dworkin, *Dewey on Education* (New York: Teachers College Press, 1959), 30.

15. Dworkin, *Dewey on Education,* 24.

16. Dworkin, *Dewey on Education*, 49.

17. Dewey, *Democracy and Education*, 354.

18. Dewey, *Democracy and Education*, 358.

19. Dworkin, *Dewey on Education*, 53.

20. Dworkin, *Dewey on Education*, 36.

21. Thomas Lickona, "Schools and Families: Partners or Adversaries in Moral Education?" in Andrew Garrod, ed., *Learning for Life: Moral Education Theory and Practice* (Westport, CT: Praeger, 1992), 89-106.

Chapter 12

Character Education Among the States

Charles E. Greenawalt, II

Since ancient times, philosophers and scholars have known that values and education are indissolubly bound together. Their connection was so obvious and important that it was virtually impossible to imagine value-free education. Even if education did not transmit values explicitly and self-consciously, it did so implicitly and by example.

Denis P. Doyle[1]

People are realizing that successful education without teaching values is impossible. We cannot have 250 million individual value systems operating in this country and survive as a nation.

Patrick McCarthy[2]

The truth of the real world is that without standards and judgments, there can be no progress....We shouldn't be reluctant to declare that some things—some lives, books, ideas, and value—are better than others. It is the responsibility of the schools to teach these better things.

William J. Bennett[3]

The task of the educator is not to cut down jungles but to irrigate deserts. The right defense against false sentiments is to [teach] just sentiments.

C. S. Lewis[4]

Schools and educators can play a powerful role second only to the influence of parents in forming children's attitudes and values. Yet to a great extent our schools are failing us.

Benjamin M. Spock[5]

INTRODUCTION

A fundamental loss of values in America has fostered a calamitous epidemic of violence and has undermined the integrity and vibrancy of the family unit while coarsening our culture and generating a steady deterioration in our quality of life. This is the belief of Dr. Benjamin Spock and an increasing legion of other social observers and analysts.

A national consensus has broadened during the past three years on the crisis of values that the United States is experiencing. Conservatives, liberals, moderates, neoconservatives, neoliberals, and communitarians all agree. Political leaders from President Bill Clinton and William Bennett to Jesse Jackson and Phyllis Schlafly have been sounding the warning to a national citizenry that is increasingly aware of the problem but increasingly despondent over what corrective measures should be embraced.

One measure that has only recently reemerged and captured a measure of public attention is character education. This chapter will examine the degree to which our laboratories of democracy—our state governments—and their educational establishments have attempted to utilize character education to reverse the trends outlined by Spock and others.

Throughout America's history, schools have had two fundamental goals: to help people become smart and good. Schools once assumed that students would learn to be better people as they developed their intellect. This no longer remains a valid assumption.

The Josephson Institute of Ethics released a study of nearly 7,000 American students that indicated that 61 percent of high schoolers had cheated on an exam during the past year, 33 percent had stolen something from a store, and 33 percent said they would lie on a resume.[6] During 1993, members of Texas Southern University's marching band were apprehended during a trip to Tokyo for stealing $22,000 worth of electronic merchandise. According to a National Retail Federation study, shoplifting cost U.S. businesses $24 billion last year, while only three to five percent of shoplifters were apprehended. Employee theft costs businesses about $9 billion per year. A 1993 National School Boards Association survey revealed that approximately 10 percent of all teachers and 25 percent of all students had been the victim of an assault. In response to these trends, 20 percent of all high school students now regularly carry a weapon to school.

In a report issued by the Princeton Religion Research Center, most Americans profess their conviction that there are few moral absolutes and that "right" or "wrong" depends on the situation. This belief in "situation ethics" rather than moral absolutes was held by 69 percent of American adults according to the center.[7] The columnist William Raspberry believes that our society has suffered because of the forsaking of moral absolutes:

> I think we've paid a very high price for our abandonment of clear-cut right/wrong pronouncements in favor of moral relativism. Our professors, our universities, and our high schools are discovering the dilemma we created for ourselves: You can't exercise moral authority while denying the authority of morality.[8]

This moral relativity has only reinforced the surge of juvenile violence that has overwhelmed our nation during the past seven years. Violence is devastating this generation; a *Newsweek* report on teen violence compared its lethal nature to the deadliness of the polio epidemic 40 years ago. Between 1987 and 1991, the number of teenagers arrested for murder increased at the rate of 85 percent. Not only are more teens committing crimes, but more teens are the victims of this contemporary crime wave. An average of more than six juveniles are killed every day, and the Justice Department estimates that about a million teens between the ages of 12 and 19 are assaulted, raped, or robbed by other youths annually.[9]

In 1993, persons under 18 years of age accounted for approximately 20 percent of all the violent crime in America. When burglary, theft, and car-theft are added to the violent crimes of murder, forcible rapes, robberies, and aggravated assaults, persons under 18 account for 29 percent of all arrests.[10]

Indeed, the "age of innocence" has ended for contemporary youth. Certainly, declining standards of behavior are most astonishing when they are seen in our children. Even the most basic kind of moral knowledge seems to be disappearing from our common culture.

Many of today's youth have a difficult time seeing any moral dimension to their actions. There are many reasons why this is true, and perhaps none are more prominent than a collapsing family structure coupled with an educational system that often eschews teaching children the core civic values that bind Americans together as a society and culture.

The need for character education was well summarized by Theodore Roosevelt, "To educate a person in mind and not in morals is to educate a menace to society." In fact, character education is as old as education itself.

HISTORY OF AMERICAN CHARACTER EDUCATION

In 1647 the first law mandating public education in the United States was adopted in Massachusetts. This law was entitled "Ye Old Deluder Satan Act," and it declared that Satan flourished on ignorance. Students were taught the alphabet from *The New England Primer* that began "In Adam's fall, we sinned all."[11] The purpose of education in puritan Massachusetts was to enable students to read the Bible. Indeed, the first education laws were enacted to enable the state to act as the agent of the church in requiring compulsory schooling for children. Patrick McCarthy, executive vice president of the Thomas Jefferson Research Center, observes that at that time, "Schooling was almost all values instructions, with a little reading and simple arithmetic thrown in."[12]

The colonies' leaders at the time of the American Revolution also believed that school had a responsibility to develop students' values. Thomas Jefferson's *Bill for the More General Diffusion of Knowledge* supported the idea that public education should instill moral principles in students. Benjamin Franklin's *Proposals Relating to the Education of Youth in Pennsylvania* outlined a curriculum that included the study of ethics.

These Revolutionary leaders harbored the belief that public education would create the kinds of citizens required in a democracy. For example, Jefferson noted:

> I know of no safe depository of the ultimate powers of society but the people themselves; and if we think them not enlightened enough to exercise their control with a wholesome discretion...the remedy is not to take it from them, but to inform their discretion.[13]

The new country's first legislators soon embarked upon a course of action that revealed the value they placed on education and its connection to character development. The Northwest Ordinance of 1787 is illustrative of the actions. It set forth a mechanism for financing public education, and its intent was clear: "religion, morality, and knowledge being necessary to good government and the happiness of mankind, schools, and the means of education shall forever be encouraged."[14] After the first few years of "common school," students were instructed either in academies, which were private secondary schools; in English-style colleges; in apprenticeships; or in other forms of professional training.

In the nineteenth century, public schools fully embraced character education through discipline, the teacher's example, and the daily school curriculum. This type of instruction is clearly seen in the *McGuffey's Readers* that were introduced in 1836 and proceeded to sell more than 100 million copies. William McGuffey used religious stories, inspirational poems, stirring exhortations, and heroic tales in his *Readers*. As children practiced their school lessons, they also learned the importance of honesty, hard work, self-discipline, responsibility, respect, caring, and citizenship.

Later in the nineteenth century, the secretary of the Massachusetts Board of Education, Horace Mann, required all public school teachers in that state to begin each school day by reading ten verses from the King James Version of the Bible "without comment." This practice, which was widely employed across the United States, was a way to assist students in developing "reason and conscience."[15]

The form of character education delivered in the public schools during the nineteenth century was firmly grounded in Protestant Christianity. As time passed, increasing numbers of Roman Catholics pressed for revisions to the type of character education in use. In Cincinnati, for example, a conflict over which version of the Bible would be read in the public schools broke into a violent conflict known as the Rifle War.

Mann and other educators who supported Bible reading, however, did so in the belief that the moral values taught in this way were universal and nonsectarian. "There is a secular morality which is not opposed to religious morality...but is the result of human experiences, is recognized by all civilized people, is taught by the philosophers of all nations, and is sanctioned by all enlightened creeds," affirmed an 1880s article in the *Wisconsin Journal of Education*.[16]

During the latter portion of the nineteenth century, numerous changes began in American society that would gradually but decisively alter the nature of U.S. schools. A few of these notable trends were increasing urbanization of society, increasing affluence of American society, and increasing religious heterogeneity. Children could spend longer periods of economically unproductive time attending school; hence, by the turn of the century, schools had enrolled significantly larger percentages of all children between the ages of 15 and 18. As religious heterogeneity escalated, schools went from basing their character education on nonsectarian Christianity to deism and later to purely secular principles.

Nevertheless, up until the 1930s, character education remained a significant goal of elementary and secondary education.

In the mid-1920s, the Institute of Social and Religious Research launched a comprehensive effort to evaluate the impact of schools upon character formation. This research was led by Hugh Hartschorne and Mark A. May. Their three-volume, 1,700-page report, "The Character Education Inquiry," concluded that the relationship between good pupil conduct and the application of a formal character education approach was slight. This research effort marked a turning point in the relationship between American public education and traditional character education.[17]

Before Hartschorne and May's research, schools were totally committed to conducting a vigorous character education program, and the nation's intellectual forces were sympathetic to this endeavor. As the study's conclusions circulated, a gradual disjunction arose and slowly spread over what educators and parents desired in the schools' values curricula and efforts. Edward Wynne tells us that this study, however, was unrealistic and was conducted from a "semi-utopian" perspective.[18]

While this study and its conclusions were fading into the mists of time, the momentum of the character education movement carried it forward through the 1930s, 1940s, and 1950s. Even though character education served our culture well over a long period of time, a number of forces, which arose after Hartschorne and May's research, surfaced and dismantled traditional character education or what Wynne refers to as "the great tradition." William K. Kilpatrick and Thomas Lickona identified these forces—logical positivism, personalism, relativism, rapidly intensifying pluralism, and increasing secularization.

These forces, their development, and their effect on character education are fully examined in other chapters. Nonetheless, the rapidly intensifying pluralism of American society and the increasing secularization of the public arena forced many schools away from their once central role as moral and character educators.[19] Many schools accepted the ideas that they should not impose any one set of values on their students, and these institutions began to profess the conviction that all values were equal and distinctions could not be made among them. Character education, if not actively discouraged, became at best unplanned and unreflective, part of the unexamined curriculum. It was abandoned to the discretion of individual teachers.

During the 1970s character education rebounded in a different guise. The forms it assumed were values clarification and moral reasoning. "Values clarification" tells children to decide for themselves under most circumstances what is right and wrong. This new approach to character education sprang from the publication of *Values and Teaching* by Columbia University professor Louis Raths in 1966. Values clarification contained no requirement to evaluate one's values against a standard, no suggestion that some values might be better or worse than others.

An alternative to values clarification, "moral reasoning," soon arose and was spearheaded by Lawrence Kohlberg. Moral reasoning tried to assist students to develop ethically valid ways of reasoning about moral issues. Nonetheless, its focus was on "process" rather than the moral content of those thoughts.

These two new approaches to character education that left students with the impression that all morality is problematic and all questions of right and wrong are in dispute have generally failed. The naive assumption behind values clarification is that students will arrive at good moral conclusions if they are given the opportunity. The actual result of these two approaches has been moral confusion.

Many schools have gone astray recently, not in the instruction of values, but in the instruction that all values are equal. Though deeply held differences exist, not all values are equal. Values are the basis of actions, and actions have consequences. Since all civilizations are embodiments of some set of values and since all values are alleged to be equal by some, all civilizations should possess the same levels of prosperity and stability. Of course, they do not.

Traditional character education provides a much more effective and realistic approach to addressing the "moral illiteracy" than do these recent curricula. In the past few years an increasing number of states have attempted to restore character education programs. The United States, however, is not alone among countries of the world in grappling with this state of "moral illiteracy" within the ranks of the young.

CHARACTER EDUCATION—INTERNATIONAL EXAMPLES

Countries across the globe are turning to their educational systems for assistance with the increasing levels of moral illiteracy among their youth. Lickona notes this trend, "The paralyzing concern of a few years ago that teaching values might...upset some people is giving way to what now seems like a self-evident truth: *Not* to equip the young with a moral sense is a grave ethical failure on the part of any society."[20]

The new international focus on character education has been highlighted recently in *The Economist*. The publication reported that the idea of character education is not new in Asia. It can be dated back beyond the time of Confucius. During the transformation of Japan from feudalism in the nineteenth century, moral education was used to protect "Asian values." At a recent conference sponsored by UNESCO, the final report noted that interest in moral education "resounded throughout." The newly industrialized countries of Asia desire the benefits of Western prosperity without what they see as the attendant evils of Western morality. Lee Kwan Yew, the former prime minister of Singapore, has warned that "If western values are adopted, cohesion will be threatened and the country will go downhill."[21]

Students in Hong Kong, South Korea, Taiwan, and Singapore all receive schooling in moral education. For example, children in Korea spend two hours each week in character education and how the virtues affect the individual, the family, and the nation. Many Asians are now worried about the decay in order, discipline, family life, basic education, and personal safety that seems to have infected the United States during the past 40 years. They passionately desire to avoid these trends.[22]

Over the past decade, divorce rates in the Asian countries noted above have climbed and teenagers are increasingly seen as unruly vagabonds. It is no coincidence that the revived interest in character education has grown as traditional virtues are thought to have declined. "There's increasing concern among educators that the next generation is going to hell," observed a World Bank economist.[23]

Consequently, the South Korean Ministry of Education has been frustrated with many parents of the country's brightest students because the Ministry believes that character education is shortchanged by these families as they focus on preparing their children for the competition to obtain entry to the best universities.

A Singapore textbook, *Confucian Ethics*, offers this advice to its students in order to retain a proper perspective as affluence increases: "Despite increasing competition in the work place, and life becoming more and more mechanical, we may still follow the Confucian path of spiritual self-cultivation and live meaningful lives with one another."[24]

PUBLIC CLIMATE AND CHARACTER EDUCATION

In 1993, the public policy research organization, Public Agenda, conducted a national public opinion study that was entitled *First Things First: What Americans Expect from the Public Schools*. In this study, Public Agenda discovered that more than two-thirds of Americans—71 percent—believe that it is more important for the schools to teach values than to teach academic subjects.[25]

When the Public Agenda researchers focused on the area of character education, they discovered that 95 percent of Americans are convinced that schools should teach honesty and the importance of telling the truth. In addition, the study uncovered that 95 percent of the populace believe that schools should teach respect for others regardless of their racial or ethnic background and 93 percent said that schools should teach students to solve problems without violence.[26]

A 1989 Gallup Poll found that 79 percent of Americans favored traditional character education in the schools. Parents with children in public schools approved of these schools conducting a traditional character education curriculum at the rate of 89 percent.[27]

In 1990 a commission of business, educational, medical, and political leaders met to examine the problems of American children. This commission issued a report called *Code Blue*, and the contents of this report were sobering. The report argued that "Never before has one generation of American teenagers been less healthy, less cared for, or less prepared for life, than their parents were at the same age."[28] The commission believed that America's youth were facing a crisis of character.

STATE CONSTITUTIONS AND CHARACTER EDUCATION

In addition to public approval of character education in the schools, state governments had traditionally placed a high value on the importance of character education. This assertion can be illustrated in a number of ways.

The first proof of this assertion is seen in the fact that all 50 state constitutions are based on higher-law assumptions. Second, the preambles of 44 states constitutions specifically refer to a deity. Finally, the constitutions of 25 states mandate character or moral education based on a confirmed knowledge of right and wrong.[29]

Despite the existence of these mandates, there appears to be no correlation between whether a state constitution mandates moral education and whether the state government actually implements a character education program. Twenty-five state constitutions mandate character education in their public schools. Surprisingly, 16 of the states that mandate character education through their constitutions have not yet officially implemented specific moral education programs. However, seven states conduct character education programs without any mandate.

Table 1 presents a comparison of those states whose constitutions mandate character education and those states that report the implementation of a character education program. Table 2 shows a classification of the states based on the type of character education program that is in effect.

TABLE 1

STATE MANDATES FOR CHARACTER EDUCATION PROGRAMS

State	Mandates	Have Objectives	State	Mandates	Have Objectives
Alabama	No	Yes	Montana	No	*
Alaska	No	*	Nebraska	Yes	No
Arizona	No	Yes	Nevada	Yes	No
Arkansas	Yes	No	New Hamp.	No	No
California	Yes	Yes	New Jersey	No	Yes
Colorado	No	No	New Mexico	No	No
Connecticut	No	Yes	New York	Yes	No
Delaware	No	No	No. Carolina	Yes	No
Florida	No	No	No. Dakota	Yes	No
Georgia	No	Yes	Oklahoma	No	Yes
Hawaii	No	No	Ohio	Yes	Yes
Idaho	No	No	Oregon	Yes	No
Illinois	Yes	No	Pennsylvania	No	No
Indiana	Yes	No	Rhode Island	Yes	*
Iowa	Yes	No	So. Carolina	Yes	No
Kansas	No	No	So. Dakota	Yes	No
Kentucky	Yes	Yes	Tennessee	No	No
Louisiana	No	No	Texas	No	No
Maine	Yes	No	Utah	Yes	Yes
Maryland	No	Yes	Vermont	Yes	*
Mass.	Yes	Yes	Virginia	Yes	No
Michigan	Yes	*	Washington	No	No
Minnesota	Yes	Yes	W. Virginia	Yes	No
Mississippi	No	No	Wisconsin	Yes	No
Missouri	No	No	Wyoming	No	No

*Did not reply   Source: Jensen and Passey, p. 31.

TABLE 2

CLASSIFICATION OF STATE CHARACTER EDUCATION CURRICULA

Has specific objectives in moral education	No specific moral education objectives	Objectives in social studies curriculum materials	Moral education objectives are determined by district
Alabama	Arkansas	California	Florida
Arizona	Colorado	Idaho	Indiana
Connecticut	Delaware	Illinois	Maine
Georgia	Hawaii	Iowa	Pennsylvania
Kentucky	Kansas	Louisiana	South Carolina
Maryland	Mississippi	Nevada	South Dakota
Massachusetts	Missouri	North Carolina	
Minnesota	Nebraska	Texas	
New Jersey	New Hamp.	Virginia	
Ohio	New Mexico	Washington	
Oklahoma	New York	West Virginia	
Utah	North Dakota	Wisconsin	
	Oregon		
	Tennessee		
	Wyoming		

Source: Jensen and Passey, p. 30.

Table 2 reveals the extent of current usage of character education curricula among the states. While 12 states have specific objectives in character education, another 12 states address character education by incorporating it as part of their social studies curricula. A study conducted by G. R. Johnson and a subsequent study by Larry Jansen and Holly Passey demonstrate that state mandates for character education have frequently been ignored. In states that conduct moral education, it frequently appears to be dictated by the "secular scholarship of the academic community...(who) have ignored the content or context of state constitutional or statutory law and followed the directives of national organizations."[30]

During the past few years, a number of states have gathered information and conducted hearings on the possibility of implementing statewide character education programs. Examples of such states are Arizona and

Kentucky. In fact, Kentucky's state government is in the process of gathering community opinion about how to proceed with the revamping of its efforts.

Meanwhile, two states, Florida and Nebraska, recently had their state legislatures vote down proposed statewide character education programs. These two states will reconsider these programs after additional refinement and amendment.

GEORGIA'S CHARACTER EDUCATION PROGRAM

In order to better understand statewide character education programs, it is useful to scrutinize one of these programs and how it functions. A good example can be found in Georgia.

In March 1991 the Georgia State Board of Education adopted Rule 160-4-2-.33. This rule required all local school districts in Georgia to provide educational opportunities in certain value concepts to all students, grades K-12. The rule was intended to extend existing values-oriented activities in Georgia while concurrently implementing the board's new program.

Georgia's requirements presented in the rule are as follows:

> 1. The local school board shall provide instruction, grades K-12, which addresses the core values concept adopted by the State Board of Education.
> 2. The local school system shall provide opportunities for practicing these values.
> 3. The local school system shall develop a plan for implementing values education, including materials and strategies to be used.

Three years of work were invested in developing the core values list. This research ranged from an extensive data search to community input gained at seven regional public hearings. Georgia's list of core values for its statewide character education program was adopted in March 1991. This list appears in Table 3.

TABLE 3
GEORGIA'S LIST OF CORE VALUES

Citizenship

Democracy: government of, by, and for the people, exercised through the voting process.
• Respect for and acceptance of authority: the need for and the primacy of authority, including the law, in given circumstances.
• Equality: the right and opportunity to develop one's potential as a human being.
• Freedom of conscience and expression: the right to hold beliefs, whether religious, ethical, or political, and to express one's views.
• Justice: equal and impartial treatment under the law.
• Liberty: freedom from oppression, tyranny, or the domination of government.
• Tolerance: recognition of the diversity of others, their opinions, practices, and culture.

Patriotism: support of and love for the United States of America with zealous guarding of its welfare.
• Courage: willingness to face obstacles and danger with determination.
• Loyalty: steadfastness or faithfulness to a person, institution, custom, or ideas to which one is tied by duty, pledge or a promise.

Respect for the Natural Environment: care for and conservation of land, trees, clean air, and pure water and of all living inhabitants of the earth.
• Conservation: avoiding waste and pollution of natural resources.

Respect for Others

Altruism: concern for and motivation to act for the welfare of others.
• Civility: courtesy and politeness in action or speech.
• Compassion: concern for suffering or distress of others and response to their feelings and needs.
• Courtesy: recognition of mutual interdependence with others resulting in polite treatment and respect for others.

Integrity: confirmed virtue and uprightness of character; freedom from hypocrisy.
• Honesty: truthfulness and sincerity.
• Truth: freedom from deceit or falseness: based on fact or reality.
• Trustworthiness: worthy of confidence.

Respect for Self

Acceptability: responsibility for one's actions and their consequences.
* Commitment: being emotionally, physically or intellectually bound to something.
* Perseverance: adherence to action, belief, or purpose without giving way.
* Self control: exercising authority over one's emotions and actions.
* Frugality: effective use of resources; thrift.

Self-Esteem: pride and belief in oneself and in achievement of one's potential.
* Knowledge: learning, understanding, awareness.
* Moderation: avoidance of extreme views or measures.
* Respect for physical, mental, and fiscal health: awareness of the importance and   of conscious activity toward maintaining fitness in these areas.

Work-Ethic: belief that work is good and that everyone who can, should work.
* Accomplishment: appreciation for completing a task.
* Cooperation: working with others for mutual benefit.
* Dependence: reliability; trustworthiness.
* Diligence: attentiveness; persistence; perseverance.
* Pride: dignity; self-respect; doing one's best.
* Productivity: supporting one's self; contributing to society.
* Creativity: exhibiting an entrepreneurial spirit; inventiveness; originality; not bound by the norm.

Source: *Georgia Values Education Implementation Guide*

How to provide value education in Georgia is a local decision. This includes the decision as to whether value education will be infused into the curriculum or be a stand-alone activity.

The state, however, has not left the school districts without any resources to implement the programs. Various program formats were suggested by the state, not only for instruction values, but also how to practice values through various activities. These activities can range from role-playing to community service.

The state also provided a list of commercially available resources on character education. These resources dealt with specific topics in the area of character education as well as staff development.

Although Georgia's state government provided no direct funding for its character education program, it gave local school districts a list of strategies to locate funds. These strategies included suggested arrangements with private industry and civic organizations that would fund various portions of the character education program. Georgia also proceeded to allocate additional state and federal grant funds to the school districts for different facets of the character education effort, such as staff development and sex and drug education.

Finally, a major advantage of Georgia's program is the provision for an evaluation of its progress. The Georgia Department of Education stresses that for a character education program to succeed, evaluation at the local level—the school district level—must be continuous and comprehensive.

NEW HAMPSHIRE'S APPROACH

The state of New Hampshire has recently initiated an indirect approach to character education for its students. Rather than implementing a statewide program in state classrooms for its students, New Hampshire has established a values program for its teachers.

This indirect approach was the result of the adoption of a new state rule, which became effective on 1 July 1993, that required educators who desire recertification to complete five clock hours of instruction in character and citizenship education. These clock hours are included in the total 50 hours of professional development that must be accumulated every three years to maintain certification.

In 1992 the New Hampshire Department of Education convened an advisory group to provide technical assistance in meeting this rule. Members of this group were not only drawn from the department, but they were also drawn from the ranks of staff development chairpersons from rural, urban, and suburban school districts; the teacher unions (AFT and NEA); the New Hampshire Principals Association; the New Hampshire School Administrators Association; as well as the New Hampshire Teachers' Academy for Character and Citizenship Education. This group proceeded to develop guidelines and a program to assist school districts in monitoring the new rule. The program developed by the advisory group now includes 67 separate staff development committees that exchange ideas, 32 regional workshop centers, and liaisons with national character education organizations.

Even though New Hampshire has not established a statewide character education program for its students, the state has recognized the paramount importance of ensuring that the state's teachers should be knowledgeable about and well grounded in character education before the state could conduct an effective program. At this time, it is uncertain whether New Hampshire will proceed to the next steps in developing a statewide character education program for its students. Not only would a detailed program with goals and timetables need to be developed, but the state would also need to obtain input from the general public. Such a step might provide additional information or perspective to improve the program as well as building public support for it.

CONCLUSION

Some states, such as Georgia, have comprehensive character education programs operational. Other states, such as New York, have only a policy statement of support. The range of programs does show that character education is being revived in America.

It is too early to report what effect character education programs will have on the morals of the students. What is known is that if a character education program is to be successful, certain program characteristics must be present:

1. Development of ongoing in-service training for all personnel in the district, from administrators to teachers.
2. Reliable information on what the community really wants and expects from the program.
3. An alliance between the community, the school, and the state.
4. Use of a public forum to educate the public about policies and procedures.
5. Sensitivity to differing opinions within the community, ensuring that a balance of all views are taken into account on every decision.
6. Development of clearly written policies supporting programs and curricula, for selecting material, and providing guidance for the implementation of the program.

Many state leaders have assumed that character education is of fundamental importance. It can be expected that as social pathologies increase among our youth other states will implement similar programs. Communities and local school boards can help in the effort to initiate plans at the state level by implementing programs of their own as examples for state authorities.

The problems confronting the youth of America need to be addressed. Character education can be a part of the solution. Jeremiah's admonition on character development remains a valuable lesson today, "Ask for the old paths and see where is the good way, and walk in it and find rest for your souls."[31]

NOTES

1. Denis P. Doyle, "Education and Values: Study, Practice, Example," in Charles E. Greenawalt, II, ed., *Educational Innovation: An Agenda to Frame the Future* (Lanham, MD: University Press of America and The Commonwealth Foundation, 1994), 2.

2. Kristen J. Amundson, *Teaching Values and Ethics* (Arlington, VA: American Association of School Administrators, 1991), 31.

3. William J. Bennett, *The De-Valuing of America: The Fight for Our Culture and Our Children* (New York: Summit Books, 1992), 57.

4. Richard H. Herold, *Report of the Advisory Council on Developing Character and Values in New Jersey Students* (Trenton, NJ: State Department of Education, March 1989), 1.

5. Benjamin M. Spock, *A Better World for Our Children: Rebuilding American Family Values* (Bethesda, MD: National Press Books, 1994), 131.

6. *Ethics, Values, Attitudes and Behavior in American Schools* (Marina del Ray, CA: Josephson Institute of Ethics, 1992), 65-69.

7. "For many, 'situation ethics' are replacing moral absolutes," *Washington Times,* 4 April 1992, 34.

8. William Raspberry, "Ethics Without Virtue," *Washington Post,* 6 December 1991, A23.

9. Barbara Kantrowitz, "Wild in the Streets," *Newsweek,* 2 August 1993, 43.

10. Michael Gartner, "Youth Crime: Ban Guns, Crack Down on Alcohol," *USA Today,* 13 December 1994.

11. Amundson, *Teaching Values,* 17.

12. Amundson, *Teaching Values,* 17.

13. Amundson, *Teaching Values,* 18.

14. Amundson, *Teaching Values,* 18.

15. Amundson, *Teaching Values,* 18.

16. Amundson, *Teaching Values,* 18.

17. Edward A. Wynne, "The Great Tradition in Education: Transmitting Moral Values," *Educational Leadership,* December 1985/January 1986, 8.

18. Wynne, "Great Tradition."

19. Kevin Ryan and Edward Wynne, "Curriculum as a Moral Educator," *American Educator,* Spring 1993, 21.

20. Thomas Lickona, *Educating for Character: How Our Schools Can Teach Respect and Responsibility* (New York: Bantam Books, 1991), 19.

21. "Teaching Asia to Stay Asian," *The Economist,* 8 October 1994, 39.

22. "Asian Values," *The Economist,* 28 May 1994, 13.

23. *The Economist,* 8 October 1994, 39.

24. *The Economist,* 8 October 1994, 39.

25. Jean Johnson and John Immerwahr, "First Things First: What Americans Expect from the Public Schools" (New York: Public Agenda, 1994), 23.

26.   Johnson and Immerwahr, "First Things First," 24.

27.   Larry Jensen and Holly Passey, "Moral Education Curricula in the Public Schools," *Religion & Public Education* 1, 2, 3 (1993): 28.

28.   D. Coats, "America's Youth: A Crisis of Character," *Imprimis* 9 (1991): 1.

29.   Jensen and Passey, "Moral Education," 28.

30.   G. R. Johnson, "Curriculum Objectives of States That Do and Do Not Mandate Moral Education" (Unpublished doctoral dissertation, Brigham Young University, Provo, Utah, 1990).

31.   *The Bible* (RSV), Jeremiah 6:16.

Chapter 13

Making It Happen: A Conversation About Character

William J. Moloney

30 OCTOBER 1994: CAPITOL CITY (WGER-TV)

Cromer: Good morning, I'm Marilyn Cromer, host of "Capitol Conversation," and today our guest is Dr. Catherine Brooks, candidate for State Superintendent of Schools.

Dr. Brooks, when you received your party's nomination four months ago, you were a virtual unknown and widely viewed as a sacrificial lamb contesting a public office held by the opposition since it was first established in 1940. Your opponent enjoys a two-to-one registration edge, has outspent you 10 to one, and has refused to debate. Despite this, the latest polls rate the contest "too close to call" and show that many regard this as the most important race in the state. Though other issues have come up, you've essentially got the public's attention by talking about just one, what you call "character education."

How do you explain what the press is calling the "Brooks Phenomena"?

Brooks: The phenomenon isn't me, Marilyn, but rather character education itself. It's a message powerful enough to overcome registration, money, and even history, and maybe just powerful enough to win this election.

Cromer: Last week your opponent described you as "out of touch with reality, unable to understand the complexity of today's educational problems, simplistic if not simple-minded; a candidate from yesterday who would do great harm to the children of tomorrow." Do you have an answer for all of that?

Brooks: Well, yes, like character education, I do have roots in the past, but this message is not only timely for the present but absolutely essential for the future. Without character education, all our children's tomorrows will be poorer in every way.

Cromer: But, Dr. Brooks, just what is character education?

1 November 1994: CHICAGO (METROPOLITAN RADIO NETWORK)

"Good morning, this is Don Henry with The Untold Story. Well, it seems that the race for the usually obscure office of state superintendent in a nearby state is grabbing national attention. Some say this year's elections are about culture or values. In this particular election, it appears to be about something called 'character education.' Many listeners have asked what that is, so here's the way it looks from here.

"It seems that educational research has discovered hard work or what grandmother used to call old-fashioned 'elbow grease.'

"Since the widely read *Education Week* featured a story entitled 'Studies Link Student Achievement to Protestant Work Ethic,' there has been a considerable spate of articles both in research and in general educational journals revolving around what is most commonly called 'character education.'

"What character education boils down to is the suggestion that there is a 'curriculum' in the schools that hasn't got a lot of attention in recent years but which is probably more important than a lot of those curriculums that have gotten attention.

"Essentially the curriculum of character education revolves around work habits and personal values (of a nonreligious nature). It places a premium on such diverse characteristics as good attendance, punctuality, persistent application, and particularly hard work. In personal relations it teaches self-control, self-reliance, the healthy aspects of competition, and respect for other people and other views. It also values family, community, good citizenship, and the need to help the less fortunate.

"In short, it seeks to instill or build character.

"The interest in character education has been heightened further by another increasingly visible phenomenon in the professional literature, and this is the pattern of extraordinary academic success being seen among Asian-American students, particularly those who are relatively new to our shores.

"Last year, Asian-Americans won all five of the top prizes in the Westinghouse Talent Search, the most prestigious science award available to American high school students.

"Further evidence of this success is the tremendous surge in Asian-American enrollment at our country's top universities. Though they represent only a little over two percent of the general population, Asian-Americans constituted 11 percent of last year's freshman class at Harvard, 21 percent at the Massachusetts Institute of Technology, and at California's Berkeley campus, nearly 30 percent.

"As awareness of the phenomenon has spread, there has naturally arisen the question, 'How do they do it?'

"One reply is that of Dr. Sanford M. Dorbusch, a Stanford professor of sociology and education who says, 'My bottom line is, there's no question these Asians are working a heck of a lot harder.' Having studied Asian-American schooling extensively, Dorbusch sees a 'powerhouse statistic in effort,' a conclusion echoed by several other studies.

"Thomas Sowell, an economist who has also written extensively on this topic, states that 'It's an old-fashioned story. If you work hard, you do well.' Very simply, he says, 'Work works.'

"The problem with the curriculum of character education is that no one in the schools quite knows where to put it. You can't quite make it into a separate course, though from time to time some people try. It can be everywhere, or it may be nowhere. We do know that the best teachers somehow incorporate much of it into whatever subject they may be teaching.

"The overheated rhetoric surrounding education and religion has made many school people wary of anything related to values. This is truly a misfortune because schools without values are poor schools indeed.

"For some educators, the astonishing work ethic of Asian-Americans or others like them is simply a societal factor that has nothing to do with school. It is simply there. Similarly, they tend to throw up their hands in the face of negative societal factors such as broken families, or weakened support systems generally.

"Such fatalistic attitudes are wrong because they devalue the worth of the school experience; they implicitly suggest that you've either got it, or you haven't, and if you haven't, don't expect schooling to make much difference.

"There is a growing body of research on effective schools that shows that the quality of a school does matter; that in particular schools with a positive ethos, emphasizing a strong work ethic and other character issues can, in fact, go far in overcoming negative influences active in other parts of the child's life.

"Another nice thing about character education is that, compared to most other curriculums, it is fairly inexpensive to implement. Mainly it takes some hard work, and, well yes, some character.

"And that's today's Untold Story."

9 DECEMBER 1994: WASHINGTON-NATIONAL PRESS CLUB (C-Span)

Fairlie: Good afternoon, I'm Irwin Fairlie. Welcome to the National Press Club luncheon. Today our topic is "American Public Education: Where We Go From Here." Our speaker is Dr. Catherine Brooks, one of the most remarkable candidates in this remarkable election year. Dr. Brooks went from political novice seeking an office her party rarely even contests to not just an upset win but a landslide. Before her election as her state's chief school officer, Dr. Brooks had been registered as an independent voter and even now refers to herself as a "partisan nonpartisan." Amazingly, exit polls showed she drew supporters almost equally from Democrats and Republicans.

By background, Dr. Brooks is a family physician and the author of four well-received books on medical history. Long active in her local and state PTA, it was concern about the education of her own three children that led her to launch a grassroots campaign revolving around the issue of "character education," a subject her victory last month has helped place on the national agenda. Welcome, Dr. Brooks.

Brooks: Thank you, Mr. Fairlie. In order to see where American public education needs to go from here, we must first look back on where it has been and what caused the problems it now faces.

The fact of America's educational decline is well known, but the nature and causes of this decline are not well known.

Though educational finance is a serious problem, it is not central to decline, *but* many see dollars as paramount and look no further. Our decline is structural in nature and best understood by comparing U.S. and foreign schools in a historical context.

American schools were long the world's best and also the most democratic. Education reached a larger proportion of the population than in any other nation, and we were the first to open higher education to other than the sons of rich men.

The bedrock strength of American education rested on the twin pillars of church and family. Following Jeffersonian precepts, government and social policy had little to do with our success.

Church and family provided a remarkable cohesiveness to this continent-wide educational enterprise. Education was basic, and the stuff of education was basics. We had a de facto national curriculum in that everybody read the same two books—the *Holy Bible* and *McGuffey's Reader*.

In other nations education was limited in scope and elitist in nature.

America gave the world its first mass democracy, and its principal handmaiden was education for the masses.

All of this, however, would change dramatically in the aftermath of World War II.

In 1945 came the dazzling zenith of American political, economic, and educational systems. The rest of the world—enemy and ally alike—lay in varying degrees of ruin and rubble, their social, economic, educational, and political systems beaten into barely recognizable fragments.

For these nations, the imperative of a new beginning was self-evident, and there was no doubt that the model for almost all postwar standards was the United States.

America, on the other hand, would enjoy more than a generation of unparalleled abundance and domination.

This period of remarkable ascendancy, however, had within it the seeds of decay. Just as the rest of the world was emulating the U.S. educational system as the key to democracy and economic success, that system was beginning to unravel in America.

For the longest time, America had educated for content. The three Rs provided the tools, but the substance of our system was content designed to ensure the transmission of the cultural heritage.

The core of the school's mission was moral education. After all, schools had emerged from the churches and even when American public education became a secular enterprise, morality remained a pervasive force.

Influenced by John Dewey and other progressives, the mainstream of American education began to move out of the era of content and into an era of "skills." The new ethos was called "life adjustment," and it rested on some very questionable and at best patronizing assumptions.

With the mass of students now aspiring to complete high school, it was felt that content or serious academic endeavor was beyond most of them, so a new softer curriculum was introduced, one which would help the less talented to accept their place in society (i.e., life adjustment).

The fundamental strength of American society and the great power of our expanding economy concealed these trends and for a time insulated us from their consequences.

In the tumultuous decade of the 1960s, the moral, economic, and political assumptions underpinning our educational system began to come apart at the same time.

In the 1970s and 1980s, America awoke to find that something terrible had happened to our schools. For nearly a generation now, we have been arguing about what did happen, who was responsible, and what we should do about it.

The curriculum of content had disappeared from all but a handful of our schools. What some called "cultural literacy" was a thing of the past.

The curriculum of skills was firmly in place, but, alas, we discovered the level of these skills was woefully inadequate when compared to our now resurgent international competitors.

Devoid of content, purveyors of inadequate skills, our schools even more alarmingly had become moral vacuums. In the grip of misguided legal doctrines and secular zealotry, we drove all vestiges of prayer and religion from our schools. With our educators trembling at the mention of the word values, we suddenly found ourselves the only nation in the Western world that did not provide and support religious studies or moral education in the curriculum of its public schools.

The collapse of discipline, the work ethic, and achievement levels could only be seen as natural consequence of these self-inflicted wounds.

At the same time these lethal trends were wreaking havoc in our schools, a parallel process of deconstruction was occurring in our society.

These events can only be called a tragedy of good intentions gone awry.

Though most social indicators relating to education and the family (e.g., drop out and illegitimacy rates) had been steadily improving since World War II, our nation nonetheless launched a vast campaign of social transformation led by the federal government that rested on the assumption that society was in great trouble and that only massive state intervention could put things right.

These series of initiatives, based upon the kind of social science exemplified by Michael Harrington's *The Other America* and Jonathan Kozol's *Death at an Early Age* came to be epitomized by what Lyndon Johnson called "The Great Society." Declaring a "war on poverty" and any other identifiable negative social indicator, the Great Society's programs would over the course of a quarter of a century have a transformational effect on America.

Unfortunately it was not the kind of transformation that had been envisioned by the decent and well-intentioned people who created and supported these programs.

Instead of getting better, things got worse. In particular the American family and the American system of public education would become victims of the very programs that had sought their betterment.

The fallacious assumption that families and schools were in such deep trouble that they required massive intervention became perversely self-fulfilling prophecies.

This process of deconstruction evolved in two distinct and mutually reinforcing stages.

The first related to expanding welfare policies which were anti-family in general and anti-father in particular.

These policies encouraged and rewarded broken family structure and illegitimacy. At the same time they penalized marriage and responsible fatherhood.

The second stage unfolded as both families and schools began to reel from the consequences of the increasingly evident failure of these social policies.

Rather than admit the failure of these policies and acknowledge the growing social pathology attached to them, the advocates concluded instead that society's problem was not "bad medicine" but rather insufficient quantities of it being administered. The constantly heard cry was our need for more programs and more money. Like the mythological general who announced the "beatings will continue until morale improves," the advocates of social intervention blamed the victim.

Central to this doctrine of "renewed effort" was that our schools must become engines of social policy. Thus began the lamentable trend toward converting schools from places of learning to all-purpose centers for "human service."

The theoretical underpinning of this movement rested upon a dangerous distrust of families. The logic was that if families weren't meeting their responsibilities then someone—i.e., the government—must do it for them.

As government policy continued to undermine the family, the situation in the schools deteriorated accordingly and nowhere more so than in our great urban centers where nearly a third of our children were to be found.

As schools lurched into a social mission for which they were sadly ill-equipped, the emphasis on their original responsibility for education and training declined.

This transformation is well illustrated by the steadily shrinking proportion of dollars and personnel invested in the classroom. Increasingly schools were staffed by nonteaching personnel whose generic purpose was to "fix" social, medical, or psychological problems.

By the 1980s, schools that had left behind the age of content and failed in an age of skills were now entering an era where the dominant reality was "school climate."

This was occurring because schools were becoming at best places of drift and unfocused purpose and at worst places of outright danger.

As the Gallup Poll on public attitudes toward education has shown every year since 1969, our people see discipline as the single greatest problem. As usual, the people and their often mocked perceptions are way ahead of the politicians and the "educrats."

At the center of this syndrome of indiscipline that affects all of our schools by varying degree is a striking decline in the educational condition of boys. From achievement rates to suspension rates, boys are clearly the big losers in today's education marketplace. Research shows consistently that these deficiencies are connected very directly to broken families in general and to father absence in particular.

Historically a central role of fatherhood has been as the guarantor of structure and positive behavior on the part of children, most particularly boys. Today, through well-intended but unknowing policy, we have seriously undermined the role of fathers in our society and in our schools.

I would summarize the connection between father absence and education decline as follows:

In every other industrial democracy in the world, public education specifically acknowledges, affirms, and supports parental empowerment in the choice of schools, the place of religious studies in the curriculum, the primacy of the family, the sanctity of marriage, and the indispensable role of parents in general and of fathers in particular.

In the United States of America public education does none of those things.

Other nations did not get where they are by accident. Their recognition of the family and the moral dimensions of education were only arrived at after centuries of bloodshed that revolved around these very issues. Out of the pain and disorder of this experience, they have found their way to enlightened social and educational policy.

The United States on the other hand was, in a relative sense, spared the trauma of the Old World.

The American experience was comparatively a remarkable, even unique, journey in which there was consensus around these volatile issues. In the absence of law and policy, American cultural cohesiveness supported consensus.

We are now at a point in our history where extended conflicts over these issues demand a new approach in both schools and society. It must be an approach that unites rather than divides and which the great mass of our people will view as affirming rather than alienating.

The restoration of family and fatherhood is an indispensable element for restoration of our schools.

The good news is that we are fully capable of doing this. We know what is wrong. We know what works; we need but summon the will to do it. Other nations have done this and so can we. It should be sufficient incentive that the stakes are nothing less than the future of our country and our children.

Fairlie: Thank you, Dr. Brooks, for these very thoughtful remarks. Owing to constraints of time, I'm going to bundle all of the questions passed forward into a single query: Does America have the time, the will, and the resources to fix all of these problems; and, in particular, are there people out there ready to create what, in your campaign, you called "schools of character"?

Brooks: Yes, Mr. Fairlie, there are—not just in my state but all across America. However long it takes, that's how much time we'll give it. No matter how great the challenge, the will of our people has always risen to meet it. And as for resources, yes, we have those, too. But remember, our most important resource is not material.

23 JANUARY 1995: BALTIMORE (WBAC-TV)

Arliss: Good morning, I'm George Arliss, host of "Schools Today," and our guest is Dr. William Moloney, superintendent of schools in Calvert County, Maryland., and a member of the governing board of the National Assessment of Educational Progress. He's here today to talk about what his district has called the New American Schools Project.

Dr. Moloney, according to what we've read, your district is making a "public offering" of some brand-new schools that you called "schools of character." One press account described them as "world-class schools unlike any others in America." That sounds pretty ambitious. What are you folks up to down there?

Moloney: We are the fastest-growing school district in Maryland. Of necessity we have to open some new schools. It occurred to us to ask why not make them the best schools in the world. Everyone talks about world-class schools, but often they have little idea of what that means. We decided to find out and then go ahead and create them.

We had extensive conversations with teachers, parents, businesspeople, and others. We had had a number of our teachers visit in other nations on Fulbrights, notably Japan. We asked those teachers: "What did you see and what can you imagine being usefully transplanted here?"

We have a sister school in Holland that also brought us useful ideas. I myself spent five years as an American educator in Europe and had an opportunity to see firsthand the schools in those nations that are today our economic competitors.

As these ideas expanded, we talked to focus groups, students, parents, and various community groups, and on the basis of all of this we are now making "public offering" of what these new schools can be like. In form they will be special "charter schools; and, yes, they will revolve around character education.

Arliss: What makes these unlike any schools in America?

Moloney: Well, there are over 100,000 schools in America, and we didn't look at them all, but I can assuredly tell you these will be unlike any other public schools and most private schools that any of us have heard of.

At this point our planning calls for these schools to have four basic characteristics. I should also note that the initial schools are elementary schools. Our plans for new secondary schools—a high school in 1996—are not as far advanced.

First, these elementary schools will pursue the core knowledge curriculum that has been the brainchild of E. D. Hirsch, the author of *Cultural Literacy.* We are already piloting that in one elementary school, and it has been very successful. This curriculum essentially says that all Americans must share a certain body of knowledge regarding the basis of our culture, our society, and most importantly, our democratic institutions.

Second, the school program will be divided into an academic day and a nonacademic day. Academics come first. In doing this we are following prescriptions of the recent report of the National Commission on Time and Learning, "Prisoners of Time." This also represents near universal practice in all other industrial nations.

We have too many kids who can't read starting the day with gym. That's over.

The third element, and one of particular power, is the notion of multi-year student-teacher relationships. One of the most counterproductive and destabilizing things we do to children is to make them change teachers every year. The shuffle, the impersonality, and the lack of commitment that results exact a very heavy price. Again we are virtually the only nation in the world that follows this odd practice.

The fourth and final item—the most important one—is to establish a school climate based on effective school principles of clear mission, high expectations, strong leadership, and strong discipline. In effect we want schools "suffused with character."

Arliss: "Suffused with character"—I like that. What does it mean?

Moloney: First think of what the real mission of schools should be. If reduced to two words, the school's central purpose is to "induce work." All children can learn because all children can work. No learning occurs without work, and no work occurs without learning. The best teachers can't learn for a student. The student must be active, engaged, motivated, and committed.

Now what is the thing that more than anything else is wrong with schools today? We polled our teachers and asked them what is the number one problem. The overwhelming answer was the "breakdown of the student work ethic." Teachers cannot rely upon students to do what they are supposed to be doing, be that homework or anything else. Our people know this. Since 1969, the Gallup Poll of Public Attitudes Toward the Public Schools every year has shown discipline to be the number one problem in the schools. Discipline shouldn't be seen narrowly as simply behavior. Most basically, it is about the work ethic.

Schools suffused with character are based on this strategy: restore the student work ethic and you will restore learning achievement and values as well.

It was for that reason the first step taken by our board of education in its campaign for reform was to adopt WORK, DISCIPLINE, AND

VALUES as the unifying themes of our entire school district.

Arliss: Talk about uniforms for public school kids. That does grab people's attention. Why uniforms? Couldn't you do all this without uniforms?

Moloney: Yes, but with uniforms it is much better. They do grab people's attention because they are powerful symbols. They stand for excellence and equity, the twin pillars of any good school.

Clothes have become a distraction in public schools. Teachers across the country tell endless stories of how clothes connect to theft, jealousy, painful contrast between rich and poor students, and in urban areas the calling cards of neighborhood gangs.

Uniforms on the other hand bespeak pride and also connect the children's minds to professionals who are excellent role models—nurses, firefighters, policemen, soldiers, athletes, etc. Uniforms also build community, school spirit, teamwork, and real pride as opposed to that cheapened variety we call "self-esteem."

Arliss: But isn't self-esteem important? Isn't the educational literature always talking about it?

Moloney: Yes, and the educational literature is wrong. Wrong about what kids want and need and wrong about what makes schools effective.

In a recent international math competition, American students ranked first in only one category: feeling good about their math abilities. They rank last in everything else. Whereas the Koreans who finished first in achievement, finished last in feeling good about their math abilities. Obviously we have the wrong kind of self-esteem and need to change that.

Arliss: Will kids buy into this?

Moloney: Absolutely, all of my experience validates this, and the best teachers and coaches prove it everyday.

Arliss: Coaches? Where do they come into this?

Moloney: Performance areas—most notably athletics, but music also—provide powerful lessons about what we need to do to transform entire schools. Often these areas are the only ones in which we really find those effective school characteristics of purpose, expectation, leadership, and discipline. I have always been impressed by two of the nine principles of Ted Sizer's essential schools: the student as worker and the teacher as coach.

Arliss: Will the school program be the same as other elementary schools?

Moloney: Most subject elements will be the same, but the organization will be different and there will be different points of emphasis. Every day will begin with an all-school convocation. This will involve morning exercises, which include the Pledge of Allegiance and patriotic songs such as "God Bless America," and members of the community can take part in the convocation. Community members—including firefighters, policemen, nurses, clergy, and doctors—can talk about their work, about values, family, and responsibilities.

The purpose of this is to not just instill character but to make values, particularly virtue, central to every child's education. As part of an effort to convey the dignity of work and responsibility, students and groups of students will be recognized for achievement.

The formal academic day always begins with reading, then math, and goes on to other academic subjects. Following the model of schools in other nations, the academic day will be shorter but more intense. There will be recess after every class and a full hour for lunch.

Nonacademic subjects, like art and music, will be in the afternoon. There will be no gym classes per se, but rather a comprehensive program of exercise, physical fitness, and sports that will be scheduled as appropriate. Counselors will not exist as a specialty area, but rather every teacher who spends several years with a child will be a counselor. Teachers will have administrative responsibilities when that is appropriate, and all administrators will teach—again following best practice in world-class schools.

Like other nations, we will not have letter grades for these young children, but regular progress reports to parents giving a balanced discussion of academic growth and character formation.

As an option, we will offer an extended day before and after school where supervised reading, study, and/or play will be available. Optional Saturday and summer activities will also be available.

Also children will have a responsibility for the upkeep of the schools. They won't replace maintenance people, but every single child will have a responsibility to do some task to help them. Once every month or so, everyone from the principal on down will come to school in their oldest clothes and spend the day scrubbing and making the place shine.

Arliss: Won't these extras be expensive?

Moloney: No. These schools will be very cost-effective, in fact marginally less expensive than regular schools even though they will be better and in session more. Parents, volunteers, and para-professionals will play a key role in extended-day activities. Parents, individually or using car pools, will be responsible for extended-day transportation.

Arliss: What has been parent response to date?

Moloney: It has been overwhelmingly positive. In part, parents have responded to the fact that children in these schools will mirror the population of our county. These are schools for all children, not schools for the academic elite. If anything they will serve better the less academic child, including special education.

The positive parental response is not surprising. Polls have consistently shown that this is what parents want—the basics: safety, discipline, well-behaved kids, values, patriotism, a strong academic foundation, responsible staff who know their children, and an environment suffused with values. This program provides that.

Arliss: Last week Dr. Catherine Brooks spoke to the Baltimore City Council on character education. Do you know her?

Moloney: No. Before the election I had never heard of her, but what I have heard I've admired. Today such people and such programs are coming forward all across the country. If not there, then here: if not here, then somewhere.

You see, character education never went away. It is just that our sense of it became clouded and confused. Character education has been a fundamental of schooling for as long as there has been education, as long as societies have been raising children. It is not an extra, but an essential. Without it societies cannot endure and still call themselves civilized. Character goes to the heart of what it means to be human.

We are now reawakened to what is required for the future of our children and our country. Perhaps our return to character education is best put by the old hymn "Amazing Grace."

"Once we were lost, but now are found,
Once we were blind, but now can see."

IV. Character Applied

Chapter 14

Strengthening Character Through Community-Based Organizations

B. David Brooks

INTRODUCTION

Historically the teaching of character and values has been shared by various members of a community. Parents and family had the primary role in shaping values and character. In addition, the community at large—store owners, community organizations, churches, synagogues, and neighbors—supported the efforts of families to teach children right from wrong. Possibly more influential than the community at large was the school. Public education, from its onset, had two major responsibilities: the first, to teach children to be smart; the second, to teach them to be good.

A fourth and often overlooked element of society responsible for the acquisition of values and character, the individual had to take responsibility for his or her behavior. The family, the community, and the school taught the language, attitudes, and skills of good character. However, the individual was responsible for acquiring and practicing these skills. The development of good character came about by practice. The family, community, or school could not be held totally responsible for the character of individuals in society. The individual had partial responsibility for good character or lack thereof.

HISTORY OF CHARACTER-BUILDING INSTITUTIONS

Until World War II there was an obvious connection between the four elements in society responsible for passing values and character on to the next generation. However, people, especially Americans, became more mobile and as neighborhoods became less cohesive the influences that historically helped shape character in individuals became weakened.

During the tumultuous decades of the 1960s, 1970s, and 1980s the influence of families and community was further eroded. Added to this erosion was the powerful, and often negative, influence of the media, especially television. It became increasingly clear that there had occurred a dynamic shift toward "doing my own thing." As a result, the thoughts of social consequences were forgotten.

Citizens now began to see life and choices from a different viewpoint. The neighborhood view became a world view. No longer were war, crime, and bloodshed left to the imagination. Individuals saw the killing of a soldier in Vietnam. People viewed graphic TV scenes of gang killings, and children sang the lyrics of songs that glorified violence and immediate personal fulfillment. The emergence of graphic depictions of violence, the making of wrongdoers into heroes, and the introduction of the idea that people are generally victims of influences beyond their control increased the move from personal responsibility and good character to a society who "did their own thing," blamed others for their failures, and lost the sense of community so vital in the handing down of core values from one generation to the next.

In spite of what is perceived as a general shift away from teaching, supporting, and reinforcing good character today there remains a set of citizens who believe strongly that character can and should be taught, that children can learn to "be good," and that society, in general, believes that there is a common core of values that all diverse elements of the society can agree upon.

While it may at times seem outdated, the ancient African saying "It takes an entire village to raise a child" is still the belief of the majority. It may be true that there is still some confusion and debate related to the strategies for teaching or developing character among the young. Nonetheless, it is increasingly clear there must be a refocusing in this area if the trends of the past 30 years are to be reversed. Along with this awareness is an emerging consciousness that one segment of the community, the family, for example, cannot do it alone.

Accompanying the gradual awakening of the need to rethink the manner in which character values are transmitted from one generation to the next are problems that still exist and include debates as to who ultimately is responsible for the transmitting of values. Some say it is the responsibility of the family and the family alone. Others see the family and the church/synagogue joined in a cooperative effort and insist that the school should teach academics and stay out of the character business. On the other hand, there are those who see the change in the family and failure of many community institutions, including the faith community, as indicators that the schools must take a greater, if not the leading role in the instilling of consensus values.

While it is true that these discussions have raged for many years, there is a growing consensus that the exclusion of one or more segments of society from the process of teaching and instilling good character decreases the chances that children will actually acquire these traits.

EXAMPLES OF COMMUNITY-BASED
CHARACTER EDUCATION

In recent years the educational establishment has taken a leadership role in the discussion regarding values and character education. A growing number of state and local education boards, curriculum specialists at the local level, and schools have initiated reviews of character education curriculum and procedures or have adopted policies related to the systematic teaching of values and character. Educators have opened this dialogue. National organizations such as the Character Education Partnership have been created to assist with raising awareness and to provide a clearinghouse for character education information. In one instance, Maryland formed a state task force to determine what core values should be taught in the classroom. The task force listed 13 character and citizenship skills that should be systematically taught.

In Baltimore, Maryland a stand-alone curriculum was purchased and placed in all elementary schools. Teachers were trained to infuse the concepts into the general curriculum. Teacher resource specialists were trained to conduct in-service-courses for other teachers in ways to infuse the curriculum into general subject areas. In the case of Baltimore City schools anecdotal reports from teachers who systematically instructed their students in the concepts and skills of good character indicate that discipline problems decrease, time on task increases, and general morale in the classroom improves.

However, in spite of the successes reported in Baltimore and other isolated schools and districts, questions remain as to whose values will be taught within the character education curriculum. Although Baltimore educators systematically developed their consensus core values with a broadly diverse community task force, there still remained the sometimes unspoken question, "Are you going to indoctrinate my child with values or character traits that are counter to what I am doing at home?" or "Whose values are you going to teach?"

While it is not possible to eliminate all doubt about the content of character education programs it is possible to alleviate most fears by changing the question from "whose values" to "what values." When a community, be it a school, a school district, or the neighborhood, enters into a discussion of character or values education the group should look at the value strands involved in character education. Looking at the four elements of character instruction will help diverse groups to understand that character education is not a "whose values" question but rather a "what values" question.

From the public school perspective there are four strands related to the issue of what values should be taught in the schools. Strand one consists of those values or principles embodied in the United States Constitution, the Bill of Rights, and other founding documents. It is generally understood that teachers not only have the responsibility to teach about such concepts as freedom of speech and freedom of the press and religion, but they should also advocate these precepts. As citizens and teachers they have an implied contract to support these principles. However, this does not imply that the principles embodied in the founding documents are static. They are, in fact, living documents that can and do change over time.

For example, it was clearly the original intention to exclude women from voting. However, as the nation grew and became more enlightened, women were given the right to vote. This demonstrates the fluidity of the founding principles.

The second strand to be considered consists of those values that are common across cultures, religions, races, economic status, and personal beliefs. It is possible with extremely diverse groups to develop a list of consensus values that all agree upon. Generally, this list will include such values or character traits as honesty, respect for self and others, courage, responsibility, perseverance, tolerance, and courtesy.

These core or consensus values and character traits should not only be taught in schools, but they should be advocated. Educators should be willing to teach about honesty and should tell students that honesty is better than dishonesty, respect is better than disrespect, and responsibility better than irresponsibility. It cannot be assumed that children hearing about honesty, for example, will automatically acquire honest habits. Therefore in addition to teaching about the value, educators must provide opportunities for practice.

In an editorial on KNX radio in Los Angeles the speaker urged an audience to remember that "Children cannot heed a message they have never heard." The simple fact is that children must hear about respect and other values in order to put them into practice.

Strand three is primarily concerned with community values. These values relate to matters that change depending on the makeup of the group or community. These values may be based upon the majority perception of the way things should be rather than a general consensus of all segments of the community. As the population in a community changes the particular value may change. For example, citizens in community A may believe that restaurants should be smoke free while residents in community B may take the opposite view. However, if citizens from community A move to community B there may be a shift in the majority point of view and therefore a new community value would result.

In relation to these community values, teachers may teach about the various points of view, but they should not advocate a particular position. Teachers can provide opportunities for students to evaluate the various positions and come to their own personal conclusions.

The fourth strand involves personal values such as religion and political affiliation. In this case, as in the case of community values, teachers can teach about the points of view but not advocate one over another. For example, one may teach comparative religions or comparative political parties. However, a teacher must not indoctrinate the students in one particular religion or political party.

As society turns back toward the systematic teaching of character and as schools take a leadership role in this swing of the pendulum it is imperative that educators make it clear that they are concerned with the first two strands and not interfering with community or personal value systems. This is important when schools or districts are internally dealing with the question of values or character education. However, understanding these strands takes on an even greater significance as cooperative efforts between schools and various elements of the community become more commonplace. As the implementation of systematic values education programs moves from isolated instances in classrooms to the cocoon of the school and out into the community, it is important that all who are involved look at the issues that may impact on the success or failure in the classroom, in the school, and in the broader community.

ISSUES FACING COMMUNITY-BASED CHARACTER EDUCATION

What questions need to be answered?

When the introduction of systematic character education has achieved success there had been an initial focus on preimplementation analysis. During this analysis several pertinent questions should be answered prior to any action. Among the most important questions:

1.   Does the systematic teaching of character education make a difference?
2.   What are the elements of an effective character education program?
3.   Can the school go it alone or should the community be involved?
4.   If the community is to be involved what procedures should be followed, who should be involved, and how should results be evaluated?
5.   Does the school or district have or does it need to create a consensus list of core values or character traits?

Does the systematic teaching of values or character traits make a difference?

A study conducted by a private research firm, California Survey Research (CSR), evaluated a program instituted in 25 Los Angeles Unified School District elementary and middle schools. The schools implemented the Jefferson Center for Character Education schoolwide character education program. Pre- and post-surveys were conducted by California Survey Research to determine if there were any measurable differences in such areas as major and minor discipline referrals, absenteeism, tardiness, and suspensions. At the beginning of the school year each teacher received curriculum materials and training. A pre- and post-survey was conducted.

According to the final report provided by the CSR, the following were found:

1.   All forms of reported discipline problems decreased from the year prior to the project.

2. Major disciplinary problems in an average month decreased 25 percent.
3. Minor disciplinary problems in an average month decreased 38.8 percent.
4. Suspensions from the past academic year decreased 16 percent.
5. Tardy students sent to the office per month decreased 40 percent.
6. Students with unexcused absences decreased 18.2 percent.
7. The median level of student participation in extracurricular
activities increased.[1]

Overall, educators involved in the project reported that results exceeded their expectations in reducing discipline problems and in providing the opportunity to teach values. Specifically, those surveyed said that the program achieved more than they anticipated: better schoolwide morale and cohesiveness, improved student awareness for their actions, a decrease in discipline problems, better student self-discipline, an opportunity to teach values in the classroom, and a common reference point to solve conflicts.

In a 1994 study conducted by the Learning Research and Development Center of the University of Pittsburgh, an additional evaluation of the previously mentioned program was conducted.[2] The STAR curriculum introduces character education content, such as the language and concepts, and also provides opportunities for students to practice skills related to such value-laden words as honesty, respect, and courage. In addition, the curriculum provides an ethical decision-making model. Both the content and the ethical decision-making model were evaluated.

When asked if the STAR program met the needs of the school in relation to character education the respondents indicated that it:

1. Meets the needs related to each social skill, reinforces social skills, and offers alternative behaviors.
2. Constitutes a core to which other social skills programs can be added.
3. Provides a language-based tool for enhancing student behavior, and thus, academic performance.
4. Emphasizes positive attitudes and behavior.
5. Is rewarding to staff as well as students.

However, in both these studies there emerged a concern that character education could not be relegated to the school alone. The fact that teachers and schools were teaching character and values was generally conceived as positive. Nonetheless, there was still the concern that parents and the community needed to be more fully involved in the effort.

What are the elements of an effective character education program?

In the November 1993 issue of *Educational Leadership*, Brooks and Kann describe 11 basic elements that, when systematically applied, increase the probability of a successful implementation of a character education program.[3]

1. Direct instruction prior to infusion into the general curriculum.
2. A language-based curriculum that introduces basic value words and concepts related to good character.
3. Focus on positive language that emphasizes the desired behavior as opposed to attention to the behaviors deemed inappropriate.
4. Contain character educaticon content and an ethical decision-making model or process.
5. Visual reminders such as posters and signs.
6. Entire school involvement.
7. Teacher-friendly materials that do not consume lengthy staff development time.
8. Adaptable to various teaching and learning styles.
9. Opportunity for student participation.
10. Parents and community involvement in planning and implementation.
11. An evaluations component.

Can the school go it alone or should the community be involved?

Developing a Character Education Program states: "Our Character Education Strategy Team [Mt. Lebanon School District, Pennsylvania] felt that the need to inform the community and staff was sufficiently important to warrant an action plan just for that purpose."[4]

Three major elements were included in the Mt. Lebanon plan. First, all employees were informed. Second, community presentations were made. Third, a handout was created to inform the community regarding such matters as district history with character education and the action plans, definitions of key terms, and resources.

It is becoming increasingly clear that effective efforts to initiate character education programs will stand a greater chance of success when parents and community are involved.

Two brief case studies

In Tyler, Texas, Larry Robinson, the chief of police, was concerned about the heavy emphasis on intervention programs and the continued influx into the juvenile justice system of young citizens. It seemed to him that crime interdiction or intervention programs were not having the desired effect on the young. No matter how many criminals were arrested and prosecuted there always seemed to be a youngster who would replace the person taken off the street.

At a conference, Chief Robinson heard about character education and began to think of this as a prevention tool. He investigated various programs and contacted the Jefferson Center for Character Education. His internal intention was to use drug seizure money to place the program in one pilot school. He wanted to determine if, in fact, the program would help reduce crime in the future.

When Chief Robinson contacted the Tyler public schools he was told that they would cooperate only if all district elementary schools were involved. To supplement the drug seizure moneys, the chief was able to secure the additional funding from a foundation in Dallas and initial planning and training were begun.

Two important factors emerged as the implementation phase progressed. It became apparent that having schools as the only players in the game was not enough. The second factor was that having been involved in the funding of the character education program, a high level of interest developed on the part of rank-and-file police officers. Many of the officers were parents themselves and had children in the Tyler schools. They saw character education as support for what they were doing at home. It then was decided that officers would be invited to adopt a school. Arrangements were made for them to receive the same training that teachers were given.

The response from the police was overwhelming. Every school had at least one office as an "adopter." During the training the officers were encouraged to look for students who were acting responsibly while away from the school. When youngsters were observed committing a responsible act the officer would "cite" them. The citation was then taken to the school by the student and the adopting officer would conduct a drawing at the end of the month. Students won star T-shirts and other donated prizes.

One positive example of the expansion of character education from the school to the community occurred as an officer pulled her police car into a convenience store parking lot. She observed a boy, 10 or 11 years old, locking his bicycle to the bike rack in front of the store. She gave a short blast on her siren and turned her lights on for a few seconds. She reported that the boy began to back away as she approached him. He nervously responded that it was his bike and that he was just locking it up. The officer told the boy that she was aware of what he was doing and wanted him to know that she appreciated the fact that he was being responsible by locking up the bike. She gave him a ticket to take back to school and explained that he should take it to the office where it would be held until the end of the month at which time there would be a drawing for a T-shirt.

Gradually, through newsletters, parents and other members of the community were included in the process of teaching and recognizing good character in the school, the home, and the community.

The success of this prevention effort in Tyler was noted by the chief of police in Duncanville, Texas. Police chief Michael Courville seized upon the success in Tyler and included the business and faith communities in the initial planning of the effort. Chief Courville wanted to take the lessons learned in Tyler and expand upon what was already known about the need to bring character education to a broader audience than the school, parents, and students.

Initially, the Duncanville effort followed the same strategies as those used in Tyler. However, there was the realization that a truly comprehensive effort should be made to expand to a larger segment of the community. After the initial implementation in the schools and the police department, the faith community and the business community were introduced to the concept of community-based character education and how they could play a role.

It is the opinion of educational and community leaders in Duncanville that the essential element of a successful character education program must include the law enforcement community, the schools, the faith community, the business establishment, community-based organizations, the PTA and other parent groups, and adults who live in the community but do not have direct or indirect contact with the schools.

From these two community-based character education efforts in Tyler and Duncanville has emerged a model for inclusion of all segments of the community in the character development of children. Tyler and Duncanville, Texas are not the only two communities to experiment with community-based character education. To various degrees communities across the country are adapting the lessons learned in these two communities to their specific needs and concerns.

As mentioned above, in the Mt. Lebanon School District in Allegheny County, Pennsylvania, character education was included in their strategic plan. From the onset of their planning, teachers, administrators, and PTA leaders realized that the school could not handle the teaching of values alone. Mt. Lebanon educators decided to include character education in their strategic plan. Three strategies were developed:

1. To establish programs for the development, implementation, and assessment of ethical and responsible student behavior.
2. To create a caring environment that ensures the success of each student.
3. To work with community groups to develop plans for students to have a variety of opportunities for involvement in community service.

The Mt. Lebanon experience along with the efforts in such diverse communities as Tyler and Duncanville, Texas, Santa Barbara and the Santa Ynez Valley in California, Woodland Hills and Bethel Park, Pennsylvania, and Windward, Hawaii, all clearly demonstrate the need to include the community in the teaching and modeling of positive values and good character.

If the community is to be involved what procedures should be followed, who should be involved, and how should results be evaluated?

It should be obvious, but is often overlooked, that the schools belong to the community. At times the "community" is considered to be those who work in the schools, the students, and their parents. In considering the implementation of a systematic character education program this view is shortsighted. The chances for success are greatly enhanced when an expanded view of the school community is embraced. Community leaders, such as Chief Courville, make it clear that each segment of the community must be aware and involved in the process.

Initially the community needs to be informed that character education is under consideration. A survey is an effective means for accomplishing this task. In addition, presentations to community groups to raise awareness and to answer questions are valuable in establishing a groundswell of support. Finally, a diverse community-based committee should be formed. The purpose of this committee is to assess what is already being done, raise questions, develop a plan, and develop a list of consensus values.

At this phase it is especially important to include critics. Quite often misunderstanding and resistance come from those who are not informed or not involved. Inclusion of skeptic or potential critics will go a long way in keeping the process moving and accomplishing committee goals.

Effective character education programs involve a carefully crafted evaluation component. This aspect of character education is often difficult because objectivity to evaluate objectivity is difficult in assessing good behavior. For example, how does one count when a student decides to not engage in teasing because it is disrespectful?

Evaluation appears to be most effective when it is tied to the consensus core values as determined by the community and when that which will be evaluated is determined locally. For example, in one school there may be grave concern about lack of academic achievement. If character traits are being taught and the assumption is made that students with good character will achieve at a higher level then one might want to evaluate the number of students on the honor role, test scores, and other indices of increased achievement. If, on the other hand, disrespectful actions are a concern, then following the systematic teaching of respect and caring might be an evaluation of the decrease in disrespectful behavior and the increase in respectful actions.

Does the school or district have or need to create a consensus list of core values for character traits?

Since it is a generally held belief that there is consensus on what constitutes core values the thinking may be, "Well, let us just get the list." The problem with this thinking is that it circumvents a vital process in the establishment of an effective character program. The fact of the matter is that there are many lists of shared values and character traits. Some have been created by state task forces, others by individual schools and districts. Some have been created by companies, both for-profit and nonprofit. Long before character education was in vogue, the Institute for Character Education offered a curriculum that had lessons based on a number of agreed-upon core values. The Jefferson Center for Character Education had a list of values and skills related to those values since the 1980s. The point is that many consensus lists exist. The majority have a similar common core of values. Some differ slightly, some not at all. While it is possible to adopt one of the existing lists, this strategy leaves part of the process unfinished. When a diverse group of individuals can discuss and agree upon values such as courage, honesty, tolerance, respect, and perseverance, then the buy-in of the group is strengthened.

How that list is created is a matter of planning that depends on many factors. Size of the group, diversity of the membership, ability to bring people together, and time are some of the factors that need to be discussed prior to formation of a representative committee.

The key is inclusion. To launch a program based on agreed-upon values everyone who should be involved should have been involved. A list can be created by an exclusive group; however, those who are excluded and feel that the list does not represent their point-of-view or who are not aware of the process that transpired to arrive at the list may make implementation more difficult.

CONCLUSION

In conclusion, it might be asked what lessons have been learned from these early attempts at broadening character education from the school to the community.

Character or values education has moved to a point where the majority of society is beginning to see the need for a community approach rather than an approach that leaves individual families and institutions working in isolation.

There are difficult questions that need to be resolved. The issue of whose values versus what values is a major concern of many. How will the school interface with such community organizations as churches and synagogues, community-based organizations, and independent youth organizations?

How will a school or school system ensure that all segments of the community are allowed to give their input and participate in forming a community-wide consensus.

What will be evaluated and how will this be accomplished?

Will schools create a new curriculum or use and adapt an existing program?

Who should be involved in the planning and how should they be selected?

In far too many cases the paramount question being asked is: Should we as a school and community be involved in character or values education at all? The answer to this question appears to rest in African wisdom. It does take an entire village to raise a child.

NOTES

1. California Survey Research, *The Values Education Project* (Van Nuys, CA: September 1991).

2. McQuaide, Fienberg, and Leinhardt, *The Values of Character* (Pittsburgh: Learning Research and Development Center at the University of Pittsburgh, October 1994).

3. Brooks and Kann, "What Makes Character Education Programs Work," *Educational Leadership,* November 1993.

4. Henry A. Huffman, *Developing a Character Education Program: One School District's Experience* (published by the Association for Supervision and Curriculum Development and the Character Education Partnership, 1994).

Chapter 15

Character and Excellence:
The Total Quality Life

John E. Murray, Jr.

INTRODUCTION

There is an idea sweeping across America. It began in the world of business and industry under the name "total quality management." The idea is often attributed to Americans such as Joseph M. Juran, Philip Crosby, and particularly, the great prophet of total quality, W. Edwards Deming. Deming enjoyed this status during his fifties in Japan, but he would be an octogenarian before enjoying a similar status in his homeland.[1]

"Total quality management" is now found under a number of aliases: "continuous quality improvement," "total quality control," "total quality performance," and others. Whatever the name, the underlying concept remains the same. It has become the byword of business in America as it did much earlier in Japan. But it is no longer relegated to business and industry. It pervades American institutions from corporations and hospitals to universities and governmental units. It requires a "cultural change" through which all members of an enterprise are "empowered" to assure continuous enhancement of quality with an emphasis on service to customers.

Total quality looks not only to the survival of the enterprise but to its development as a major force in domestic and global competition. The creative energy of workers is harnessed to work "smarter" if not harder. With an emphasis on "leadership" instead of "management" and with the chief executive officer of the enterprise as well as division leaders taking on the character of "first among equals," every process within the enterprise is continuously improved because every worker is obsessed with the idea of continuously enhanced quality.

In the years following World War II, the great demand for consumer products led American business to emphasize quantity and, quite literally, to ignore quality. American management indulged the conclusive presumption that it was invincible. In the 1960s, the arrogance of American management that global U.S. economic dominance would never end was shared by many Europeans.[2] A generation later, however, there would be headlines in American newspapers like one in the *Washington Post* which read "Kiss No. 1 Goodbye, Folks." By the early 1990s, political economists were predicting Japanese and European economic dominance in the twenty-first century.[3] The enormous success of our global competitors was frustrating to American business leaders. A flurry of books disparaging Japanese trade practices appeared[4] together with popularized accounts of the perils of Japanese intentions.[5] While demands for "level playing fields" in international trade were exacerbated to the point of threatening drastic sanctions and trade wars, American business was not only learning about total quality but beginning to pursue it with a vengeance.

The gross neglect of quality in American manufacturing had lasted for more than three decades after World War II at a horrendous cost. Japanese products became the clearly preferred, highest-quality products for manufacturers and consumers.[6] The loss of market share and even whole industries placed many American corporations in jeopardy. At times, the search for solutions can only be described as frantic. While the 1982 publication of Deming's book, *Out of Crisis*, is often viewed as a milestone in the recognition of total quality, it was a 1980 television documentary that made Deming an overnight celebrity.[7]

Here was an unheralded American who had attained celebrity status in Japan three decades earlier. Within four years of his entry, the Japanese had established the Deming Prize in 1951 for individual and corporate excellence in statistical theory. It became the ultimate prize in Japanese business. Emperor Hirohito conferred a medal on Deming at a time when few Americans knew of his existence.[8] From 1980 until the time of his death on 20 December 1993, however, W. Edwards Deming achieved his belated celebrity status in his homeland.[9] Yet, in keeping with his philosophy of perpetual, continuous improvement, he was "never satisfied."[10] Deming seminars were held everywhere.[11] One could discover an institute or college of total quality, under the names of the other gurus, Crosby and Juran. Corporations devoted entire departments to total quality. In 1987, the U.S. Congress created the Malcolm Baldridge Quality Award which became the great quality prize sought after by American corporations[12] while Europe later developed the European Quality Award.[13]

Indeed, a total quality revolution has occurred in America. As it spreads beyond manufacturing to service and even nonprofit enterprises, more Americans continue to learn of it. Total quality demands that we reject the inevitable tendency to leave well enough alone.[14] It allows workers from the CEO to the housekeeping staff to feel a sense of dignity and creative energy in continuously improving the work they perform. The fascinating question is, should total quality be relegated to one's job, or is there an equally plausible argument for a total quality life?

A TOTAL QUALITY LIFE—THE VIRTUOUS LIFE

We think of the total quality concept as one that was created quite recently, no earlier than the 1950s in Japan. Some may recognize the precursors to Deming who announced total quality concepts in America and Japan earlier in this century. When, however, we consider the pervasive slogan of total quality, "Doing the right thing right the first time,"[15] we discover a similar statement made much earlier, "The temperate man does the right thing in the right way at the right time." This is a quotation from Aristotle's *Nichomachean Ethics* in the fourth century, B.C. "Doing the right thing right the first time" is not only a principle of business and management, it is a high ethical principle.

Even modern ethicians agree that Aristotle's ethical system, with all of its imperfections, is the only ethical system deserving of study. Aristotle concentrates on the virtuous life, the development of the good or virtuous habits of prudent judgments or choices which necessarily manifest justice, fortitude, and temperance or moderation. Thomas Jefferson taught us that our society requires not only smart people but virtuous people. James Madison insisted that the virtuous citizen is indispensable to that noble experiment in democracy called the United States of America.

Americans, however, have rejected the standards of virtue because those standards presume to tell us how to live. The virtuous life requires continuous improvement. The ancient Greeks did not speak of sin. Rather, those who did not continuously improve by developing whatever talents they possessed were treated with disdain. The ancient Greeks understood the external standards of virtue. In America, however, there are no external standards. Each of us pursues a "lifestyle" and "marches to his own drummer." We reject any external standards of how we ought to live whether those standards come from the home, the school, or the church. We pursue a standard of absolute freedom where only the individual decides what is right or wrong. External standards of any kind are viewed at best as statements of opinion which are the product of nostalgia and lost innocence.[16]

The ordinary religion of most of our universities is relativism and nihilism.[17] During the last two years of his recent presidency of Harvard University, Derek Bok complained that Harvard and other universities failed to promote the moral growth of its students.[18] He worried about students leaving Harvard and other universities believing that one view of morality is necessarily equal to any other view, i.e., morality is, necessarily, only a matter of opinion. The contemporary ethicist Alisdair MacIntyre suggests that we have developed a new philosophy of "emotivism" where the only question is whether any particular action is comfortable for the actor, i.e., "How do you feel about it?" We replace "bad" or "good" with personal approval or disapproval and the result is moral chaos.[19]

The most famous pediatrician in the history of the United States, Benjamin Spock, who told millions of parents how to live, spends the twilight of his life in despair over the decline of spirituality in our society.[20] Parents no longer tell their children how to live and any suggestion that schools adopt standards of value is undermined with the question "Whose values?" Since we cannot agree on any list of values, we reject *all* values and stand moral philosophy on its head by treating education in the moral virtues with disdain. We are quite willing to announce slogans such as "just say no to drugs," but we are totally opposed to answering the question "to what do we say yes?" Some years ago, the *New York Times* best-seller list included a book called *Why Johnny Can't Read*. A more recent book is called *Why Johnny Can't Tell the Difference Between Right and Wrong*. With rare exception, it has become totally unfashionable to even speak of conduct that is "wrong." [21]

With some justification, we have been called a society of moral illiterates who display total ignorance of prudent judgments by making all of the wrong choices. The greatest nation in the world—the only remaining superpower—leads the world in many wonderful technological achievements, and we rightly preach freedom and democracy to the rest of the world. At the same time, we lead the industrialized world in crime, divorce, violent deaths of children, child abuse, abortion, and incarceration. We cannot build new jails fast enough, but we continue to assure new supplies of prisoners with a 500 percent increase in teenage pregnancies since the 1960s. It is not coincidental that there has been a 500 percent increase in violence over the same period or that seven of ten juvenile offenders come from broken homes. Most of the inmates of state prisons did not live with both parents while they were growing up and the majority were born to teenage mothers. As of 1991, these inmates had 826,000 children under the age of 18. It is no wonder that, for children born in 1980, 22.2 percent of white children and over 80 percent of African American children will be welfare dependent before reaching age 18.[22]

Our children no longer face the threat of nuclear holocaust, but they are twice as likely to be murdered and three times more likely to commit suicide as were their parents. Children are killing each other every day in our society where there is one gun for every 1.25 Americans compared to one gun for every 258 Japanese. In 1991 and 1992, firearms killed more Americans than the total killed during the entire Vietnam War. We have two defense budgets in the United States, the Pentagon budget of some $300 billion and what might be called the domestic defense budget of more than $425 billion to protect each other from ourselves.

Thirty years ago, one of every ten families was headed by a single parent. Now, almost one of every three families is headed by a single parent. Just 15 years ago, the experts told us that the children of divorce are resilient. Today, every study from Cambridge, Princeton, California, and elsewhere clearly demonstrates that children almost never get over divorce.[23] The effects are entirely negative and often last a lifetime. The second leading cause of suicide among 17- to 24-year-olds is this age group's problems dealing with divorced parents. A University of Chicago study calls no-fault divorce "a failed experiment," but we are not listening.

After all, we live in a no-fault society where no one is guilty of anything. We continue to adhere to the teaching of Sigmund Freud even though we now know that his theories are about as scientific as the theories of Phil Donahue. Freud taught us to repress guilt and that teaching provides perfect support for our ersatz philosophy of "emotivism"—again, whatever makes *you* feel comfortable is the right thing to do even if that amounts to a repudiation of the virtuous life.

What solutions have we, as a society, applied to these and other pathologies? We are surfeited with bromides and palliatives. We indulge euphemisms such as "sexually active" instead of accurate depictions because we are afraid to use more precise language such as "fornication." "Fornication" suggests actions which are wrong while "sexually active" is a neutral and nonjudgmental phrase.[24] Our solution to weapons in schools is metal detectors, but there is no metal detector outside the school yard where toddlers are gunned down through indiscriminate drive-by shootings. The U.S. government pays for condom ads with an admission that it is not a real solution to the problem of illegitimate births or AIDS. Tens of thousands of Americans die from all of these pathologies. They die because they do not know how to live. They have never heard of the moral virtues of prudence, justice, fortitude, and temperance.

A dysfunctional educational system allows for high levels of ignorance in traditional subjects as well as ethics. When American grade school and high school students consistently finish near the bottom on international comparisons and when the president of the Princeton Testing Service says that American students are first only in video watching, the educational establishment argues with the comparisons. Yet, even the president of the second largest 835,000-member teachers' union feels compelled to say that such arguments might be relevant if we were doing well, but "we are doing terribly."[25]

The massive ignorance of virtues is exacerbated by the unwarranted assumption that we understand them. Most Americans believe they understand the concept of justice, but justice is a complex concept that must be studied to be understood. It is not part of our DNA. As for the virtue of fortitude, innumerable gangs in our society practice a perversion of fortitude or courage by extolling members who have successfully killed someone with a handgun with special commendation for a member whose victim was a police officer. The virtue of temperance or moderation has been extinguished in our instant gratification society where the standard is clear: no one should wait for any pleasure, regardless of the circumstances, and it is impossible to have too much of a good thing. Moderation in all things is translated into gluttony and licentiousness. This massive ignorance of other virtues precludes any possibility of making prudent choices.

The total quality revolution in business has been adopted by most of our corporations out of a fear of survival. It is now time to recognize that there must be a total quality revolution in all of society if our society is to survive. We need total quality management not only to make our corporations more competitive. The concentration from cradle to grave must be on a "total quality life," a virtuous life, where genuine prudence, temperance, justice, and fortitude prevail and where anyone failing to observe these external standards is treated with disdain. The inalienable rights to life, liberty, and the pursuit of happiness can be guaranteed only if our entire society accepts the truth that the virtuous life is the only life that allows us to be safe, free, and happy.

Virtues and vices are habits. The pathologies of our society are the result of developing bad or vicious habits. The virtuous life may be stated in the words of the current total quality movement: To practice the virtuous life, one must develop the habit of doing the right thing right the first time in all of our actions. It is not enough that we do the right thing right the first time in relation to a manufacturing or service process. We must do the right thing right the first time in relation to children, wives, husbands, neighbors, and every other member of society including ourselves. In the words of total quality guru Philip Crosby, the goal should be a complete life of "zero defects." This, indeed, is a very high goal but this *is* the virtuous life and it is within our grasp.

To understand the virtuous life, education in the virtues must pervade every school in America. But that alone is insufficient. It must also be emphasized by our corporations, our labor unions, our churches, and government at all levels. Only then will value education be restored to the fundamental institution of our society, the family. The pervasive total quality concept is capable of not only producing geometric economic benefits by making American business more competitive. A total quality revolution in every facet of life can lead us from our current state of societal chaos to a rational society that recognizes responsibility as well as freedom. It can also teach us the eternal lesson that true joy is found exclusively in caring for others and carrying their burdens.

CONCLUSION

Finally, it is time to recognize the critical complement to the virtuous life, the spiritual dimension. To assure value neutrality, we have made a studious and successful effort to eliminate the last scintilla of religion from our schools and any public place. Present constructions of our Constitution forbid any mention not only of God or religion but of spirituality. The latest assault would remove even a moment of silence for individual student reflection. A Christmas scene or Menorah in any public place will immediately inspire litigation because we are obsessed with value neutrality. Constitutional law scholars are anything but comfortable with the ambiguous and often contradictory pronouncements of our courts in these matters. Our value neutrality, however, leaves a void that suggests no external standards of any kind.

Many people of faith would agree with those who resist the return of prayer in public schools or other public places. But we have gone well beyond the neutral exclusion of religion in such places. There is a genuine lack of respect for religion or spirituality which often appears as an obsession to eradicate it. It is viewed as that "soft and sentimental stuff," like the study of moral philosophy which is not considered to be a real discipline because its subject matter is only a matter of opinion.[26] Like moral philosophy, however, theology is a real discipline. For people who believe, faith is the most rational of all acts. It is not the opium of the people. It is the foundation of the virtuous life through the love of God and neighbor.

Whatever our religious convictions or lack thereof, we must be a society of faith. We must have faith in our basic values. We must have faith in our institutions, and we must have faith in each other. That pervasive quality of faith as well as moral values can be restored to our society. It cannot be accomplished through legislation or judicial fiat. It can only be accomplished through a moral consensus that everyone in our society is expected to live a total quality life.

NOTES

1.   While the gigantic contribution of Deming must be recognized, there were many others including the much underrated Dorian Shainin and early quality missionaries from the United States to Japan such as Western Electric's W. S. Magil, Homer Sarasohn, and Charles Protzman. Their students included Masaharu Matsushita, Takeo Kato (Mitsubishi), Hanzou Omi (Fujitsu), Bunzaemon Inoe (Sumitomo), as well as Akio Morita and Masaru Ibuka of Sony. Moreover, all of the American quality gurus were preceded by the great Kaoru Ishikawa who had developed, before Deming, quality principles in effect today.

2.   One of the prime illustrations of this view is found in the 1967 best-selling book by French author Jean-Jacques Servan-Schrieber, *The American Challenge* (*Le Défi Americain*), in which he described how American multinational firms such as Ford and IBM were conquering Europe. He wrote, "We are being overtaken and dominated, for the first time in our history, by a more advanced civilization."

3.   See, e.g., the 1992 book by political economist and dean of the Sloan School of Management at MIT, Lester Thurow, *Head to Head*. See also *The Consequences of the Peace* by James Chace. See also the article in *U.S. News & World Report*, vol. 112, no. 13 at 36 (1992), which reads, "Twenty-five years ago, Europeans were preoccupied with le défi americain, the American challenge described by French author Jean-Jacques Servan-Schrieber. Today the talk is of le défaut americain."

4.   See, e.g., *Trading Places* (1988) by Clyde V. Prestowitz, Jr.; *Yen! Japan's New Financial Empire and Its Threat to America* (1988) by Daniel Burstein; *The Enigma of Japanese Power* (1989) by Karel van Wolferen; *Agents of Influence* (1990) by Pat Choate; *Japanese Power Game* (1990) by William J. Holstein; *In the Shadow of the Rising Sun* (1991) by William S. Dietrich; and *Unequal Equities* (1991) by Robert Zielinski and Nigel Holloway. See also the novel by Michael Crichton, *Rising Sun*.

5.   The novel *Rising Sun* was made into a film. A more recent novel is even more disparaging and suggests a revenge motive —*Debt of Honor* by the popular writer of thrillers, Tom Clancy.

6.   American consumers accepted Japanese electronic products with very few exceptions. It was also interesting to visit manufacturing plants where American managers displayed the latest Japanese manufacturing equipment but felt compelled to add a shrug of the shoulders as if to say "What can we do? The machine and service are simply better."

7.   The NBC documentary *If Japan Can...Why Can't We?* aired on 24 June 1980.

8.   Americans tended to explain Japanese success on factors other than quality—the culture of teamwork, homogenous people, loyal workers, and the "unholy" alliance of government banks, companies, and unions that precluded a level playing field. While these factors are certainly not to be discounted, they failed to explain why the General Motors Framingham plant required 31 hours to assemble a car when a Toyota plant only required 16 hours, or why the GM plant averaged 135 defects per car when Toyota had only 45 defects, or why GM required almost twice as much space as a Toyota facility or why GM required a two-week parts inventory when Toyota needed only a two-hour supply of parts for its assembly line.

9.   As reported by John A. Byrne in *Business Week*, 10 January 1994, Deming did not land his first key American client until 1979. William E. Conway was the chief executive of Nashua Corporation, an office and computer products manufacturer, facing competition from Japan. On his trips to Japan, Conway later reported, "All they talked about was Deming." Conway hired Deming notwithstanding considerable skepticism from his colleagues after the first interview with Deming when one colleague told Conway that Deming appeared to be "a nut." For four years, Deming presented four-day seminars for every Nashua employee and Nashua fortunes rose. Byrne suggests that Deming's Nashua success led to the 1980 NBC documentary.

Deming is often described as having been difficult. In the same piece, Byrne characterizes Deming as "cranky, obstinate, and obscure." Others report that Deming would often call business leaders "stupid." Thomas Murrin, former guru of total quality at the Westinghouse Electric Corporation, later deputy secretary of commerce in the Bush administration and currently dean of the Duquesne University School of Business Administration, generally concurs in this description of Deming upon his first meeting at Westinghouse. Like Byrne, however, Murrin would join in the general characterization of Deming as the godfather of total quality.

10. In the same *Business Week* article (see note 8), John Bryne remembers a scene in 1991 when Deming lectured to some MBA students and wrote that phrase on the blackboard. Bryne also suggests that Deming "remained unsatisfied that management's interest in quality was deep enough to ensure lasting improvement." He describes Deming's last hurrah in California when, in December, just before his death, Deming lectured while sitting in a wheelchair tethered to an oxygen tank.

11. It is reported that Deming's fees were as high as $25,000 per day.

12. Among the winners of the prize, corporations such as Motorola, Xerox, and Westinghouse have demonstrated an almost obsessive pursuit of total quality. Quite recently, AT&T won both the Malcolm Baldridge Award and the Deming Prize for Quality, which CEO Robert Allen likened to winning the World Series and the World Cup on the same day.

13. Joseph Juran participated in establishing the 28 criteria which are used to determine the winner of the Malcolm Baldridge Award. Deming and Crosby were critical of that award. While the three experts agree on the quintessential importance of quality, they manifest different perspectives. Deming was interested in providing customer satisfaction through products and services at low cost requiring continuous innovation and improvement which the Japanese call *kaizen*. Juran was particularly concerned with a product's fitness for use while Crosby looked at quality from an engineering standpoint in terms of conformance to precise standards and requirements. Crosby's famous phrase, "Do it right the first time and achieve zero defects," had become a slogan of the total quality movement. The phrase is typically recounted as "Doing the right thing right the first time." The European Quality Award is bestowed by the European Foundation for Quality Management and is similar to the Baldridge Award.

14. Even though competitiveness has emerged as a national priority, recent advances in U.S. competitiveness induced a number of media suggestions that the United States had won the international competitive game. Somehow, we were to believe that we had totally overcome poor quality as well as the high cost of capital and outmoded manufacturing processes. When the recessions in Japan and Europe were added to this mix, pundits were again proclaiming the invincibility of the United States as the leader in global economics. Fortunately, chief executive officers, university presidents, and labor leaders are convinced by a margin of two to one that the United States will continue to face great economic

challenges for the indefinite future. *1994 Competitiveness Index* (Washington, DC: Council on Competitiveness, July 1994).

15. The origins of this phrase are seen in Philip Crosby's phrase in note 13, *supra*.

16. On 15 April 1993, Senator Daniel Moynihan addressed 800 civic leaders comprising the Association for a Better New York. Moynihan was celebrating the 50th anniversary of his graduation from Benjamin Franklin High School in New York City. He compared the New York of 1943 with the New York of 1993. In 1943, there were 44 homicides committed with guns; in 1993 the number was 1,499. In 1943, there were 73,000 people on welfare; in 1993 there were 1,000,000 welfare recipients. In 1943, 3 percent of babies were born out of wedlock; in 1993, 45 percent were born out of wedlock. Moynihan concluded that these pathologies were based on the decline of the family. The message was not well received. One leader complained that Moynihan's statements were based on nostalgia and lost innocence.

17. In this century, we have reached the zenith of relativism and its ultimate end, nihilism. We are surrounded by deconstructionists and reductionists in our philosophy, our literature, and our law. There are no universal truths or values. Everything is culturally determined, i.e., morality is a matter of geography.

As suggested by Harvard philosopher Robert Nozick in his book, *Philosophical Explanations*, any claim to the validity of social or political principles is an ideological superstructure generated and maintained by ruling powers. Rationality does not exist because our activities can be reduced to a variety of factors. They may be the product of repressed desires causing us to play roles created in early childhood, or they may be induced by external stimuli or internal biochemical and electrical activity in our brains and our current hormone imbalances. The reductionists also claim that our cultural patterns including marriage, religious attendance, childbearing, friendship, and even suicide are not explicable by the reasons normally suggested but by the needs of society or self-interested economic calculations.

Not all of these theories can be true. But that does not matter to the reductionist whose sole and exclusive purpose is devaluation—the destruction of human dignity, so that we can all share in the consciousness of lower self-esteem.

18. Earlier, Bok had defended the higher education establishment against the criticisms of Bill Bennett, a Harvard graduate who became secretary of education and later Drug Czar. During the last two years of his presidency, however, Bok began to sound very much like Bennett. These views will be found in Bok's book, *Universities and the Future of America* (1990).

19. Alasdair MacIntyre, *After Virtue*, 2nd ed. (Notre Dame, IN: Notre Dame University Press, 1984).

20. At a news conference at which he discussed his new book, *A Better World for Our Children: Rebuilding American Family Values*, Dr. Spock said, "We have lost a lot of our spirituality and our beliefs. The sad state of our society shows we can't get along without our beliefs."

21. A rare exception is smoking. The smokers of America are the lepers of our society who are treated not only with disdain but with contempt. While the medical evidence against smoking is overwhelming and a moral consensus against it is desirable, one cannot help but wonder why we have failed to achieve moral consensus on the other pathologies of our society which may be at least as damaging as smoking. There appears to be more sympathy for the drug addict than for the tobacco addict. There is sympathy for the mother of the illegitimate child. There is understanding for the student who lacks diligence and can barely read. There is even some sympathy for the confessed murderers of one's parents. And where is the moral consensus concerning infidelity?

22. We have not even begun to consider the calamity of the tens of thousands of crack or cocaine babies born each year. These children will never be able to shoulder the burdens of life without complete assistance from a society with neither the means nor the will to render such assistance.

23. Consider the studies cited by Barbara Dafoe Whitehead in the famous *Atlantic* magazine cover story, "Dan Quayle Was Right," or the 22-year study by Judith Wallerstein in California, or the work of Sara McLanahan of Princeton or Kathleen Kiernan of Cambridge. They arrive at identical conclusions. Children of divorced and single parents are more likely to be poor, to have emotional and behavioral problems, to drop out of school, to abuse drugs, and to become embroiled in the criminal justice system. Girls of divorced parents are more likely to have a premarital birth in their teens and boys are more likely to be out of work. One of the more fascinating findings is that children who lose a parent through death, on the other hand, do not manifest these problems. Even children who are raised in a family of bickering parents, i.e., where there is no physical abuse, show no ill effects from these surroundings.

Critics raise the question of whether children should continue to live with parents who are physically or psychologically abusive. The obvious answer is no. The National Commission on Children, however, reports that physical or psychological abuse occurs in only 10 to 15 percent of marriages. While that is far too many, it is emphatically not the principal cause of the overwhelming number of divorces (the rate has quadrupled since the 1960s). Divorce occurs essentially because one of the partners would feel more comfortable by dissolving the marriage.

24. It is common to hear Americans including parents and the surgeon general of the United States proclaiming that "Our children will be sexually active, won't they?" One will never hear the same people say "Our children will fornicate, won't they?" Current U.S. policy seems to suggest that we can convince our children and others to forbear smoking, but it is impossible to convince them to avoid illicit sex. Of course, this contradiction is resolved if our domestic policy is viewed as suggesting that "illicit" sex is impossible because there is no external standard that would disfavor voluntary sex of any kind with the exception of sex with children. When one considers the pregnancies of 12- and 13-year-olds, however, even the exception is in some doubt.

25. Statement of Albert Shanker, president of the American Federation of Teachers, as quoted in the *New York Times*, 29 December 1991.

26. Harvard professor of divinity Harvey Cox offered a course at Harvard, "Jesus and the Moral Life," that saw the largest subscription to any undergraduate class in the history of the university to that time. One thousand students subscribed in 1987. When asked how the academic world, especially Harvard, viewed Cox's success, a professor of social ethics at Harvard Divinity School, Ralph Potter, summed it up in a word: "harshly." *New York Times*, 22 May 1988.

Chapter 16

Character and Public Policy: Reinventing the American People

Robert Royal

INTRODUCTION

What keeps the United States united in the 1990s? In many ways this is a silly question. America is the most powerful nation on earth, one of the wealthiest, and by any significant measure the most successful democracy in all of human history. Millions of people around the world would gladly come here (and do yearly), not only because America promises prosperity, but because it also offers a reasonable welcome within and a solid defense against threats from without. We are far from being a perfect nation. But judged by world-historical standards, as G. W. F. Hegel and his late unlamented Marxist followers used to put it, we aren't doing so badly either.

Why, then, worry about what holds America together? Simply stated, many of us sense that amid the conflicting claims of multiculturalism, Afrocentrism, feminism, the men's movement, children's rights, right-to-die advocates, gays and lesbians, radical environmentalists, and codependency theorists, some common center has been lost. We seem to be failing even to transmit or maintain basic standards of civil behavior. The brittleness of much of our public discourse and the tendency to read discrete problems as evidence of vast social pathologies are only two symptoms of our anxiety. In some profound way we have become divided and confused about the basic constitution of our civic life.

The American Founders talked about the virtues and character necessary to sustain a free citizenry and professed a virtual creed of liberty. By contrast, some today regard a strong belief in universal civic principles and popular habits as the very definition of tyranny, a threat to pluralism, and an intolerance toward difference. In the past decade the term *Ayatollah* has often been applied to American leaders, secular or religious, who have advocated strong action to arrest decline in civic behavior, personal morals, or public manners and action to restore some common notions of civil life.

Most shapers of American opinion seem to think that reasonable defense expenditures coupled with energetic social justice programs are a sufficient glue for American society. But we have just had an object lesson in this matter. The former Soviet Union had enough weapons, manned by an enormous number of troops, to deter any outside attack. "Star Wars" research notwithstanding, the Soviets had assembled an extremely powerful fighting force that could have both protected the homeland and intimidated other nations for the foreseeable future. Soviet weakness was not technical, organizational, or even economic. Money could still have been found for defense and domestic food subsidies for years to come, even if the United States' sheer ability to produce wealth would have led eventually to a definite superiority over the Soviets. What collapsed in the Soviet Union was faith in the Marxist creed among the Marxist leaders themselves.

The West in general and the United States in particular could easily follow a similar path to disorder and decay. America has shown itself to be a remarkably stable polity, and it is not likely to break up into contending republics any time soon. Yet we should not be deceived by our own seemingly adamantine economic, technological, and military strength. Only the confident spirit behind them, in communion with our religious and republican heritage, keeps our system alive. We have had our laughs over the "vision thing," but the alternatives remain: either find vision or perish. Perhaps our deepest problem at present is that we seem occupied with visions of precisely the wrong kind.

BLURRED VISION

Instead of real vision, what we have been pursuing for some time are political mirages. To expect the federal government to solve current widespread doubts about American society and our experiment in liberty is about as realistic as was expecting the Politburo to solve the disenchantment with Marxism in the former Soviet Union. Washington is the source of the skepticism, not the cure. Politicians are often described as being "out of touch" with the rest of the country. But the rupture is far deeper than that. Liechtenstein has been described as a "bank masquerading as a country." Washington has become an enclave of politicians, federal and District bureaucrats, lobbyists, journalists, and pundits masquerading as a popular government.

Washington may marginally help or, more usually, hinder independent initiatives in the private and social spheres. As the Eastern Europeans have learned, however, society—even civility itself—can be severely distorted by governments operating on abstract principle with delusions of grandeur. At best, decent governments may be trusted to keep up simple projects like the interstate highway system, national parks, and museums, and to deliver, when necessary, lethal military force. Occasionally, governments may do things that marginally reinforce civic virtue. But barring a truly great spirit in the White House—someone like Abraham Lincoln, who would understand the shape and limits of what the state may do to encourage a healthy civil society—we must look elsewhere for moral and civic reconstruction.

DIVERSITY IS US

A nation that boasts it rose *E pluribus unum* ("Out of many, one") must always value the plural. What is good in contemporary multiculturalism continues to remind us that our experiment as a nation is not like the experience of most other countries. The French are French, Norwegians are Norwegians, and Greeks are Greeks because each of those groups has a common history, language, and culture. Americans have never been united simply in that way. Pluralism is our native condition.

Yet the American Founders did not aim at a nation that would consist merely of several tribes making camp and trading with one another. They envisioned *unum* arising *e pluribus*, and already had some evidence that the process was under way. Occasionally, for good causes, they exaggerated such popular unity as already existed. John Jay, for example, writing in *The Federalist Papers*, says he had often noted with satisfaction that

Providence has been pleased to give this one connected country to one united people—a people descended from the same ancestors, speaking the same language, professing the same religion, attached to the same principles of government, very similar in their manners and customs, and who, by their joint counsels, arms, and efforts, fighting side by side throughout a long and bloody war, have nobly established general liberty and independence.[1]

The details of this portrait are, of course, a pious fiction. The Germans in Pennsylvania, Dutch in New York, Swedes in New Jersey, and French Huguenots in South Carolina would have been surprised to learn of their common ancestry. The Quakers, Catholics, Jews, and diverse Protestant bodies scattered throughout the early American republic professed no common religion. And in the 1780s even language and basic political beliefs were not as uniform as Jay here suggests.

And yet Jay's general point is correct. Popular customs and attitudes toward government had made Americans, for all their variety, a new and united people. In fact, in its grandest sweep, the thinking of the founding generation of Americans expressed the belief that this new understanding of human nature and political life had universal validity—and could be implemented, wherever conditions were right, with enormous increase in human happiness.

Curiously, at the very moment when American institutions are more open than at any time in their history to people of diverse backgrounds, the implied universality behind that openness is no longer the starting point for contemporary discussions of American unity. In great part, this stems from the fact that the Left has dominated recent American intellectual life. Over the past few decades the Left and a good portion of the old liberals have abandoned belief in universal principles and a common humanity, let alone more sophisticated concepts of person and community. Their obeisance to the holy trinity of race, gender, and ethnicity has enlarged the American prospect in minor ways. But it has discredited—at least in the eyes of the Left—the old American claim of equality before the law and fair public treatment of all. Such concepts are now denigrated as masks for the oppressive ideologies of dominant groups and "cultures."

Conservatives and old-style liberals have been decrying such readings of American institutions for some time. But the situation is now so desperate in intellectual circles that even some old radicals have woken to the dangers. Todd Gitlin, for example, a leading radical sociologist at Berkeley, recently lamented this privileging of difference and denial of universality by the Left:

As a result, we find ourselves today in a most peculiar situation: the left and right have traded places, at least with respect to the sort of universalist rhetoric that can still stir the general public. Unable to go beyond the logic of identity politics, the disparate constituencies of the cultural left have ceded much political high ground on the right.... Ronald Reagan's genius lay in his ability to demarcate common ground on the right. Unless it learns to speak its own language of commonality, the shards of the left will be condemned to their separate sectors, sometimes glittering, sometimes smashed, and mostly marginal.[2]

Gitlin's history is open to question, but his empirical observations are not: today the most emphatic denials of our common humanity and the greatest threats to a future course based on such an ideal come from precisely those intellectual sectors that once prided themselves on their independence from narrow nationalism and provincialism of any kind.

The old American desire to welcome diversity has, we have come to learn, practical as well as theoretical limits. For example, the school system of Montgomery County, a suburb of Washington, claims that it must handle 16,000 foreign students who come from 150 countries and speak 101 languages. Fairfax County, another Washington suburb, has 17,000 foreign-born students from 150 countries who speak 75 languages. The Washington area is somewhat unusual in this regard, but it differs from other urban centers only in degree, not in kind. The desire to take into account the various "cultures" within school districts like these is a generous impulse, but no public school districts can really afford the time or money to do more than make some gestures at recognizing diversity on this scale. Schools just have too many other immediate tasks.

We have probably passed beyond the point where John Dewey's vision of the public schools as training centers for "democratic living" retains much validity. Even the original conception was, to put it mildly, highly optimistic. Only because families and communities had already largely shaped students to live in pluralist America were the schools even remotely capable of tying together their diverse backgrounds. Absent such efforts by others, the schools will be in over their heads.

In most instances, parents still try to encourage their children to participate in the mainstream culture. Why come to America in the first place if you do not wish in some way to do that? To participate does not mean to surrender everything from your particular background to some abstract "American" ethos. All immigrants to these shores, which is to say everyone's ancestors—including the native American peoples who migrated here during the last Ice Age—have had to adapt to new American conditions. But there are better and worse ways to negotiate the changes America requires.

As Peter Skerry has just shown in his enlightening *Mexican Americans*, two models of immigrant participation in the mainstream have emerged in recent decades.   To oversimplify somewhat a detailed and nuanced argument, in Texas people of Mexican origin are often severely discriminated against, Skerry says, but they practice an old-style ethnic politics—just as Jews, Poles, Irish, and Italians did earlier—that has drawn them into the larger community and has generally resulted in social and economic success.   By contrast, Mexican Americans in California are subject to less severe discrimination, but Mexican American leaders there practice the group-grievance politics that emphasize separatism and special treatment.   Not surprisingly, Mexican Americans in California have done far less well than their Texas counterparts, in terms of both social integration and economic advancement.

The broad lessons here may be that the older model not only succeeds in practice but is better able to handle discrimination.   Much of the blame for the lower rate of Mexican Americans' success in California has to be laid at the door of the group leaders who have mistaken their personal needs as spokesmen for the welfare of their people.

The desire to preserve "cultures" cannot excuse this kind of political and economic damage.   Looked at clearly, the very notion that "cultures" are perfectly preserved in America dissolves before our eyes.   African Americans may continue, even unconsciously, African ways in their lives and thought, but no existing African country has a "culture" that corresponds to African American culture.   Whether we think of jazz music or rap, street life in Harlem, or rural life in Mississippi, black American culture is inextricably intertwined with American life.   As Arthur M. Schlesinger, Jr., puts it: "Self-Africanization after 300 years in America is playacting."[3]

Furthermore, the cultural traffic is not one way.   Mainstream America has been changed incalculably by minority figures.   It would be difficult to imagine modern American society without Martin Luther King, Jr., Duke Ellington, or Colin Powell.   Any programmatic effort to separate mainstream and black America can result only in the impoverishment of both.

The same is true of Asian American, Polish American, and Arab American groups.   People of foreign backgrounds who have not been changed by their involvement with mainstream American culture are rare indeed.   In almost all cases, original cultures can be preserved only within some highly protected and vulnerable enclave that cannot long stand the centrifugal energies of its own young people. Separatism can be maintained here, but it exacts a price.

IN SEARCH OF A MODEL

Our way of life has been enriched by multiple and conflicting social currents in the past, and our search for common bases of civic life should not reduce that richness to some bland common denominator. But is there any model on which Americans can draw to recover a more universal vision? And if we can identify such a model, is there sufficient will to carry forward the renewal needed to turn around some serious decay?

The answers to both these questions are quite uncertain. We have become so accustomed to the notion that individual whims and the claims of "cultures" trump all larger social demands that any attempt to set up a model, however circumspect and ample, will be immediately decried as dictating a single standard for diverse "communities." And yet Americans continue to share some deep common agreements that we need to make explicit in our public language.

Zbigniew Brzezinski has argued recently that the greatest challenge now facing the West and America in particular is a moral challenge:

> America clearly needs a period of philosophical introspection and of cultural self-critique. It must come to grips with the realization that a relativist hedonism as the basic guide to life offers no firm social moorings, that a community which partakes of no shared absolute certainties but which instead puts a premium on individual self-satisfaction is a community threatened by dissolution.[4]

The United States is also a leader, a model, and a potent cultural influence for the rest of the world. If we are unable to restrain ourselves at home, we will inevitably transmit that uncircumcised spirit abroad, to the detriment of people around the world.

How to begin the task of reform? We must first take up the difficult reconstruction of public discourse so that we are again allowed to speak of ethics, morals, and even manners as the very basis of our personal lives and social institutions. America's Founders were not ashamed to speak of truths with a moral and religious content: "We hold these Truths to be self-evident, that all Men have been endowed by their Creator with certain unalienable Rights." The American theologian John Courtney Murray has argued that, at the very least, this brief phrase affirms three things: there are universal truths; we can know them; and we—we Americans—hold them because they guarantee our liberty as a nation and our dignity as human beings.

We are in crisis on many fronts precisely because we have forgotten our own roots and separated the realms of freedom and moral truth. We have all read John Rawls's *Theory of Justice* and think abstractly fair and impartial institutional practices are enough for the just society. But the genius of the American system is that its foundations are sunk quite a bit deeper than that.

An unexpected source has recently shed some light on these questions. John Paul II's encyclical on morality, *Veritatis Splendor*, deliberately takes up the issue of conscience, human freedom, and social order. John Paul accepts the view that conscience is inviolable and that human freedom is one of God's sacred gifts to man. He denies, however, the view held by many people in developed democracies that skepticism and relativism are a bulwark against the tyranny of one narrow faction. The pope argues to the contrary that where certain views of the human person and human society are not widely embraced, democracies will fall not only into crisis but into bondage. Democracies throughout history have ended in tyranny precisely for want of devotion to that social creed. Weimar Germany, for example, had a democratic constitution provided by the sociological genius Max Weber; it had checks and balances and duly elected officials. Nevertheless, it put Adolf Hitler and the Nazis in power.

As Americans, we have a high respect for the rights of conscience. But if the pope is right, we have been reaping the consequences of a one-sided emphasis on conscience to the exclusion of truth for some time now. He quotes the great English convert John Henry Newman: "Conscience has rights because it has duties." Everyone from the pope to President Bill Clinton has been speaking about duties and responsibilities lately. The difference is that the pope is willing to spell out precisely what people should do with their freedom. You cannot hope to encourage responsibility by taking it away through governmental paternalism.

To reassert this moral *pons asinorum* is not a simple exercise in nostalgia for a lost moral consensus. There have always been limits to what a democratic polity can tolerate. Thomas Jefferson could say in a moment of carelessness that it did not matter to him if his neighbor believed in no god or 20: "It neither picks my pocket nor breaks my leg." But the Sage of Monticello could afford to indulge such sentiments only because the cultural horizon of the world in which he lived made disagreements on basic morals few, whatever differences in theology existed.

Having lived to see both the rise of strange gods and the widespread eclipse of fundamental moral reasoning, we cannot be so nonchalant. Our pockets are picked and our legs broken, and we face even greater threats to life and liberty every day because of the absence of religion in some quarters and the presence of false gods in others. The United States should not become a theocracy, but our moral and religious challenges must be met with moral and religious responses that, while allowing for pluralism, also strongly assert the American creed of free people freely accepting responsibility for their own future.

THE THERAPEUTIC CHALLENGE

Almost 30 years ago, before the social landscape was marked by some of the greatest recent changes, the sociologist Philip Rieff observed:

> Americans no longer model themselves after the Christians or the Greeks. Nor are they such economic men as Europeans believe them to be. The political man of the Greeks, religious man of the Hebrews and Christians, enlightened economic man of 18th-century Europe (the original of that mythical present-day character, the "good European"), has been superseded by a new model for the conduct of life. Psychological man is, I suggest, more native to American culture than the Puritan sources of that culture would indicate.[5]

Rieff went on to observe that the "therapeutic" had made a clean sweep of all the other models.

Today, therapy has become the almost universal language for discussing our social problems. For some reason, we now think it humane and democratic to tell people that they are not responsible or free. We speak glibly of people "recovering" from addictions to violence, drugs and alcohol, love, and even religion. When poor young men are violent, we blame the lack of role models. Society itself is accused of a homophobia that needs treatment. Vice President Al Gore has written in his environmental book, *Earth in the Balance*, that we are a "dysfunctional civilization" in "deep denial" about our abuse of nature.

There is a grain of truth in all these characterizations, but we must be extremely wary of their implications. For instance, when the federal government steps into the health business, unless health is very carefully defined, politically driven "therapies" and reeducation programs may expand enormously. Let us be clear: social therapy, like health care reform and the desire to become multicultural, is a secondary question.

It is another political mirage that sets up an intermediate term as the final principle on which our society rests. After we have been freed of our irrational compulsions by therapies, have seen to our health, and have welcomed the contributions of those previously marginalized, we still have the same task before us: deciding how we are to live together. We may pass beyond psychological and sociological irrationality, but we will still face the question of what is morally and socially rational.

Paradoxically, the United States' very stability and success have lulled many people into believing that the abandonment of moral language in favor of the language of therapy or inclusiveness carries no costs or potential dangers. Yet civilization, as Freud pointed out while writing of its discontents, has a price. It requires, even in the esoteric context of Freudian therapies, finding ways to sublimate and channel selfish and socially destructive "natural" impulses into more fully human ways. Not all calls to modify the natural are mere repression; something naturally human interacts with our more animal nature to produce the strange rational animal that is a human being. The deep skepticism many people display in teaching sexual restraint to the young or expecting civic amity among adults reflects not so much a difference of ethical opinion as a tiredness at performing the tasks of civilization.

REINVENTING A PEOPLE

Recognizing the vital role that popular virtue plays in our kind of political system may lead us to look elsewhere than to government for the source of, and remedy for, our troubles. In modern America, accepting this truth will be hard. We are tempted to assume that the people are all right; it is just the politicians who have gone crazy. In comparative terms it is true, the people are more stable, less given to large abstractions, and generally more virtuous than the hard-driving campaigners they usually elect to public office. Yet there are good and bad currents evident among the American people.

Despite the breakdown of the family, the spread of pornography and violence, and the growing tendency to look to the federal government for solutions to social problems, the American people still display some old virtues. They tend to believe in hard work, fair treatment of one another, and sound moral and religious principles. The replacement of the nation's old WASP leadership and the ridicule it has received in some intellectual circles, however, has given even stalwart Americans the notion that the basic unifying themes of our history have disappeared.

The most urgent task facing us as a society is to learn to restate those themes in ways that speak to our current discontents. The alternative will not be a "diverse" nation but disaster. As Alexis de Tocqueville wrote:

> Without ideas in common, there is no common action, and, without common action, there may still exist human beings, but not a social entity. In order for society to exist, and, even more, to prosper, it is then necessary that the spirits of all the citizens be assembled and held together by certain leading ideas; and that cannot happen unless each of them comes from time to time to draw his opinions from the same source, and unless each consents to receive a certain number of ready-made beliefs.[6]

We still find such beliefs implicit in many American practices. We need to make them explicit.

Rather than reinventing government, we should concentrate on reinventing the American people. This far more pressing task is neither a sentimental nor a nostalgic one. We need to face current problems in the light of the truths we have held since our founding. Those truths wedded human dignity, which arose from religious respect for the value of all persons, with republican realism about political institutions. The Founders were willing to risk that a people given control over its own destiny would respond to the challenge. Whatever our current crises, we are not meeting them with our deepest spiritual and moral insights.

To begin with, we need to rethink several large questions simultaneously, especially what kinds of lessons current law and governmental practice are teaching the people. Somehow, for example, we have come to think that government payments give us dignity while support from family, church, and neighborhood make us dependent— virtually the opposite of our former beliefs and clearly a self-deception.

This mentality carries an additional cost. Where government moves into more and more social sectors, it inevitably tends to homogenize the very diversity that so many claim to cherish. American higher education, for example, used to be wonderfully diverse, with denominational, all-male, all-female, black, and other specialized schools filling various needs. Several decades into federal support for schools and guaranteed student loans, diversity is talked about a great deal. But, in fact, every institution is now required to be "diverse" in absolutely uniform ways.

This should be a cautionary tale for all sectors of society that see federal action as a simple solution to their problems. We were more diverse and more unified when we were less commanded to be so by federal legislators.

We also need a transfusion of new terms into the public sphere. Local community, industry, and agriculture form the living matrix for individuals and families, and our public speech used to reflect that truth. It may seem a paradox, but the people of a large republic like ours feel more a part of the national ethos when they are more closely a part of local life.

The mass media, particularly television, have fostered a false sense of interconnectedness. Despite our ability to follow events anywhere in the world, we feel more distant from one another at home than at any time in our past. We need to reexamine not only the amount of violence, but the glorification of sex and corruption on television. We also need to rethink entirely what powerful modern communication technologies mean for our way of life. The ancient Athenians thought Socrates corrupted the young, but even Socrates did not have their attention six hours a day.

It is no mere coincidence that in almost every portrayal of the future, from George Orwell's *1984* to *2001: A Space Odyssey*, complex machinery and political control are seen as, together, enfeebling or threatening the human race. Prospects for grand schemes like the data superhighway and universal medical services should prompt us to recall such warnings. Our primary task is to find ways to be less, not more, dependent on single mechanisms. Popular unity can accommodate diversity; bureaucratic uniformity and machinery cannot.

If we embrace more vigorously universal principles of human freedom and responsibility against all mechanical explanations of human behavior and against all reductive visions of human society, we may be able to escape the false unities of current politics. Relying on millions of individuals is a risk, because those individuals will be irresponsible as well as responsible, will abuse freedom as well as use it. America's Founders studied history, and they knew most democracies ended in tyranny. They took the risk.

Unless we wish to become a new kind of society under a different form of government, we must return to that basic faith—the faith that millions of free individuals working together in a free society that rewards and honors virtue, and discourages and blames vice and dependency, create the only unity finally worthy of us as Americans.

NOTES

1. John Jay, *The Federalist Papers*, ed. Clinton Rossiter (New York: New American Library, 1961), no. 2.

2. Todd Gitlin, *Harper's*, September 1993, 20.

3. Arthur M. Schlesinger, Jr., *The Disuniting of America: Reflections on a Multicultural Society* (New York: Norton, 1992), 103.

4. Zbigniew Brzezinski, *Crisis*, May 1993, 41.

5. Philip Rieff, *Triumph of the Therapeutic* (New York: Harper and Row, 1966), 58.

6. Alexis de Tocqueville, *Democracy in America*, vol. 2 (New York: Vintage Books, 1945).

Chapter 17

Character in the Marketplace

Earl Hess

INTRODUCTION

The focus of this chapter is on character and its relationship to our economic order. I do not approach the subject with a wealth of scholarly credentials but rather from the wisdom gained through nearly 35 years of founding, shaping, and growing my own business.

I began the venture as a chemist in private practice, well prepared technically to practice my profession but not armed with business school management skills. Although these two elements are normally considered prerequisite to business success, experience has taught me that there exists a third which undergirds the first two and without which neither has any meaning—namely the core values of the business founder. In that area I was richly endowed by a family and community that instilled through instruction and example the attributes of honesty, caring, respect, tolerance of differences, and serving others.

During these years I have tried to keep abreast of the rapid changes in science and technology and have learned the basics of business administration through either study or sometimes painful experience. But most significantly, I have learned how the core values referred to earlier can find expression in every aspect of a business venture when planted and nourished there.

As I anticipate retirement, Lancaster Laboratories, Inc. is no longer one chemist in private practice with a couple assistants but a thriving 520-person organization nationally known for its services provided in the environmental field and to the food and pharmaceutical industries. But it is also recognized, in addition to its technical competence, as an organization where values find expression in many ways in its style of doing business.

With this personal introduction, allow me to make some general observations before beginning the main body of this chapter.

GENERAL OBSERVATIONS

First, our economic order is foundational to our society's health. None of us can say we live above it. It is the "stuff" of our physical existence—the food, clothing, and shelter bought with moneys derived from our own specific occupation. In an age of mushrooming technology and specialization, we have become a highly interdependent society, far removed from our primitive ancestors who were largely self-sufficient. This shift from an independent to dependent lifestyle is actually the reason for our economic order. In the earliest times the caveman was completely independent and there was no trade. The first trade was by barter. One man excelled in hunting, another in farming, and they exchanged goods. Soon money became a universal medium of exchange, and as our society became more complex so did our economic system. Today, even those with Ph.D.s in the subject seem almost overwhelmed by its complexity. At least very few of them reach the same conclusion when presented with the same economic data!

Second, our complex economic order is highly dependent upon the morality of its players. A person's character is put to the test directly when the opportunity for economic gain pressures him or her to take something less than the high ground in business dealings. We have currently all kinds of examples of unscrupulous behavior: (1) the series of Wall Street scandals where insider trading brought inordinate wealth to a few by taking it from the many, (2) the savings and loan debacle, (3) companies compromising product safety for economic advantage, or (4) laboratories taking shortcuts in collection of data, putting at risk the health and safety of many.

A Norman Rockwell sketch illustrates most simply and best the dependence of our economic order on the character of its players. The sketch, appearing I believe as a *Saturday Evening Post* cover some time during the 1940s, depicts a butcher weighing a chicken on an old-fashioned scale. The chicken lies on some wrapping paper, and nicely concealed under the paper is the butcher's finger pressing down on the scales. But unseen by him is the *buyer's* finger (an older lady with the most serene look on her face) pushing up on the scales. (Who knows what that chicken really weighed?) This drawing hangs in our company's training room, and I use it in introducing our ethics training program to illustrate two points: (1) All of us are involved in the marketplace, as consumers at least if not as "businesspersons." (2) True character is revealed when moral values come into conflict with economic values and when we can violate moral values to our own economic benefit *without* being caught.

Finally, I have developed in recent months a diagram that helps me understand the necessary elements and their configuration in the creation and maintenance of a business (or any other organization) where ethical practice is a way of life for every employee and in every business transaction.

FIGURE 1

Values: Foundation of the Organization

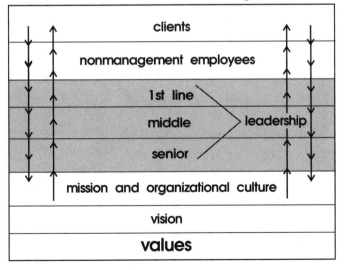

As indicated earlier, it is my firm belief that the integrity of an organization (or lack of it) begins and centers on its founder and/or current CEO. His or her values are incorporated into the *vision* of the entrepreneur and then, as the business forms and matures, into its corporate culture. That culture is no longer the property of its founder but is embraced by the organization's senior leaders.

But only after that culture is transmitted through various ranks of the leadership team does it become active in the most critical area, the interface between line employees and the customer. In recent years, many companies have made major commitments to total quality management, and they measure their success in terms of customer feedback. I have broadened the total quality concept to that of a total ethics process. Such includes not only a commitment to total quality but to a consistent living out of all corporate values as measured by the feedback not only of customers but of all stakeholders.

The main section of this chapter will tell the story of our company's journey in that quest.

ESTABLISHING A CORPORATE ETHOS THAT REINFORCES CHARACTER

In the early years of our corporate life, we operated without formal mission statements or codes of ethics. Did that mean that we did not have a mission or conduct ourselves ethically? Of course not. The group was small and informal, we were seeking our business niche by experimenting in a number of areas, and the tone of our conduct was set by the actions of the leadership. In fact, the character of those formative years became the bedrock on which our organization could grow in succeeding years.

In about 1980, when we seemed to have found our business niche, a mission statement seemed appropriate. It is significant as I reflect on that statement (still our current one) that we chose to define not only *what* we do, but *how* we are committed to doing it. The "what" part seems rather unexciting (independent laboratory services in the fields of chemistry and biology), but it has been valuable in guiding us to "stick to our knitting" when there is a temptation to wander outside our defined area. The *how* part of the statement commits us to the provision of quality service with a client focus, to conduct ourselves ethically, and to be good stewards of the resources that come our way.

Lancaster Laboratories' Mission Statement and Principles—A Credo

We will provide quality independent laboratory services in the chemical and biological sciences by:

- fully understanding and always meeting the requirements of those we serve;
- relating to our clients, coworkers, suppliers, and community in a fair and ethical manner;
- managing our growth and financial resources so we can serve our clients well, preserve our independence, and maintain our meaningful and enriching workplace.

This generic statement of the what and the how of our business has served us well, but of course it became necessary to develop more specific expressions of each. A variety of technical literature is available to clients setting forth the specifics of our technical offerings. We have also set forth documents outlining our procedures for assuring technical accuracy. In 1988, we set out on a total quality management (TQM) path and in so doing have merged our prior commitment to technical accuracy with an intensified commitment to identifying and meeting client needs. All full-time employees have received 15 hours of total quality training and have incorporated into their professional development plan at least one quality goal.

It was about four years ago at a company leadership retreat and planning session that I as founder made my first noises concerning my gradual retirement from the business. One of the small work groups responded by asking the larger group to help identify what my unique contributions to the business were and therefore what would be lost from the business when I retire if an effort were not made to preserve it. Identified first was my entrepreneurial spirit, but a close second was my persistent commitment to ethical practice. Out of that retreat came a "Corporate Culture" task force which has evolved over these four years into the current Ethics Committee.

The statement of purpose of the Ethics Committee follows. Although this group originated in the leadership retreat, the committee now consists of a cross-section of all employees.

Statement of Purpose

It shall be the responsibility of the Ethics Committee to:
- encourage and maintain commitment among employees to our core ethical values;

- act as a think tank in developing a "total ethics process" for orienting new employees and maintaining a high level of awareness and commitment of all within our organization;
- serve as a monitoring/oversight group for that process.

To date, the major effort of the group, in collaboration with our training department, has been to offer an ethical fitness training course to all employees. This course, taught in three two-and-half-hour sessions, is derived from a program developed by Rushworth Kidder of the Institute for Global Ethics.[1] The ethical fitness approach of Dr. Kidder is described in a recent book, *How Good People Make Tough Choices*.[2] I personally have elected to be trained as a trainer and offer about half of the instruction. The training sessions develop as follows:

Development of Moral Awareness

Through videotape and sharing of current events stories, we develop a sense of urgency for the issue not only in our workplace but in society in general. Using recent historical events (e.g., the Exxon Valdez, Chernobyl), we demonstrate how a deteriorating moral climate combined with the power of new technology threatens the very existence of our world in the twenty-first century. More specifically we look at the responsibility that we have to be competent and to be ethical in providing laboratory data, because the health and safety of society are dependent upon us.

Defining Core Values

Immediately following the awareness development is a simple exercise of setting forth core values that we would like to embrace as guiding principles in our work together. Not surprising, from one class to another, there is a striking similarity. Words like "honesty," "respect," "responsibility," "tolerance," and "caring" appear almost unanimously. Our Ethics Committee has produced a document described as our corporate Statement of Values by synthesizing and integrating the material gathered from these exercises. I take special satisfaction in the values statement, not only because of its content, but because it represents a document drawn from the employee ranks, not an edict handed out by management.

Statement of Values

Lancaster Laboratories' heritage has as its core the ethical treatment of everyone involved with our business. As a corporate community, we embrace our heritage of integrity and strive to live by the following principles:

- Fairness and honesty in all our relationships;
- Mutual trust;
- A respect for ourselves and others;
- A sense of caring that leads us to act responsibly toward each other in society, now and in the future;
- Loyalty to our clients and one another;
- A spirit of open-mindedness as we deal with all;
- Dedication to service;
- Good stewardship of our resources;
- A commitment to flexibility and continuous improvement.

We each take personal responsibility to live these values in all of our dealings, knowing full well our pledge may involve difficult choices, hard work, and courage.

As can be readily seen, character as we define it in our workplace goes beyond simple honesty in the way we collect our data and report it to clients or refrain from stealing company property or from each other. It embraces issues like caring—about each other, our clients, our vendors, our community; of respect for and tolerance for those different from us—in ethnic heritage, in religious faith, yes, even in lifestyle.

Our values statement is proving to be a very valuable and useful document. It acts as a filter through which our actions and/or company policies are judged. If there is an inconsistency, then we must examine our policies or actions. I wear a note on my name tag that simply says, "If I'm not living our values, challenge me."

A recent occurrence illustrated this principle beautifully and demonstrated that the values statement is a live document, not something gracing our literature file or boardroom walls. A given client required that all employees working in his project be subject to drug and alcohol testing. This included about half of the total workforce. When we prepared to comply, there was, of course, a release form for each employee to sign. In the form was some legal "hold harmless" language. A group of employees came to company leaders carrying the release form in one hand and our values statement in the other. "How are these consistent?" they asked. "They are not," we agreed and modified the release form to their satisfaction!

Defining and Analyzing Ethical Dilemmas

One of the unique aspects of Dr. Kidder's ethical fitness training[3] is its focus on the really tough ethical dilemmas faced when two of our core values would seem to draw us in opposite directions. He describes these as right/right dilemmas while basic right/wrong situations are referred to simply as moral temptations. After some classroom instruction, discussion, and practice, students divide into small groups and share ethical dilemmas that they have faced or are familiar with, looking at each through four windows: truth versus loyalty, self versus community, short term versus long term, and justice versus mercy. In so doing and in subsequent sharing with the class, students grapple with real-life situations from either work or family life and come to understand that some common principles underlie most of what they deal with.

Understanding and Applying Decision-Making Rules

Three common decision-making rules taught by philosophers are then set forth as practical down-to-earth ways of resolving dilemmas: (1) ends based, otherwise known as consequentialism or utilitarianism; (2) care based, often referred to as the golden rule or the reversibility concept; and (3) rule based, often referred to as Immanuel Kant's categorical imperative. Students go back into their same groups as mentioned above, and attempt to solve their dilemmas through one or more of the decision-making rules. Oftentimes when no clear solution is evident, a creative alternative develops to help resolve the matter.

The net effect of our ethical fitness training has been truly remarkable. We have agreed on a set of values, which we will attempt to live up to. We feel comfortable in challenging each other if we experience deviation from them. Additionally, we have provided each employee with a common language (very comparable to TQM language) for the discussion of the ethical aspects of any work or personal situation. Most of all, we have established the importance of character in their work and personal lives.

But a training course at the beginning of one's work experience is not enough. Concepts will soon gather dust if not actively used in daily life. With training now behind, except for new employees, the Ethics Committee is focusing its attention on keeping the issue alive. An ethics bulletin board displaying current issues, a "dilemma of the month" column in our internal newsletter, recognition for those best exemplifying our values—all are appearing as ongoing activities.

Recently a company-wide survey was made to assess how well we are living our values. Ninety percent of employees completed the survey giving satisfactory ratings in most areas. In areas of sensitivity and teamwork the ratings were slightly less positive, pointing to the need for training and development in those areas.

Using recently commercialized human resource software called *SynergEASE*[4] (which we were privileged to beta test), we are now addressing the issue of more systematic recruitment of new employees. The competency requirements of each job class are identified by a combination of dimensions unique to that position. Included at all levels are dimensions which parallel our values statement. Thus, we can systematically screen and interview not only for technical competence but for values that match our own. Such a process, which requires a day's specific training for all interviewers, is now in place. It is too early to tell what impact it will have.

Another activity is a review of our performance appraisal system. It is only natural that employees will respond in those areas for which they are held accountable. If raises and promotions are based solely on technical or financial achievement, then corporate leadership sends a message that living our values is secondary. The *SynergEASE* software will be helpful here as well. By assessing an individual employee's adherence to the corporate values, job plans can include goals for improvement in those areas considered weak. Progress against such goals can be measured and made part of performance assessment.

THE SIGNIFICANCE OF LEADERSHIP DEVELOPMENT IN MAINTAINING AN ETHICAL CULTURE

To this point I have stated that the ethical tone of a business organization is clearly set by its senior leader(s), and have emphasized the importance of positive character traits in line workers if the customer is to be served in a totally ethical manner. But there is one important link that has not been discussed, those commonly referred to as middle management or supervisors. (I prefer to call them first and second tier leaders.) They represent the critical link in connecting senior leaders to line workers by owning and modeling corporate values in their work lives. It is obvious that the old style of command and control management does not harmonize with our corporate values. In fact, conventional managers do not even fit into a total quality culture where empowerment is critical to the success of the process.

Our success in developing leaders who model our culture is based on a search for those who see themselves first as servants and second as leaders. Such leadership styles are promoted by groups such as the Greenleaf Center for Servant-Leadership[5] and by authors such as James Kouzes, Barry Posner,[6] and Stephen Covey.[7] Two themes emerge from our experience which are consistent with those set forth by these gurus:

First, a leader to be effective must see himself or herself in the role of a servant.

Second, effective leadership begins with embracing and modeling core values such as trustworthiness, integrity, caring. James Autry in his book titled *Love and Profit* sums it up by saying, "workers want to know how much you care before they care how much you know."[8] Kouzes and Posner in their book *The Leadership Challenge* identify five qualities of outstanding leaders: enable others to act; model the way; challenge the process; encourage the heart; and inspire a shared vision.

In their second book, *Credibility*, they relate these characteristics to virtues of integrity, trust, etc. I think it is obvious how these characteristics are consistent with our company's statement of values.

We thus have two building blocks for our leadership development, the basic instruction in ethical fitness taken by all employees and the opportunity to develop leadership skills as described above. Two other elements are about to be offered. The first are seminars in development of psychological hardiness. Every leader who takes his or her job seriously is well aware that carrying responsibility for others is stressful. How to deal with stress to remain hardy through such times is, of course, important to a leader's long-term well-being.

Finally, we are using the materials of Edward de Bono concerning lateral thinking as action tools for leading groups in problem solving, avoiding conflict, and turning opposing energies into synergistic ones.[9] De Bono's "Six Thinking Hats" process guides us in techniques of group process and team building that support values such as respect, tolerance, cooperation. Developing the skills within our leadership team to engage in as well as to lead groups in lateral thinking will empower them to exemplify in their leadership many of the values which we uphold.

The four areas in leadership development described thus far hang together in the form of a diamond, as developed by James P. (Pat) Carlisle,[10] our human resources consultant who works with our training group in delivering these development experiences. At the four corners are the development tools we've already discussed, which when used together give rise to what he calls the totally credible leader.

FIGURE 2

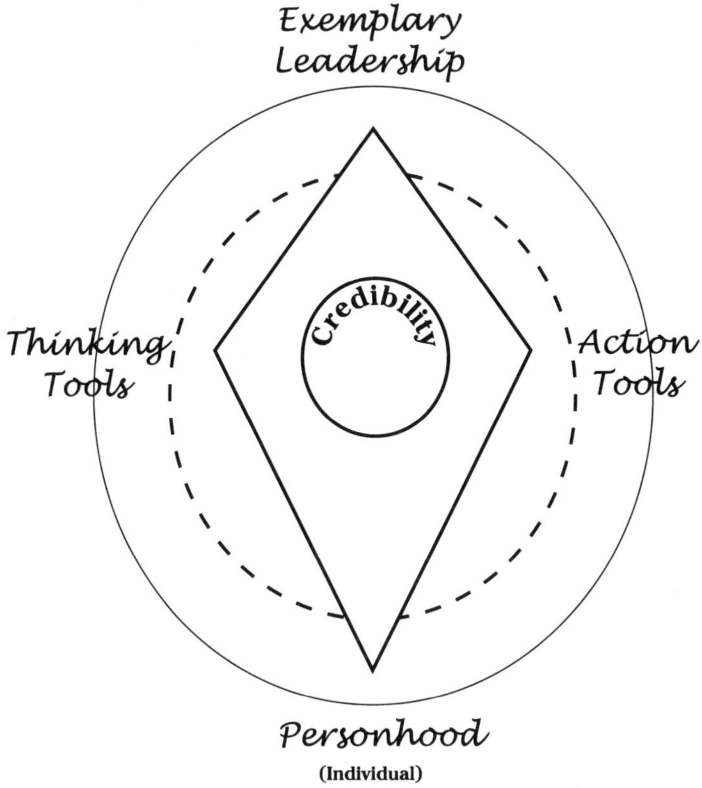

Exemplary
Leadership

Thinking
Tools

Credibility

Action
Tools

Personhood
(Individual)

SUMMARY AND CONCLUSIONS

Our economic order frames our human existence. It becomes more complex as we become more specialized in our vocational skills and thus more interdependent. In this interdependent society, technical and business skills alone are not enough. They must be undergirded by people of character exhibiting the core values of honesty, caring, respect for others, etc.

Lancaster Laboratories, a company which I founded 34 years ago, has been for me not only a chemistry lab but one where beliefs that I held with respect to ethics in business could be tested. We have in the last few years put into place a total ethics process, comparable in approach but much broader in scope than the total quality process popular in American companies today. It has elements comparable to TQM, including a strong educational program for all employees, tied in with ongoing awareness, recognition, and challenge. A tangible and very useful product of the educational process is a corporate statement of values. Evaluation of our progress is being monitored with a new computer software tool that also is of value in the screening of recruits for their fit with our values.

Finally, the development of special skills in our leadership teams enables them to "talk the talk" and "walk the walk" and provides employees with the knowledge that ethical conduct is expected and valued. It brings out their best not just in technical achievement but in qualities of character that strengthen our company.

NOTES

1.   For information, write: The Institute for Global Ethics, 21 Elm Street, Box 563, Camden, ME 04843.

2.   Rushworth M. Kidder, *How Good People Make Tough Choices* (New York: Morrow, 1995).

3.   Kidder, *Tough Choices*.

4.   Development Dimensions International, *SynergEASE* (Bridgeville, PA).

5.   For information, write: The Greenleaf Center for Servant-Leadership, 921 E. 86th Street, Suite 200, Indianapolis, IN 46240.

6.   James M. Kouzes and Barry Z. Posner, *The Leadership Challenge* (San Francisco: Jossey-Bass, 1987); and *Credibility* (San Francisco: Jossey-Bass, 1989).

7.   Stephen R. Covey, *The Seven Habits of Highly Effective People* (New York: Simon and Schuster, 1989); *Principle Centered Leadership* (New York:

Summit Books, 1990); and A. Roger Merrill and Rebecca R. Merrill, *First Things First* (New York: Simon and Schuster, 1994).

8.   James A. Autry, *Love and Profit* (New York: Morrow, 1991), 17.

9.   Advanced Practical Thinking Training, *Official Edward de Bono Thinking Methods* (Des Moines, IA); Edward de Bono, *Six Thinking Hats* (New York: Little, Brown, 1986); and *Lateral Thinking* (Larchmont, NY: International Center for Creative Thinking, 1990).

10.   For information, write: Carlisle Leadership Group, 1722 Niblick Avenue, Lancaster, PA 17602-4826.

Chapter 18

Character and American Compassion, Past and Present

Marvin Olasky

INTRODUCTION

Did the nineteenth-century understanding of compassion work? Almost all observers could see that jobs existed for the able-bodied and willing except during occasional periods of business panic. And all agreed that living conditions for many of the urban poor, particularly in crowded Manhattan, were terrible (the 1880 census showed six wards in lower Manhattan with over 200,000 persons per square mile).

The debate, however, centered over the direction of movement: for how many was dire poverty a short-term curse? To what extent did charity and challenge help individuals escape poverty and to what extent was upward mobility a result of economic growth? Was it fair that most would advance—but some very slowly—while those unwilling to work would not advance at all? Should we observe the snapshot of poverty or watch the moving picture of general upward mobility?

Charity organizations presented favorable statistics of their work, but numbers can mislead. Observers' reactions varied greatly based on the perspectives they brought to their analyses. On the one hand, many turn-of-the century Jewish and Christian magazines regularly reported challenge and response: volunteers convinced a man who had become used to dependency "that he must earn his living"; a woman who had become demoralized "was worked with, now through kindness, again through discipline, until finally she began to show a desire to help herself."[1] On the other hand, early twentieth-century muckraking magazines suggested that little was changing and that all should share in the wealth.

Jacob Riis, a writer who hauled heavy cameras up flights of stairs hour after hour, day after day to provide striking photographs of dull-eyed families in crowded lower Manhattan flats, argued that government welfare made life worse by creating an "incentive to parents to place their children upon the public for support";[2] material distribution to the able-bodied, by the state or private charities, led to "degrading and pauperizing" rather than "self-respect and self-dependence." Riis praised New York's Charity Organization Society and "kindred organizations" for showing "what can be done by well-directed effort" and understood that progress was incremental and tied to economic growth.[3]

Others, however, argued that compassion required "coercive philanthropy"—the taxation of all—which would "establish among us true cities of God."[4] "Social misery and wrong" could be ended by officials with "a genuine and earnest and passionate desire for the betterment of mankind." Welfare programs could "become the outer form of the altruistic spirit—the unselfish, loving, just nature of the new man."[5]

TRUE COMPASSION: SUFFERING WITH

Part of this revisionist definition was based on the revived 1840s idea of man as naturally good and productive unless a competitive environment warped finer sensibilities. While early twentieth-century reporter Ray Stannard Baker saw that *suffering with* compassion was having an impact—"Whenever I went downtown to see [the] work [of one mission] I always came away hopeful"[6]—he was disappointed that many did not undergo change. One-by-one compassion was based on handpicking of fruit ready to be harvested, but an apple-grabbing machine presumably could motor through the orchard. Baker distinguished the old understanding from what he hoped could be a new one by titling one of his articles, *Lift Men from the Gutter? or, Remove the Gutter? Which?*[7]

For those working within the biblical understanding of compassion, the question was not either/or; the goal was to remove as much of the gutter as possible so that no one would have to live in it. Yet they had the grim expectation that some would seek out parts of the gutter that remained, or

build new sections and sometimes drag their children and others into it—
"the poor you always have with you." While Social Darwinists gave up
at that point, those who believed the story of the prodigal son argued that
times of torment were not wasted; it was sometimes necessary for some
to hit bottom before they were ready to move up.[8]

One Charity Organization Society official conveyed this understanding:

> the question which we try through investigation to answer [is,] Are these
> applicants of ours ready to work out with us...some plan which will result in
> their rescue from dependency...? If such elements are entirely lacking—no
> basis of good character, no probability of final success—then we do not
> assume the responsibility of asking societies or churches or private persons
> to help, and may even, if our advice is asked, urge them to refrain from blind
> interference with natural educational agencies."[9]

The goal was not "that poor families should suffer, but that charity
should accomplish its purpose." Mission workers steeled themselves to
bid farewell to those who would not accept the challenge to change.
Some who left never came back, but as one volunteer wrote, "the
prodigals commonly returned confessing their weakness and laboring
earnestly to prove their penitence."[10]

Such thinking was unacceptable to those who saw no need for hearts to
change. Greeleyites and Bellamyites saw sins but not sin, evil acts but not
evil and believed that problems originated in social conditions not moral
corruption. "[A]lmost all social thinkers are now agreed that the social
evils of the day arise in large part from social wrongs."[11] Since actions
were determined by environmental factors, a good environment would save
all. Compassion gradually came to mean acceptance of self-destructive
behavior and postponement of pressure to change until all were in a good
environment.[12]

Since theological liberals believed that persons freed from material
pressures also would be freed from the sinful tendencies arising from those
pressures, a focus on material need emerged. One novelist described the
extent to which material comfort was believed to drive moral progress:

> the world is constantly growing better and happier....[T]here can hardly be
> any doubt about this [when one sees] the changes which the century has
> brought about in the people's health, education, and comfort....People are
> better housed, and for that reason, among others, their morality has
> improved.[13]

If utopia could be attained through mass redistribution, personal compassion was unnecessary. Compassion could become synonymous with sending a check or passing redistributionist legislation.

PROFESSIONALISM AND CROWDING-OUT

A new stress on professionalized social work accompanied increased government action. The New York Charity Organization Society's Summer School of Philanthropy, established in 1898, soon became the Columbia University Graduate School of Social Work.[14] One Charity Organization Society official worried that professionals were being "exalted...at the expense of the volunteer," and noted a "certain opinionated and self-righteous attitude in some of the trained social workers [who saw the world as a stage] upon which we professional workers are to exercise our talents, while the volunteers do nothing but furnish the gate receipts and an open-mouthed admiration of our performances."[15]

National Conference of Social Work president Owen Lovejoy announced in 1920 that social workers would have a new kind of task. While volunteers had endeavored "to ameliorate evil social conditions, to lighten the burdens of poverty, to reduce the volume of ignorance, combat the ravages of disease and otherwise labor diligently to assuage the flood of human sorrow and wretchedness," social workers and their allies would be "social engineers" capable of creating "a divine order on earth as it is in heaven....[S]imply making the earth a place that will be humanely endurable and stopping there [is] an intolerable belittling of the innate qualities in man."[16]

In short, Horace Greeley's idea that all (even the voluntarily idle) were entitled to a piece of the pie gained vast intellectual and theological support in the early twentieth century. Just as it was considered unfair within liberal theology that anyone should go to hell, if there was a hell, so it was unfair that anyone should physically suffer in this life. The universalistic theology that all must be saved, regardless of beliefs and actions, was matched by a universalist sociology that all must receive provision.

Other changes followed. If provision of material aid was primary, programs could be measured by the amount of material transferred, and nonquantifiable considerations could be overlooked. The nineteenth-century concern that state charity would supplant private efforts—the "crowding out" effect—was turned upside down: some began to call for less private charity, arguing that such efforts let government off the hook. "It became evident in many communities that so long as private agencies, including charity organization societies, continued to care for those families eligible for a pension, it would be easy for the state to evade the responsibility."[17]

One Philadelphia group was praised for no longer helping widows, for only when private groups went on strike would "public funds ever be wholly adequate for the legitimate demands made upon them."[18] Increasingly, some saw charitable organizations as a sign of government weakness rather than as a sign of social strength. As professionals increasingly dominated the realm of compassion, opportunities for charitable work decreased and volunteers departed. At the United Charities of Chicago by 1915, "interested laymen were as likely to be consigned to a desk job as they were to be assigned to a family." When board members at one organization wanted more involvement, its president announced, "our staff is so well organized that there is very little for our Board Members to do...."[19]

Boards did, however, retain one major function—fundraising: "Under the exacting gaze of a freshly certified professional elite, boards were remodeled into fundraising bodies...." Increased economic segregation and mediated compassion allowed the better-off to "measure community needs through abstractions: publicity, lectures, the photographs in annual reports. Communications innovations, like professionalization, separated the twentieth century donor from the object of his largesse. [Donors] could exercise the obligations of stewardship at a safe remove from the problems they were helping to solve."[20]

By the 1920s, a University of Chicago sociologist found that suburban residents were unlikely to venture into poor areas. One woman explained, "[the slums are] too dirty and besides it's too dangerous. I can't see how anyone could get a kick out of doing that. Merely the idea of it is nauseating to me."[21] A willingness merely to spend money grew as the desire to expend time decreased: "Like some of Shakespeare's characters [rich people] have developed a habit of flinging purses at the least provocation and crying: 'Spend this for me!'"[22] One wealthy Chicagoan, when asked why her peers were not involved in person-to-person activity, said, "Organizations look after everything, and they give to them, so why think about it?"[23]

By the 1930s, the long-term trend toward redefinition was already on its way to making cash king. Decreased personal action was easy to justify when problems seemed overwhelming, and when an emphasis on

Community Chest cash transfers provided "the ultimate in bureaucracy—an anonymous public supporting anonymous machinery supporting anonymous clients."[24] Philanthropy had become "as cold as payment of taxes," one journalist noted, "indeed the objectives of the two are often the same."[25] The New Deal emphasis on compassion as income transfer was generally accepted because the ground had long been prepared.

In 1938, one editor wrote:

> [P]ersonal conscience in the United States has fallen to a new low in our history as a nation. It has been largely lost to our sight in all the din and dither that have been raised about that other moral concept, the social conscience, which, we are constantly reminded, has a nobler and more widely embracing function. And, the more we hear of the one, the less we hear of the other. The personal conscience has been steadily submerged; the very foundation upon which any broader conception of individual responsibility towards society must rest is being washed away.[26]

Influenced by ideas of the Left, many social work leaders argued that emphasizing individuals was a "trivial and reactionary" practice that

> imposes on the individual the cruel burden of adapting himself to a psychotic society, and, insofar as it succeeds, constitutes a brake on social action.... [T]rained social workers in the relief field are helping fundamentally to bring about a new social order [through] the reorientation of clients from the still prevalent viewpoints of rugged individualism to the newer social philosophy dictated by the interdependent, complex society of today.[27]

REDISTRIBUTIONISM TRIUMPHS

The *Oxford English Dictionary* has as its second definition of compassion "The feeling, or emotion, when a person is moved by the suffering or distress of another, and by the desire to relieve it...." Similarly, *Webster's Third International Dictionary* defines compassion as a "deep feeling for and understanding of misery or suffering and the concomitant desire to promote its alleviation."[28] The implications of these definitions substantially depart from the one Noah Webster offered in 1834: "suffering with another; painful sympathy...."[29] The older definition demands personal action, the other two a mere "feeling" that requires only a willingness to pass a bill or send a check.

By the 1960s, one lecture series emphasized the new conventional wisdom: "the age-old plague" of poverty will end as soon as "proper direction" and "imaginative planning" bear down on it. "We have reached the stage where old concepts of charity and almsgiving no longer apply.... There will always be the need for the spirit of generosity and neighborly benevolence, but it will act on a higher and happier level." That happier level was massive wealth redistribution, based on "a five-year or a ten-year or a 50-year plan...to end this abject poverty."[30]

While liberal theologians planned tours of the celestial city, Lyndon Johnson declared his intention to create "a Great Society: a society of success without squalor, beauty without barrenness, works of genius without the wretchedness of poverty."[31] Johnson's legislative triumphs of 1964 and 1965—the Economic Opportunity Act, food stamp legislation, Medicare, Medicaid, public works programs, and so on—were immense. The speed of passage, unrivaled since the New Deal, showed a disregard for real-life effects, and was more remarkable in not being prompted by the mood of crisis so evident in 1933.[32] Great Society legislation was truly a triumph of faith, the social gospel walking on earth.

Yet, as nineteenth-century charity leaders had warned, government programs lacked true compassion and tended to produce social folly at the margin. The War on Poverty meant that some Detroit auto workers could earn more by quitting their jobs and joining job-training programs; in Johnson, Rhode Island, 73 parents of children in a poverty program owned more property—58 homes and 113 cars—than typical nonpoor residents.[33]

Reports of such inequities were embarrassing but underlying materialist assumptions predominated. One administration official said, "The way to eliminate poverty is to give the poor people enough money so that they won't be poor anymore."[34] One columnist wrote that for $12 to $15 billion a year (two percent of the gross national product) "poverty could be abolished in the United States"—as if a change in material circumstances would inevitably alter attitudes that, left unchanged, would create new poverty.[35]

Books of the period generally equated compassion with redistribution and argued for compassion not just to widows, orphans, and other victims but to those who had victimized themselves and wished to continue in self-destructive pursuits.[36] Some of these books claimed to be based on the Bible, and others were explicitly Buddhist; the common theme was compassion as "a vision that dissolves division" and that teaches "seeing the unity in things."[37] Attempts to distinguish the deserving from the undeserving "[legitimize] inequality...."[38]

The political agenda in this use of compassion was evident: "Only through greater reliance upon programs that offer the promise of opportunity as envisioned in the Great Society is the nation likely to reject policies of negativism and retrenchment for a more compassionate response to poverty in America."[39]   The National Council of Churches called for "the extrication of stewardship from its almost indelible association with economic capitalism." Douglas Hall demanded "a new look at the socialist alternative" and a "search for new forms of community—including a 'New Economic Order' that can more adequately reflect our faith's concern for justice, equality, and mercy."[40]

COMPASSION TODAY

By the 1980s, observers such as Clifford Orwin noted abundant misuse of "compassion": "Our century has hardly seen a demagogue, however bloody and monstrous his designs, who has not known how to rally compassion and mine its potential for sympathetic moral indignation."[41] Writer Mickey Kaus noted that Americans were supposed to have "compassion for the unmotivated delinquent who would rather smoke PCP than work. Compassion makes few distinctions—we are all in Mario Cuomo's 'family'—which is why a politics based on mass-produced compassion leads naturally to the indiscriminate dispensing of cash in a sort of all-purpose socialized United Way campaign."[42]

Despite such warnings, a bull market in compassion raged throughout the 1980s, particularly on the issue of "homelessness." The *Washington Post* typically used "compassion" as a euphemism for "more heavily funded": when Speaker of the House Tip O'Neill favored more spending on the homeless, his "compassion was the size of his frame."[43] O'Neill's successor Jim Wright was likewise praised, as was Washington, D.C. Mayor Marion Barry.[44] Professor Dwight Lee concluded, "The notion that compassion toward the poor requires favoring expansion of government transfer programs has achieved the status of revealed truth."[45]

As the 1980s came to an end, compassion also meant "leniency": Chicago lawyers asked a judge for compassion when sentencing a sheriff's deputy for selling cocaine;[46] California lawyers asked a jury to have compassion for an accused murderer by letting him off.[47] Baseball star Steve Garvey asked for compassion for having exercised passion through bigamy or trigamy.[48] At times the word was even less defined: a music reviewer complained that an LP record was filled with "make-out ballads" for "the wine-and-cheese crowd," but was saved by "the mix of spiky aggression and compassion."[49] A California music group was praised for trying to "communicate" the idea of compassion in a "noncognitive way."[50]

TRAGIC CONSEQUENCES

There are many more ludicrous examples, but the misconception is more tragic than comic. In 1990, *New York Times* employee Nathaniel Dunforth sought to

> fulfill a long-standing dream by quitting [his] job...[and taking] a position at half the pay as a caseworker with New York City's Child Welfare Administration....I lasted two months....Paperwork ruled the office; social work was secondary. I got more forms and documents on my first day than I had seen in seven years at the *Times*....[Cases] would be shifted from desk to desk, getting "attachments"—more forms for the caseworker to fill out. They would eventually reach our supervisor, to sit for a few more hours and a few more "attachments"....Meanwhile, in various parts of the city, the children and the sympathetic adults trying to help them were left to fume....The tragedy is evident in the lament that 'I had a calling; it was that simple. I wanted to help."[51]

Dreams also have died among many poor people. Prior to the 1960s entitlement revolution, marriage was both a social and economic contract. Economically, it was a compassionate antipoverty device that offered adults affiliation and challenge while providing children with two parents. So strong was support for marriage in the 1950s that 85 percent of single pregnant women got married before their babies were born. Those who did not had a second option: placing a child for adoption. Fewer than one in ten pregnant women chose single parenthood for fear of social ostracism and lack of financial support.[52] While marriage under pressure certainly was not optimal, it did not leave a woman alone. Placing a child for adoption also was difficult, but one result of the marriage/adoption emphasis was that children had fathers during their early years.

In the 1960s, as part of the new definition of "compassion," government obligations to single mothers increased while marital obligations decreased. As no-fault divorce laws spread, women knew that husbands were allowed to be unfaithful with little penalty. Sociologist Jack Douglas noted:

> Almost all women have enough economic common sense to realize that the marriage contract has been tremendously devalued by the legal changes. Since any potential husband can fly free of his family at the first impulse, women have far fewer incentives to get married, even when they are pregnant.[53]

The reduction of social and financial barriers to single parenting made it seem logical to raise children alone, even though they often grew up not only materially poor—three out of five were in poverty—but emotionally impoverished as well. Their mother's husband, in essence, was the federal government. These children never knew what it was like to have a father who could love and discipline them.

Many programs described as "compassionate" were actually the opposite, since they made neighborly or familial help less likely. To gain a full share of government-funded services, pregnant teens had to be on their own, without support from families or children's fathers. While there was no clear evidence that government entitlements led women to become pregnant, they did influence decisions to choose parenting or adoption, marriage or welfare dependency, and living at home or in an apartment. Adolescents were aware of opportunities for government support and "did not consider the expense of raising a child as a barrier" to setting out on their own.[54] To a teenager, monthly AFDC stipends looked like a great deal, and they were available only if bonds were broken. As single mothers moved into their own apartments, government spending was actually reducing the level of true compassion by providing incentives for social isolation.

NEEDED: A RETURN TO TRUE COMPASSION

At a reunion of Johnson administration officials in Austin, Texas, 25 years after the War on Poverty fired its first cannonade, the mood of reminiscence was akin to William Wordsworth's memory of enthusiasm following the French Revolution: "Bliss was it in that dawn to be alive...."[55] Sargent Shriver exulted that the Reagan years had not really damaged Great Society programs, most of which were "still in existence, all helping millions of Americans today." *New York Times* columnist Tom Wicker proposed that it is time to stop moaning and instead drink a toast to "vision and aspiration, confidence and compassion."

Vision, aspiration, and confidence were all there. But was compassion? Not if the word is given its historical definition—and we need to bring back that original understanding. Not only is the current misuse notorious, but current confusion among those who really want to help shows no signs of abating: "Washington, like cities across America, is doing a rotten job of housing its homeless. But I haven't a clue as to how to do it much better."[56] "Some great revision in our assumptions or in our actions is required. But because I feel genuinely caught in this dilemma myself, I am not now advocating any particular resolution."[57]

Today, while Americans sit and debate, or increasingly give up, generations are being lost. Crack babies in inner-city hospitals tremble and twitch uncontrollably. Teenage mothers, alone with squalling children, fight the impulse to strike out. Men in their twenties call job-holders "chumps" and go on a rampage in Los Angeles. Women in their thirties, abandoned by husbands, wait for their numbers to be called in cold welfare offices. Homeless men, aged beyond their years, line up impatiently at food wagons and then shuffle off to eat and drink in alleys smelling of urine.

The good news is that the impasse can be resolved. Many lives can be saved if we recapture the vision that changed lives up to a century ago. In one sense, we have thought ourselves into this social disaster, and we can think ourselves out of it. The key to the solution is an accurate definition of the problem. To arrive at that definition, we need to repack into our understanding of compassion both the theory and the practice of *suffering with*, mutual obligation, and challenge.

This chapter was originally Part II of an article entitled "American Compassion, Past and Present" which appeared in June 1992 in the newsletter Philanthropy, Culture, and Society *published by the Capital Research Center in Washington, D.C. Part I appeared in the April 1992 edition of that same newsletter.*

NOTES

1. *The American Hebrew* LII (11 February 1898), 448.
2. Jacob Riis, *The Children of the Poor* (New York: Scribner's, 1892), 277-78.
3. Jacob Riis, *How the Other Half Lives* (New York: Dover edition, 1971), 199.
4. Richard Ely, American Economic Association founder, from a speech given 4 December 1891, before the Evangelical Alliance convention in Boston.
5. R. M. Newton, *New York Journal*, 24 December 1899, 39.
6. Ray Stannard Baker, *The Spiritual Unrest* (New York: Stokes, 1910), 157.
7. *American Magazine*, July 1909.
8. Many mission workers modeled their practice of compassion on the biblical pattern, in which God frequently let the Israelites see the consequences of their beliefs and would not show compassion until they repented.

9.   Edward T. Devine, New York Charity Organization Society secretary, "The Value and Dangers of Investigation," *Proceedings of the Section on Organization of Charity*, 1897, 91-92.

10.   Arthur Bonner, *Jerry McAuley and His Mission* (Neptune, NJ: Loizeaux Brothers, 1967), 64.

11.   William D. P. Bliss, ed., *The Encyclopedia of Social Reform* (New York: Funk & Wagnalls, 1897), 270.

12.   Simon N. Patten, *The New Basis of Civilization* (Cambridge: Harvard University Press, 1968; originally published 1907), 205. Patten noted his allegiance to the "heretical doctrine that the depraved man is not the natural man."

13.   Hall Caine, "Mission of the Twentieth Century," *Chicago Tribune*, 30 December 1900, 37.

14.   Names during the transitional period were the New York School of Philanthropy and the New York School of Social Work.

15.   Mary Richmond of the Baltimore Charity Organization Society, quoted in Roy Lubove, *The Progressives and the Slums: Tenement House Reform in New York City, 1890-1917* (Pittsburgh: University of Pittsburgh Press, 1962), 199-200. In 1893, Anna Dawes delivered a paper on "The Need for Training Schools for a New Profession"; in 1897, Mary Richmond followed with a much-discussed paper, "The Need of a Training School in Applied Philanthropy."

16.   Owen R. Lovejoy, "The Faith of a Social Worker," *Survey* 44 (8 May 1920), 209.

17.   Frank Dekker Watson, *The Charity Organization Movement in the United States* (New York: Macmillan, 1922), 398-99.

18.   Watson, *Charity Organization Movement*.

19.   Kathleen McCarthy, *Noblesse Oblige* (Chicago: University of Chicago Press, 1982), 136, 146.

20.   McCarthy, *Noblesse Oblige*, 147, 167.

21.   Clarence Elmer Glick thesis, quoted in McCarthy, *Noblesse Oblige*, 167-68.

22.   "Billions for Practical Piety" *Literary Digest,* 26 January 1929, 28.

23.   Results of interviews by Harvey W. Zorbaugh, quoted in McCarthy, *Noblesse Oblige*, 170.

24.   Walter I. Trattner, *Homer Folks: Pioneer in Social Welfare* (New York: Columbia University Press, 1968), 221.

25.   Allan Herrick, *You Don't Have to Be Rich* (New York: Appleton-Century, 1940), 201, 202. Herrick noted that relief was once "personal, direct, frank, and above board," but in the new pattern "the giver never sees the object of his bounty....Whether the recipient is made happy or is embittered by the gift, is unknown to him. Giving is impersonal, indirect, mechanized."

26.   J. Donald Adams, "The Collapse of Conscience," *The Atlantic Monthly*, January 1938, 9.

27.   Grace Marcus, "The Status of Social Casework Today," *Compass*, June 1935, 5-12.

28. *Webster's Third New International Dictionary* (Springfield: Merriam-Webster, 1986), 462.

29. Noah Webster, *American Dictionary of the English Language* (New York: N. and J. White, 1834), 167.

30. R. M. MacIver, ed., *The Assault on Poverty: And Individual Responsibility* (New York: Institute for Religious and Social Studies, distribution by Harper & Row, 1965), 1-3. The placement of a colon followed by "And" in the title seems unusual, but was apparently designed to emphasize the responsibility of readers to take action. The War on Poverty turned out to be an assault on individual responsibility, without the colon.

31. *Public Papers of the Presidents of the United States, Lyndon B. Johnson,* 1963-64, no. 431, 819.

32. See Doris Goodwin, *Lyndon Johnson and the American Dream* (New York: Harper & Row, 1976).

33. Merritt Ierley, *With Charity For All* (New York: Praeger, 1984), 179.

34. Quoted by Stewart Alsop, "After Vietnam— Abolish Poverty?" *Saturday Evening Post,* 17 December 1966, 12.

35. Alsop, "After Vietnam," 12. Alsop, however, predicted that social universalistic proposals would be a hard sell if they would result in transferring income, no questions asked, to "the drunks and the drug addicts, as well as bad people, immoral people and just plain lazy people....[T]he deepest and most instinctive opposition to the idea derives from 'the Puritan ethic,'" and only if that ethic was attacked could universalistic proposals receive widespread acceptance.

36. These books include titles such as *The Philosophy of Compassion, The Veins of Compassion, The Power of Compassion, The Beauty of Compassion, Truth and Compassion, A Spirituality Named Compassion,* and *Tear-Catchers: Developing the Gift of Compassion.*

37. Christina Feldman, "Nurturing Compassion," 23, and Jack Kornfield, "The Path of Compassion," 25, in Fred Eppsteiner, ed., *The Path of Compassion: Writings on Socially Engaged Buddhism* (Berkeley: Parallax Press, 1988).

38. David E. Purpel, *The Moral & Spiritual Crisis in Education: A Curriculum for Justice and Compassion in Education* (Granby, MA: Bergin & Garvey, 1989), 35. Regarding education, Purpel asks, "Why do we single out a group for 'graduating with honor?' Does this mean that those who are not in this group are without honor?" Purpel, *Moral & Spiritual Crisis,* 37.

39. Sar A. Levitan, George Washington University, *Programs in Aid of the Poor,* 5th ed. (Baltimore: Johns Hopkins University Press, 1985), 138.

40. Douglas John Hall, *The Steward: A Biblical Symbol Come of Age* (New York: Friendship Press, 1982), 79-81.

41. See Clifford Orwin, "Compassion," *The American Scholar,* Summer 1986, 309-33.

42. Mickey Kaus, "Up from Altruism: The Case Against Compassion," *The New Republic,* 15 December 1986, 17.

43.   *Washington Post,* 22 December 1987, A2.

44.   *Washington Post,* 17 November 1984, A1.

45.   Dwight Lee, *Public Compassion and Political Competition,* booklet published in the Contemporary Issue Series (no. 35) by the Center for the Study of American Business, Washington University, St. Louis, September 1989, 14-15. Lee also observed, "To suggest that government transfers should be reduced, or even tightly constrained, is to risk being rebuked as heartless."

46.   *Chicago Tribune,* 28 September 1989, 2.

47.   *Los Angeles Times,* 28 September 1989, II-1.

48.   *Los Angeles Times,* 24 September 1989, 7.

49.   *Chicago Tribune,* 28 September 1989, 13E.

50.   *Los Angeles Times,* 27 September 1989, VI-9.

51.   Nathaniel Dunford, "N.Y.C., True to Form," *New York Times,* 10 April 1990, A21.

52.   Maris Vinovskis, *An "Epidemic" of Adolescent Pregnancy?* (New York: Oxford University Press, 1988), 25.

53.   Jack Douglass, University of California at San Diego, "Pro-Family Laws Can Help Revitalize Family Life," unpublished manuscript, cited in "New Research" section of *The Family in America,* April 1987.

54.   Judith S. Musick, Arden Handler, and Katherine Downs Waddill, "Teens and Adoption: A Pregnancy Resolution Alternative," *Children Today* November/December 1984, 26. See also Arden Handler and Katherine Downs, *A Statewide Study of Teenage Parents and Adoption,* final report for the Ounce of Prevention Fund, Chicago, 1984.

55.   Quotation from William Wordsworth in *The Oxford Dictionary of Quotations* (Oxford: Oxford University Press, 1979), 577.

56.   William Raspberry, *Washington Post,* 16 December 1989, A31.

57.   James S. Fishkin, *The Limits of Obligation* (New Haven: Yale University Press, 1982), 171.

Chapter 19

Character and Public Discourse

Richard C. Harwood

INTRODUCTION

Today there is a deep conflict of vision over the direction of public discourse—and thus the very nature of public character itself. One thrives in an environment of "civic dissonance"; it assumes that the way in which to move society ahead, to win battles in public life, is to actively embrace a divisive and acrimonious approach to public discourse. This vision demands keen gamesmanship and nerves of steel, and it calls for little exercise of public character.

The alternative vision is grounded in civic engagement, a form of public discourse in which there is robust give-and-take in society, always informed by an underlying desire and spirit among people to try to solve problems together. Public character is essential to this alternative; it guides civic engagement. More importantly, civic engagement itself produces and nurtures public character.

The choice between these competing visions may seem self-evident, but our current practices simply defy such logic. The overlay of civic discord and bombast is so broad and deep that it smothers the development and practice of public character. And yet, experience tells us that just beneath the murky surface of civic dissonance—within both individual Americans and the communities they form—rests the essence of a strong public character.

If we want to engender and exercise public character in America, then Americans must embrace fundamental changes in the nature of public discourse. That will require making a choice between competing visions. It will mean embracing civic engagement.

UNENDING CIVIC DISSONANCE

Civic dissonance now engulfs public discourse, creating a kind of drumbeat of unnerving public noise—like the constant playing of television static at its highest volume. Americans hear this annoying public discourse each day: it comes in the form of shrill bickering, one-upmanship, shouting and yelling, acrimony, sensationalism, and deep conflict.

Some dissonance within society, of course, is helpful and necessary. The friction it causes can spur people to rethink their assumptions and to change the lens through which they view an issue or challenge. Dissonance can give rise to creativity in people and provide the conditions for deep and lasting learning. Over time it can help to coalesce public thought, and it can ensure that public action is not driven by superficial swings in the public mood. No doubt, people expect, and even welcome, some dissonance in their private and public lives. As with any good, heated argument, dissonance often has a kind of natural evolution or rhythm—while it may reach pitched levels, we eventually expect there to be resolution.

But the dissonance we experience today is not momentary or passing in nature. Rather it is constant and overwhelming; too often there is no resolution in sight. Indeed, there is no natural rhythm to it other than the unnerving civic noise we hear and the crippling effect it has on public life. This dissonance squeezes out of public discourse the room we need for discussion, for listening, for exploration; the result is that people begin to believe that we cannot deal effectively with social change and solve public problems. Thus, the dissonance we experience unsettles people, putting them on edge and producing anxiety; it leads people to believe that there is no common ground to be found, prompting them to feel cornered and trapped. Dissonance creates such a skewed focus that what is real and authentic to people becomes noticeably absent from public discourse, making people frustrated and angry.

As civic dissonance grips America, and as people see no viable alternative, a host of social norms take hold, including self-centeredness, shallowness, recklessness, and a lack of accountability. These norms run counter to people working together in a spirit of civic engagement; they slowly eat away at our public character. They prompt within people a fear of the unknown and give others the opportunity to manipulate that fear. They produce among people a sense of disconnectedness from anything larger than themselves. They create the desire within people to put on blinders, to go it alone with little regard for others.

NEED FOR CIVIC ENGAGEMENT

It is not possible for a democratic society to work under these conditions. Surely politics cannot work—that much we see each day. But there is more to be concerned about than just "politics." Civic dissonance and the social norms it engenders inform the ways in which media, corporations, and civic groups relate to public life. Moreover, increasingly it drives the basic interactions of individuals with their neighbors, local shopkeepers, and coworkers. And it shapes the ways in which people view their own responsibilities within the public realm.

Our concern then about public discourse cannot be limited solely to political debates over grand issues but must focus also on the ordinary and often the seemingly mundane. Indeed, in a democratic society, the forms of everyday discourse that are prompted by a small daily newspaper, that occur over a backyard fence between neighbors, that are framed by organized interest groups are inextricably intertwined. They are dependent upon each other; they give rise to one another. The nature of these daily activities must be examined seriously, and acted upon, if there is to be an affirmation of public character and a greater exercise of it.

The urgent demand for public character is obvious if one looks at the many challenges America confronts—from the need to lower persistent federal deficits, to improving local education, to keeping families together, to raising children. None of these challenges, or any others, can be met without *courage* to raise the challenges for discussion and to face up to reality; *understanding* of diverse needs among people; *compassion* for others; seeing another person's *perspective*; the ability to *agree to disagree*; a sense of *responsibility* for what is demanded of oneself; *judgment* in order to make informed decisions; *will* to act. These attributes make up public character, they are the essential characteristics that help to form it.

Civic engagement, public discourse that has the qualities of give-and-take and a spirit of people working together to solve problems, cannot occur without public character. The very act of civic engagement helps to produce attributes of character—serving to embed and nurture them within people, to make them a part of a person's very nature.

LOSS OF PUBLIC SENSIBILITIES

Unfortunately, we live in a time when public discourse suffers from a constant degradation that is producing civic dissonance and that has assumed a momentum all its own. Each day it is possible to see the corrosive effects of this trend on our public character.

The 1994 health care reform debate was a brutal and bloody battle in which proponents of competing proposals took part in malicious name calling, finger pointing, and the questioning of each other's basic motives. In our own research, citizens and civic leaders report that this dissonance left them with little room to think about and weigh the merits of various ideas; they say that people were pressured to make choices long before they were ready, producing a sensation of being trapped, a fear that their personal health care coverage might be endangered. Thus, many people began to believe that no reform was better than some reform. The acrimonious debate left people feeling that they could no longer be concerned about the fate of others. All bets were off in terms of trying to walk in someone else's shoes.

Not long ago a public opinion researcher I know told me of a technique they use when polling in small towns on high-visibility issues. I was drawn into her story when she said that her firm cares little about the survey results. Confused, I asked why then do the polls? Grinning, she responded that her "interviewers" ask people questions that create fear within them about possible actions. This spurs the rumor mill in town, with one person calling the next, with each version of the rumor more outlandish than the one before. This enables the pollster's client to vilify their opponent and ultimately to declare victory. But at what cost to the community? Residents lose the opportunity to exercise the courage to face up to a tough issue and to make judgments about what to do. They can absolve themselves of having to take responsibility for their own future.

Our research on public meetings has revealed a consistent and troubling pattern: in these settings, major issues of concern to people quickly become fragmented and polarized. Consider the issue of community growth. Not long after it is raised in a public meeting, the discussion often will be taken hostage by both pro-development and stop-all-growth factions. Public officials will then listen to whichever side shouts the loudest or protests the longest. Yet in communities across America we find that most people struggle to strike a balance on growth issues; they tend not to support either extreme. But, despite their desire for a reasonable solution, people feel there is little room in the public debate for discussion. Thus, they find themselves either adopting an extreme position or turning their backs entirely on the public square.

Many of the "new tools" now touted to reengage Americans in public discourse literally can serve to undermine public character. For instance, computer bulletin boards—which futurists say will provide the new public square as virtual communities form—often create even more civic dissonance in public discourse; indeed, observers have said that increasing amounts of "flaming" are occurring online—people making defamatory and sometimes lurid remarks to one another. Listen to talk radio—which often is hailed as a cornerstone of electronic democracy—and one also hears discussions marked by sharp, vitriolic rhetoric. Televised town meetings increasingly are no different: producers will instruct audience members to ask questions that corner guests, thus serving to create conflict and dissonance. That, we are told, makes for good television. Meanwhile, people are not expected to hold themselves accountable for their remarks or thoughts; the notion of responsibility is missing.

Finally, think about this scene: We have all watched as someone seeks to return a garment to a clothing store and fails to get the kind of response they expect from the salesperson. Quickly the purchaser's voice will fill with rage; they will berate the salesperson—often questioning that individual's integrity and intelligence. A discussion over a simple piece of clothing soon degenerates into a shouting match. This kind of scene is not an isolated event, it is becoming a part of everyday life in America. For instance, it is now a frequent incident at airport ticket counters when flights are delayed or canceled; as people verbally attack bus drivers when they pull up late to a scheduled stop; and in schoolhouse interactions when parents lash out at a teacher, blaming him for their child's failure to learn the multiplication tables.

A pronounced nastiness now pervades public discourse. In an interview we conducted for one of our reports, a Des Moines woman said about the quality of public discourse, "I want to hear more about the issues, not mudslinging." Yet in public encounters people seem able to call each other names with remarkable ease. They are quick to point fingers of blame at others, with little reflection upon their own responsibility. The manipulation of people's fears and emotions is now a staple of modern public affairs management.

There is little room for productive exchanges among people today. Too many times public discourse is over before it ever has the chance to truly unfold. Indeed, too many debates are undermined by polarization. As a man from Los Angeles once told us in an interview,

> there are a number of issues in this country where there seems to be very little gray area. And that's something I am afraid of in this country—the polarization. You've got to be this way, or you've got to be this way. If you're not for it, you're against it.

A central feature of civic dissonance is that many of our public interactions seem to be dehumanized. There is, simply put, a lack of civility. This is not to say that public discussions need more "love" or "friendliness"; the definition of civility is not the pursuit of a happy-go-lucky, feel-good democracy. Rather we have misplaced our public sensibilities—the unspoken rules of what it means to be part of a community. We lack the basics of civil conduct which speak to the need for people to be able to engage one another, to agree to disagree, to fight for a cause and still treat each other with common decency and consideration.

The souring of public discourse now permeates America. Perhaps it is most evident in the nation's daily political life—in the ways in which we debate major public issues and conduct political campaigns. But it can be heard too in the tenor of people's voices on talk radio and at local public meetings. We can see it in our most common interactions, such as when we return a piece of clothing to a store or talk with our child's teacher.

We live in a time when civic dissonance has become the prevailing framework for public discourse. And with the spread of civic dissonance, there is an atrophying of public character. Equally alarming is that in some people, such as our young, public character may never have the chance to form fully. As one college student told us in an interview about his generation's view of public life:

> What we have is a silent protest going on [about public life]. You have a generation slipping into a dream world. I have friends who are saying "screw it." People are disillusioned, escaping...so you have people disappearing into the cracks.

THE EMPTY PUBLIC SQUARE

Modern-day public discourse is a reflection of an empty public square in which the basic relationships among citizens and between citizens and their public institutions have broken down. The result is that there are too few possibilities for individuals to engage in civic-minded discourse. Indeed, civic dissonance is now becoming institutionalized in America. Many observers recognize this deteriorating situation, but unfortunately many of their solutions fail to mitigate it. In fact, they actively contribute to it.

Take the relationships that Americans hold with an array of public institutions that affect their daily lives from media to government to corporations. Many people now believe that these institutions neither understand their concerns nor act in ways that reflect those concerns. These institutions are felt to be cold, distant, and faceless, even ruthless in the ways in which they conduct their public business. Our research suggests that these beliefs contribute immensely to people's angry and strident interactions with institutions, and thus to civic dissonance.

Many institutions are now responding to the public's anger by making attempts to "listen"—to convince people that their concerns are understood, that indeed there is an ongoing conversation taking place. Signs of these responses are ubiquitous: scores of town meetings are being held, polls are being taken, listening tours are under way.

Ironically, these attempts often produce even deeper public cynicism and even greater civic dissonance. Too often they draw on the techniques of public relations and end up being little more than window dressing. For instance, government officials will seek citizens' input by setting up a complex system of public meetings; yet the focus of these meetings often is a sales pitch by government leaders for a predetermined plan of action. Newspapers will go out and "listen" to readers and, despite readers' pleas to cover issues in ways that help them to understand the issues, journalists will continue to report stories through a prism of conflict and of winners and losers. Corporations will announce they want to be connected to the communities in which they operate, so they send corporate officials out to meet with community leaders. Results of the road show may find their way into a new ad campaign or a CEO's speech, but they will not penetrate the larger corporate structure to inform those actions that reflect how a company actually views its relationship with a community.

Too often, little real engagement and listening occurs as our public institutions seek to engage the public. Moreover, the lenses through which institutions view the public and their concerns do not change, and the practices of institutions are not altered in any discernible way. What emerges, ultimately, is a public whose basic sense of disconnection and frustration only grows.

The ways in which organized interest groups approach public discourse also produces civic dissonance. With increasing regularity, or so it seems, many organizations are placing more emphasis on "positioning" themselves than on working with others to solve problems. There seems to be a singular bottom line to their calculations: to grab headlines and to win arguments.

Indeed, time and again I have heard people who work in interest groups say they are unwilling to come together with others out of fear that their organization will not be able to distinguish itself from its opponents or even from fellow travelers. If that were to occur, they say, they could not maintain their membership or raise necessary funds. In this environment, civic dissonance becomes a crutch by which to sustain the very existence of an organization.

Perhaps surprisingly, civic organizations such as neighborhood associations and clubs also have become purveyors of civic dissonance. Increasingly, citizen groups feel they must mirror the political practices of society's larger institutions if they are to have an effect. So, as people gather in these local groups, they emphasize the techniques of how to push their preset agenda, rather than to explore and weigh all sides of an issue. This response is seen regularly on "NIMBY" issues—Not in My Backyard—in which there is citizen resistance to attempts to locate a landfill or a transition home for the mentally ill near a residential neighborhood. Thus, civic organizations, which exist in order to engage people in problem solving, become one more tool of civic dissonance.

Then there is the public itself. As Americans' confidence in government and the political process has plummeted, people have become more defensive in their public posture, leading them to contribute to the civic dissonance they actually abhor. They are fearful that public decisions will work against their interests, that they will be gouged by a new tax bill as others get tax breaks, or that a new road cutting through their community to make a commute easier for someone else will lower their property values or undermine the integrity of their community. People's belief that the political process is incapable of producing fair decisions causes them to react in self-centered and acrimonious ways.

Contributing to this civic dissonance is what Robert Hughes has called "the culture of complaint," in which people are fragmenting themselves into competing tribes—each with its own set of claims, each having complaints about others, each seeing itself as a victim of societal trends and actions. What emerges is a politics driven by an "us versus them" mentality in which common ground is not the goal; rather people jockey to divvy up the public square.

Civic dissonance is a result, and a product, of an approach to public life in which people perceive that their rights take precedence over responsibilities and balance. It is an approach that tends to be absolute in its quality, one based on the staking out of nonnegotiable positions. Its goal is to maximize personal gain and to make as little contribution to the commonweal as possible.

WORSHIPING A FALSE GOD

Unfortunately, as these conditions have taken hold, a false panacea has emerged to find and to listen to "the public": the surveying of Americans. These polls come fast and furious, with results reported daily in the news media. In a world consisting more and more of "virtual realities," polls have become our virtual public discourse. They are an attempt, albeit a feeble one, to create a public voice in the midst of an empty public square.

But the almost nonstop polling of America insidiously deepens civic dissonance. Polls tend to fragment people's concerns, failing to reflect the kinds of connections that people experience in their daily lives. They require people to make judgments about issues long before they have had the chance to understand and talk with others about them. They force people to choose among solutions to problems that are based on simplistic political divisions, missing people's sense of complexity of problems and the kinds of cross-cutting responses they typically seek.

What's more, rather than being used as a tool for problem solving, poll results have become weapons of public life. Results are manipulated to buttress a preconceived position, to accentuate the negative, and to put others on the defensive. And rather than providing the insights that might lead to sustainable actions, poll data too often serve to deepen social polarization and fragmentation by creating camps of people, with more emphasis being placed on that which divides people than on the common ground they share.

Instead of providing the healthy friction necessary for learning and creativity, the civic dissonance we experience today puts a halt to public discourse. It stops real thinking at the point at which people need to work through a problem to reach a deeper understanding; it shuts down discussion, just when we need most to create new and unexplored possibilities for action by talking with each other; it stifles people's ability to find ways to work together.

OUR MISSING PUBLIC CHARACTER

The ill-effects of civic dissonance are reflected in the erosion of the very fundamentals of our public character. The nature of public discourse today gives people license to disavow ownership of public problems and the responsibility to address them. There is little accountability for one's words or claims—anything seems to go. The great irony of this situation is that while people can say whatever they want, genuine attempts to challenge another person's thinking often are taken as an affront to that person's dignity and basic motivations. Indeed, people are not challenged to summon the courage to face up to an issue, learn about it, think it through, and wrestle with implications. Larger public concerns are discounted if they fail to address our seemingly unlimited private concerns. Compassion is relegated to therapeutic television and talk-radio shows. Sacrifice occurs at times of convenience; it is viewed almost as a relic of American life.

Civic dissonance gives rise to a society in which public character cannot take shape because the essence of what it means to be part of something larger than oneself is stripped out of public life. People and groups are approached as islands unto themselves, as atomized consumers of the public square, barking out individual wants and desires. We do not challenge ourselves to think as *citizens*, as people connected to one another with a shared destiny.

Until relatively recently, conventional wisdom seemed to hold that Americans liked the winner-take-all nature of public discourse. Through the process of battle, people would have their say and their interests would become known. The battle itself was seen as a means to engage people. Perhaps some observers thought that this kind of discourse was a true reflection of the combative, individualistic tradition of America.

But in *Meaningful Chaos*, a report the Harwood Group prepared for the Kettering Foundation on how Americans come to engage in public life, we found that this highly charged, fragmented, self-centered, and shallow approach to public discourse actually serves to push people away from the public square. Americans told us that too often they cannot find meaning in this discourse; that it fails to reflect their deeper concerns; that it does not capture their aspirations and dreams. They do not believe that it leads to improving people's lives. Americans yearn for an alternative.

EMERGENCE OF PUBLIC CHARACTER

The conflict of visions over the direction of public discourse is indeed a fight for America's public character. Neither public discourse nor public character can exist in the absence of the other; and effective public problem solving cannot occur without the presence of both.

Civic engagement embeds and nurtures public character within people. By actively engaging with others, people gain, for instance, a sense of understanding, compassion, courage, and responsibility. They hold themselves accountable for their own words and deeds. They move from raw, uninformed opinion to making judgments. Civic engagement can produce within people, both as individuals and as members of a community, the will to act. Here are some examples that illustrate the effect that civic engagement can have on public character.

Take discussions on education and public schools, for instance. These discussions often are riddled by civic dissonance. People are quick to blame teachers and administrators for our troubles; they are unwilling to support efforts to improve schools with either their money or time. Often they are concerned only about their own child's education, and believe that they hold little responsibility for addressing school problems.

Yet as people engage in give-and-take discussions on education, the prevailing civic dissonance dissipates. People are quick to consider the challenges that teachers and administrators face daily; they weigh different perspectives on what has gone wrong and what can be done; they begin to reflect on their own behaviors and past statements. As people talk with one another, they say that they want schools to restore order and to find ways to meet their basic educational mission so that *all* children can learn, not just their own. Equally important, they say that schools alone can not, *must not*, be left to educate children—that education can improve only if parents, civic organizations, educating institutions (e.g., libraries), and others play significant roles. Here is how a woman from Seattle, interviewed for one of our reports, put it:

You know, there comes a time when we need to change the way we think about schools. Everybody needs to become involved—no matter what [their] age—to give just a little time, because it's not just the mothers and fathers who have children in school. It's everybody's...society's responsibility to make sure that those kids are given an education.

What emerges from civic engagement on education is a vision for schools that includes parental and community responsibility at its core; it calls for people to make sacrifices. Through civic engagement, people begin to take ownership of their *public* schools. The individual and collective will to act begins to form.

Another example is the issue of crime. Recent public discourse on crime has been framed largely around survey findings indicating Americans' deep concern about their personal safety and their desire to get tough with criminals. This has led many public leaders to call for increasingly severe measures in attempts to prove their toughness to the voting public. In the 1994 mid-term elections, the game of one-upmanship led to a frenzy of proposals from candidates and sitting public officials alike. Without any alternative to consider, the public cheered such rhetoric.

Yet as people engage in public discussions on crime, a much different tone and prescription come to the fore. No doubt citizens say they want criminals punished, but they also say that society should provide more opportunities for people to succeed before they get into trouble. In short, people want public responses to crime to reflect a constellation of social values often depicted as being mutually exclusive: nurturing, responsibility, and accountability. This desire could be heard in interviews we conducted on crime in Tallahassee, Florida. After talking about longer sentences, boot camps, and more cops, inevitably the conversation would turn to comments like this one by a Tallahassee woman: "We have to start with young people...an ounce of prevention is worth a pound of cure." Or a man who said, "It all goes back to the root problem of...the family." Or a woman who made this observation: "We need to put a higher priority on raising kids."

Civic engagement on crime issues gives people the room they need to step away from demagogic appeals and to look seriously at the problem. When that occurs, a public voice emerges that suggests society must punish people who do not follow its laws, but which first gives people every opportunity to succeed. Through discourse, people exercise judgment—balancing their compassion with their notion of responsibility. They articulate what it means to hold one another accountable. They set society's expectations for public character itself.

The issue of rural health care offers a good example of how civic engagement can enable people to reach a deeper understanding of the challenges that others face and what that can mean for solving problems. In states with rural areas, there often is a debate over whether every community should have a full-service hospital, regardless of its population and whether the hospital can support itself economically. In Georgia, where we are conducting work on health care reform, a superficial gauging of the public would suggest that a deep divide exists between rural and nonrural residents on this issue. On one side are residents who strongly oppose closing hospitals, and on the other side are those who say that it is not cost-effective to keep every hospital open.

But a strange thing happens as Georgians talk together about this dilemma. When given the simple choice of whether to have a full-service hospital, rural Georgians of course seek to protect their health care security. Yet when given room to talk freely about possible alternatives to full-service hospitals, rural Georgians say they are willing to close their hospitals *if* they can have immediate access to primary care facilities and transportation to emergency services. Most often, nonrural Georgians wholeheartedly embrace this solution, saying they did not realize what rural Georgians were truly seeking. Once they do, this solution seems both fair and sensible.

These conversations on rural hospitals show that people are able to discover among themselves a way out of dissonance. Unfortunately, too often people are pushed into a corner, forced to take a position which can lead to gridlock and block the possibility for new solutions to emerge. Then civic dissonance wins over public character.

Another health care example demonstrates that people often see gray areas in public life, and that they want to avoid offering shrill, simplistic, and divisive answers to tough questions. Through civic engagement, people can gain the courage to face reality and to hold themselves accountable for their own views.

In California, for example, one woman, unprompted by anyone else in a discussion group we held, raised an article in the *Los Angeles Times* about a Siamese twins' case that had captured the attention of America. The twins had been separated, and one had passed away while the other's life hung in the balance. The cost of the twins' care was astronomical.

In a world of civic dissonance, the debate on this issue would take on the same markings as debates, for instance, on abortion, end-of-life decisions, and gun control. People would be forced to make a simplistic "either/or" choice—in this case on whether medical dollars should be spent on these children—as if that is all there is to decide on a complex issue. Then, if that simple choice was part of a survey, the finding would be touted by one side or the other as the truth on what should be done, and then, quickly, before anyone had the opportunity to even think about the issue, a heated, polarized debate would be joined.

But when asked what she thought about the issue, the Los Angeles woman said that she was not sure—that it is a tough question and that she needed to think about it. Rather than offer a knee-jerk response, she said that she wanted more room to talk with friends and family about the issue, to listen to their views and to explore what she believed. Others in the group had a similar response.

CREATING PUBLIC CHARACTER

The deepening of civic dissonance closes off possibilities for a democratic society to work. It breeds public anger and cynicism. It produces a mistrust among people of one another and of the institutions that affect their lives. And it creates within people anxiety about society's ability to act effectively on the challenges it confronts.

Today civic dissonance is driving people away from the public square. Americans now believe that there is far too little room within public discourse to talk, listen, explore, learn, and find ways to address public problems. This dissonance, which has gained a momentum all its own, leads to social norms of self-centeredness, shallowness, recklessness, and a lack of accountability.

There is a yearning within Americans to bring resolution to the civic dissonance we experience daily. People want to find ways to work together to improve public life.

But to achieve resolution, Americans must embrace a vision of public discourse that is based not on civic dissonance, but on civic engagement. This vision is guided by the vigilant exercise of public character. Moreover, through the very pursuit of civic engagement, public character is created, embedded, and nourished within people.

But to pursue a vision of civic engagement will require renewing our public sensibilities. We will need to listen, to ask questions, to challenge each other in ways that encourage Americans to come back into the public square, rather than to flee it. We must stand ready to agree to disagree— sometimes even vehemently. There must be present the belief that it is far better to search for that which people share in common than to emphasize that which divides people. There must be the willingness among people to participate in genuine give-and-take, particularly when discussions are heated and filled with tension.

Civic engagement also will require that Americans have the courage to face reality. Public character is revealed, indeed often forms, when people wrestle with the tough choices before them and the hard trade-offs that go with those choices. It emerges when people spend time seeking to understand points of view different from their own, and when they are willing to rethink their own views. It surfaces when people begin to believe that they hold personal responsibility for ending civic dissonance and for finding ways to act effectively on public problems. And public character grows when people assume that they must hold themselves and others accountable for their own words and deeds.

Through productive civic engagement, the necessary dissonance for people to learn and to rethink their assumptions is created. At the same time, however, civic engagement also allows people enough room for ambivalence so that they can have the courage to say "I'm not sure" or "I don't know," and then to continue to search for an answer.

The responsibility to create an environment of civic engagement must be embraced at all levels of society. Surely, the often acrimonious debate that occurs in the halls of Congress and throughout our national political scene must change. But the focus of our efforts must not be relegated to America's formal political debate. Rather our focus must be on the series of vital and intertwined civic relationships in our communities and daily lives that give rise to public discourse throughout the nation.

Thus, each individual has within his or her own power the ability to alter the nature of public discourse. This power should not be underestimated. Civic engagement can begin to occur as people talk with one another in their neighborhoods, in workplace discussions, and when they interact, for instance, with a salesperson while returning a piece of clothing to a store or with a teacher when discussing their child's education.

Institutions also must act to change the ways in which they approach the public square, including media, corporations, and organized interest groups. To pursue their interests, these institutions must rely less on creating acrimony, divisiveness, and hype, and place more emphasis on making sound arguments that have a ring of authenticity to people. They must seek to forge genuine relationships with the public by listening to people's concerns and making sense of those concerns, rather than trying to find the public's "hot buttons" to manipulate and to sway public opinion. They must seek to engage people in public discourse, rather than merely to sell people on a bill of goods and to hope for blind acceptance. They must create more public settings with an eye toward enabling people to participate in give-and-take discussions that do not degenerate into shouting matches among organized groups.

America faces two visions over the direction of public discourse. One vision would continue to produce the civic dissonance we experience now. The alternative suggests that we must embrace a form of public discourse grounded in civic engagement. The answer will tell us about the very nature of our public character today and in the future. The choice is ours.

Chapter 20

Sport, Character, and Virtue

Randolph Feezell

INTRODUCTION

I think it is the commercials that did it. Most American sports fans have
seen them. You are watching a college athletic contest, time-out is called
and the commercial advertisements begin to drone. Then he appears. He
is poised, articulate, and successful—I mean really successful! He is
probably the CEO of a major corporation. He smiles and explains that he
was once a second-string guard at State University. The camera pans to
old footage of a State game where number 68, playing courageously with
no face mask, is leading a sweep into the end zone—of course. He tells
us that playing sports taught him hard work, determination, competitive
drive, and teamwork, just those qualities of character that he needed in
order to be successful in mega-business. Yes, intercollegiate athletics is
really important. Now back to the game.... The announcers then mention
that State University is currently under investigation by the NCAA for
recruiting violations, tampering with transcripts, using substitute test-takers
for scholar-athletes, providing free cars for players, and illegally providing
bail money and support for drug rehabilitation. Character, you say?

I confess at the outset that I find this issue vexing. Something like the
character-building view of sport appears to be part of the prevailing
orthodoxy of the sportsworld. It is not just the NCAA public relations
people who want to persuade others of the moral importance of

participating in athletic competition. Coaches, administrators, educators, and the ordinary person down the street are often heard rejoicing in the lessons taught, the values conveyed, and the virtues developed by playing sports. Former President Gerald Ford offers not a unique but surely a quintessential expression of this orthodoxy.

> Broadly speaking, outside of a national character and an educated society, there are few things more important to a country's growth and well-being than competitive athletics. If it is a cliche to say athletics build character as well as muscle, then I subscribe to the cliche.[1]

On the other hand, it is difficult not to be skeptical of this cliche, not simply because it is trite or hackneyed or held by Gerald Ford and the majority of coaches we happen to have met. In *Sport: A Philosophy Inquiry*, Paul Weiss considers the character-building view of athletics, only to dismiss it for what seem to be good reasons. In the context of ruminating on the attraction of athletics he describes the plausible view that good habits of character are developed by facing athletic challenges. However, to take the position seriously we would have to assume that most aspects of character are not formed much earlier than the age of sports participation. Moreover, it is not obvious that the character of children is developed by the sports experiences they often have, in which winning is overemphasized, injuries occur, and character is scarcely exemplified by screaming parents and coaches who lack self-control. "Sport does not, at least for some children, help them grow properly as bodies, and may hinder their growth in character."[2]

In addition, the studies of social scientists have not been particularly kind to the orthodox view. One author concludes his review of 10 years of research on the socialization effects of college athletic participation by saying that "the basic conclusion must remain that there is little valid evidence that participation in college athletics has any effect on the character of the athlete."[3] Another article's title sums up in a pithy manner the skeptical thesis: *Sport: If You Want to Build Character, Try Something Else.*[4]

Also, we should not overlook the evidence of personal experience, however anecdotal and limited it might be. As I look back at my own experience, starting on ragged little baseball diamonds and cracker-box gymnasiums and ending with athletic competition for one of the major college athletic powerhouses in the country, I do not associate playing sports with building whatever character I happen to have. In fact it may have helped produce something akin to cynicism when I hear the pious declamations of Ford-like moralists. Institutions are poorly served by the charade of moral justification when they do nothing more than talk a good moral game. On the other hand (and it is just this interminable "on the other hand" that makes the issue so vexing) I think athletic participation has been important in the moral development of my oldest child, continues to be for the second, and I expect it to be for the youngest two. And then there's my philosophical colleague who told me that whatever character he happens to have was largely formed by participating in sports. What are we to make of so much conflicting evidence? What can a philosopher contribute to this issue?

There are a number of questions related to sport and character-building that are philosophically interesting and relevant. Certainly the question whether sport does, in fact, cause the development of good character is in part an empirical one. But there are a host of other issues that can be addressed philosophically. What is it to have character? Good character seems to involve the question of virtue, for virtues are taken to be beneficial or prescribed traits of character. What is a virtue such that participation in sports might develop it? If sport did develop character or virtue, how would it do this? Are there moral dangers involved in sports participation? Are there natural threats to building character in sport? Which virtues might we expect to be developed by playing sports? Are there virtues specific to sports participation? Are there other important virtues that we would not expect to be developed by sport? If there are, are they important for good character? Is there anything distinctive about sport, such that playing sports is especially important in developing character or virtue?

I would like tentatively to answer some of these questions by looking at some recent work in moral philosophy on the virtues.[5] In *After Virtue*, Alasdair MacIntyre offers a conceptual account of the virtues that is particularly powerful as a way to get at some of the above questions. He argues that the natural home of the virtues resides in sustaining what he calls "practices," which, as we will see, include playing a given sport. He says of his theory that "this kind of conceptual account has strong empirical implications; it provides an explanatory scheme which can be tested in particular cases."[6] Hence, his theoretical account might help us make sense of the conflicting evidence found in various empirical studies concerned with sport and character. I will focus upon several of MacIntyre's main theses about the nature of virtue and the unity of a life. These arguments suggest that the character-building thesis, if successful at all, is incomplete or offers a thin view of character. I will also look at some other treatments of virtue and character to reinforce the view that sport only contingently and incompletely provides an arena for character formation.

VIRTUE AND SPORTS

In *After Virtue*, MacIntyre attempts to write a philosophical history that will help us understand the problematic characteristics of our current moral discourse. For MacIntyre our current moral debates are characterized by disagreement because the rivals in these debates move validly from incommensurable moral premises. The problem is that "we possess no rational way of weighing the claims of one against another,"[7] this because we possess these premises as mere fragments, dislodged from the historical context in which they originally and specifically made sense. We experience moral language in an odd and paradoxical manner, because we take moral reasons as impersonal criteria for action yet the incommensurability of conflicting principles suggests that our ultimate moral principles are arbitrary, our moral positions nothing but expressions of private attitudes and feelings. MacIntyre's tour de force reconstructs the story of how we supposedly got ourselves into this mess, why we are unable to see this because of the prevailing ahistorical ways of doing moral philosophy, and how we might now confront this situation. The enlightenment project of justifying morality had to fail and our emotivist, bureaucratic modern culture is the inevitable result. Only Friedrich Nietzsche seemed to diagnose accurately the moral ills of modernism. We are left, in MacIntyre's view, with either an acceptance of Nietzsche's view that rational justification of morality fails and morality is "a set of rationalizations which conceal the fundamentally non-rational phenomena of will,"[8] or a return to some kind of premodern (or postmodern?) Aristotelian view of morality. To understand the dilemma of modernism and especially to appreciate the Aristotelian option, MacIntyre's narrative reconstructs the development of the notion of virtue in the ancient world and later. By the time the reader reaches the unifying chapter on the nature of virtues he has encountered rich discussions of the virtues as lived and written about in Homeric society, in the Athens of Sophocles and Plato, and later Aristotle, and in the world of New Testament writers and medieval thinkers.

The problem, of course, is the dazzling diversity of these accounts of virtues. Homer emphasizes physical excellence embodied in the warrior. Aristotle emphasizes *phronesis* and the virtues of an Athenian citizen.

Faith, hope, and love are emphasized in the Christian tradition. Homer emphasizes qualities of character necessary for fulfilling specific social roles. Aristotle stresses the role of virtue in relation to the *telos* of human nature. Christian virtues are also understood teleologically, but the good life for the Christian is in substantial ways quite different from the good life for the Athenian. Then there's Jane Austen's notion that seems to combine the Homeric emphasis on social roles and Aristotelian teleology, and Benjamin Franklin's insistence on the virtues as useful.[9] What could these disparate accounts have in common? Is there a "core conception of a virtue" that can be derived from these different notions? MacIntyre's strategy is to understand virtue in relation to what he calls a "practice." Consider his central theses on the nature of the virtues.

MacIntyre's View of Virtue and Practice

> By a "practice," I am going to mean any coherent and complex form of socially established cooperative human activity through which goods internal to that form of activity are realized in the course of trying to achieve those standards of excellence which are appropriate to, and partially definitive of, that form of activity, with the result that human powers to achieve excellence, and human conceptions of the ends and goods involved, are systematically extended.[10]

The first thing to note about MacIntyre's notion of a practice is how very broad it is. He mentions as examples such activities as farming, science, architecture, portrait painting, and chess. Even politics, in a sense, and helping to run a family could involve participation in a practice. For our purposes, however, one thing is quite clear. To play a sport is to engage in a practice. MacIntyre specifically mentions football and baseball in his discussion.[11] Crucial to his analysis is the distinction between internal and external goods. Suppose I teach my child to play baseball and he becomes an excellent young player. He might receive public recognition, a college scholarship, and even a professional contract. That is, he might achieve a variety of *external* goods—fame, education, money—from playing baseball. These are goods that can, logically, be achieved by engaging in other activities. For example, he might become well known and respected in a community by starting a small business while still in high school. On the other hand, there are goods internal to the playing of baseball that cannot be explained, experienced, or understood apart from the specific context of the practice. For example, becoming an excellent line-drive hitter is an internal good in baseball.

The list of possible internal goods associated with the practice of baseball appears to be quite long, including all of those skills necessary for becoming an excellent player or coach.

"A practice involves standards of excellence and obedience to rules as well as achievement of goods."[12] Internal goods arise because practices involve standards of excellence, ways of performing better or worse in achieving precisely those goods. This means that practices develop as skills and abilities are advanced. Thus, practices have histories. They develop authoritative internal standards that provide objective criteria for performance. For example, in baseball it is understood that coaches know more about how the game ought to be played. That is, they understand the tradition and try to show young players how to play better or well.

> External goods are...characteristically objects of competition in which there must be losers as well as winners. Internal goods are indeed the outcome of competition to excel, but...their achievement is a good for the whole community who participate in the practice.[13]

This point is also quite obvious in the context of sports. For example, Babe Ruth's power transformed the way in which higher levels of baseball are played. Dick Fosbury transformed high jumping, and defensemen in hockey played differently after Bobby Orr's tremendous achievements. These are the most obvious examples, but successful innovations in playing and coaching specific sports appear often in less obtrusive ways. On the other hand, external goods like money, power, and fame are not typically communally shared. Little League all-star teams contain only a few players from the league; the headlines can mention only the hero; college athletic scholarships are limited; the Yankees need only so many catchers. Now, how are we to connect these insights to the notion of virtue?

> A virtue is an acquired human quality the possession and exercise of which tends to enable us to achieve those goods which are internal to practices and the lack of which effectively prevents us from achieving any such goods.[14]

Whenever we engage in a practice we necessarily involve ourselves in a community of shared expectations, goals, and standards. As MacIntyre says, we subordinate ourselves to others with whom we share the experience of the practice. Certain things immediately follow from this. We must recognize both the authority of the tradition which has developed the standards informing a practice, and authorities who are knowledgeable about the tradition and its standards. Some will be better than others in acquiring the abilities that enable a participant to achieve the goods internal to a practice. Those who are better deserve their lot. Participants must take risks since they may fail in achieving internal goods. To become better they must be honest about their shortcomings and respect authority. The conclusion about central virtues is easily purchased. MacIntyre insists, also, that such central virtues are required to sustain practices "whatever our private moral standpoint or our society's particular codes may be."[15] Hence, this scheme could satisfy the absolutist's thirst for cross-cultural moral unity while retaining the relativist's sense of moral particularity.

We are now able to offer some initial tentative conclusions about sport and character in light of MacIntyre's account. Given the definitions of a practice and a virtue, it is easy to see why the character-building view is so plausible. The young athlete needs to develop a keen sense of himself and his abilities in relation to the traditions of his sport. His development or simply his participation will require a certain honesty about himself, a respect for coaches who embody the tradition, a sense of who deserves or merits playing time, a feeling about the need for cooperation to achieve shared goals, courage in the face of failing to achieve standards, and persistence or determination in the attempt to achieve his goals. Since an athlete will participate in a variety of practices in life, if he really acquires or possesses justice, honesty, courage, and determination, because they enable him to achieve goods internal to his sport, he will benefit throughout life. At the same time, another interesting conclusion appears to follow. It may be unsurprising that sports, as practices, might be occasions for the development of virtues. However, there is probably nothing distinctive, in this respect, about playing sports. The same could be said for participation in any practice. Contrary to what Gerald Ford might say, at this point the same arguments apply to arts, sciences, crafts, and so forth. If engaging in such practices might occasion the development of some central virtues, then the important thing is for young people to commit themselves substantially to some practice, not any specific one, like a sport. One might as well learn to play the violin rather than soccer.

Other Related Views

Our conclusions are reinforced by considering Iris Murdoch's reflection on some related matters. For her, ethics ought to be concerned with the question, How can we make ourselves better?[16] She answers this question in the context of her view of human nature as essentially selfish, anxiety-ridden, and defensive.

For Murdoch, the locus of moral development resides in experiences of "unselfing," in which the self pierces the veil of vanity and self-absorption and begins to see things as they are. While not claiming anything exclusive about the realm of the aesthetic, she emphasizes the moral power of experiences of natural beauty and art, in which the "brooding self" gives itself over to the reality of the world and forgets its obsessions. Good art confronts us with a more objective and less jaded sense of things.

As I suggested, Murdoch does not claim that art is preeminent in its role as educator of our moral vision. Recalling Plato's mistrust of the artist and his emphasis on mathematics as a *techne*, she suggests that the virtues appear in many different kinds of human activities besides the arts. In sciences, crafts, and intellectual disciplines we see displayed "such concepts as justice, accuracy, truthfulness, realism, humility, courage as the ability to sustain clear vision, love as attachment or even passion without sentiment of self."[17]

Here we are none too far from MacIntyre's focus on the virtues required for the pursuit of goods internal to practices. Murdoch's stress on virtue as clear vision reinforces MacIntyre's sense of why the virtues are crucial to practices. For both, the self finds itself related to something over against which it must realistically come to be related. Murdoch says: "In intellectual disciplines and in the enjoyment of art and nature we discover value in our ability to forget self, to be realistic, to perceive justly."[18] I would add here that participating in sports may be able to educate us likewise, and that is, once again, why the character-building view of sport should be taken seriously. Having said that, we might briefly pause to consider the downside of Murdoch's view before returning to MacIntyre's analysis.

If, as Murdoch suggests, the virtue-enhancing possibilities of an activity like a sport might reside in the way it occasions a sense of honesty, justice, and humility (as selfless seeing of the way things are), then the extent to which young sports participants are not taught or helped to see things as they are will be morally inhibitive. Sport is a fecund area for dreams and fantasies, and wishful reveries are as much or more a part of the adult's experience as the child's. Think of the archetypical Little League parent who pushes, goads, resents, blames, and punishes. All for the sake of a loving dream of athletic fame and wealth for a child whose talents might be limited and whose interests are sometimes even more meager. A child needs to be taught not only to have a keen sense of his strengths, in order to nurture ambition; he must also come to realize and have a keen sense of his own limitations, in order to make wise judgments about the plan of his life. Murdoch mentions several difficult moral decisions, like situations involving care of the retarded or elderly, sustaining an unhappy marriage, or pursuing important goals that conflict with family relationships. For her, good moral judgments involve seeing.

One of the central barriers to building character in sport is the inability of people to perceive things truly.[19] Sometimes it is a matter of ignorance, as when a parent simply does not know enough about the traditions of a sport to realize a coach does understand who deserves to play or when a child simply does not have enough natural ability to succeed in a given sport. Sometimes it is simply a function of illusion, as Murdoch says.[20] But the external pressures on the activity or practice are severe, as MacIntyre's further analysis shows.

As we have seen, when we engage in a practice we encounter others, in both an immediate sense and a historical sense. Hence the virtues mediate, in a positive sense, our human relationships internal to the practice. But something else happens in the historical life of practices.

> Practices must not be confused with institutions. Chess, physics and medicine are practices; chess clubs, laboratories, universities, and hospitals are institutions. Institutions are characteristically and necessarily concerned with...external goods. They are involved in acquiring money and other material goods; they are structured in terms of power and status, and they distribute money, power, and status as rewards.[21]

In the context of sports little needs to be said to interpret this point. We live in an age of massive commercialization of sports, beginning now even at the high school level and continuing through the college and professional levels. MacIntyre's distinction between practices and institutions, between internal and external goods, provides an enlightening way to view this much talked about and much criticized phenomenon. Institutions are required to sustain practices, but the institutionalization of a practice carries clear moral dangers. When the primary focus of a practice is on competition for contingent external goods provided by institutional structures, a natural tension develops between the virtues required to attain internal goods, and qualities of character, vices, that may be helpful in pursuit of fame, wealth, and power.

The ideals and the creativity of the practice are always vulnerable to the acquisitiveness of the institution...the cooperative care for common goods of the practice is always vulnerable to the competitiveness of the institution...without justice, courage and truthfulness, practices could not resist the corrupting power of institutions.[22]

In large part, in our social context, the goods of wealth, fame, and power are tied to the ethos of winning. The ethos of contemporary sport, related to the orthodoxy of character building, emphasizes winning—sometimes at all costs. "Show me a good loser and I'll show you a loser." "Winning isn't everything, it's the only thing." "If winning isn't important, why do they keep score?" Now, paradoxically, we are in a position to see why the emphasis on winning, in the context of the institutional pressures associated with practices, can undermine the very moral message that is central to the orthodox view. For if winning is the key to achieving external goods, and the pursuit of external goods is overemphasized, then one may as well cheat to get the goods, that is, to win. But to cheat is to admit that the overruling reason to engage in a practice is to achieve external goods. It is to ignore the internal goods of the practice, the standards of excellence generated by the tradition, and the virtues required for pursuing and perhaps achieving such excellences. To cheat, as MacIntyre says, "so far bars us from achieving the standards of excellence or goods internal to the practice that it renders the practice pointless except as a device for achieving external goods."[23]

Such a view is very much what Christopher Lasch has in mind when he speaks of the "trivialization of athletics."[24] In the tradition of Johann Huizinga, Callois, and other play theorists, he sees sport as a form of play precisely because it involves a game, an arbitrary construction of rules for no reason other than making the activity in question possible.[25] "The degradation of sport, then, consists not in its being taken too seriously but in its trivialization. Games derive their power from the investment of seemingly trivial activity with serious intent."[26] In MacIntyre's language, the point of sport as a practice is seriously to engage in the pursuit of relatively trivial internal goods. We do not take sport seriously when we allow the wholesale invasion of external goods as its primary raison d'être. To do that is to ignore the internal goods of the practice. Again, paradoxically, it appears that the more appropriate way to defend sport's moral possibilities is to emphasize the "worthlessness" of sport; not to see it as a path to wealth and fame but as an occasion for momentary, enjoyable commitment and the achievement of a particular kind of excellence. We really appreciate and love baseball when we appreciate

Ryne Sandberg's second base play or Will Clark's swing, not just wins and losses. We love the tradition and enhance the moral possibilities of a given sport when we view such excellence as shared goods constituting the possibilities available for young players if they care to attend justly, honestly, and courageously to their sport.

Surely the most important sense of winning and competing courageously is to see winning as an internal good of significant yet trivial proportions. Perceiving sport as "splendid futility" is perceiving it without illusion, in Murdoch's sense. We can still stress the value of winning as important because it is an essential part of the practice of a sport. But surely to overemphasize the value of winning is to diminish the numerous other internal goods of sports, and it is to point in a direction in which it becomes more difficult, not less, to be a good person. I suspect that the epithet associated with being a "winner" or being a "competitor" often has more to do with being ruthless than having good character. Yet the moral discourse associated with sport muddles the issue. Since "winning" is so tied up with achieving external goods in our social context, and to "win" one must "compete," being competitive becomes the key virtue in sports. As MacIntyre says, "in any society which recognized only external goods competitiveness would be the dominant and even exclusive feature."[27] This is because external goods are much more the object of competition because of institutional and commercial pressures. So in our social and economic context the pressures are enormous. Perhaps it is not surprising that the mythical State University of the first paragraph of this chapter is faced with such a mess.

Still, although the psychological and economic forces that inveigh against the moral possibilities of sport are great, other problems remain. MacIntyre stresses the importance of the virtues in sustaining practices. But some practices may be evil.[28] Or, for our purposes, some practices may be relatively trivial in relation to other important human activities, for example, having a good jumpshot versus being an excellent neurosurgeon. Our commitments to a particular practice and the virtues sustaining our participation may conflict with other parts of our life.[29] An athlete might be universally admired for his courage and heroism on the athletic field, while he is miserable in sustaining his family, his friendships, and his other interests. After all, as Murdoch suggests, we are really interested in how we become better. That is why the character-building thesis is of interest. How do the virtues associated with sport fit into life as a whole? Can the playing of sports contribute to making our life a unity, so we can order the goods of different practices?

VIRTUE AND THE UNITY OF A LIFE

MacIntyre attempts to place the virtues in a large context by offering a rich and provocative discussion of human action and the self. Briefly, the major error committed by both analytic philosophers and the Sartrian brand of existentialism has been to interpret human action atomistically, ignoring the way in which action is embedded in a historical or narrative context that makes it intelligible. If I interpret some piece of human behavior I must appeal to the intentions of the agent; but these intentions can be made intelligible only by referring to a larger "setting" or a narrative history.[30] For example, driving west out of the city might be driving to the country to buy apples, momentarily escaping suburban boredom, leaving one's wife, going to see one's parents, testing a used car, and so forth. As MacIntyre says, "We place the agent's intentions...in causal and temporal order with reference to their role in the history of the setting or settings to which they belong."[31] This means that "narrative history" is necessary to interpret human actions and the self must be understood in terms of the way in which it is situated in the narratives it acts out.

This narrative conception of selfhood is fundamental for moral philosophy, because the question of what I ought to do can only be answered by placing my action in some larger narrative context. Human life is both unpredictable and teleological, since we are not quite sure what will happen to us, but we live as if our lives are moving toward certain ends, some of which are particular to individual lives, some of which we share with others.[32] MacIntyre sums up his main thesis:

> A central thesis then begins to emerge: man is in his actions and practice, as well as in his fictions, essentially a story-telling animal. He is not essentially, but becomes through his history, a teller of stories that aspire to truth. But the key question for men is not about their own authorship; I can only answer the question, "What am I to do?," if I can answer the prior question, "Of what story or stories do I find myself a part?"[33]

Now we are in a position to place the question of the virtues in a larger context. If my life is fragmented into a series of roles and a multiplicity of practices, how do I understand my life as a whole, as a unity, such that I can order the conflicting demands of the segments of my life? If the virtues sustain a variety of practices, how can I see my life as unified, such that the virtues still maintain their traditional Aristotelian role in relation to the teleological character of a human life? And for our purposes, how can we relate the answer to the character-building view of sport?

MacIntyre's answer echoes Socrates' profound response to these issues, although MacIntyre frames his answer in terms of the medieval conception of quest rather than the problem of the unexamined life. For MacIntyre, the "unity of a human life is the unity of a narrative quest."[34] But it is a quest which is typically Socratic. It is a seeking for answers to the ultimate moral questions of life without quite knowing what the answers would look like. It is understanding the problem of conflicting goods associated with the multiplicity of life's practices and seeking a notion of the good that would schematize these conflicts. In short, it is the attempt to answer the great Socratic question, How ought I to live?

The virtues sustain not only practices but our quest for the good. Courage, persistence, truthfulness, and justice are as much required in our quest for how best we ought to live as for our pursuit of goods internal to practices. However, for our purposes it is quite clear that something else is required. In this quest we seek understanding and good judgment concerning the relative merits of competing goods. We pursue philosophical knowledge, and for that we must develop the requisite intellectual virtues. To wonder about the good life we must develop a sense of reflectiveness, curiosity, questioning, skepticism, rationality, and wisdom. In short, we must become philosophical. The good life, the virtuous life, as Aristotle insisted, requires both intellectual and moral excellence. We need "the virtues necessary for philosophical inquiry about the character of the good," as MacIntyre says.

If it is intuitively clear why the character-building view of sport is plausible when we consider the way in which the virtues sustain practices, I think it is just as clear that participation in sports has no intrinsic connection to the development of intellectual virtue. No doubt certain strategic skills are developed when someone learns to play and coach a sport. Understanding and quick judgment are called for. But what we are talking about here involves larger philosophical issues about the nature of the good life, and learning how to turn a double play or when to squeeze bunt appears to have nothing to do with answering Socrates' fundamental question. I suspect that the evidence for the claim must, necessarily, be anecdotal, but we know a number of things about contemporary sports that should make us skeptical about any connection between sports participation and becoming more reflective. We know that parents and coaches are often ready to sacrifice the long-term educational interests of their children and players for athletic success. From red-shirting junior high football players to the educational exploitation of college athletes, the stories are legion. One searches in vain for a coach to take the point of view described by MacIntyre. For example, John Wooden's "Pyramid of Success" mentions the following character traits: industriousness, friendship, loyalty, cooperation, enthusiasm, self-control, alertness, initiative, intentness, condition, skill, team spirit, poise, confidence, competitive greatness, ambition, adaptability, resourcefulness, fight, sincerity, honesty, integrity, reliability, patience, and faith.[35]   Not mentioned in this laudable list are wonder, questioning, Socratic ignorance (uncertainty), skepticism, reflectiveness, and critical ability.

Let's close this section by performing a thought experiment. This thought experiment may only show that, given the current conditions under which sports exist, a certain kind of virtue is probably rather rare in the sports world, not that sports can never, in principle, be the vehicle of intellectual development. I suspect the outcome depends on the education. First consider these quotes from famous football coaches.[36]   "I will demand a commitment to excellence and to victory, and that is what life is all about" (Vince Lombardi). "Winning isn't everything, but it beats anything that comes in second" (Paul Bryant). "Winning is living" (George Allen). "Every time you win, you're reborn; when you lose, you die a little" (George Allen). "No one ever learns anything by losing" (Don Shula).[37]

Now consider another kind of coach who believes that participating in sports can really be morally and intellectually profitable. Imagine his speech to his players, and consider whether this jars our expectations. "Gentlemen, I know you've all had coaches who say things like 'Winning is living,' but I'm not one of them. I want you to look honestly at what you're doing. You're playing a rather silly game. Compared to other human endeavors it is relatively insignificant. Don't ever let your sport consume your life to the detriment of the other great goods in life. Sport is wonderful because it offers you an opportunity to commit yourself to a highly enjoyable physical endeavor. In doing this, sports can dramatize great moments of the human condition. You ought to see it as art, not war. In saying this, I don't want to sound as if I am a final authority, for what I want you to do is really to think about the nature of your commitment to this game, and how it stands in relation to the rest of your life. I want you to think about what really matters in life and what kind of person you are. Is life about winning and victory, solely? I am not sure: I suspect it's not. Such a thesis sounds simplistic, even silly. What is success? Is it being famous and wealthy? What is happiness? Is it just becoming a great athlete? What will life look like after you quit playing sports? Is the value of competition as great as you find in our culture? What I want most from you is to play this game as well as you can, to enjoy it to your utmost, and to think as well as you can about the kinds of questions it occasions. As for me, I'm not too sure about the answers to these questions, but I think reflecting on them is an important part of life and profoundly changes the nature of the person asking such questions. If you want to learn about life, read about Socrates, not famous coaches or athletes." Sounds otherwordly, doesn't it?

GOOD CHARACTER AND SPORT

Throughout this chapter it has been assumed that "character" or having "good character" must have something essentially to do with virtue, since character must be described in terms of those traits or dispositions that we take to be constitutive of it. It is as if "character" means being virtuous, in a broad sense. Is there a way to look more specifically at character, to provide a more unified account of our talk about its development and presence? Let me say at the outset that I'm skeptical about pinning down such a notion in a very tight manner. I'm not sure that our talk about having character is governed by the sorts of rules that would allow for a philosophical definition. I offer my own account because I think it helps us to understand something central about this area of our moral discourse, not that I have succeeded in defining what it means to have character or good character.

I take my lead from some interesting remarks made by Anthony Quinton in an essay called "Character and Culture."[38] He is interested in resuscitating the concept of character both in our cultural life and as an object of philosophical interest. After sketching a view of character he attempts to provide a historical account of its decline and he describes its principal enemies in our everyday moral life. What is character? Quinton claims "it is in essence resolution, determination, a matter of pursuing purposes without being distracted by passing impulse."[39] He believes this view is consistent with Plato's emphasis on prudence, courage, and moderation, since these virtues "are all dispositions to resist the immediate solicitations of impulse."[40] For example, as Aristotle also understood, courage is a response to our natural feelings of fear, while prudence is "settled resistance to whim."[41] Quinton sums up his notion of character or important qualities of character.

They are, generally speaking, ways of deferring gratification, of protecting the achievement of some valued object in the future from being undermined by the pull of lesser objects near at hand.[42]

It is the disposition or habit of controlling one's immediate, impulsive desires, so that we do not let them issue in action until we have considered the bearing of that action on the achievement of other, remoter objects of desire. Understood this way, character is much the same thing as self-control or strength of will.[43]

I find this a valuable general view of character, especially if it is conjoined with Murdoch's view of human nature as essentially selfish, self-preoccupied, and self-absorbed. For the desires that we must naturally battle are often those that insulate an inflated ego and prohibit the kind of objective seeing that is the foundation of virtue for Murdoch. In the context of sport and character we are interested in the possibilities for moral education provided for children, adolescents, and young adults by participation in sports. If the young are not always moral barbarians, they certainly do usually need the kind of training that responds to the immediate and often selfish impulses described by Quinton and Murdoch. It is possible now to construct a more specific account of character based on the moral psychology we have just outlined. Of what qualities does character consist? I offer this list in no particular order.

First of all, I associate character with a kind of strength that forces one properly to take responsibility for certain negative events that befall a person. Such events might make one look bad in the eyes of others and oneself. It is the courage to take responsibility for defeat and failure when appropriate, to be honest about one's self. I know of no neat term for virtue that sums up this quality, but it is obviously a kind of responsibility. It is akin to a kind of self-reliance, and its opposite is the perpetual whiner, blamer, and excuse-monger. John McEnroe's lack of this quality is expressed in his constant paranoid complaints to officials, as if he has experienced more unfair and incompetent officiating than anyone else in the history of tennis. Lack of this quality is apparent throughout the sport world when officiating is blamed for defeat.

Character requires avoiding the impulse to succeed by cheating. A person of character is just or fair, in more than one sense. He is unwilling to take unfair advantage of another in order to gain his own advantage, and he is attuned to merit. He comes to see the way in which things are due, justly, to persons.

Character requires trustworthiness. In any social context reliable persons who resist the impulse to violate shared agreements are valued.

A person with character resists the impulse always to see things solely in terms of the way his own life is affected. Qualities like generosity, benevolence, and respect for others are important parts of character. Likewise, sensitivity to the social dimension of living produces a kind of civility in the person with character.

Surely character requires the resistance to impulses that might allow us to give up easily when life is difficult. Persistence and determination are important.

A person of character, in overcoming intense self-absorption, will appreciate the larger scheme of things and thus will have a diminished sense of his own importance. He will have a good sense of where his own abilities fit in various hierarchies of excellence. I agree with Murdoch when she stresses the centrality of the virtue of humility.

A person with character develops some sense of good judgment about what matters in life. In fact, it is this sense of good judgment that is the ground for resisting immediate impulses. As Quinton notes, "Strength of character, by holding in check impulses excited by what is immediately present, allows the cognitive harvest of our reasoning powers to have an effect on what we do."[44]

A person with character manifests a certain harmony, a balance among the parts of his character. There is a certain unity that provides a basis for what we might call the integration of the self. In short, all of the qualities of character seem to fit nicely and work harmoniously.

Finally, a person with character also is able to carve out a space for the particular goods of his own existence, and in making wise judgments about other competing matters, understands when it is important to remain committed to his own idiosyncratic plan of life. A person with character has integrity, in this sense.[45]

Quinton contrasts the characterless self of everyday morality with a self characterized by "cultivated and disciplined modes of choice, by which passive appetites are held in check and so brought into contention with longer term purposes."[46] For me, this broadening of vision involves judgment about my own situation in the larger scheme of things and the requirements of living with others whose claims equal my own. Character requires a self who is responsible, just, trustworthy, generous, respectful, civil, determined, humble and unpretentious, reasonable and wise, balanced, and has integrity. Whereas Quinton says that character is "comparatively unspecific, unlike abilities and skills,"[47] I think these relatively specific dispositions are a part of our concept of character. I agree with Quinton that character is a "fairly hard-won achievement,"[48] since developing these traits requires strength of will, practice, and sound judgment.

CONCLUSION

Now we are in a position to offer some tentative conclusions about the claim that sport builds character. Does sport build character? The best that can be said for this view is that sport can help build a part of character, especially if coaches and parents are good moral educators. But the notion of "character" is sufficiently rich and complex and the social, economic, and psychological pressures are so great that we should expect a very mixed moral result from sports participation. This is precisely what the empirical studies seem to show. As we have seen, the corrupting power of the institutionalization of sport and thus the emphasis on the pursuit of external goods produces an atmosphere in which the internal goods are often underplayed or compromised. Winning, as the avenue to external goods, becomes the dominant ethos, and moral shortcuts naturally evolve. With the competition for external social goods comes the diminution of generosity or benevolence as key virtues specific to sports participation. Likewise, with fame, power, and money at stake, psychological variables like those described by Murdoch work against the virtuous seeing of the way things are. Thus the character-building view is a fragment. It ignores these difficulties and seems to focus only on those instrumental virtues that help us achieve the goals we might have in a competitive, business-oriented social world.[49] It also has little or nothing to say about the importance of becoming reflective in working out the very questions that commitment to sports occasion.

In short, my answer to the question Does sport build character? is the uninspiring "It depends." We are served best by attending to Ludwig Wittgenstein's admonition to beware of our simplifying "craving for generality," respect particularities, attend to the phenomena, and see how various human experience is. If our task in life is to become better and help our children likewise, then participating in sports may help a person to become more responsible, fair, respectful, and determined. Unfortunately, it may have precisely the opposite effect. And I doubt that it has anything to do specifically with becoming wiser about how we ought to live. But thinking about the issues discussed in this chapter may produce a greater sensitivity concerning what we might do if we are really serious about the moral possibilities of sports.

NOTES

1. Gerald R. Ford, "In Defense of the Competitive Urge," in David L. Vanderwerken and Spencer K. Wertz, eds., *Sport Inside Out* (Fort Worth: TCU Press, 1985), 247. The essay originally appeared in *Sports Illustrated* (1974).

2. Paul Weiss, *Sport: A Philosophic Inquiry* (Carbondale, IL: Southern Illinois University Press, 1969), 29.

3. Christopher Stevenson, "College Athletics and 'Character': The Decline and Fall of Socialization Research," in Chu, Segrave, and Becker, eds., *Sport and Higher Education* (Champaign, IL: Human Kinetics, 1985), 264.

4. Ogilvie and Tutko, "Sport: If You Want To Build Character, Try Something Else," in Chu, Segrave, and Becker, eds., *Sport and Higher Education* (Champaign, IL: Human Kinetics, 1985), 267-73; see also Dorcas Susan Butt, *Psychology of Sport*, 2nd ed. (New York: Van Nostrand Reinhold, 1987), especially Chapters 9, 10.

5. See Gregory E. Pence, "Recent Work on Virtues," *American Philosophical Quarterly*, 21 (October 1984): 281-97 for an informative overview.

6. Alasdair MacIntyre, *After Virtue*, 2nd ed. (Notre Dame, IN: Notre Dame University Press, 1984), 196.

7. MacIntyre, *After Virtue*, 8.

8. MacIntyre, *After Virtue*, 117.

9. MacIntyre, *After Virtue*, 180-85.

10. MacIntyre, *After Virtue*, 187.

11. MacIntyre, *After Virtue*, 187, 190. It is interesting to note that MacIntyre's notion of a practice is helpful in distinguishing a game from a sport. In his sense, sports are practices, whereas a game is not necessarily a practice. See also Bernard Suits, "The Elements of Sport," in Osterhoudt, ed., *The Philosophy of Sport: A Collection of Essays* (Springfield, IL: Charles Thomas, Publisher, 1973), 48-64. The essay also appears in Morgan and Meier, eds., *Philosophic Inquiry in Sport* (Champaign, IL: Human Kinetics, 1988), 39-48.

12. MacIntyre, *After Virtue*, 190.

13. MacIntyre, *After Virtue*, 190. The point is wonderfully exemplified in an anecdote described by David Halberstam in *Summer of '49* (New York: Morrow, 1989), 175. Ted Williams' passionate devotion to the art of hitting caused him to give tips to opposing players. The Boston owner, Tom Yawkey, asked him to stop helping the competition. Williams was quoted as having responded to his owner, "Come on... The more hitters we have in this game, the better it is for the game. Listen, when you're coming towards the park and you hear a tremendous cheer, that isn't because someone has thrown a strike. That's because someone has hit the ball." Williams was interested in a shared internal good; Yawkey's interest was in external goods.

14. MacIntyre, *After Virtue*, 191.

15. MacIntyre, *After Virtue*, 192.

16. Iris Murdoch, *The Sovereignty of Good* (New York: Schocker Books, 1971), 78.

17. Murdoch, *The Sovereignty of Good*, 89.

18. Murdoch, *The Sovereignty of Good*, 90.

19. Think of John McEnroe's behavior in this respect. The problem concerns his incivility and lack of respect for an opponent. But the incivility and disruptive behavior seem to be a function of his seeming paranoia, as if referees are always out to get him, or he is at the mercy of their incompetence. In fact, a more realistic judgment would be that referees sometimes err but are for the most part accurate in their judgments.

20. Murdoch, *The Sovereignty of Good*, 93.

21. MacIntyre, *After Virtue*, 194.

22. MacIntyre, *After Virtue*, 194.

23. MacIntyre, *After Virtue*, 191.

24. Christopher Lasch, *The Culture of Narcissism* (New York: Warner Books, 1979), 194-97.

25. Lasch, *Culture of Narcissism*, 191.

26. Lasch, *Culture of Narcissism*, 195; see also Randolph Feezell, "Play and the Absurd," *Philosophy Today*, 28 (Winter 1984): 319-28. Lasch describes sport as "splendid futility."

27. MacIntyre, *After Virtue*, 196.

28. MacIntyre, *After Virtue*, 196.

29. MacIntyre, *After Virtue*, 201-02.

30. MacIntyre, *After Virtue*, 204-08.

31. MacIntyre, *After Virtue*, 208.

32. MacIntyre, *After Virtue*, 215.

33. MacIntyre, *After Virtue*, 216.

34. MacIntyre, *After Virtue*, 219.

35. Eitzen and Sage, eds., *Sociology of North American Sport*, 3rd ed. (Dubuque, IA: Brown, 1986), 55.

36. Eitzen and Sage, *Northern American Sport*, 60.

37. This last quote by Don Shula is particularly interesting, since it appears to be so patently false. One wonders why he would say something like this.

38. Anthony Quinton, *Character and Culture*. The essay originally appeared in *The New Republic* (1983). I will refer to the pagination of the essay as it appears in Sommers and Sommers, eds., *Vice and Virtue in Everyday Life*, 2nd ed. (New York: Harcourt Brace Jovanovich, 1989).

39. Quinton, *Character and Culture*, 614.

40. Quinton, *Character and Culture*, 614.

41. Quinton, *Character and Culture*, 614.

42. Quinton, *Character and Culture*, 615.

43. Quinton, *Character and Culture*, 615.

44. Quinton, *Character and Culture*, 615.

45. MacIntyre, *After Virtue*, 203, 241-43.

46. Quinton, *Character and Culture*, 620.

47. Quinton, *Character and Culture*, 614.

48. Quinton, *Character and Culture*, 614.

49. In *Quandaries and Virtues* (Lawrence: University of Kansas Press, 1986), Edmund Pincoff distinguishes between instrumental virtues and noninstrumental virtues. Noninstrumental virtues include aesthetic virtues (both noble, e.g., dignity, and charming, e.g., wittiness), meliorating virtues (including mediating virtues, e.g., tolerance, temperamental virtues, e.g., cheerfulness, and formal virtues, e.g., politeness), and moral virtue.

Chapter 21

Influencing the Character of Entertainment Television: Ethical Dilemmas of Prosocial Programming

William J. Brown and Arvind Singhal

INTRODUCTION

The character of our nation is not only reflected in our media culture, but is also influenced by it. Decades of research by George Gerbner and his colleagues at the University of Pennsylvania have documented the socialization effects of the American media on popular culture. If it is true that what we role model produces behavioral tendencies, and behavioral tendencies develop into habits, and habits form character, and character determines destiny, then we must seriously consider how to ethically promote prosocial values, beliefs, and behavior through the popular media. In this chapter we discuss the use of prosocial television programming as a means to promote social development.

The use of television to promote social development has generated ethical dilemmas that will affect several billion television viewers during the 1990s. Development is defined as a widely participatory process of directed social change in a society, intended to bring about both social and material advancement.[1] Television has a greater potential impact on social development now than ever before in human history. Several countries are systematically producing television programs with prosocial messages. Prosocial television content refers to televised performances that depict cognitive, affective, or behavioral activities considered to be socially desirable by most members of a television audience.[2] Ethical concerns regarding the responsible use of television are prompting television producers and officials to reduce the antisocial effects of television by increasing the prosocial content of television programs.

While the use of prosocial television programs raises several ethical dilemmas (as we will show later in this chapter), literature on television ethics is severely limited. Television ethics represents a relatively neglected and undeveloped field of inquiry. Existing research focuses primarily on specialized themes such as television news ethics.[3] The purpose of this chapter is to investigate the use of prosocial television, to review relevant theory on communication ethics, and to address several important ethical dilemmas that individuals should consider as television's influence grows during the 1990s.

TELEVISION'S GROWING INFLUENCE

As television audiences increase worldwide, entertainment television is rapidly replacing educational television. Entertainment television is comprised of televised performances intended to capture the interest or attention of individuals, giving them pleasure and/or amusement. Educational television refers to a televised program of instruction and training intended to develop an individual's mental, moral, or physical skills to achieve a particular end. Entertainment programs are highly popular and are now crowding out educational television programs. This trend is occurring because entertainment programs attract larger audiences, are viewed for longer periods, and generate greater profits than do educational programs.

Despite the sustained growth of entertainment television, little is known about the prosocial effects of entertainment television programs. There are several reasons for this limited knowledge. First, television programs are commonly categorized into a dichotomy that separates entertainment television from educational television. In the past four decades this dichotomy has been reified in the way television and its effects have been discussed and researched. For example, before cable television, "entertainment television" was often referred to as "commercial television" and "educational television" was called "public television."

These arbitrary labels complicate research on the effects of television programs.   Educational programs like *Sesame Street* can be highly entertaining, and entertainment programs like *ER, The Cosby Show, Shogun,* and *The Day After* can be highly educational.[4] The prevailing notion that entertainment television entertains rather than educates limits a researcher's framework by underestimating the importance of entertainment television's educational and social influence.

A second reason for the paucity of research on the prosocial effects of entertainment television is the emphasis on studying television's antisocial effects.   Antisocial is defined as cognitive, affective, or behavioral activities considered to be socially undesirable by most members of a social system. Of the many thousands of studies conducted on antisocial television effects, we identify four major research strains: the harmful effects of television violence,[5] the effects of promoting inaccurate health-related information on television,[6] the portrayal of negative (and often discriminating) images of women and children on television,[7] and the unrealistic depiction of interpersonal and social relationships on television.[8]

In contrast, relatively few studies have focused on the prosocial effects of entertainment television.[9] Therefore much less is known about the effects of television programs that are intended to have positive social impacts than is known about the unintended antisocial effects of entertainment television.

THE GROWTH OF PROSOCIAL TELEVISION

The idea of producing entertainment television programs for prosocial purposes is not new. However, the use of human communication theories to promote specific prosocial beliefs and behaviors through entertainment television programs (not just commercials) is a relatively new practice.[10]

On several occasions, television producers in the United States have incorporated prosocial messages into entertainment television programs. During the 1970s, Norman Lear launched the popular CBS television series *All in the Family* to address ethnic prejudices and to encourage racial harmony in America. The highly acclaimed ABC miniseries *Roots*, viewed by 32 million U.S. households, and its sequel, *Roots: The Next Generation*, viewed by 22.5 million U.S. households, promoted the value of egalitarianism.[11]   Another television miniseries studied, *Shogun*, positively affected viewers' attitudes toward the Japanese; the series increased viewers' knowledge of the Japanese language, history, and customs, and increased their desire to be socially closer to the Japanese people.[12]

Research indicates that exposure to even a single prosocial television program can produce enduring cognitive and behavioral changes in viewers. The television movie *The Day After* significantly increased viewers' attitudes about preventing nuclear war.[13] *The Great American Values Test*, a 30-minute television special designed to promote prosocial values, significantly increased viewers' pro-environmental and pro-egalitarian beliefs and behaviors.[14] Although most of the studies of prosocial television programs indicate only modest effects, they reveal the potentially beneficial impact of prosocial television content.

Numerous organizations maintain a presence in Hollywood in order to influence U.S. television producers to include social issues in an episode of a television series. These "Hollywood lobbyists" (social cause groups) occasionally are successful in getting their issue presented on prime-time television, and thus raise public consciousness about that issue.[15]

Educational institutions also have made contributions to the production of prosocial messages. For example, the Harvard University School of Public Health instigated the "designated driver" television campaign to prevent drinking and driving. By March 1989, the designated driver concept appeared in 35 different prime-time series on U.S. network television.[16] As social problems facing many countries become more acute, as is expected with the growing AIDS crisis and widespread drug abuse, more prosocial television content is likely to be broadcast during the 1990s.

ETHICAL THEORY AND PROSOCIAL TELEVISION

The expanding use of television for social development raises important ethical concerns that need to be discussed. First, we discuss perspectives provided by several key ethical theorists to define and evaluate the ethics of prosocial media. Then we discuss four ethical dilemmas associated with prosocial television.

Aristotle's "golden mean" concept suggests that messages should be tailored to address an audience in the "prime of life," balancing the extreme characteristics of young people and old people. Aristotle emphasized that ethical conduct is attained by actions that are intermediate between extremes, and that moral knowledge and ethics are produced collectively. Consistent with Aristotle's ethical theory, several media planners have created prosocial messages that are addressed to the "golden mean" of modern societies, focusing on the common needs of most people. However, using prosocial media to address only these audiences may lead media planners to ignore needs of other demographic groups, especially minorities.

Other media planners have created prosocial messages consistent with John Stuart Mill's "principle of utility," which judges an action to be ethically appropriate only when it produces the greatest amount of good for the greatest number of people in a society. Creating prosocial messages that produce the greatest good for the greatest number of people is difficult to implement because someone must define what constitutes the "greatest good."

Immanuel Kant's ethic of the "categorical imperative" has also influenced ethical theory in the media. Kant believed that a good act was one which the actor would be willing to see universalized and that every person should be considered as an end rather than as a means to an end. Media policy based on Kant's view would suggest that every individual in society should have an equal opportunity to receive beneficial media messages, and that the focus of such messages should be first to help the individuals, not just to change the individuals to achieve a government's objectives.

The ethical view presented in this chapter is closely related to Kantian philosophy. We suggest that common human values should be considered in producing prosocial media messages. Minnick (1980) noted that Albert Schweitzer defined ethics as nothing more than reverence for life. Schweitzer's definition implies that moral judgments are built upon commonly accepted values. Ethics emerge from enduring social values rather than from logically defensible propositions.[17] Thus, ethical communication has a dimension of social identity.[18]

We define ethical communication as that which upholds and protects an individual's freedom, equality, dignity, and physical well-being. Communication media are ethically employed when they are not the limiting factor in addressing individual and social needs.[19] If the media fail to uphold and protect basic human values, or limit people's access to resources that provide their basic needs, then it is used unethically.

ETHICAL DILEMMAS OF PROSOCIAL TELEVISION

An evaluation of prosocial television according to our definition of ethical communications has revealed four important dilemmas: the prosocial content dilemma, that is, how to distinguish prosocial from antisocial television content; the sociocultural equality dilemma, that is, how to ensure that prosocial television upholds sociocultural equality among viewers; the unintended effects dilemma, that is, how to respond to the unintended consequences of prosocial television; and the prosocial development dilemma, that is, how to respond to those who argue it is unethical to use television as a persuasive tool to guide social development.

The Prosocial Content Dilemma

Previously we defined prosocial television as televised performances that depict cognitive, affective, or behavioral activities considered to be socially desirable or preferable by most members of a particular social system. Distinguishing prosocial content, however, is difficult when people do not have common moral and ethical values. There is some consensus about certain prosocial issues in most societies. For example, almost everyone would agree that child abuse is wrong, that violence against women should be stopped, and that it is good to "say no" to illegal drugs. However, the best ways to prevent the abuse of women and children or to prevent drug abuse are hotly disputed, and a lack of consensus exists regarding many social issues.

During the past two decades one of the most controversial social issues in the United States has been abortion. In a 1972 episode of *Maude*, the middle-aged star of the television series decided to get an abortion rather than bear an unwanted child. This episode set off a controversy with U.S. right-to-life organizations, who demanded equal television attention to their position on abortion. In 1985, an episode of *Cagney and Lacey* showed a right-to-life group picketing an abortion clinic, causing tremendous consternation among pro-abortion groups in the United States. For those favoring abortion, the *Maude* episode was considered to be prosocial (based on freedom of choice to abort a child), but for those against abortion, the *Maude* episode was considered to be antisocial (based on the right to life of an unborn child). Similarly, picketing the abortion clinic in *Cagney and Lacey* was viewed as prosocial by right-to-life advocates. Ted Turner, an outspoken abortion-rights advocate, invigorated this controversy once again when he broadcast *Abortion: For Survival* on his TBS network. Turner's opponents wanted equal time on TBS.

At the heart of the prosocial content dilemma is determining who will decide for whom, what is prosocial and what is not. In most Third World nations, including those broadcasting prosocial television programs, the government overseeing the media usually decides what is prosocial. History reveals horrendous abuses by governments who have used the media to promote antisocial beliefs and behaviors, leading many countries to limit or eliminate government regulations of the media. Yet in many countries governments have used the media ethically and responsibly for prosocial purposes.

Unfortunately, the assurance that the media will be used for prosocial purposes is not greater in nations where the responsibility for prosocial media is left to television producers and commercial advertisers. Such a responsibility shift creates problems for television producers and advertisers who usually avoid addressing controversial social and educational issues. For example, U.S. television networks have resisted the broadcast of condom advertisements. While entertainment television programs depict numerous sexual behaviors every day in America, the depiction of condom use is virtually nonexistent.[20] Although Americans want to reduce teenage pregnancy and the AIDS epidemic, the networks' policy on condom advertising exists because people disagree about the consequences of making condoms the answer to these problems.

The reconciliation of prosocial programming in free market economies like the United States (where television systems are commercially driven) is in itself an ethical dilemma.[21] The ongoing contention against commercial television's depiction of tobacco and alcohol use illustrates the difficulties encountered when judging the prosocial and antisocial content of media messages. Many Americans feel that they should have the freedom to decide whether or not to use alcohol and tobacco products, and that restricting information regarding the use of such products is wrong. However, others feel that it is unethical to promote products that encourage potentially harmful beliefs and behaviors.

In summary, the prosocial content ethical dilemma results from differing views about what beliefs and behaviors benefit society and which ones are detrimental. Regulation of television content, as is often the case in Third World countries, is vehemently resisted in the United States. Yet if the decision about prosocial television content is left to commercial networks, some of the most important prosocial messages may never reach millions of American television viewers. Balancing the freedom of the broadcast media with the need for more prosocial television is an ethical dilemma every nation must face.[22]

The Sociocultural Equality Dilemma

A second ethical dilemma in using prosocial television concerns the problem of ensuring sociocultural equality, that is, providing an equal treatment on television of various social and cultural groups. Sociocultural equality means regarding each social and cultural group with the same value or importance.[23] In nations with a high homogeneity index, a measure of a country's sociocultural diversity, there is a high degree of consensus regarding a society's normative beliefs and behaviors. In Japan, where the homogeneity index is 99 percent, people have fewer problems agreeing on what is prosocial than do people in the United States, where the homogeneity index is 50 percent.[24]

The sociocultural equality dilemma is heightened when prosocial television programs are exported to other countries. Television programs are imbued with the sociocultural values of the society where they are produced. The threat of "cultural imperialism" generates great concern about the sociocultural impact of imported television programs. For example, the influence of Western entertainment television programs was one factor that contributed to the Iranian revolution. Disdain for the "immoral" sexual relations depicted by several American-produced dramatic television series fueled the Iranian fundamentalist movement against Westernized secularism.

The Unintended Effects Dilemma

A third ethical dilemma brought about by the use of prosocial television is the problem of unintended effects. Social development is a complex phenomenon whose consequences are not easily predictable. Undesirable and unintended consequences can result from the diffusion of prosocial messages, as officials in Iran discovered. Reluctance to depict condom use on U.S. television, as mentioned earlier, demonstrates how a fear of unintended consequences can discourage broadcasts of prosocial content. Many parents fear that television content intended to encourage sexual responsibility might encourage sexual promiscuity instead.

As evidenced by thousands of studies on antisocial television effects, unintended consequences of entertainment television programs are common. To illustrate this problem, the present discussion will focus on two popular U.S. television series, *Miami Vice* and *All in the Family*. Of these series, *All in the Family* was intended to be somewhat prosocial, and *Miami Vice* was not intended to be either prosocial or antisocial.

In the early 1970s, CBS broadcast a mildly prosocial and highly acclaimed situation comedy, *All in the Family*. The series focused on ethnic prejudices through the depiction of a highly bigoted character, Archie Bunker. While the program attempted to point out to viewers the absurdities of their own ethnic prejudices, some already prejudiced viewers became even more prejudiced in their beliefs.[25] Similar findings resulted from studies on the impact of the television miniseries *Roots*[26] and *Roots: The Next Generation*.[27] Viewers of these two television series became more aware of racial issues, but did not become less prejudiced.

NBC's popular crime-drama series *Miami Vice* illustrates that even seemingly insignificant events in entertainment programs may lead to sizable unintended behavioral effects on television viewers. U.S. gun-shop owners noticed a remarkable effect on the gun-buying behavior of *Miami Vice* viewers during the 1980s. Shortly after Detective Sonny Crockett began sporting a shark-gray Australian-made 5.56-mm Steyr AUG, a semiautomatic assault rifle, on episodes of *Miami Vice*, gun shops across the United States were flooded with customer calls asking how they could buy one.[28] Although *Miami Vice*'s producers never claimed they were trying to promote social responsibility, NBC was likely surprised to learn the degree to which *Miami Vice* promoted gun sales and had become the fashion leader in assault weaponry in the United States.

The Prosocial Development Dilemma

Even if a society agrees on a set of prosocial beliefs and practices, can maintain a reasonable degree of sociocultural equality, and can control unintended effects of prosocial television, is it ethical to systemically attempt to use television as a persuasive tool to guide social development?

Research on television effects indicates that we should be concerned about the antisocial effects of television. It is virtually impossible to produce "value-free" or "socially innocuous" entertainment programs.

The idea that persuasive communication is unethical and, therefore, should be avoided in television production denies the reality of what past research indicates. Television persuades people; how much, is debatable. Even if one percent of a population is persuaded to change a belief or behavior on account of watching television, that is still an important change. Persuasive communication cannot and should not be eliminated in a democratic society.[29] Therefore, arguing that it is unethical to use television to promote prosocial beliefs and behaviors seems unreasonable and inconsistent with democratic freedoms.

However, unequivocal promotion of prosocial television for social development can also represent an untenable ethical position. When there is disagreement about the rightness or wrongness of certain social beliefs and behaviors, it becomes obvious that what is considered to be prosocial by any group of people, whether that group represents the majority of a population or the highest court of the land, should not be uncritically promoted on television. Whether or not it is ethical to produce prosocial television depends on a number of factors, including the nature of the belief or behavior being promoted, who decides the prosocial status of a certain belief or behavior, and what effects the promotion of a certain belief or behavior are likely to have on an audience. Thus, the ethics of using television as a persuasive tool for social development is inextricably intertwined with the three other ethical dilemmas that were discussed earlier.

CONCLUSION

In summary, we have discussed four ethical dilemmas associated with the use of prosocial television: the ethics of distinguishing prosocial and antisocial content in television programs, the ethics of ensuring sociocultural equality in prosocial programs, the ethics of dealing with the unintended effects of prosocial television, and the ethics of using television as a tool to guide social development. As television audiences continue to expand, and as the number of prosocial programs increase, an understanding of these ethical dilemmas becomes crucially important.

Promoting prosocial change through television requires responsible communication which demands a commitment to the moral responsibility of protecting the public.[30] Since television is already used as a persuasive tool, the ethical use of television calls for the provision of accurate, timely, and freely distributed information that protects the voluntary choices of television viewers.[31]

Entertainment television has a complex social impact on its viewers. If societies are to use television for social development, then the production of prosocial television content should not be discouraged, despite the ethical dilemmas associated with its effects. Television consumers who are unhappy with the antisocial effects of entertainment television should become more actively involved in determining the kind of content they desire.

Prosocial television can improve the quality of our lives, but if we are to encourage its use, the responsibility for television content cannot remain on the shoulders of commercial sponsors and networks prone to avoid prosocial programming content, or on government officials who can arbitrarily decide what is prosocial and what is not. The ethical use of media must be based upon the imperative of protecting our freedom, equality, dignity, and physical and psychological well-being. In the case of prosocial television, ultimately, the ethical dilemmas will be decided by television viewers.

NOTES

1. E. M. Rogers, "Communication and Development: The Passing of the Dominant Paradigm," in E. M. Rogers, ed., *Communication and Development: Critical Perspectives* (Newbury Park, CA, 1976), 121-33.

2. J. P. Rushton, "Television and Prosocial Behavior," in D. Pearl et al., eds., *Television and Behavior: Ten Years of Scientific Progress and Implications for the Eighties*, vol. 2 (Bethesda, MD: National Institute of Mental Health, 1982), 248-58.

3. T. W. Cooper, "Ethics, Journalism and Television: Bibliographic Constellations, Black Holes," *Journalism Quarterly* 2 (1988): 450-55, 496.

4. R. I. Kulman and J. T. Akamatsu, "The Effects of Television on Large-Scale Attitude Change: Viewing 'The Day After,'" *Journal of Applied Social Psychology* 13 (1988): 1121-32; E. L. Palmer, *A Pedagogical Analysis of Recurrent Formats on "Sesame Street" and "The Electric Company,"* a paper presented at the International Conference on Children's Television, Amsterdam, June 1978; and M. J. Shatzer et al., "Adolescents Viewing 'Shogun': Cognitive and Attitudinal Effects," *Journal of Broadcasting and Electronic Media* 3 (1985): 341-346.

5. F. S. Andison, "Television Violence and Viewer Aggression," in G. C. Wilhoit and H. de Bock, eds., *Mass Communication Review Yearbook 1* (Beverly Hills, CA: Sage, 1980), 555-72; E. Donnerstein, "Pornography and Violence Against Women," *Annals of the New York Academy of Science* 347 (1980): 227-88; E. Donnerstein and L. Berkowitz, "Victim Reactions in Aggressive-Erotic Films as a Factor in Violence Against Women," *Journal of Personality and Social Psychology* 41 (1981): 710-24; N. M. Malamuth and E. Donnerstein, eds., *Pornography and Sexual Aggression* (New York: Academic Press, 1984); D. P. Phillips, "The Behavioral Impact of Violence in the Mass Media: A Review of Evidence from Laboratory and Non-Laboratory Investigations," *Sociology and Social Research* 66 (1982): 386-98; D. P. Phillips and J. E. Hensley, "When Violence Is Rewarded or Punished: The Impact of Mass Media Stories on Homicide," *Journal of Communication* 3 (1984): 101-15; and D. Zillmann and J. Bryant, "Pornography, Sexual Callousness, and the Trivialization of Rape," *Journal of Communication* 4 (1982): 10-21.

6.   H. J. Barnum, Jr., "Mass Media and Health Communications," *Journal of Medical Education* 50 (1975): 25; M. B. Cassata et al., "In Sickness and in Health," *Journal of Communication* 4 (1979): 73-80; M. C. Long, "Television: Help or Hindrance to Health Education," *Health Education* 3 (1978): 32-34; D. T. Lowry and D. E. Towles, "Soap Opera Portrayals of Sex, Contraception, and Sexually Transmitted Diseases," *Journal of Communication* 2 (1989): 77-83; F. A. Smith, "Health Information During a Week in Television," *New England Journal of Medicine* 286 (1972): 516; and A. S. Tan and G. K. Tan, "Television Use and Mental Health," *Journalism Quarterly* 1 (1986): 107-13.

7.   M. B. Cassata and T. D. Skill, *Life on Daytime Television: Tuning-in American Serial Drama* (Norwood, NJ: Ablex, 1983); M. Downing, "Heroine of a Daytime TV Serial," *Journal of Communication* 2 (1974): 130-37; R. K. Goldsen, "Throwaway Husbands, Wives, and Lovers," *Human Behavior* 4 (1975): 64-69; R. M. Liebert et al., *The Early Window: Effects of Television on Children and Youth* (New York: Pergamon, 1973); G. Noble, *Children in Front of the Small Screen* (Beverly Hills, CA: Sage, 1975); and G. Tuchman et al., eds., *Hearth and Home: Images of Women in the Mass Media* (New York: Oxford University Press, 1978).

8.   A. Alexander, "Adolescents' Soap Opera Viewing and Relational Perceptions," *Journal of Broadcasting and Electronic Media* 3 (1985): 295-308; N. L. Buerkel-Ruthfuss and S. Mayes, "Soap Opera Viewing: The Cultivation Effect," *Journal of Communication* 3 (1981): 108-15; R. Estep and P. T. MacDonald, "Crime in the Afternoon: Murder and Robbery on Soap Operas," *Journal of Broadcasting and Electronic Media* 3 (1985): 323-31; B.S. Greenberg et al., "Sex on the Soap Opera: Afternoon Delight," *Journal of Communication* 3 (1981): 83-89; B. S. Greenberg and D. D'Alessio, "Quantity and Quality of Sex in the Soaps," *Journal of Broadcasting and Electronic Media* 29 (1985): 309-21; D. T. Lowry, et. al., "Sex on the Soap Operas: Patterns of Intimacy," *Journal of Communication* 3 (1981): 90-96; and J. C. Sutherland and S. J. Siniawsky, " The Treatment and Resolution of Moral Violations on Soap Operas," *Journal of Communication* 2 (1982): 67-74.

9.   P. P. Amato and A. Malatesta, *Effects of Prosocial Elements in Family Situation Comedies*, a paper presented at the 37th Annual Conference of the International Communication Association, Montreal, Canada, 1987; W. J. Brown, "Effects of 'Hum Log,' a Television Soap Opera on Prosocial Beliefs in India," *Dissertation Abstracts International* 01A (1988): 20; S. J. Ball-Rokeach et al., *The Great American Values Test: Influencing Behavior and Belief Through Television* (New York: Free Press, 1984);   S. J. Ball-Rokeach et al., "'Roots: The Next Generation'—Who Watched and with What Effect?" *Public Opinion Quarterly* 45 (1981): 58-68; M. C. G. Berrueta, *The Soap Opera as a Reinforcer of Social Values*, unpublished master's thesis, Iberoamericana University, Mexico City, 1986; B. Gunter, "Television as a Facilitator of Good Behavior Amongst Children," *Journal of Moral Education* 13 (1984): 69-77; S. E. Harvey et al.,

"Primetime Television: A Profile of Aggressive and Prosocial Behaviors," *Journal of Broadcasting* 23 (1979): 179-89; V. O. Lovelace and A. C. Huston, "Can Television Teach Prosocial Behavior?" *Prevention in Human Services* 2 (1982): 93-106; W. J. Porter and W. Ware, "The Frequency and Context of Prosocial Acts on Primetime Television," *Journalism Quarterly* 2 (1989): 359-66, 529; M. Sabido, *Handbook of Social Value Reinforcement* (Mexico City: Televisa, 1982); A. Singhal and E. M. Rogers, "Television Soap Operas for Development in India," *Gazette*, 41 (1988): 109-26; A. Singhal and E. M. Rogers, "Prosocial Television for Development in India," in R. E. Rice and C. Atkins, eds., *Public Communication Campaigns*, 2nd ed. (Beverly Hills, CA: Sage, 1989), 331-50; and A. Singhal and E. M. Rogers, "Entertainment-Education Communication Strategies for Family Planning," *Populi* 2 (1989): 38-47.

10.   W. J. Brown, *The Role of Entertainment Television in Development Communication*, a paper presented at the 39th Annual Conference of the International Communication Association, San Francisco, CA, May 1989; and W. J. Brown et al., "Pro-Development Soap Operas: A Novel Approach to Development Communication," *Media Development* 4 (1989): 43-47.

11.   S. J. Ball-Rokeach et al., "'Roots: The Next Generation'—Who Watched and with What Effect?" *Public Opinion Quarterly* 45 (1981): 58-68.

12.   M. J. Shatzer et al., "Adolescents Viewing 'Shogun': Cognitive and Attitudinal Effects," *Journal of Broadcasting and Electronic Media* 3 (1985): 341-46.

13.   R. I. Kulman and J. T. Akamatsu, "The Effects of Television on Large-Scale Attitude Change: Viewing 'The Day After,'" *Journal of Applied Social Psychology* 13 (1988): 1121-32.

14.   S. J. Ball-Rokeach et al., *The Great American Values Test: Influencing Behavior and Belief Through Television* (New York: Free Press, 1984).

15.   K. C. Montgomery, *Target: Primetime: Advocacy Groups and the Struggle Over Entertainment Television* (New York: Oxford University Press, 1989).

16.   E. M. Rogers et al., *Proceedings from the Conference on Entertainment-Education for Social Change*, Annenberg School of Communications, University of Southern California, Los Angeles, CA, 1 April 1989.

17.   W. Minnick, "A New Look at the Ethics of Persuasion," *The Southern Speech Communication Journal* 65 (1980): 352-62.

18.   J. W. Cheseboro, "A Construct for Assessing Ethics in Communication," *The Central States Speech Journal* 20 (1969): 104-14.

19.   T. M. Martin et al., "Balance: An Aspect of the Right to Communicate," *Journal of Communication* 2 (1977): 158-62.

20.   D. T. Lowry and D. E. Towles, "Soap Opera Portrayals of Sex, Contraception, and Sexually Transmitted Diseases," *Journal of Communication* 2 (1989): 77-83.

21.   The unique dilemma of producing prosocial media messages in free market economies represents an important subject that requires an in-depth analysis beyond the scope of our present discussion.

22.   A version of this article, presented at the 40th Annual Conference of the International Communication Association, 23-29 June 1990 in Dublin, Ireland, contains an expanded discussion of this dilemma.

23.   W. B. Gudykunst and Y. Y. Kim, *Communicating with Strangers* (Reading, MA: Addison-Wesley, 1984), 5.

24.   G. T. Kurian, *The Book of World Rankings* (New York: Facts on File, 1979).

25.   N. Vidmar and M. Rokeach, "Archie Bunker's Bigotry: A Study in Selective Perception and Exposure," *Journal of Communication* 1 (1974): 36-47.

26.   K. K. Hurr and J. P. Robinson, "The Social Impact of 'Roots,'" *Journalism Quarterly* 55 (1978): 19-24.

27.   S. J. Ball-Rokeach et al., "'Roots: The Next Generation'—Who Watched and with What Effect?" *Public Opinion Quarterly* 45 (1981): 58-68.

28.   A. Alexander and J. Stewart, "Detective Sonny Crockett: Leader in Fashion Weaponry," *The Honolulu Star-Bulletin*, 19 September 1989, B1.

29.   E. P. Bettinghaus, and M. J. Cody, *Persuasive Communication*, 4th ed., (New York: Holt, Rinehart, and Winston, 1987).

30.   D. Weiser, "Two Concepts of Communication as Criteria for Collective Responsibility," *Journal of Business Ethics* 7 (1988): 735-44.

31.   J. A. Jaksa and M. S. Pritchard, *Communication Ethics: Methods of Analysis* (Belmont, CA: Wadsworth, 1988).

About the Contributors

DON E. EBERLY is president and co-founder of the Commonwealth Foundation in Harrisburg, Pennsylvania, an institute committed to civic, democratic, and economic renewal. He is also the founder of the National Fatherhood Initiative, a national civic group seeking to restore the role of fathers in American society. Mr. Eberly has written extensively on economics and social policy issues. He is the author of *Restoring the Good Society: A New Vision for Politics and Culture* (Baker Books, 1994) and editor of *Building a Community of Citizens: Civil Society in the 21st Century* (UPA, 1994). He received his M.A. from George Washington University and his M.P.A. from Harvard University.

B. DAVID BROOKS is president of the Jefferson Center for Character Education in Pasadena, California. Dr. Brooks trains law enforcement officers at the University of Southern California and is a consultant to various city and national agencies regarding character education, gangs, violence, and vandalism. He is a member of the board of directors of the Character Education Partnership based in Washington, D.C.

WILLIAM J. BROWN is professor and dean of the College of Communication and the Arts at Regent University, an all-graduate institution in southeastern Virginia. Dr. Brown has published a number of articles on the production and social impact of entertainment-education messages with prosocial values and beliefs designed to improve the quality of life and address critical social problems.

347

ERIC E. EBELING is assistant professor in the College of Education at Texas Tech University, where he teaches graduate courses in the history and philosophy of education. His research interests include the role of families and communities in education, school reform, and the history and future of American education. Dr. Ebeling was awarded his Ph.D. from the University of Maryland, College Park.

RANDOLPH FEEZELL is professor of philosophy at Creighton University in Omaha, Nebraska. He is the author of *Faith, Freedom, and Value: Introductory Philosophical Dialogues* (Westview Press, 1989), *How Should I Live? Philosophical Conversations About Moral Life* (co-authored with Curtis Hancock, Paragon House, 1991), and numerous articles and book reviews in various areas of philosophy including ethics and philosophy of sport. Dr. Feezell received his Ph.D. from the State University of New York at Buffalo.

CHARLES L. GLENN is professor of educational policy and chairman of the Department of Administration, Training and Policy Studies in the Boston University School of Education. He has served as the executive director of the Office of Educational Equity in the Massachusetts Department of Education. Dr. Glenn is the author of *The Myth of the Common School* (University of Massachusetts Press, 1988) and *Choice of Schools in Six Nations* (U.S. Department of Education, 1989). He received his A.B. from Harvard College, his Ed.D. in administration from Harvard, and his Ph.D. in religion and modern culture from Boston University.

CHARLES E. GREENAWALT, II is assistant professor of political science and assistant director of the Center for Politics and Public Affairs at Millersville University, Millersville, Pennsylvania. He also serves as senior policy associate for the Commonwealth Foundation. Dr. Greenawalt is the former director of policy development and research for the Senate of Pennsylvania. He received his Ph.D. from the University of Virginia.

RICHARD C. HARWOOD is president of the Harwood Group, a public issues research and innovations firm in Bethesda, Maryland. He is the author of two nationally acclaimed reports, *Citizens and Politics: A View from Main Street America* and *Meaningful Chaos: How People Form Relationships with Public Concerns*. Mr. Harwood has served on the policy staffs of U.S. presidential, congressional, and local election campaigns. He received his B.A. in political economy from Skidmore College and his Master of Public Affairs degree from the Woodrow Wilson School of Public and International Affairs at Princeton University.

EARL HESS is founder, chairman of the board, and chief executive officer of Lancaster Laboratories in Lancaster, Pennsylvania. Throughout his career, Dr. Hess has served with distinction as a scientist, entrepreneur, and community leader. In 1994 he completed a term as a director of the U.S. Chamber of Commerce. Dr. Hess received a B.S. degree in chemistry from Franklin and Marshall College and a Ph.D. in organic and biochemistry from the University of Illinois.

WADE F. HORN is director of the National Fatherhood Initiative and an adjunct faculty member in the School of Public Policy at Georgetown University. He is also an affiliate scholar with the Institute for American Values in New York City. Dr. Horn previously served as commissioner for Children, Youth and Families and chief of the Children's Bureau within the U.S. Department of Health and Human Services. He has a Ph.D. in child clinical psychology from Southern Illinois University.

CHARLES R. KESLER is director of the Henry Salvatori Center for the Study of Individual Freedom in the Modern World at Claremont McKenna College, where he is also associate professor of government. He is the co-editor with William F. Buckley, Jr. of *Keeping the Tablets: Modern American Conservative Thought* (Harper and Row, 1988) and editor of *Saving the Revolution: The Federalist Papers and the American Founding* (Free Press, 1987). Dr. Kesler received his Ph.D. in political science from Harvard University.

THOMAS LICKONA is professor of education at the State University of New York at Cortland and currently directs the Center for the Fourth and Fifth Rs (Respect and Responsibility). He has also been a visiting professor at Harvard University and is an internationally respected authority on moral development and values education. Dr. Lickona is the author of *Educating For Character: How Our Schools Can Teach Respect and Responsibility* (Bantam Books, 1991). He holds a Ph.D. in psychology from the State University of New York at Albany.

WILLIAM J. MOLONEY is superintendent of schools in Calvert County, Maryland and a member of the governing board of the National Assessment of Educational Progress. He directs the New American Schools Project in his school district and is an active consultant, speaker, and writer on education reform issues. Dr. Moloney has also served as an adjunct education professor at Lehigh University in Bethlehem, Pennsylvania. He received his Ph.D. from Harvard University.

JOHN E. MURRAY, JR. is president of Duquesne University in Pittsburgh, Pennsylvania. He has written extensively in the area of contract law. His books include *Murray on Contracts* (Bobbs-Merrill/Michie, 1991) and *Sales and Leases (National and International Transactions)* (Murray and Flechtner, West, 1993). His civic activities in Pittsburgh include work with the Allegheny Foundation and the Allegheny Conference on Community. Dr. Murray received his B.S. from LaSalle University, his J.D. from the Catholic University of America, and his S.J.D. from the University of Wisconsin.

MICHAEL NOVAK is a theologian, author, and former U.S. ambassador who currently holds the George Frederick Jewett chair in religion and public policy at the American Enterprise Institute in Washington, D.C., where he also serves as director of social and political studies. He was the recipient of the 1994 Templeton Prize for Progress in Religion. Mr. Novak has written 25 influential books on the philosophy and theology of culture and authored over 500 articles, monographs, and reviews. In 1981 and 1982 he served as the head of the U.S. delegation to the United Nations Human Rights Commission in Geneva, Switzerland, with the rank of ambassador. He holds degrees from Stonehill College and the Gregorian University in Rome and received an M.A. in history and philosophy of religion from Harvard University.

MARVIN OLASKY is professor of journalism at the University of Texas at Austin and a senior fellow at the Progress and Freedom Foundation in Washington, D.C. Dr. Olasky is also editor of *World* magazine and the author of 11 books of history and cultural analysis, including *The Tragedy of American Compassion* (Regnery Gateway, 1992). He received an A.B. from Yale University and a Ph.D. in American culture from the University of Michigan.

KEITH J. PAVLISCHEK is director of Crossroads, an educational and public policy program of Evangelicals for Social Action. He is also the author of *John Courtney Murray and the Dilemma of Religious Toleration* (Thomas Jefferson University Press, 1994). Dr. Pavlischek holds masters degrees from the Institute for Christian Studies and Westminster Theological Seminary and a Ph.D. in religion, ethics, and society from the University of Pittsburgh.

ROBERT ROYAL is vice president and Olin Fellow in religion and society at the Ethics and Public Policy Center in Washington, D.C. Dr. Royal is the author of numerous articles in national publications and among the books he has published are *1492 And All That* (Ethics and Public Policy Center, 1991), *A Century of Catholic Social Thought* (Ethics and Public Policy Center, 1991), and *Play, Literature, Religion: Essays in Cultural Intertextuality* (State University Press of New York Press, 1992). He has a Ph.D. in comparative literature from the Catholic University of America.

ARVIND SINGHAL is assistant professor in the School of Interpersonal Communication at Ohio University. He is currently a visiting professor at Bangkok University where he is helping to establish Thailand's first doctoral program in communication. Dr. Singhal has published numerous articles and one book on the diffusion of prosocial messages and effectiveness of organizational communication strategies that contribute to the development and improvement of social conditions.

CHRISTINA HOFF SOMMERS is associate professor of philosophy at Clark University in Worcester, Massachusetts. Dr. Sommers is the author of *Who Stole Feminism? How Women Have Betrayed Women* (Simon and Schuster, 1994) and other works on feminism and American culture and ethics and moral theory. In 1992, she was appointed by the secretary of education to serve on the federal committee that oversaw accrediting agencies. Dr. Sommers received her B.A. from New York University and her Ph.D. from Brandeis University.

JAMES Q. WILSON has been James Collins professor of management and public policy at UCLA since 1985. Previously, Dr. Wilson was Shattuck professor of government at Harvard University for 26 years. He is the author of extensive publications on urban problems and the prevention of delinquency and has advised four U.S. presidents on crime, drug abuse, education, and other crises of American culture. Dr. Wilson has been elected a member of the American Academy of Arts and Sciences and a fellow of the American Philosophical Society. He was awarded his doctorate from the University of Chicago.